Studies in Media Management

The MOVIE BUSINESS

AMERICAN FILM INDUSTRY PRACTICE

Edited by A. William Bluem and Jason E. Squire

COMMUNICATION ARTS BOOKS

HASTINGS HOUSE, PUBLISHERS

New York

For BEVERLY   *For MOM, DAD, GAIL and WALT*

Fourth Printing, November 1976
Fifth Printing, February 1979

Library of Congress Cataloging in Publication Data
Bluem, A. William   *The movie business.*
(Studies in media management) (Communication arts books)
1. Moving-picture industry—U. S. Addresses, essays, lectures. I. Squire, Jason E., author. II. Title.
PN1993.5.U6B58   658'.91'791430973   79-38238

Cloth Edition: ISBN 0-8038-4665-7
Paper (text) Edition: ISBN 0-8038-4667-3

Published simultaneously in Canada by
Saunders of Toronto, Ltd., Don Mills, Ontario

Designed by Al Lichtenberg
Printed in the United States of America

CONTENTS

Part Two: FINANCING AND BUDGETING FILMS

Part Three: FILM COMPANY MANAGEMENT

Part Four: PRODUCTION—PRELIMINARIES

Contents

Part Eight: THE NEW TECHNOLOGY

APPENDICES

EDITOR'S FOREWORD

Alfred North Whitehead observed that the justification for a university is that it "preserves the connection between knowledge and the zest for life, by inviting the young and the old in the imaginative consideration of learning. The university imparts information, but it imparts it *imaginatively*."

Perhaps it is commitment to this verity which brings so many to the calling of film education—embracing instruction by film as well as study of film—on the American campus. Everywhere, faculty have begun to employ film in formal courses of instruction as well as in myriad related "enrichment" applications and, everywhere, young people who are not actively making films are sitting in darkened classrooms and auditoria, contemplating and enjoying films of all styles, varieties and intentions. The university has become the film study center for our civilization, and all who participate in campus life are intellectually influenced and spiritually shaped by the medium which has come to play so vital a role in the "imaginative imparting of information."

As this enthusiasm has spread, curricula of established film departments have undergone continuing revision, while faculties of new departments have sought to include more diverse interests in instructional planning. The outcome of this creative ferment is witnessed in broad new academic programs which examine or utilize film in all of its capacities and modes—as *an art*, as *a stimulant to learning*, as *a determinant of social attitudes and behavior*, as *a shaper of habit, custom and culture*, and as *a vast economic enterprise*. It is in service of the latter that this volume—the fourth in the *Studies In Media Management* series—was planned.

A. Wm. Bluem
General Editor
Studies In Media Management

PREFACE

This book is devoted to one kind of film—the feature motion picture made for theatrical release. Within our examination of this dominant kind of film production, only those specific considerations underlying the business aspects of creating and showing such films to an audience are given stress.

We have observed that many schools and departments already have devised various instructional programs which reflect this important element of film study. Seminars, workshops and regular courses dealing with the economics of the film industry are increasing in number as faculties and professionals alike move to offer students a systematic appraisal of the realities of getting their work to the market place. Of corollary significance is the fact that academic specialists from the disciplines of law and economics, as well as practicing professionals, are beginning to join film departments with both regular and adjunct faculty appointments. Further, many programs offered in this area are available to the professional, whether beginner or veteran, as well as to regular degree candidates.

Regrettably, however, little serviceable textual material is available to teachers and students with specialized interest in the business of film. There are some rather formidable economic studies in which the industry is examined principally from the view of social scientists specializing in industrial organization or business administration.

Such works, however, not only are out of date, but were somewhat too theoretical and abstract to be of use to the professional film-maker even when first published. More often than not, subsequent efforts along these lines have been nothing more than revised versions of what is sometimes the very enemy of erudition, style and literary invention—the doctoral dissertation. The true professional, after all, is probably less interested in economic theory than in how he may achieve success—both *d'estime* and *d'fou*—while still preserving his personal and artistic integrity.

We have designed and prepared this book because it is our conviction that there is no better way to confront the practical, procedural problems of a mercurial film industry than through the first-hand experience of professionals. We have, therefore, invited as contributors to this volume persons who successfully occupy creative decision-making posts along the industry firing line. They were asked to relate their experience within the life-cycle of a commercial feature film to what comes before and after they have committed their own skills and talents to the whole. In short, the sum of their individual knowledge and expertise is pooled here for the benefit of the serious professional—whether arrived or aspiring—who seeks a better understanding of any part of that process by which successful commercial features achieve their state of being. This book follows the cycle—from development of story and screenplay through produc-tion, distribution, exhibition, and final accounting—as it is witnessed and given forward thrust by those who are actively involved.

The editors wish to express their gratitude to many people who extended their kind personal assistance while this work was in preparation. First and foremost, appreciation is extended to our contributors, each of whom has taken time to explain his individual responsibilities, express his hard-won opinions, and generally help to clarify our view of the inner workings of the movie business. Special thanks are also due Arthur Knight, Bill Chaikin, Don Kopaloff, Ken Rotcop and Joe Friedman—all of whom offered useful and construc-tive comments upon the original outline. For valuable help in prepara-tion of the manuscript we are grateful to Marion Robinson, Andrea Fischel, Diane Olsen, Gloria Verish and Karen Connell Hold. Finally, our deepest gratitude is reserved for Lou Greenspan, whose enthu-siasm gave us encouragement, whose experience gave us insight, and whose editorial labors provided a substantive contribution to this volume.

A. William Bluem   Jason E. Squire
Syracuse, N.Y.   New York City

INTRODUCTION

LOU GREENSPAN

As I look back over the past half-century, it seems that there was hardly a time when the motion picture industry was not in "a state of crisis." First, talking pictures disrupted established patterns. Next, radio became a threat. Then the depression was upon us, followed by World War II, which was immediately followed by the advent of television. In each case the motion picture industry suffered a fall-off at the box office, and in each case the movie business was consigned to oblivion.

Yet the picture business has survived, and it undoubtedly will continue to survive and grow even stronger, despite those prophets of gloom and doom who have been predicting its decline and fall through all of these years. Today, despite the fact that "free" television is available to 90% or more of the homes in this country, millions of people still gladly pay money each week for the privilege of seeing a movie

LOU GREENSPAN has been Editor of the *Journal* of The Producers Guild of America since 1959. His editorial background includes reporting and editorial service with *Variety* and *Hollywood Reporter*. Mr. Greenspan also served with Hollywood studios during the '30's and early '40's and has served in a variety of important service capacities for the motion picture industry. He has been a guide, friend, defender and dutch-uncle to the movie business throughout his long and distinguished career.

inside a movie theatre. This kind of theatrical patronage in a country where television has reached near-saturation proportions can hardly be construed as a symptom of a dying industry.

But this has not been enough to stop pessimistic conjecture and speculation about the future of the film business. Some continue to believe that the survival of the American motion picture is still in doubt—and they point to a number of recent developments in Hollywood's film industry to support their contention. They interpret as signs of disintegration the inevitable changes that have brought about the decentralization of major companies and the resultant new status for the independent producer. They also point to the rise of a new and possibly threatening element—the conglomerate. They see something ominous in the production overseas of more and more pictures—some of which might perhaps not be produced at all if they had to be made in Hollywood. They hear persistent rumors to the effect that the major studios are planning to destroy themselves by selling off their real estate—and perhaps building one central studio complex.

A hasty evaluation of these reports, rumors and speculations might well give the impression that the film industry is actually fighting for its life. A closer look at the situation, however, reveals that the developments which are taking place are the results of measures which are designed to strengthen and fortify the industry's capacity to fashion successful motion pictures in a period of changing conditions.

Many observers have erroneously reasoned that the rise in independent film production in Hollywood has been at the expense of the major studios. It is true that many producers and a number of stars who were formerly under contract to major studios are now making films on an independent basis. But this hardly implies that the major companies are falling apart. It does mean, however, that part of the structure under which Hollywood films are made is undergoing alteration to conform with modern concepts of doing business. The most salient example of this alteration is the fact that most of the films produced independently not only rely on the distribution facilities of the big companies, but also count on them for their financing.

There is every reason to be optimistic about the simple truth that fewer pictures are being made. In the 1930's and the early 1940's Hollywood's studios ground out an average of between 500 and 600 pictures a year and they geared their plants accordingly. Today, with the emphasis on quality instead of quantity, studios are turning out less than half as many. As a consequence, the vast film-making facilities at some of the larger studios are not being used to full capacity. Yet the present moves to streamline studio operations, to cut down on unnecessary overhead, and to effect economies are far from being last-ditch efforts to keep afloat. It would be more accurate to say that the industry is emerging from a period of evolution stronger than ever.

We can be equally optimistic in observing that at a time when the production costs of top quality films are at an all-time high it is only reasonable to assume that the selectivity of pictures would be greater in proportion to the lesser quantity. Despite the complaints of exhibitors, one of the reasons fewer feature productions are coming out of Hollywood is that pictures are getting more playing time than ever before. We must recall that distributors and producers campaigned for years to eliminate double features for that very reason. We can't overlook the fact that this short-sighted policy has now been corrected in most situations in the country.

The mind of man has never designed an entertainment as wide in its appeal and as all-embracing in its scope as the movies. But because of the increased competition for the entertainment dollar, those on the gloomy side have been too grim in their predictions. There has been too much loose criticism of the picture business. Some of it has been unfair, and the more hopeful aspects of motion pictures have not been stressed sufficiently. Often the critics fail to recall that Hollywood's batting average is better than that of the book publishing business, the stage and other media. The motion picture industry still turns out a proportionally larger number of hits than one finds among books and Broadway shows. A book selling 100,000 copies or even less, for example, becomes a best seller. A picture, however, must play to at least 20 million persons just to be considered average. Some pictures of record have sold to 100 million or more. There is little wrong with the future of an industry capable of doing that kind of business.

The challenges of the next decade are clear. The production arm of the industry is well aware that it takes better than average entertainment to capture and hold today's elusive movie audiences. The public waits not only for bargains or specials in products they buy, but also for what they believe is sure-fire entertainment before they buy their tickets. This situation is sad in some ways, because no one picture can be everything. Many fine films have had relatively poor attendance, although they have held worthwhile amusement, interest or emotional appeal. Yet if one considers the pressure groups now operating upon Hollywood, the wonder is that pictures which do manage to please many people are released.

Still, the primary challenge is to create varied entertainment. The industry must continue to make pictures which reflect some of the serious realities of life, but it must also satisfy those who want less sophisticated pictures, who want travel, comedy, love stories and an endless variety of diversions. Further, as Hollywood looks to the future it becomes more and more evident that the producer, the distributor and the exhibitor must work together in selling the picture to the public.

Can the challenges be met? Of course they can. We live in a world where change itself is all that is predictable. But difficulties ahead can hardly be more critical than those that were met and solved in the first 70 years of this century—seven decades in which the lasting vitality of the motion picture has been demonstrated. It is pretty safe to predict that the movie business is here to stay.

PART ONE

Developing the Story and Screenplay

Among a number of realities which affect the economics of movie-making, the most insistent is a fundamental and pervasive dependence upon the screenplay. The screenplay, after all, is the only tangible representation of a picture before it reaches celluloid. Key pre-photography business judgments are based upon it; financing agreements are often set on the strength of it, and pictures are budgeted from the screenplay. Yet the role of writer—the creative force who sets all other film arts in motion—is peculiarly ambivalent, for when it is all over he has lost identity with the form of what he created. In his essay here William Goldman considers the unglamorous realities of scripting for a non-linear medium in a linear way, but also stresses the creative freedoms as well as economic rewards of screenwriting.

The crucial link between the creative screenwriter (seller) and the production entity (buyer) is the literary agent. Two west coast representatives, Lee Rosenberg of Adams, Ray & Rosenberg and Lew Weitzman of the William Morris Agency, describe procedure in a small and large agency, respectively. Each points out that the literary agent must operate at two levels, advancing his client's career with careful guidance while at the same time circulating a client's work among producers and production/distribution companies. One aspect of the literary agent's work cannot be undertaken without attention to the other.

In the large production organization, it is the story editor who must remain closest to new literary trends. J. Kenneth Rotcop describes the roles and functions of story editors, who are responsible primarily for examining potential screen material in the variety of forms on which it may occur—novel, play, outline, treatment, complete screenplay or any other words-on-paper format. While Rotcop details the various phases through which such material may move as it passes from idea to earliest stages of pre-production, the major legal questions which may arise during this process are described by Saul Rittenberg, who focuses particularly upon difficult questions of copyright protection and acquisition of the property. An analysis complementary to Rittenberg's work is provided by M. William Krasilovsky, who has structured a useful, historically-based overview of legal subtleties which are inherent to the entire field of literary rights and permissions.

THE SCREENWRITER—A GOLDEN TIME

WILLIAM GOLDMAN

". . . There are no sure-fire commercial ideas anymore . . .
and there are no unbreakable rules. . . ."

The movie business as we know it is dying or dead. It is the best time ever for anyone who wants to be a screenwriter. Now one can write anything. Since no one knows any more what will or won't go, almost anything has a chance of getting made. If I were 19 right now instead of 39, perhaps I wouldn't be a novelist at all. Now it seems possible for a writer to say what he wants through film and make a living at it.

I have been writing screenplays for about five years; I have been writing novels for 12 to 15 years. And I suppose I've made 30—maybe 50—times as much money writing screenplays as from the hard-cover sales of my novels. One of the things that no one tells an eager author in college is that if he writes a novel, the chances are that he won't get it published. And if he does get it published, he might make a thousand dollars or maybe even two. It takes years and years to become an established fiction writer, and one can hardly support a family this way. No one buys hardcover books anymore. There aren't more than three or four writers who can actually make a living out of

WILLIAM GOLDMAN is a distinguished novelist and screenwriter whose original screenplay for *Butch Cassidy and The Sundance Kid* won him an Academy Award. He has written several novels—including *The Temple of Gold, Soldier in The Rain* and *Boys and Girls Together*—and the screenplays for *Harper* and *The Hot Rock*.

hardcover fiction writing. Filmwriting, on the other hand, not only pays, it overpays. And it is a way for one to exercise his craft and still feed his children—both critical aspects of a writer's life.

Some authors start out, no doubt, knowing they want to write screenplays. I am basically a novelist and fell into screenplay writing rather by misinterpretation. It happened at a time when I was in the middle of a monstrous novel called *Boys and Girls Together*. I was hung up in the thing, and to try to unstick myself I wrote a 10-day book called *No Way To Treat A Lady* which was published under another name. It is a short book with 50 or 60 chapters. Cliff Robertson got hold of it and thought it was a screen treatment rather than a novel. At the time he had a short story called *Flowers for Algernon*, which eventually became *Charly*, and for which he won an Academy Award. He asked me to do the screenplay but, without even waiting to see my work on it, he got me a job as play-doctor for a film he was doing in England, and I never got to do *Flowers* after all.

The whole sequence of events did prompt me to learn more about screenwriting. I bought the only book available—called *How To Write A Screenplay*, or some such title—and discovered that screenplays are unreadable. The style is impossible and must be dispensed with. It always has those big capital letter things that say: "305 EXT. JOHN'S HOUSE. DAY." I realized that I cannot write this way. Instead, I use run-on sentences. I use the phrase "cut to" the way I use "said" in a novel—strictly for rhythm. And I am perfectly willing to let one sentence fill a whole page. I'll say such things as: "We're running down the street as we cut to the so-and-so." I double-space it properly, but I never want to let the reader's eye go.

A writer needs to find his own style, something he is comfortable with. For example, I use tons of camera directions, all for rhythm. It breaks up the directors, who shoot the scenes the way they want them anyway. But it *looks* like a screenplay and yet it is *readable*. My brother, who also writes screenplays (*The Lion in Winter*), doesn't use the standard form either. The standard form cannot be read by man or beast.

Anyone wanting to be a screenwriter should write a screenplay —not an outline or a screen treatment or a novel that then has to be adapted. One of the reasons that Hollywood is dying is that there is such incredible waste. A studio can have a million dollars tied up in a property between the time it is purchased as a novel and the time a script is ready. And this is aside from subsequent production costs. If an author writes a screenplay, it is already there to be seen and judged. The company can say right off, "Yeah, we'll shoot it," or "No, we won't." If it sells, it pays the bills. And, besides this essential aspect, it is a legitimate and honorable kind of piece to write.

Background reading and research can be important for a writer. For one thing, sometimes he just stumbles upon something that really grabs him and that he knows he wants to do something with. It was way back in 1958 or '59 that I first came across the material about Butch Cassidy and was moved by it and knew I wanted some day to write a movie about it. I continued researching the subject off and on for 10 years, finding things to read that added background and depth. There is a lot available on Cassidy but almost nothing on Long-baugh (Sundance). Larry Turman, a good friend who produced *The Graduate*, was very important in helping me to structure it.

Since I am basically a novelist, it never occurred to me to ask for advance money on "spec" based on an outline that I might sell to someone. I just wrote as if I were writing a novel. This is an unusual occurrence, at least for a Class A picture. The professional screenwriter usually doesn't just write an original screenplay and then look for a market. If he makes his living as a screenwriter, what he probably does is "buck-shot" it. That is, he writes 10 outlines and circulates them, hoping that one of the 10 clicks and someone gives him money for it. He then writes the full screenplay with financial backing.

I wrote the first draft of *Butch Cassidy and the Sundance Kid* in 1965 and showed it to a few people, none of whom was interested. I rewrote, really changing it very little, and suddenly, for whatever reason, everyone went mad for it. Five out of the seven sources in Hollywood who could buy a screenplay were after it. It was this unexpected competition—not my particular skill with the rewrite—that sent the price so high.

Authors who write in various forms of fiction and non-fiction as well as screenplays often have two agents, one on each coast. The one on the west coast handles the film material while the New York agent handles all of his other manuscripts. It was my Hollywood agents, Evarts Ziegler, who handled all the negotiations for *Butch Cassidy*. My only contact with the deal was that he called me in New York every day to keep me posted on the bidding and warn me to stand by the phone to get his call when the bidding was over. It was up to me to give the final okay. It was finally bought by Fox.

No doubt many authors write a film imagining a certain actor in a specific role. Right from the beginning I had Paul Newman in mind. Actually, as I wrote the picture originally, I saw Paul Newman and Jack Lemmon in the main roles. Jack Lemmon had just done a movie called *Cowboy*—this was 10 years ago—and I thought he would do a fine Butch Cassidy. Paul Newman had just done a movie about Billy the Kid and I saw him as the Sundance Kid. As the years went on, Lemmon disappeared from my mind but Newman agreed that he would play the Sundance Kid. Then, when George Hill (who was eventually signed as director) read the script, he mistakenly assumed that Newman was going to play Butch. When that happened, Newman, who wasn't really eager to play Sundance, was delighted to change roles. Then the long search began for the actor who would play the Sundance Kid. Every star in Hollywood was up for it. There were arguments about certain choices. Under such circumstances an author doesn't have very much power. Long ago, Hollywood decided that the way to keep people quiet is to overpay them. An author paid all that money should go home and count it and be content. I was in there arguing, and so were others who had more influence, notably Newman and Hill. We finally won the battle, and Robert Redford, who in those days was not nearly so well known as some of the other candidates, got the part.

Fortunately for the entire project, George Roy Hill was hired as director. There are only a couple of directors in all the history of the world who have had three films that have brought in $15-million. One of them is an Englishman named David Lean and the other is not Mike Nichols or Arthur Penn or Cecil B. DeMille or Alfred Hitchcock or Billy Wilder or Elia Kazan or George Stevens. It is George Roy Hill. Because he is not publicity happy, he is not well known outside the business. His first Broadway directing job, *Look Homeward, Angel*, won a Pulitzer Prize and he has many fine television credits. He is an extraordinarily gifted director.

How close is a writer allowed to the actual production? To a degree the answer lies in how big a writer he is. The bigger his name, the more he is likely to have a say about the details of production. Generally, the answer is that the writer gets as close to the production as his director allows. The production is really the director's baby. If he has faith in the author's judgment, he will be more willing to tolerate his presence during filming. If the director doesn't want him, there is nothing the writer can do about it.

An author is blessed if he has a director who is interested in working closely with him as he prepares for production. The time when the author is most essential is in the story conferences with the director prior to filming. It is during these very crucial days that he tells the director over and over again exactly what he meant. And sometimes an author really hasn't written what he meant. Talking it all out in minute detail with the director can clarify the content and insure the director's chance of a clean and accurate interpretation. It is during these conferences that scenes are cut, added or otherwise modified. In *Butch Cassidy*, for example, the screenplay was changed, but never basically. Certain scenes were cut; the musical numbers were added, but the thing that makes the movie work—the basic relationship established between the two men—was left essentially unchanged.

In one specific instance, I had written an atrocious scene, the opening scene of Robert Redford and the card game. Everyone said, "Get rid of it! It stinks!" And I kept saying, "I know it stinks, but it's the best I can do." And all the time that I was going through that pressure, George Hill kept saying, "You're not going to change it! You're not going to change it!" George knew how to make it play. He took the scene and put it in sepia, which gave it an old look. And he had what is probably the longest close-up in modern film history on Bob Redford. It's about 90-seconds of solid Redford, and the scene really plays. He gets a tremendous tension out of it. This is a striking example of how a good director can take even a rotten scene and make it work.

I went out to Hollywood in June of '68. George Hill was already there. And for about 90 days he and I met every day, spending most of each day talking about every aspect of the script and coming up with ideas for it. These meetings lasted until mid-September and included a two-week rehearsal period prior to actual filming. Until the filming began, then, I was involved in many decisions that were made, but the final work necessarily was that of the director. I returned in the middle of production for one week of shooting at the studio between location work in Utah-Colorado and that in Mexico. On this visit, I saw four or five hours of rushes that George had shot in Utah-Colorado and gave him my reactions. That basically was my total contact with the actual production of the film.

My own feeling is that I don't want to be around on a film I have written. There are times when an author can be helpful. In *Butch Cassidy*, for example, there were a couple of scenes mis-done. Had I been around, I could have said, "Oh, no, no, no, no—I meant this." You see, they were actually mis-written and I didn't realize it until I saw them on film. They are not, incidentally, in the final film. Had I been around, I could have said, "I mis-wrote that. Don't play what I wrote; play it this way."

Generally, however, I don't like to be around for two reasons. First of all, because I am the screenwriter, nobody really wants me around. If a line is mis-spoken with the proper emotion or spoken properly without the proper emotion, there can be problems between the writer who thinks the actors are ruining his lines and the actors who resent the author's presence. And similar tensions can arise between director and author over interpretation. Secondly, although there is nothing more exciting than your first day on a movie-star-laden set seeing all your dreams come true, by the second day you are bored with it. By the third day, everything is so technical that you are ready to scream, "Let me out of here!" The idea of standing around for 72 days of shooting, bothering people and saying such insignificant things as, "The line is: 'There's the fireplace' not 'Where's

the fireplace,' " is madness. Since the author just doesn't know when
he might be really helpful, he might as well stay away and avoid the
agony for himself and everyone else.

I was really fortunate. Over-all, I happen to be delighted with
Butch Cassidy. In many ways it is better than what I wrote; in many
ways it isn't, and in many ways it's different. My script was much
darker and, I think, would not have been so successful. And most of
the credit for its coming off so well I give to George Hill, its director.

Writers are basically secondary in Hollywood; they tend to be
forgotten. But ask *any* director and he will tell you he is only as
good as his screenplay. There is no picture without a script. When
you read that Joseph E. Levine announces a new $8-million picture
from a novel he has bought, that's nonesense. No one knows what a
film will cost until there is a screenplay. There is no film; there is no
anything at all in this world until there is a screenplay. A screenplay
is gold. And right now, with movie companies fragmented and dying
and with money coming from all kinds of strange new sources, it is
a golden time for kids to write screenplays. It's a whole new and
unpredictable ballgame. There are all kinds of things people will take
a chance on that they never would have risked earlier. There is material being made into films now that would never have made
it a few years ago. Perhaps the audience wasn't there for it earlier.
Studios in the old sense are dying. They are all going to be housing
developments. But there will still be sound stages. As long as a movie
like *Joe* can be made for less than a quarter of a million dollars and
have the appeal it has had, movies will continue to be made. They
just will cease being made on those massive sound stages with 85
technicians sitting around doing nothing. This is the change that
is coming about right now and opening it all up for the young, eager
screenwriters. It's all up for grabs.

In the old days, a studio might buy a property because it looked
"good" for Tyrone Power or another big star that they had under
contract. Those days are gone. Nothing is a sure thing. The number
of memos sent from one executive to another explaining why they were
right to turn down *The Graduate* and *Bonnie and Clyde* would fill the
Library of Congress. Nobody knows.

What movies get made reflect the executive mentality; what
movies are successful reflect the audience. Everybody wants to say
that movies are the province of the young. It seems to me that there
is a young audience which makes a tremendous hit of *M*A*S*H* or
Butch Cassidy and there is an older audience which makes a tremendous hit of *Airport*. But beyond it all, nobody really knows which
films will be big. There are no sure-fire commercial ideas anymore.
And there are no unbreakable rules. Classically, Westerns have vil-
lains. *Butch Cassidy*, however, the most successful Western ever made,

has no tangible villain, no confrontation in the usual sense. Perhaps the success of the movie with the kids is in this very concept of the "super-posse," a force that follows them and makes them do terrible things that they cannot control.

I believe that all truths are known. Everyone knows that war is hell and that he should love his neighbor. One of the mistakes the academics make is that when they dissect a poem, they forget that it is supposed to be pretty or that it has an emotional content. They concentrate on Shelley's philosophy or political inclinations. Well, that's not why Shelley wrote the poem; that's not the creative impetus that drove him to it. And I believe that movies are a rotten medium for making didactic statements. We know them before we go in and we don't want to be lectured. We know we are not supposed to dislike people because of the color of their skin or their national origin or their religion. But some of us do, and that's a problem. Now if the writer can involve us in the specific individual people—a Black, a Spaniard, a Jew—without making it a preachment, then he might rock us and cause us to assess our philosophical thinking. *Shop on Main Street* does this.

I love movies and I enjoy writing screenplays enormously. In addition, it's how I support my family. If it were the only kind of writing I did, however, I think I would find it desperately frustrating. When I write a novel, I take it to my editor. He says, "This stinks and I want you to change it." If I agree with him, I say, "Okay," and I change it. If I don't agree with him, I can say, "Goodbye." It is my baby and I can fight to the death. I can either not get it published at all or get it published as I want it elsewhere. At least it is *my* fight to make if I choose. In films, an author doesn't have that right. In films, he must assume that it will be the director who will be ultimately responsible for what the finished product is and whether it will work or not. And, of course, there is no guarantee that he will get a director who will listen to him.

One thing that really pleases me about movies today is that advertising and publicity and critical reviews don't mean anything any more. In other words, a movie like *M*A*S*H** can be made with relative unknowns by a director whose only other film was a disaster, and on opening day people are lined up around the block. *Butch Cassidy* opened in New York to pretty crummy notices but tremendous business. If *Bonnie and Clyde* had been a play, it would have closed on Saturday, because it got three terrible notices before it opened from the *New York Times* critic who had seen it at a film festival. Happily, the reviews are totally unimportant on a film. No one except maybe the critic's mother is going to go to a film or stay away from a film because he says it's good or it's bad. Movie audiences will not be lectured to. It is a golden time.

THE LITERARY AGENT—TWO VIEWS

LEE G. ROSENBERG
LEW WEITZMAN

MR. ROSENBERG — *The Small Agency*

". . . It is the agent's primary job to help his client develop to the fullest extent of his talents. . . ."

The basis of operation for a small agency such as ours is not necessarily the established writer, who is in constant demand, and whose services command substantial salary. Rather, the small agency can emphasize new writers who have had very little exposure to the motion picture business and to television. Selecting as clients those judged the most talented, the agency promotes them as fully as possible, believing that their growth and the agency's growth are interdependent. Not the least reason behind the success of such an arrangement is the dramatic about-face the industry has made in its attitude toward young people. Since 1965, in reaction to certain social upheavals, the feeling has grown that if one is over 30 he is over the hill. While such an opinion is not valid, it has helped to create a great demand for new writers. The small agency has thrived on this demand.

An agency like ours represents a variety of authors, including

LEE G. ROSENBERG is a partner in Adams, Ray and Rosenberg, a literary agency in Los Angeles. Educated at the Choate School and Harvard (B.A. 1956), Mr. Rosenberg held various production positions in films and television before co-founding his agency in 1963.

LEW WEITZMAN is a literary agent at William Morris Agency, Inc. in Beverly Hills. He served in a similar capacity with MCA Artists Ltd., and as an associate agent with other firms before joining William Morris.

screenwriters, television writers (sometimes one and the same, of course), playwrights and novelists. Novelists, however, are more generally handled by agencies in New York. New York agencies represent very few, if any, screenwriters. With the west coast emphasis upon film, an agency such as ours becomes an outlet for New York agencies for the published works of their authors. Occasionally we work with a writer from the genesis of a novel through its screen version, but in such an instance we assign responsibility for publication of his novel manuscript to an agency in New York, making certain commission arrangements to accommodate the circumstances.

Playwrights, too, come within the scope of the small agency. We might, for example, represent them in the licensing of their plays here in Los Angeles, through such local theatres as The Gallery and The Mark Taper Forum. In fact, this is an area in which we hope to expand activity in the near future. Playwrights based primarily in New York and wishing to translate their works to film, as well as European writers wishing to work in American films, are also potential clients. Young, unknown producers as well as directors in need of management to assist them in breaking into the field are often handled by the small agency. A writer may seek to matriculate into a producership—and here, too, we can perform a significant service. At the moment our own agency does not handle performing talent. We feel the time and energy required for that are such that we would not be able to maintain a desired level of effectiveness on behalf of the type of client we now handle.

It is no doubt pertinent to note that while an agency such as ours does, on occasion, handle novels for publication, we are generally more interested in a manuscript in the basic form of a play or, most desirably, a screenplay. Clearly, a novel is less viable than a screenplay, because it involves an investment for acquisition which then must have added to it an investment for development of a screenplay. The risk is great. On the other hand, the original screenplay is there. It may require rewriting, but it is there in essence for quick evaluation, not only by the agent but by potential buyers. The screenplay eliminates a lot of guesswork.

For example, film rights for a novel might cost $100,000. Then, to develop a screenplay from it would cost an additional $35,000 to $100,000, without any sure guarantee of its quality. While starting with an original screenplay might involve as much as $200,000 for the rights, it may be evaluated as a screenplay without the risk of time and money that is inherent in the adaptation of a novel. The screenplay, after all, is the final blueprint of a film.

To begin a study of agent/client symbiosis, let us examine a writer's initial problem: finding and engaging an agent.

Securing an agent is a critical and often difficult accomplishment for the unknown writer. First of all, just saying one is a writer doesn't make it so. Second, once one has written something, the product must be read by others who might be impressed with its potential. Reading takes time. Once a writer has something to offer—novel, play-script, screenplay—he can, through a number of devices, attempt to interest an agent. Consider the direct telephone call, for example. The impression of personality and intellect he might create on the phone for an agent willing to take the call, is possibly more important than coming to the office and saying, "Here's my script." Getting the agent to take his call may depend upon whether the agent has received a prior contact about the writer from someone he trusts, or whether he has received a letter from the writer that sounds reasonable, intelligent, and perhaps reflects the writer's ability to communicate and the originality of his point of view. Basically, the inventive applicant is likely to attract the interest of even a busy agent who might agree to listen to him. Sometimes writers put ads in the "trades" to secure an agent.

However he manages it, after the initial connection, he then must put a manuscript on the agent's desk. Sitting and conversing accomplishes little. The agent must read the script. And this necessity points out the greatest problem of all: finding time for reading. With all the other demands upon his time, an agent is fortunate to find an hour a day to devote to reading. Following the submission of his manuscript, the writer must be patient.

If the agent is impressed with the manuscript, he calls the writer and tells him he likes the work—perhaps with a few reservations—and arranges a meeting to talk things over. Considering this meeting a first date which may lead to marriage, the agent inevitably projects his own personal chemistry while at the same time he seeks to get acquainted with the author as a person. As in a marriage, one never knows whether he has married the right girl until he has lived with her for a few years. At this first encounter, the parties begin to assess each other. The agent describes his reaction to the material as a sample of the author's work and an index of his ability to handle the visual medium: how he dramatizes and how he writes dialogue and action. The agent will also include his judgment on the saleability of the script.

This initial procedure is relatively the same in all agencies, whatever their size. There is, however, one significant way in which a small agency such as ours modifies the process. The agent explains to the writer that his script is going to be recommended for reading by other partners in the firm. A large agency usually doesn't have time for this extra consideration. In an enterprise involving so subjective a judgment on the part of the reader, however, there is likely to be added insurance of success if the three or four agents comprising the firm are all enthusiastic about the property. If just one of the group is positive in his reaction, it would be inappropriate for him to sign the writer to an agreement. For the alliance to succeed, there must be mutual trust and genuine enthusiasm between agency and client, and the broader the exposure between the two the more confidently they can work together.

In contrast to the west coast, film-oriented agencies, the publication agents in New York rarely have a contract with a client. A novelist who takes three years to write a novel is not likely to shift his loyalties very often. In the faster-paced world of film and television, however, the agent must have constant fluid contact with the market and with his client. In this world, general and specific problems and the loneliness of the writer are daily rather than annual or even triennial issues. It is not good business sense to ignore these needs.

The initial contract between agency and author is generally a document that provides an "out" for the writer if he is not employed for a certain period of time. He can say, "I'm cancelling the contract," and, unless he has earned a salary within the stipulated time, he is free to separate himself from the agency. Again, a client might come in and say, "Look, I'm not happy with you. You're not functioning well. I'm not getting anywhere." There might be adequate reason for the agency to allow him to break the contract, even though legally he has no right to leave. The agency must be realistic. If forced to stay under what he considers intolerable conditions, a client may give the firm the worst kind of public relations.

There are, however, poor conditions that may prevail in the relationship which can be improved. Perhaps there has been such insufficient or inadequate communication between the writer and his agent that the writer feels his interests are being neglected. His complaint may clarify the situation and initiate satisfactory correction. The contract then binds agent and client together for a "cooling-off" period. In this instance, the contract allows the agency to hold the client legally while everyone has an opportunity to reassess his position and his attitudes. If the parties still can't resolve their differences, the agency may then allow the writer to go with another agency under an agreement to split commission with the other agency. Or, if real hostilities prevail, the agency may release their client completely.

By permission of the Writers Guild, the duration of a contract is a maximum of two years for the initial term and two-and-a-half years for the renewal term. An agent may, of course, contract for a shorter period, such as one year, if he chooses. However, since the initial investment in attempting to introduce and sell a new talent is substantial, one year is generally not long enough for the agent to get any returns for his efforts. But by building on what the agent has done that first year, a client might move on to another agent and subsequently find work in a deal for which groundwork had been laid by the first agent. A two-year bond, therefore, is usually desirable for both parties.

Once the contract has been signed, the agent begins the process of submitting the material to potentially interested parties. He will decide who among his list of studios, producers, story editors, directors, actors, distributors and the like, might be interested in this specific property. In some instances, it may be just two or three people who seem particularly good prospects. Perhaps, for example, the property is basically a director's script and particularly suited to the talents of directors X, Y and Z. The agent submits the script to the three, perhaps even simultaneously to save time and even to stir up a little competition for the property. Another property might be submitted to as many as 40 separate possible interests within as short a time as 48 hours. The aim, of course, is to stimulate maximum response. An agent with more than one positive response to a property is obviously an agent in clover.

While there may be occasions when a very limited submission is made, in today's highly horizontal, fragmented market institutions such as studios and distributors rarely buy just a manuscript. An agent must be inventive in putting together a saleable package. He may need to coordinate several interests, combining writer with director and/or star, and then take this package to a studio. The ultimate source of the money is usually the studio or the independent production company. An individual with sufficient funds to make such a deal on his own is a rarity. No matter how many parties are involved, the agent remains with the negotiations through the general licensing and establishing of rights. Thereafter, the property is in the hands of the party who buys it.

As the agent moves in to close the deal he tries to nail down as many specific details as possible. If he is dealing with people whom he knows, and who are resourceful and knowledgeable of the standards of the industry, and who have studio bureaucracies backing them, he is usually safe in making verbal commitments. With anyone other than a studio, however, he will be wise, before proceeding, to insist that a memorandum agreement be drawn up and, in extreme cases, that the funds be put in escrow. Proving damages in a renege on a verbal agreement is excessively difficult and costly. Our agency, for example, executes a seven-page *deal letter* outlining the substantive points, including the price, the general rights acquired and certain other exotic stipulations which may be implicit in a given case. Details are set down so that a lawyer can actually draft a contract from our letter. Once the *deal letter* has been initialed by the parties concerned, we then, for our own agency records, put it into a *deal memo* including the client's name, the commission, the buyer's corporate designation, and the starting date of services. After the deal has been made, there is an administrative period for the agency while the contracts are being drawn and payments are being made. The agent can help to keep communication lines open between writer and producer and try to work out problems which might arise from misunderstandings or differences of opinion. It is the agent's obligation to continue to serve the best interests of his client. This is not to suggest that most producers are exploiters. Many deals go very smoothly in happy alliance. It is the agent's primary job to help his client develop to the fullest extent of his talents.

MR. WEITZMAN — *The Large Agency*

> "... *Authors and their agents are as much interested in getting the material off the ground as they are in making high-priced, high-class deals. The aim, after all, is to get the material produced.* ..."

When an agent looks at material, he's looking for a number of things, some of them quite intangible. He's looking for professionalism, of course. Many would-be writers unwisely submit manuscripts in all shapes and forms, probably not really knowing what a screenplay is and how the mechanics of it are set up. An agent is much more likely to look at a script if it is in proper form, indicating professional know-how on the part of the author. Beyond this criterion, he looks for the kind of material that he thinks makes sense in today's market. Can it be cast? Can it be done on a reasonable amount of money? Does it have something to say? Does it provide a measure of entertainment, an ingredient that is—as much as anything else— the name of the game?

Although our agency does not direct each script toward a specific audience—youth, minority group, elderly, or whatever—at the same time, we are aware that certain studios and producers have keyed themselves to certain types of productions. Consequently, if something comes in along certain lines, the agent will be more specific as to how this material can best be presented and where it should be presented. For instance, material dealing with children and animals and turn-of-the-century whimsy, certainly suggests Walt Disney Productions. A script involved with today's students, campus riots or personal stories about people trying to make certain things happen, suggests material for young filmmakers. This is not to say by any means that the agent is simply trying to get on some current bandwagon. But in his day-to-day dealings with various producing companies, directors and other filmmakers, he tries to keep abreast of their desires and needs. Then, when something comes across his desk that he thinks falls into a given category, he will at least be better prepared to move in the right direction with it. His job is, in essence, to be the efficient middle-man between seller and suitable buyer.

At best, the agency business is greatly dependent on personal judgment and educated guesses. There is no guarantee that anything that comes across the desk will appeal to any person at a particular time. Appeal is a matter of mood—specific mood of the individual and general mood of the times—a matter of attitude and feeling about what producers are looking for when they read material. Perhaps also, however, it depends on the agent's intuition from his own experience and from past and present conversation with a given buyer in assessing what this buyer is looking for and what product to offer him at a given time. It does appear at present, for example, that there is a great deal more acceptance for the original screenplay material than there used to be. Conditions are such that there is a reluctance on the part of motion picture studios to get involved in the long and expensive process of buying a novel, finding a producer and then negotiating for the services of a screen adapter to prepare the material for production. Whenever the filmmakers can get involved with a completed screenplay, even if it be at first draft stage, they are more likely to be interested in the project. This situation results largely from the vast modification of the typical studio organization that has occurred over the past few years. They no longer have stables of writers, producers, directors and actors that they can assemble and assign to this or that project. Now they look for a script as nearly ready for production as possible.

Once an author-client has a saleable manuscript to show, the agent goes through his lists of potential buyers and communicates with them, to let them know what he has, how he feels about it and why he thinks the material has special merit for them. This contact can be by a phone call, by going to see them at the studio or, in certain cases where he feels the material needs to get out fast, by sending a letter with the material itself to the prospective buyer.

The agent often feels the need to move with speed, because there may be other materials around of a similar nature. Naturally, the "firstest with the mostest" is the guy who sells.

While some agencies use a "shotgun" technique when submitting a manuscript, making it generally available to all of their buyer-contacts indiscriminately, our agency tends more and more to be specifically selective in our submissions, attempting to reach the one or two people we feel are really likely to be in the market for one particular piece. These would be people who in our judgment would also have the best chance of getting the project off the ground. To be successful in these judgments an agent must not only know his potential market extremely well, he must be in constant, even daily, touch with the individual buyers to assess their needs. In a small agency, one or two agents must cover the whole town. In a larger agency like ours, on the other hand, the individual agent has a limited number of prospects to cover and can take the time to know them well. He would, then, probably have an advantage in making selective submissions. In the large agency an individual agent would be one of five or six men within a department of the firm. And one agent might be responsible for perhaps three studios plus a certain number of independent producers. This limitation allows him to give more time to each. While each agent has his own "rounds" to make to keep up with what is going on, he has access to all material and properties represented by the agency. He must, therefore, also keep in close touch with his associates who might be submitting some of the same material to his own list of potential buyers.

Although the order of events varies to suit the agent or a given need of the day, a typical day in the life of an agent can be fairly easily predicted. He is likely to spend the morning in his office, either making calls or attending meetings. He might have lunch with an author-client or a prospective buyer to talk about material. The afternoon he will spend visiting the studios and talking to producers and even to clients who are on assignments, checking to see how things are going and what new situations or needs might have developed. By late afternoon, he will return to the office to complete calls which came in regarding materials and services for various clients. There is no set situation, of course; rather, each agent develops for himself the kind of operation with which he feels most comfortable.

The purpose of making regular daily rounds is, as indicated, to be in close and constant contact with the producers in order to keep them informed of the material that is available and to learn first-hand what their specific needs are at the moment. Even beyond the strictly business aspect of it, however, is the importance of developing a good personal rapport with potential buyers. An agent is, after all, a sales representative. If a potential buyer knows him and trusts him personally, obviously the buyer is going to have more faith in his opinions and the product he has to sell.

An author will normally leave the entire matter of negotiations in the hands of his agent. There are some well-established professional writers who will say, "Listen, I expect to get this kind of deal for it, and I won't settle for anything less. So make these people aware of what I want." But generally, the agent must consider the market and what kind of deals are being made. Then he puts a price on the material that is not excessive, but at the same time protects the interests of his client.

When the agent receives a positive response on a script, he informs his associates that a prospective buyer is interested. This check lets the other agents in the department know that they should not close out a deal on that property elsewhere without further conference and coordination of efforts. The agent next gets in touch with the author of the screenplay and advises him of the situation. He tries to give him a little background on the buyer's position in the industry: what he has done, what he is working on currently, and what sort of deal or arrangement he has with a financing organization. Then they discuss price.

One way that the agent and the author can control who might buy the material is through the price they put on it. If, in fact, an important, high-priced writer is being approached by a person who has little reputation in the industry, he might be willing to gamble on the man, but his price might be placed so high that the would-be buyer would be hard pressed to meet it. But authors and their agents are as much interested in getting the material off the ground as they are in making high-priced, high-class deals. The aim, after all, is to get the material produced.

Whatever the circumstances, all negotiations are delicate and need careful handling. Perhaps a writer already in the marketplace has received a certain price for past materials. This can help to shape a deal. If, on the other hand, the writer is young and not established, there may be a good deal more jockeying insofar as price is concerned. The agent tries to establish a price area and a price level that he thinks is compatible with the market and protects the client's interests. With the concurrence of the client, he then approaches the buyer with the terms outlined. When the agent puts a price on the material, the buyer may claim that the price is out of line and counter with a lower offer. Then the agent returns to his client, perhaps suggesting, "He is saying this; I think we can get that." It's a matter of give and take, of what the agent thinks the market will bear, and how eagerly the producer wants the material, and how badly the client thinks he has to have the deal. "Get all you can, but don't blow the deal," is often the client's instruction. There's nothing like a good haggle!

Of course deals are blown, and sometimes rightly, because client and agent refuse an offer they feel is too low for a good property. If there is a timelessness about the piece and money is tight, then it might be wise not to sell just for the sake of a deal. As the market improves, they should be able to get a fairer price. On the other hand, there are certain pieces of material that have a great feel of the contemporary in them. Those an agent will try to move as soon as possible, because within a short period of time their worth will drop and maybe even disappear.

Today, agents are trying more and more to negotiate not only with flat money situations for the writer and his material, but, in addition, with the proviso that the writer share in the profits of the venture. That is, he might be assigned "a piece of the action," or a percentage of the profits. If he can't get a percentage, the agent might attempt to have certain other monies taken out of first profits of a picture as a deferment which would be shared by the producer, the writer and anyone else who is written into the deal.

This arrangement might very well cut down the buyer's initial investment. This is not to say that for a prestigious writer an agent won't try, and often succeed, in getting him all of his money up front, plus a profit participation. But with the present state of the economy in this business and with projects being budgeted at much lower prices than they have been in the past, it is necessary to make deals based upon certain monies in front and, in addition, certain monies to be paid once the producer gets the project off the ground. That is, other monies would start at principal photography of the picture, with more monies paid at the close of photography or at the first general release of the picture, plus possible participation in the profits. Writers are not, however, likely to share in gross receipts. Nevertheless, in anticipating the possible impact that the growing cassette business may have on film, some agencies are now including a proviso in the writer's contract that he be entitled to share in the proceeds from cassette sales, either on a "gross" or "net" arrangement.

Under these various arrangements, a writer is actually putting faith in his own work, and anticipating income from its production, rather than a flat payment up front for his screenplay. If the picture turns out to be a great hit, such a deal can be far more profitable for the writer than an outright flat price.

It would be remiss not to discuss another very important characteristic of the business today. A real sign of the times is the tendency for the literary agent to be concerned with more than just selling the writer's material. Often he finds himself attempting to work the manuscript into a so-called "package deal." In the motion picture vernacular, a "package" is a saleable coalition of two or more elements of a potential motion picture. It may be a piece of material and a producer; it may be the material and the director; it may be the star and the director; it may be the producer, director, actor and script, or any one of a number of other combinations. Invariably, it does include the material as one essential and integral part of it, and very often, too, the producer or director as another essential part.

In working up such package deals, the large agency or the multi-service agency has a built-in advantage. When an agency represents not only writers, but producers, directors and actors as well, it has the ability to work on behalf of all clients at close range. Through its writers, the agency knows what material is available or potentially available, while at the same time through its producer, director and actor clients it can keep close tabs on their needs and desires. The agency that services all of the talents should have a definite advantage as it attempts to package material and people together. In such a packaging a literary agent within the firm would work very closely with the firm's talent agents. For instance, the literary agent might get a call from a talent agent saying, "Dustin Hoffman is looking for this or that." The literary agent would look through his material to see what is on hand and might even discuss with a couple of his writers what he understands Hoffman's needs to be. Then he would see what he could do about forwarding the material that he felt was right to Hoffman's agent—to let him take a look at it and see what he has to say. If, however, the agent can't complete the package within his own agency, he will always go to the outside because, obviously, the inclusion of those elements which fit is most important. He must never force an element that does not fit or let the package die for lack of an element the agency does not represent.

There can, of course, be disadvantages in prepackaging, or being tied up with a deal involving more than one element. Anytime a literary agent arranges a situation between his writer and a director, star, producer or combination thereof, he may place the material in a slower market. No matter how hard he tries to get just the right combination, sometimes part of that particular package is not held in such high regard at one place or another. It may take longer to get responses from certain places if some elements are not held in esteem. Naturally, an agent will try to avoid putting the kiss of death on a project by involving a director who has a bad reputation. Nor for that matter does he or a director want to get involved with a piece of material that has been seen all over town, unless the director was of such prominence that his presence in the package would practically guarantee the project.

But there is another side to the question of the value of packaging. The chief source of money for production is still the institution, the studio. Once a manuscript has been shown to the studios and passed over on its own merits, there is a great reluctance in this town to revive the material for another go, perhaps as part of a package. And in the past few years the motion picture studio has changed from all-out production units into financing-distribution bodies—virtually banks of a sort—interested in backing a ready-made package rather than developing the various elements from within. As noted earlier, there are almost no staff producers, directors, actors or writers affiliated with studios today. Given their present situation, the studios are understandably more interested in the package deal than in just a script coming in from the outside. An agent finds, then, that more and more he is not submitting a manuscript to a studio or production company directly. Rather, he approaches the producer, director or star who might be interested in entering a package deal with his manuscript that in turn would spark interest in a studio with the money to finance his project. In this manner the agent achieves his greatest satisfaction—the successful production arrangement—and, with a great deal of good fortune, a creative as well as profitable venture.

THE STORY EDITOR

J. KENNETH ROTCOP

"... The story editor must be flexible. He must allow the writer to be comfortable, and not feel any pressures beyond those that are going to be caused by the script itself...."

The primary responsibility of the studio-based story editor is to locate worthwhile story material and help both creative and managerial personnel in bringing such material to fruition in production. A story editor must be able to recognize good drama. He must be able to appraise submissions in light of industry and studio standards for success, and he must be sensitive to the creative efforts involved in readying the material for production.

Although the story editor deals with many already-published literary properties, he is often expected to consider the original story submitted in a script form, and it is useful for our purpose to trace the progress of a script from its submission to the initial production stages within a studio. Such description may help the aspiring story editor to understand the realities—not to mention complexities—of this particular professional task. Needless to say, the processes described below will vary from situation to situation. I have based my observations primarily upon my direct experience with Avco-Embassy.

J. KENNETH ROTCOP is primarily a writer who served also as Executive Story Editor for Avco-Embassy Pictures. Mr. Rotcop has written for various TV programs, including the award-winning CBS documentary series, *Images and Attitudes*. Three of his screenplays are presently in pre-production.

Seven out of every ten scripts submitted come in from a literary agent. No studio can afford to accept unsolicited material simply because, once having turned a submission down, they might be sued if they ever should make a film with a similar theme. The safeguard, therefore, is submission through an agent, and there is an unwritten code in effect between studios and legitimate agencies which protects the studio.

The remaining three out of ten scripts submitted come in from independent producers who buy material and then submit a script for studio consideration. The producer may buy a book and hire a writer to write a screenplay; or he may buy a screenplay that has been written on speculation; or he may develop his own story idea and hire a writer to write a screenplay. If it's a producer-submitted property, the studio story editor will, of course, work with the producer in all further matters related to the screenplay.

For sake of exposition, let us first deal with the agent submission. If the agent is excited about the work—and if he is known to have sound judgment—the story editor personally will read the project. If the material comes from a writer who is well-known, the story editor himself will read the project. If neither the agent nor the writer is established, the story editor will turn the project over to a reader.

Most studios have four to ten readers on staff. Their task is to read the screenplay and prepare a summary of the story. The reader summary will include such additional information as story locale, settings, the era in which it takes place, and such miscellaneous information as whether a particular actor or actress under studio commitment would be good for a certain role, or what director with a studio commitment might be interested in this particular screenplay. Finally, the reader includes his personal evaluation of the story. If the reader feels it should be given consideration, the story editor will then read it. If the reader sees no hope for it, the story editor probably will not read it. The system may seem callous, but the story editor must have confidence in the judgments of his readers because he does not have time to read all submitted material. In a two-year period, Avco-Embassy received some 1,800 scripts—all from professional writers—and no man can intelligently read 900 scripts a year.

Once a script has gotten initial story department approval, the summary is ready for internal studio distribution. In the old days, when studios had various directors and producers under contract, the summary would be sent to each—and perhaps even to the stars under contract. Based on *their* interest, the studio might proceed with the project. After reading a summary, a particular producer might ask for the script. If it appealed to him he might tell the studio head that it was a project he wanted to do. Now, of course, the studios will not make as many commitments. Few directors and producers are under contract, let alone stars. If a reader likes a piece of material, it goes to the story editor, who then reads it. If he is in agreement with the reader, and if he feels that the project should be bought by the studio, he turns the material over to an executive whose job it is to negotiate for that screenplay.

The price of a screenplay is dependent on many factors. The writer's reputation is significant, but the desirability of the work itself is important, too; and, if several studios are bidding on it, the price will jump accordingly. Price will also be influenced by whether there are top stars like Paul Newman, Steve McQueen, or Barbra Streisand who wish to commit to the film. Attaching successful directors with good track records to the project would also affect the price of the script. The negotiating studio executive will need to know whether such people are tied into the package, or have expressed interest in the material. He should also know how expensive it is going to be to convert this screenplay into a completed film. Is it a costume piece? Does it require many extras? Are there many speaking parts? Should the film be shot on location, or can it be shot on the back lot? Since the first job of the negotiator in fact consists of his getting a rough estimate of a budget for the film, he turns it over to still another executive—a specialist in cost estimating who reads a script and prepares a "topsheet." A topsheet is simply an estimate of what it will cost to make that film. (See pp. 76-86). Normally, 10% of the top-sheet budget estimate is considered as purchase price for the script. With that figure as a point of departure the negotiator and the writer's agent begin their bargaining.[1]

As this stage is reached, the story editor again enters the process. Based on his recommendations, the negotiator will have to decide whether the script is ready to shoot, or whether in fact it needs a rewrite, or whether it calls for a "polish" (which is really a minor rewrite), or whether it needs some very intensive work. Whatever the screenplay requires is incorporated into the contract. In other words, a writer is hired on the basis that he will do a rewrite, or polish or second draft that is acceptable to the company. The story editor's role and function continues to change as work on the script progresses. Let us assume that the writer is now hired to do a second

[1] For examples of what writers are paid, consider the minimums set by the Writers Guild. Assuming the writer is working on a motion picture budgeted at over $1-million, a minimum salary for a screenplay, with treatment, is $13,000; without a treatment, $4,000 less. A rewrite alone is worth $4,000, as is a treatment alone. An original treatment, though, is $6,000, and for providing the story alone, a writer can expect a $4,000 minimum. (See Appendix II)

draft and a polish. This is the normal sequence. A meeting is now held, and all executives who have read the first draft of the screenplay bring their notes. There is some discussion, and the notes are given to the story editor, who must extract from that material the information which must be considered as the writer begins his second draft. A producer or a director may have been assigned to the picture at this point, and if so, they, too, sit in with the executives and pass *their* notes along to the story editor. In many cases, however, neither a producer nor director has been added at this point.

Guided by the executive discussions, the story editor next will tell the negotiator how much time he feels is necessary for the writer to prepare the second draft. The time allowed will vary according to how intensive the rewrite must be. Because some writers do not like to be rushed, they are usually given a minimum of six months to do a rewrite. On the other hand, some writers will do their own thing for the first five-and-a-half months, and finish everything in the last two weeks. It is important to the negotiations, not to mention the ultimate success of the enterprise, that the story editor know his writer—and have rapport with him. He must become his confidant during the period when the writer is under contract to the studio.

Assuming all is in order and the negotiations and understandings are settled, the first story conference is scheduled. Sometimes a director and/or producer will be brought in, and sometimes only the story editor meets with the writer. If a director and a producer are brought into that conference, it is the job of the story editor to make sure that they and the story editor are in complete agreement as to what changes should be made. They are not to cause confusion by giving different opinions once the writer is in the room. The writer must get as straight and as direct a point of view as possible about what is to be included in a rewrite of the screenplay.

After the first story conference, the writer begins his work. How often he meets with the story editor after that is up to both of them. Some writers like to call the story editor every time they get a bright idea, and just kick it around with him. Some writers like to turn in pages every evening, and others wait until they have 20 pages they think are solid, and then turn those in. Still other writers do not want to see the story editor or have anything to do with him until the second draft is completed. The story editor must be flexible. He must allow the writer to be comfortable, and not feel any pressures beyond those that are going to be caused by the script itself.

The major problem for story editors, of course, arises when there are major inconsistencies between the writer's version of the story and the studio's. My feeling is that if we give the writer sufficient time—if we give him, in fact, six months to do a rewrite on something that might be done in three weeks—then these problems are minimized. If there is leeway to work in, then the writer can do it his way first. After all, nobody knows the story better than he does. It is his story; he has created it. He knows those people better than anyone else. What is important is that he get it down on paper, so that we know those people as well as he does. The major problem is not that a writer will argue for a point or argue to keep a character a certain way. The major problem is that the writer, in his head, knows a character—or a scene—very well. He simply has not put it on paper that way. He has not been able to get across that point which he feels he knows inside.

Once the screenwriter sells a screenplay, he knows that he now becomes part of a team. He knows now that he no longer owns that project himself. In a way, this is a very sad state of affairs. In June, 1970, The Writers Guild lost this point to the studio executives. The Guild wanted the writer also to be considered as an executive on a project, but they lost this point. The writer became an employee, and the studio became boss. Sometimes it has been difficult for the writer to understand that. If he does not like the situation, he has two alternatives—either drop off the project and get paid only a portion of what the final payment would be for a finished screenplay, or buy the screenplay back and take it to another studio. His third alternative is to accept the changes and revisions which the studio feels it must have. In nine out of ten cases a good story editor will allow the writer to do it his own way first, and only if he writes himself into a hole will he then be made to do it "the studio way."

As the second draft nears its completion, the story editor must now consider the screenplay not only in light of those criteria and standards by which he judged the original draft as suitable for production by his studio, but also by various additional criteria established by the studio executives. In considering the second draft, the story editor must determine whether the writer has captured all of the elements that were discussed in the earlier meeting. Do the changes work? Are there some changes which seemed good when first proposed but which do not work now? If so, should they be taken out? Is the story, in fact, better now than it was in the first draft? Is it clear and easily understood? Are there holes in the script— areas or aspects in the development that make no sense? Are characters doing things out of character? Are promises made at the beginning of the script not fulfilled later?

The editor must also consider basic economics which can be affected through script changes. Is every single scene necessary? For a scene in which two characters walk in the rain, it will be necessary to use a rain machine, which creates additional expense. Is it necessary that that scene be played in the rain? Could it not play as well in the sunshine? The story editor must ask himself such questions. Another scene may require a "mob"—meaning extras. The story editor must first ask himself if the mob scene is essential to the development of action, and if he decides it is, he must then consider the size of the mob.

It should be stressed that all studio executives also read the second draft. A studio normally will have a three or four week reading period in which to consider a new version. Executives read the screenplay and make additional notes. Then another meeting is held, and now the executives and the story editor decide how near they are to the *final draft*. This procedure is essential simply because a screenwriter may lose sight of the original story altogether in a second draft. Many times it turns out to be inferior to the first draft. If the point of view has been lost, then new decisions must be made. Should the studio allow a third draft to be written by this screenwriter, or is he "written out"?—implying that the writer has now written to the best of his ability on this particular story and it may in fact be necessary to bring in another writer.

These are the negative possibilities. Hopefully, the second draft will be acceptable and deemed almost ready for production. If all do agree, the last step is "polish." At this point a director is usually assigned to the picture. The director will also recommend changes as polishing gets under way. His suggestions are based on his knowledge of things that won't work—that may look good on paper, but will look terrible on film. There may be certain scenes which the director feels cannot be made to come through at all. The director's notes, as well as the producer's are collected, and now the producer, the director, and the screenwriter will meet with the story editor to make all final suggestions for the polish.

Now the work of the screenwriter and the story editor is drawing toward conclusion. A polish is usually a quick brush-up, requiring no more than three or four weeks until it is finished, submitted and approved. While the polish has been going on, the producer has been in touch with actors and actresses. He has hired a casting director, and has worked closely with budget analysts. He has probably been engaged in 30 or 40 other functions while the screenplay is undergoing its final polishing. Once the screenplay is finished, a shooting schedule is set and a starting date is agreed upon.

During the final period it is essential that the writer and director spend at least a week in close discussion. Any questions the director might have are answered by the writer during this week, because in nine out of ten cases the writer does not accompany the production team when the film is made. Once that final screenplay is approved, it then becomes the director's baby, and the screenwriter is for all intents and purposes finished with his job. He goes on to other work and the story editor moves to new projects.

What I have described above is a fair representation of the process by which an *original screenplay* is brought to the production stage in a typical studio. The cast of characters and sequence of events will vary slightly from studio to studio, and situation to situation. I have also tried to outline the role and responsibility of the story editor within the studios, stressing his dual commitment to the creative and the business imperatives which are a part of the motion picture game.

It must be noted, however, that a great many stories which eventually become *films* are not initially submitted as screenplays. Publishing houses, for example, send newsletters to the studios dealing with book manuscripts that they have bought. *Thumbnail descriptions*—six to eight lines of what the material is about—are included for the attention of story editors. *Publishers' Weekly* actually compiles these thumbnail sketches from all the publishing houses. This information comes in to the story editor, as well as the *Kirkus Report* which independently offers the same service to studios. From these and a hundred other sources come possibilities for films. It is necessary, therefore, to review this process from a different vantage point, in this case putting emphasis upon the specific stages through which complete screenplay development is carried, by describing practices and defining terms which are in common use among story editors, writers and literary agents. The review of procedures outlined above was based upon submission of an original *screenplay* and we are now considering the process of developing the screenplay out of an idea, sketch, novel, stage play or any other possible source.

An idea or story is read and liked by a studio, which then has two alternatives: it can either buy the material outright, or *option* it for a payment equivalent to about one-tenth of the purchase price. The option usually gives the studio a 12-month hold on that project, during which time it has the exclusive right to develop a screenplay out of that material.

A writer may be hired on what is called a "step deal," a deal in which the writer simply gets paid a certain amount after each step. In the first step the writer is invited to submit a *treatment*, which is simply a description of how the writer would treat the manuscript cinematically if invited to write the screenplay. Many writers write a treatment in the informal mode of a letter or memo to the story editor. The treatment might include observations about characters, changes in locale, and other suggestions for combinations and permutations of plot, character and situation which would make the story work as a film.

After the treatment comes in to the story editor and is distributed to all executives for approval, the studio has one of three choices: (1) It can admit that it is too difficult to turn this property into a film and drop the project—or the option—at that time. (2) It can decide that the treatment does not capture the flavor of the book, and drop the writer. Another writer is then brought in on a step deal to write another treatment. (3) The studio can approve the treatment and move the original writer on to the next step, which is developing the *story line.*

In a story line the writer is literally telling the story editor how the story should go. Much of this is also done in informal style because most writers work much better if they are writing directly to somebody. The story line can run anywhere from 10 or 15 pages to 120 pages in length. The writer is now telling the story simply and explicitly almost as one would tell a story to a child. When the story line comes in, a studio again has three choices: (1) drop the project completely; (2) drop the writer and bring on a new writer at this point; or (3) pay the writer for this step and continue with him to the next, which is the *breakdown.* In a breakdown the story is broken down into component scenic units. In example—"Scene One: Mary Lou comes out of her apartment and runs into Tom Smith, and they decide to go off to the country together. Scene Two: In the country, they're having a picnic. Suddenly a bull attacks them, and they have to run for their lives." That is a breakdown—a brief description of what every scene in the picture will entail. The breakdown is submitted to the studio executives, who still have their three choices. If the breakdown is approved, the writer is moved to the fourth step, which involves preparation of the *first draft.*

In the first draft each segment of the breakdown is expanded, dialogue is added, as well as appropriate action, descriptions of character mood and other details. In our example, the Scene One described above now becomes:

EXTERIOR. APARTMENT HOUSE. SAN FRANCISCO. DAY.
Mary Lou comes out of the apartment. She is chicly dressed. She is 26 years old. She walks down the street and runs into Tom Smith.

TOM (surprised)
Mary Lou! How nice to see you!

MARY LOU (smiling)
Tom! What a pleasant surprise to see you here.

This is the extent of the first draft, which brings us to the point at which we began our initial description of what happens when a screenplay is submitted.

STORY AND SCREENPLAY:
NEGOTIATING FOR RIGHTS AND WRITERS

SAUL RITTENBERG

". . . In most cases, the services of an attorney would be advisable. . . ."

The problems involved in securing film rights to an idea, story or screenplay in any of its possible stages of completion are of varying difficulty, depending upon the complexities of the particular case, but they do require some familiarity with various laws—including those of copyright. In most cases, the services of an attorney would be advisable. While it is impossible to consider all of the variations and ramifications of this complex field, I can set forth some typical examples of legal considerations which are involved in this aspect of the motion picture business.

Let us begin with the example of an independent producer who wants to make a picture and is looking for material. He finds a published work—a book, a play, poem or song—anything, and he wants to get the legal right to make a film based upon it. At this point it

SAUL RITTENBERG engaged in private law practice in Los Angeles and Beverly Hills for over 20 years before becoming Executive Head of the Metro-Goldwyn-Mayer, Inc. Studio Legal Department in 1956—a post he held for the next 15 years. Mr. Rittenberg is a member and former officer/ trustee of the Copyright Society of the U.S.A. and the Los Angeles Copyright Society. He is a member of the American Bar Association, Section of Patent, Copyright and Trade Mark Law.

can be assumed that if the work is *published* it is protected by a copyright made available under the Federal Copyright Code which was passed in 1909 and has been amended a number of times since. If the work is *not published* it still may be protected in certain cases under the Federal law, or under what is referred to as *common law copyright*, which is the copyright existing under the general *non-statutory law* of the various states. One basic difference between Federal Copyright and Common Law Copyright is that the latter protects only material which has *not* been "published."

Now that statement is subject to many complications—and a producer would be wise to work very closely with his lawyer on such matters.

To proceed: if the material in question is protected under federal copyright, the identity of the copyright owner can be established. Normally it might be the author, but the registration system at the United States Copyright Office permits recording of *assignments of copyright* and of licenses under that copyright. Those records can be searched—either by the Copyright Office, which charges certain established fees for the service, or by a private firm. I know of two private firms of attorneys who will provide the service for a fee. These firms have skilled personnel and very fine records. The producer's lawyer should investigate those sources and determine with whom he should work. If the property is not copyrighted, the search for the copyright proprietor may be more difficult, but even if nothing about the property is recorded anywhere, it is normally not a problem to find out who the owner is (usually it would be the author), and that is with whom negotiations are conducted.

A copyrighted property *is* genuine property, like an article of furniture or a parcel of land. It either must be bought outright, or leased. The term "lease" is not used very much in copyright law but one can secure a license, or partial rights to the property. An independent producer would best be advised to take an option on the material—meaning that he pays a small amount of money down against an ultimate purchase price which is paid only when and if he gets a script written, puts a package together, and arranges some financing. His risk at the "front end" is thus considerably reduced. Options represent only a right to buy at a given time, or a right to obtain rights. Option agreements are made with the copyright owner. This could be the publisher, but usually is the author. Normally, a reasonable option price ranges from 5% to 10% of the purchase price. Although one can in some cases pick up an option for a few dollars, it is worthwhile to pay some reasonable amount for it. If the optioning party pays very little for it, he may not be able to secure effective enforcement of his rights later on.

Proceeding further, the producer now has, in effect, optioned time—time to try to put a production deal together. He has taken an option for the purpose of buying whatever rights can be negotiated. His agreement—if it is soundly drawn—should say that during the option period he has the right to create adaptations, motion picture scripts, treatments or whatever else he intends to create. Indeed, if the option agreement does not stipulate the right to adapt the property, it may later be claimed that this right was not granted. That is one of the pitfalls the motion picture lawyer should recognize. Occasionally the attorney representing the owner of the property will insist on a provision that—if the option is not exercised—whatever written material based upon the original is completed during the option period will revert to the copyright owner. If a producer hasn't been able to put his package together, then he may have to give up what work he has done. This then becomes a matter of negotiation. The producer's attorney may argue that the costs of his client's creative effort during the option period should be paid for by the copyright owner, whose lawyer might well argue in turn that this could be done, but only if and when the new material can be "put to work" by the copyright owner.

The reason the owner wants some kind of hold on what is done is that he must protect his own interests in the event that he options the material again. Assume, for example, that a novel has been developed into a screenplay by a producer who fails to complete his project and "drops" the option. If another producer optioned the property for similar purposes, the copyright owner might find himself in a difficult position if he did not also own the work done by the first producer. The copyright holder may say to the original optioner: "I want the rights to whatever you do with my novel if you drop the option because you may work in a direction that the next man in line may also want to take. He would have no knowledge of what you have done but might create something quite comparable, in which case you could claim that I passed your treatment on to him and he merely copied what you did. I can't get into that situation. You have in effect 'clouded my title'—you have made it difficult for me to sell it to another purchaser if you don't go ahead with the picture."

Thus far, I have tried to mention merely a few of the complexities and pitfalls in acquiring the rights to potential motion picture story material. We should next deal with legal questions which may arise as the material is developed into an actual screenplay.

Once a producer has acquired rights to an idea or story, the next step is to get something written, which means dealing with a writer, unless the producer is also a writer. Let us assume that the producer wants to employ a professional motion picture writer. He must recognize first that he will have to meet Writers Guild contractual obligations. The Guild has negotiated contracts with the major companies and most of the other producing companies since the 1940's, and their contract is long and complicated—covering a variety of subjects. It establishes minimum rates which must be paid for a treatment, for a screenplay, or for revisions. Over the years certain restrictions have been established in regard to what rights can be acquired by a producer who is buying original material. The legal specialization involved here is called the "separation of rights" field. The Writers Guild has been successful in bringing about limitations upon the rights which a producer or a motion picture company can acquire when purchasing non-exploited material, and a motion picture lawyer has to be completely familiar with these. The rights which are withheld are not of a nature that would affect motion picture development. The Guild's purpose, rather, was to reserve to the author the peripheral values that might grow out of a successful picture based on the material. If a producer or company buys motion picture rights, it usually will also get the right to put the picture on television. It can usually get the right to do a television series using the characters. It can almost always get remake rights—meaning the right to do substantially the same story over again. It can usually get sequel rights —meaning the right to do additional pictures using the characters. Normally, the author will reserve stage rights, publishing rights, radio rights, and live television rights, subject to various restrictions and limitations which may become the subject of somewhat complicated negotiation. If we understand that whatever is settled is subject to the Writers Guild agreement* we can turn our attention to some other problems which may arise in contract negotiations between a producer or company and the writer.

Most professional writers have what is called an "established" salary. They have reached the point where they know they can get a certain amount of money, so the sum is mentioned immediately upon going into negotiation. Then the bargaining begins. If the producer or company can afford it, they pay it. If they cannot afford it, they will try to reduce it. There is no difference between that kind of bargaining and bargaining in any other kind of business. It is all a matter of market standard value. The producer, of course, seldom deals with a writer, but with the writer's agent. Almost all writers have agents, or attorneys, or both. Some agents are better than others and they make better bargains. Prices can go to absurd extremes, but too much of that kind of price-driving can hurt the industry. However, in recent years, I think, the peak has been seen and prices are now

* For a more detailed analysis of the Writers Guild basic contract, see Appendix II.

going down. You can always get good prices, however, for top material and top writers.

Once price is agreed upon, the contract is formulated. The normal deal is straight employment, wherein the writer is engaged as a salaried employee of the producer. Sometimes the producer will make what is called an "independent contractor deal"—normally established at the suggestions of the writer's tax lawyers—or the deal may be a "loan-out" from a company controlling the writer's services. The differences are largely technical.

The contract sometimes provides for week-to-week employment at a certain salary per week. In negotiation, the period of time in which the writing must be completed is sometimes determined and set forth in the contract. This pattern is more often used when a writer is employed to do revising, polishing, or specialized writing. The more usual arrangement with a writer is called "a deal contract," which means that for a given price he will deliver a treatment, a screenplay or whatever is stipulated. These contracts also follow a pattern, in which the amount the writer is to be paid for each step of the work, and the length of time for such steps of work is predetermined. It may be a flat deal where no options are involved, or it may be an "option" or "step deal" where the writer does his work in steps. At the end of each step the producer may have the right to terminate or continue the contract, through treatment, first-draft screenplay, and the final screenplay.

I have barely touched upon the full range of legal questions related to rights and contract negotiation in the development of story and screenplay, but I hope I have given the reader sufficient information to suggest the importance of obtaining professional advice and guidance in this area.

MOTIVATION AND CONTROL OF CREATIVE WRITING *

M. WILLIAM KRASILOVSKY

". . . The principle of copyright as a privilege granted in order to induce creative work is well established. . . ."

An individual in Detroit has been waiting for the world to beat a path to his door in order to purchase his ideas. He advertised in *Variety:*

IDEAS FOR SALE

Gentleman with prolific imagination has several original story ideas suitable for developing into novels, stage plays, television scripts or movies. Unique themes of the caliber of *The Graduate, Alfie, The Pawnbroker, The Red Shoes, The Bicycle Thief,* etc. available to Studios, TV Packagers or other recognized professionals.

M. WILLIAM KRASILOVSKY is a member of the New York law firm of Feinman and Krasilovsky. He served formerly as counsel to Warner Brothers Music Companies and as associate counsel to the American Guild of Authors and Composers. Mr. Krasilovsky is a co-author (with Sidney Shemel) of *This Business of Music* and *More About This Business of Music.* He has lectured for the Practicing Law Institute and contributed articles to *Copyright Society Bulletin, Performing Arts Review* and *Columbia Teachers College Magazine.*

* The author is pleased to acknowledge the valuable research assistance of Alexis Krasilovsky of Yale University in the preparation of this article reprinted from *Performing Arts Review*, Vol. I, No. 1, 1969, by permission of the author.

Undoubtedly, this gentleman honestly believes that he has property rights to these great ideas which are capable of commercial
transactions the same as one can deal with a ton of steel, a bunch of
bananas or a copyrighted script. His assumption is wrong inasmuch
as ideas are protected only to the extent that the originator can keep
his ideas to himself through non-disclosure, except insofar as he can
establish a contractual relationship with the would-be purchaser
through express or implied agreement. Most offers of ideas actually
result in immediate rejection by the "recognized professionals" sol-
icited in the *Variety* ad.

W. C. Fields accepted an idea submission of gags from a
stranger only after placing the following condition upon the relationship:

> If you would like to submit a couple of scripts gratis and I
> am able to use them, who knows, both parties being willing,
> we might enter into a contract. My reason for injecting the vile
> word "gratis" is that we get so many letters from folks who,
> if we answer even in the negative, immediately bring suit for
> plagiarism. Whilst we have never had to pay off, they some-
> times become irritating no end.

Even in this case, W. C. Fields' irritation was without end because a California court gave a judgment to the idea merchant who
brought suit despite the acceptance of the condition.[1]

The irritation of persons who fall into trouble by accepting the
submission of ideas can underline the reason for rejecting property
rights to the bald idea. If the law were to protect ideas as the private
property of the first person to think of them it would create chaos
in the entire field of the arts. Idea protection would reward the
indolent and restrain the energetic author or artist from expressing
himself to the public.

The United States Copyright Office states:

> Ideas, plans, methods or systems cannot be copyrighted. It is
> only the particular manner in which an author expresses him-
> self in his writings that can be protected by copyright. The
> ideas, plans, methods or systems that he describes, or that are
> embodied in his works are not copyrightable.

Another statement of this Office is:

It is not possible to register a claim to copyright in the idea for

[1] The lyric of a song sung by Danny Kaye and written by Sylvia Fine illustrates
the problems of idea acknowledgment. In describing a presentation of "Manic
Depressive Pictures," the lyrics state: "Screenplay by Glotz, from a stage play by
Motz, from a novel by Sock, from a story by Block, from a chapter by Rock, from
a sentence by Stoke, *from an idea by Croak, based on a Joe Miller joke.*"

a motion picture, television program, story or any other kind of work.

This absence of protection for ideas was a basis of denying relief to Orson Welles in a law-suit against CBS for a reproduction of a portion of his famous *War of the Worlds* radio show. The Court found that Welles had truly conceived of the idea of presenting the original radio dramatization by means of radio news announcements describing a contemporaneous invasion of Martians. Nevertheless, the rule of law applied was that ideas *per se* are not copyrightable, but only the expression of the ideas are the subject of copyright.

The basic authorization of copyright statutes is found in the United States Constitution authorizing Congress:

> . . . to promote the progress of science and the useful arts, by securing for limited times to authors and inventors the exclusive rights to their respective writings and discoveries.

Note that this short provision contains restrictions and distinctions which emphasize the peculiar nature of copyright. The rights are, first of all, for "limited times" after which they are to be in the public domain. (These limied times are presently for two successive terms of 28 years but, due to copyright revision attempts in recent years, new expirations have been deferred since 1962.) The second essential point is that "authors" are to receive right of copyright and that connotes originality and creativity. A third item to be noted in this Constitutional provision is that protection of copyright is extended to "writings" which necessarily excludes ideas and other unexpressed creative output and has even been held to exclude protection to *titles*.

The most important point to note in the Constitutional provision is the over-all philosophy expressed in the statement of purpose of promotion of the progress of science and the useful arts. This demonstrates the concern of enriching culture for the public as a whole rather than recognition of any inherent natural right of an author. As early as 1826, the then leading lobbyist for copyright, Noah Webster, showed his failure to accept the concept of copyright as a privilege in the following words:

> I do not see why an interest in original literary composition should stand on different grounds from all other personal property. . . . Literary composition (is) a species of property more peculiarly a man's own than any other, being a production of a man's mind or inventive facilities . . . while a horse or an acre of land, which a fool may obtain by muscular exertions, is a permanent inheritable estate.

He also said:

The right of a farmer and mechanic to the exclusive enjoyment and right of disposal of what they make or produce is never questioned. What then can make a difference between a product of muscular strength and the produce of the intellect?

One early advocate expressed the argument of "sweat of the brow" quite literally and in his own poetic style as follows:

. . . we possess as absolute a right over our thoughts as we have over the brain cells whose rhythm gives to the sensational impulses the thought form, and whether we use the thought form to mould words with our mouth or bricks with our hands, the product is equally our property.

These arguments have been consistently rejected and the principle of copyright as a privilege granted in order to induce creative work is well established. This motivating factor of copyright was stated by the Supreme Court in the following language (which unfortunately stresses economic incentive without reference to right of control of manner and extent of use):

. . . encouragement of individual effort by personal gain is the best way to advance public welfare through the talents of authors. . . . Sacrificial days devoted to such creative activities deserve rewards commensurate with the services rendered.

This would seem to be a finding that "personal gain" is the best way to motivate the writer. It would seem quite an adequate answer to works such as *Valley of the Dolls*, the *Batman* television series, and many a popular magazine article or story. It does not seem a complete answer to the following Sinclair Lewis question:

One of the most curious questions about a writer and one least answered in biographies, is why he ever became a writer at all; why . . . he should choose to sit alone year after year making up fables or commenting upon what other and livelier citizens do.

A. H. Maslow's general answer is:

Clearly creative behavior is like any other behavior in having multiple determinants. It may be seen in innately creative people whether they are satisfied or not, happy or unhappy, hungry or sated. Also it . . . may be compensatory, ameliorative or purely economic.

The purely economic motivation of a truly creative author is described in sorry tones by Eugene O'Neill in connection with a movie right sale:

> . . . you may understand what my feeling is about a film sale of a favorite play I know Hollywood will distort. Let's consider *The Hairy Ape*. It remains one of my favorites. . . . I sold it because, with two homes and ranch overhead on my neck, I had to sell it or sell some of my annuities whose income pays the alimony. . . . I tell you I was not going to see the film—nor read one word about it—nor even admit that it exists, I sure mean it! But all the same I will always feel guilty.

Fortunately for O'Neill, he was able to assuage his guilt some time later when he received a cable saying that Jean Harlow, as America's foremost actress, wanted O'Neill, as America's foremost dramatist, to write an original screenplay for her. He was asked to reply as to terms in a collect cable of 20 words. His reply read:

> NO! NO! NO! NO! NO! NO! NO! NO! NO! NO! NO! NO! NO!
> NO! NO! NO! NO! NO! NO!   O'Neill

A constructive role of economic reward as a motivation to the writer must, of course, be recognized. Rudyard Kipling's biographer notes that when Kipling was faced, in the first year of marriage, with a bank failure and loss of all but $100, he merely turned more assiduously to his writing and soon recouped his fortunes as "lack of ready cash was no great obstacle to a man who could always sell his wares." Also, when James Joyce was a failing medical student, he turned to his writing as a means of earning a livelihood as a serious occupation rather than avocation. Undoubtedly, if writing were not a source of economic return controlled by the writer as businessman, we would find that many an otherwise capable writer would devote his writing talents to currying favor with his subject as a form of prostitution of pen rather than objectively setting forth his best efforts. The old saw that art is most effectively produced by a starving artist in a cold garret is no longer accepted.

The adequately fed and housed writer or artist can better devote his time to writing rather than to selling real estate or potatoes. He can fulfill the roles summarized by Alexis Krasilovsky as being quite apart from any economic motivation:

> . . . the ego can be interpreted as the writer's need to communicate with the reader, to delay the immediate gratification of the inspirational vision through a barrier of language and form; while the super-ego represents the writer's most moralizing sense of submission to an artistic devotion inflated to the importance of religion.

This super-ego spiritual communion was described by James Joyce:

> This supreme quality is felt by the artist when the esthetic image is first conceived in his imagination. The mind in that mysterious instant Shelley likened beautifully to a fading coal. The instant where that supreme quality of beauty, the clear radiance of the esthetic image is apprehended luminously by the mind which had been arrested by its wholeness and fascinated by its harmony is the luminous silent stasis of esthetic pleasure, a spiritual state very like to that cardiac condition which the Italian physiologist Luigi Galvani . . . called "the enchantment of the heart."

Although appealing, this "enchantment of the heart" cannot be accepted as the source of most creative activity in the field of writing and the arts. Most copyrights are obtained nowadays not by the lonely artist submitting to a compulsion to express himself but by persons, collaborators, firms and corporations who have other motivations. A statement by the president of McGraw-Hill called attention to the very prolific field of writing in science and engineering which he found to be very unrewarding in direct economic gain and yet to have other indirect economic motivations. He said that the busy scientist or engineer who spends some 20 years in producing his magnum opus writes for personal satisfaction and professional prestige rather than for the limited royalties involved. The indirect returns, he finds, are promotions, better jobs and higher consulting fees. All of these, however, are consistent with copyright's power to control publication and publisher towards achieving most prestigious presentation. The corporate publisher of scientific and engineering works must make substantial investments in preparing manuscript for publication, often with only limited marketing potential, and economic control over selling price is essential to justify this investment.

Many modern day creative works are by highly impersonal "authors" in the form of giant corporations employing dozens or even hundreds of individuals working under corporate supervision and control towards one creative result. Any modern motion picture, for example, may utilize teams of writers, composers, lyricists, choreographers as well as executants in the form of directors, conductors, costumers, make-up men, hairdressers and, of course, actors and actresses. The millions of dollars that have become customary budgets for films cannot be expected to be invested unless maximum economic control of the product is possible. Accordingly, the employee-for-hire who is the human author or composer for film works has only such rights as his contract provides, and for copyright purposes the corporate employer is the "author" with all resultant privileges. Thus does MGM keep tight control over *Gone With The Wind* so that no television showing can diminish theatrical audience, and so does the corporate owner of *Around the World in 80 Days* reject $3½-million for television use of the film. On the other hand, Otto Preminger could not restrain television showing of *Anatomy of a Murder* even on grounds that necessary cutting to allow commercials hurt the artistic integrity of his film, and George Stevens had similar limited rights with respect to *A Place in the Sun*. Both suits were based on right to screen credit and integrity of work rather than copyright.

The right of control is a natural and essential part of copyright. Abraham Kaminstein, the Register of Copyrights, has said:

> Copyright as it now exists combines two elements: control and remuneration. Take away the first and you no longer have copyright; you have patronage. Within the next few generations I feel sure that there will be strenuous efforts in every country, developed as well as developing, to take the author's control over his work away from his copyright, or to restrict it sharply, leaving him with rights of remuneration on which limits are placed . . .

In the United States today we have several aspects of copyright which are without right of control. Any non-dramatic work can be publicly performed if not for profit, such as by a municipal band playing in a park or a poetry reading in school or club. In the highly commercial area of phonograph recordings, any musical composition can be recorded under a compulsory license of two cents per record once the copyright owner has permitted any first recording to be released. Juke box use of recordings for public performance, even though for profit, is also exempt from copyright protection under present law. This practice of exemptions and compulsory licenses of works otherwise under copyright is also utilized in a number of countries for permitting local translations, with a view towards serving public demand rather than private ownership.

The general right to control uses of creative works is often recognized as essential to forestall the artist from emulating Gauguin in burning his paintings. The world has copyright to thank for the Pulitzer Prize-winning play *Long Day's Journey Into Night*. Eugene O'Neill let the manuscript out of his hands only on written condition that it not be opened for 25 years after his death. His publisher, Random House, agreed to this condition and honored it after O'Neill's death, only to find that as the copyright devolved to O'Neill's widow upon his death, she insisted upon the release of the play for stage performance and for publication by Yale University Press.

The right of control of use of copyrighted works also encourages early and broader release of certain works. Curtis G. Benjamin of McGraw-Hill has remarked concerning medical books especially:

> Frontier research must be proved and published in the professional journals and accepted conclusively at this stage before it can appear in medical books, for the physician and the public must not be given false information or false hopes.

Lord Macaulay expressed another view of periodical publication not being available for book use without author's control. He said, upon learning of American publishers taking advantage of lack of copyright:

> . . . if they are to be republished, it is better that they be republished under the eye of the author and with his corrections rather than with all the blemishes inseparable from hasty writing and hasty printing. . . . The public judges, and ought to judge, indulgently of periodical works. They are not expected to be highly finished. Their natural life is only six weeks. Sometimes their writer is at a distance from the books to which he wants to refer. . . . He may blunder; he may contradict himself; he may break off in the middle of a story; he may give immoderate extension to one part in a few words. All this is readily forgiven if there be a certain spirit and vivacity in his style. But as soon as he republishes, he challenges a comparison with all the most symmetrical and polished of human compositions.

The author's right to choose his medium is even more important in the highly diversified forms of media that technology makes available today.

The right to remain unpublished or to limit forms of publication is actually a right of privacy. In their precendental article on privacy, Warren and Brandeis cited copyright principles as follows:

> . . . that the protection afforded to thoughts, sentiments and emotions expressed through the medium of writing or of the arts so far as it consists of preventing publication is merely an instance of enforcement of the more general right of the individual to be let alone.

Dean Chafee called attention to the perpetual right under common law (as distinguished from limited rights under statutory copyright) with regard to unpublished letters, as follows:

The letters of James McNeill Whistler are lost to the world because a crabbed niece would not allow his chosen biographers to print them. Suppose that a new manuscript of Poe should be discovered tomorrow. His descendants could keep it hidden if they so desired and according to judicial dicta could do so forever.

Of course, as in the case of *Long Day's Journey,* the heirs of a deceased author may also release for publication an otherwise unavailable work. Certainly, if property rights are to be respected in unpublished works, it is more desireable that society look to a living person for a negotiated release than to have to be controlled by a dead hand from the grave.

Society may also consider itself enriched by the very right of privacy and limited publication which, in the short view, may bar publication. At least, through assurance of privacy, the author is less restrained in his expression of thoughts. Professor Alan Westin, in his recent book on privacy says:

> . . . the democratic society is strengthened when individuals have a sense of personal autonomy since it produces traits that are desirable in citizens of a free state: independent thought, diversity of views, and non-conformity.

Each of these traits was admirably displayed in the 1968 statements on television following the President's State of the Union message. However applicable use of the word "privacy" may be in the context, nevertheless it is that which encouraged James Farmer, ex-ambassador Reischauer, William Buckley, Daniel Moyanihan, Floyd McKissick and others to a spontaneous give-and-take within minutes of the close of the President's message. The "spirit and vivacity" mentioned by Lord Macaulay so many decades ago with respect to periodical publication were the goal at the expense of symmetry, polish, research and even logic. Undoubtedly some of the participants would refuse to allow publication of their remarks, but there is no doubt that the dialogue produced on the spot was more valuable to the public than even the most polished and definitive printed statement. In this and other oral statements, the right of control may be a more essential motivation of public statement than is economic reward.

The right of control also encourages enrichment of archives for limited scholarship and historical purposes. Papers of public officials are a frequent subject of archive storage but there are many others. The Copyright Office itself furnishes an archive function of unpublished lectures, dramas and musical works which are registered for copyright in unpublished form. Eugene O'Neill told the story of a particularly productive period in his life when he thought he was God:

I'd finish them and rush down to the post office to ship them to Washington to be copyrighted before somebody stole them . . .

The odd result, however, was that his diligence of obtaining exclusive control by copyrighting the unpublished plays was not matched 28 years later when he forgot to renew the copyright and therefore permitted them to fall into public domain where they were freely available in authentic preserved form and were published without his permission.

An admirable Library of Congress Archives project is found in its 850 recordings of poetry. Poets who consented to record their voices in the projects included Robert Frost, William Carlos Williams, Langston Hughes, Marianne Moore and Lionel Trilling. Yet, the foreword to the catalogue shows that less than half of the recordings are available to the public. (Copyright only covers the poetry itself, not the performer's rendition, but it may be assumed that the Library of Congress has an obligation in the nature of contract with some of the individual poets not to release their recorded renditions.)

In the ever-changing balancing of the scales of public interest and private incentive, the courts have evolved some exceptions called "fair use." This is best illustrated in the generally recognized right of critics and reviewers to quote portions of copyrighted works without asking permission or paying for the use. Chief Judge Leon R. Yankwich of the United States District Court for the Southern District of California has cited the following considerations to be given in determination of fair use:

(1) The quantity and importance of the portions taken;
(2) their relation to the work of which they are a part;
(3) the result of their use upon the demand for the copyrighted publications.

The interesting aspect of fair use is the risk involved by the prospective user. Of course a *bona fide* book reviewer can rely on fair use, but can a dramatist allow a character to enter on stage whistling a few bars of *Happy Days Are Here Again*? Can a magazine article describe a news event by quoting a few lines of a poem recited in a courtroom? Ofttimes even *Time* Magazine will prefer to give a copyright credit when it might rely on fair use, but to the credit of the *New Yorker* it may be noted that they went to court to establish their rights to limited quotation in a non-fiction article involving the *Perils of Pauline*. The very nature of risk involved in fair use is what makes it flexible and appropriate to an ever-changing world of publication and new media.

Chief Justice Warren and Vice President Humphrey were in the audience when the United States Marine Corps band played, without copyright clearance, some very impertinent variations on songs. The then-President was the butt in: (sung to tune of *Davy Crockett*)

> Built himself a fortune through the FCC
> Lyndon, Lyndon Johnson, the buck-skin buccaneer.

And Richard Nixon was described to the tune of a Cole Porter tune in:

> I've got it under my skin
>   The White House, Deep in the heart of me
> So deep in my heart it's really a part of me
>   I've got it under my skin

In this use of parody and satire, the Gridiron Club was in the company of Sid Caesar who was allowed to use portions of *From Here to Eternity* to the extent needed to bring to mind the portions of the plot that were the subject of satire and parody. Similarly, *Mad* Magazine was permitted to use limited portions of lyrics in "Louella Schwartz Describes Her Malady" (*A Pretty Girl Is Like a Melody*) and "The Last Time I Saw Maris" (*The Last Time I Saw Paris*). The Court in that case noted that the Constitutional purpose of copyright is promoting the progress of art. In this regard, the Court said that "financial reward is but an incident to this general objective" and that there is a fear that the art of parody, which has thrived from the time of Chaucer, would be stifled if its propriety were tested entirely on the precise amount appropriated from the original. "We believe," said the Court, "that parody and satire are deserving of substantial freedom, both as entertainment and as a form of literary criticism. . . . Many a true word is indeed spoken in jest."

As previously noted in discussing the Constitutional basis of copyright, the *originality* of a work is a *sine qua non* of copyright. Judge Jerome Frank said with regard to copyright, that "original" means that the particular works "owes its origin" to the author. This is to be distinguished from "novelty" or "newness" which is a requirement of the sister field of patents claimed by inventors. The distinction is interestingly put in an oft-quoted decision of Judge Learned Hand as follows:

> If by some magic a man who had never known it were to compose anew Keats' *Ode on a Grecian Urn*, he would be an author, and, if he copyrighted it, others might not copy that poem, though they might, of course, copy Keats'.

As far-fetched as this example may seem, the possibility of coincidental original authorship occurs frequently in cartography, directory compilation, photography and music in its simpler forms. As we approach the days of electronic authorship through computers and in electronic music composition, the frequency of coincidence of originality may increase. A computer can have an intake of a thousand earlier works and come out with a combined factual answer utilizing many sources. Works of electronic music can merge, twist, bend and even develop themes and treatments of a hundred prior composers. The editorial work of earlier public domain sources can result in "coincidental original" editorship worthy of copyright to two or more "authors," but the more disturbing question is how is the original author of contributing portions to be identified, much less compensated?

Originality has not always been appreciated with the same fetish-like devotion that is now accorded through copyright laws. William Hazlitt said:

> Homer appears the most original of authors, probably for no other reason than that we can trace the plagiarism no further . . .

Goethe said:

> The most original modern authors are not so because they advance what is new but simply because they know how to put what they have to say as if it had never been said before.

Zimmerman, in a recent issue of *Musical Quarterly*, stresses the frequent plagiarism of composers as great as Handel with the observation that mercantilism had its effect in the world of art in the 16th Century when the publisher and not the patron sought economic return rather than communion with the arts. He searches back to the 1st Century when Quintillian said:

> (there is) a universal rule that we should wish to copy what we approve in others . . . (and) . . . improve upon the good things and vie with the original in the expresion of the same thoughts . . .

An early Supreme Court case of *Emerson* v. *Davies* in 1845 held:

> In truth, in literature, in science and in art, there are, and can be, few, if any, things which, in an abstract sense, are strictly new and original throughout. Every book in literature, science and art, borrows and must necessarily borrow, and use much which was well known and used before. . . . If no book could be the subject of copyright which was not new and original in the elements of which it is composed, there could be no ground for copyright in modern times, and we would be obliged to ascend very high, even in antiquity, to find a work entitled to such eminence. Virgil borrowed much from Homer; Bacon drew from earlier as well as contemporary minds; Coke exhausted all the known learning of his profession; and even Shakespeare

and Milton . . . would be found to have gathered much from the abundant store of current knowledge and classical studies of their days . . .

As previously noted, copyright is a privilege granted by the government in order to motivate original expression. As such, there is a continuing need to observe that copyright maintain its function of incentive of artistic expresion rather than to hamstring other creative expression. Principles of fair use and compulsory licenses assist this delicate balance of interests, but the law of the market-place is of even greater importance in supplying copyright clearance for the ever growing variety and volume of derivative uses.

The current Copyright Law Revision Bill now before the Senate defines a "derivative work" as:

A work based upon one or more pre-existing works, such as a translation, musical arrangement, dramatization, fictionalization, motion picture version, sound recording, art reproduction, abridgement, condensation, or any other form in which a work may be recast, transformed or adapted. A work consisting of editorial revisions, annotation, elaborations, or other modifications which, as a whole, represents an original work of authorship, is a "derivative work."

Familiar examples of derivative works are *My Fair Lady, South Pacific,* and *West Side Story* of the Broadway stage; the television adaptations of *Batman* and *Charlie Brown* comic strips; motion pictures such as *Gone With The Wind* and *Around the World in 80 Days* and the numerous translations of books from abroad. There are two sides to the question of copyright in each derivative work; the right to make the new version in the first place and the right to stop others from copying the new version in the second place.

A promotional statement used during the Canadian *Expo '67* described a modernistic conglomerate as "a fusion of sound, film and architecture designed to bounce the participant and make him rummage through his mind and spirit." This combination of the arts and its goal of making the observer a "participant" through his "mind and spirit" brings to mind the definition of culture offered by Ortega y Gasset: ". . . that which a man has in his possession when he has forgotten everything that he has read."

Derivative works often do more than bring to mind a forgotten plot applied to modern times, such as *West Side Story* or *Damn Yankees.*[2]

[2] *Damn Yankees* as a Broadway play gave appropriate credit to being based on the book *The Day the Yankees Lost the Pennant.* However, they neglected the earlier credit to Goethe's drama, *Faust,* which was the basis of Gounod's opera and Thomas Mann's novel and which, in turn, was based on Christopher Marlowe's *Dr. Faustus,* which was also the inspiration of a Rembrandt etching and a cantata by Marius.

Jerome Kern was found to be sufficiently cultured to have a subconscious plagiarism in the writing of *Dardanelle*, and undoubtedly many a creative author or composer finds similar difficulty in distinguishing inspiration of the muses from appreciation of an earlier work.

Culture has a way of absorbing and digesting bits and fragments of musical, literary and artistic expression into an accumulated fund from which it is difficult to distinguish originality from copyrighted works and works of publc domain. Susan Sontag has noted that the accumulative nature of knowledge which we used to restrict to science is tending to appear in the arts as well. She has pointed out:

> Art does not progress, in the sense that science and technology do. But the arts do develop and change. . . . The most interesting works of contemporary art are full of references to the history of the medium; so far as they comment on past art, they demand a knowledge of at least the recent past. As Harold Rosenberg has pointed out, contemporary paintings are themselves acts of criticism as much as creation. The point could be made as well of much recent work in films, music, the dance, poetry, and (in Europe) literature. Again, a similarity with the style of science—this time with the accumulative aspect of science—can be discerned.

Miss Sontag has found that much of modern art's creative role is in the "idea and concept." This is the very thing that copyright is designed to *exclude* in the interest of motivating an expression of the idea and concept in concrete form.

In the light of cultural and technological changes, we must be continually aware that the border between creative author and cultural consumer is becoming more of a penumbra. Creative roles are more frequently recognized in the user, be he a film producer, opera director or recording artist, and for his part the original author is often closer through tape recorders, Xerox machines and other technical instruments to the bald idea purveyor. It may be that copyright has been purposely kept narrowed to the chain of title attributed to the basic expression because of difficulties of tracing and of bookkeeping. Perhaps computers can assist in broadening this aspect to include other recognizable creative participants. It may also be that some historic or romantic notion of lonely artists working independently helps to preserve the right of copyright owner from stopping further development of his brain-child (as distinguished from the world of parents) but there too, a simple analysis of registrations will show the corporate and partnership status of most works registered, and the resultant reduction in principles of inviolable paternity. The question remains as to whether mere financial return under fair distribution principles would suffice if copyright were broadened to reward all creative participants and to permit maximum permutations. ASCAP and BMI, the music clearing houses that control nearly all copyrighted music in the United States, are demonstrations of the minimal or non-existent demands other than fair compensation once a work is initially released to the public. Also, the compulsory two-cent license for phonograph reproduction of music, with its results of maximum variations on any one theme regardless of original owner's taste, has not worked noticeably against the public's cultural needs despite a few rock-and-roll versions of old standards.

The end question remains whether ideas which have reached public acceptance through protected expression enough to become part of a national culture are to be the sole province of the purchasers of copyright or those authors who manage to keep ownership in themselves. If the marketplace is sufficiently active, it would seem that the limited terms of copyright is a safe period of mercantile monopoly. But when the owners refuse to show up for trading in the market, we might consider applying the same principles of eminent domain that are available in real estate when public need is evident.

PART TWO

Financing and Budgeting Films

If the creative wellspring for all movies is in the form of words committed to paper, the true source of any film is in the form of cash on the barrelhead. To illustrate this major point, Rick Setlowe *capsulizes an assortment of fresh potential financial sources available to producers engaged in the endless quest for backing, while* A. H. Howe *describes the role and concerns of a picture financier—in this case the Bank of America— of the more traditional variety. Howe's contribution dispels a number of myths about bank financing.* Robert Gilbert *covers essential international financing considerations in his discussion of sources for foreign film subsidies which potentially are available to American producers.*

The financial demands of a picture are found in the budget itself, where valid figures are critical to all final decisions regarding whether or not production can proceed. The budget must be considered in light of the screenplay it represents, and in proportion to the projected commercial strength of the picture. Equally important, the budget must be prepared before actual photography is initiated. The final essay in this section is devoted to the crucial problem of accurately budgeting feature films. The "topsheet" of the budget form used by Universal Pictures is described by Marshall Green *and* Tim Donahue, *who also give attention to practical problems which arise when financial guidelines must be given specific application.*

HOLLYWOOD'S NEW FINANCIAL TRICKS*

RICK SETLOWE

{ ". . . In the new Hollywood "system," anything goes as long as it makes sense, and, of course, its money back. . . ." }

American filmmakers—the liveliest of artists and businessmen—have always had the inherent imagination and ingenuity to surmount any crisis. Pic-by-pic, a whole new ballgame of independent production, outside financing and major distribution deals emerged in 1970.

With the established studios in a major financial bind but their distribution arms nevertheless still requiring a flow of product, the filmmaker sought out and attracted an exotic array of outside financial backing ranging from an oil-affluent Indian tribe, to cereal companies

RICK SETLOWE was recently named Vice-President in charge of Creative Affairs for ABC Pictures Corporation. A graduate of the University of Southern California, Mr. Setlowe has completed graduate studies at Stanford and the University of California. He served on the staff of *Daily Variety,* was a reporter and editor on the San Francisco *Examiner,* and has contributed frequently to *TV Guide, Time* and *Life.*

* Reprinted from *Daily Variety*, 37th Anniversary Edition, Oct. 27, 1970.

EDITORS' NOTE: In mid-1971, Mr. Setlowe asked that the following note be added when the above material was published:

The article was written as journalism to appear in September 1970, and as such is an accurate reflection of conditions in the film industry at that immediate period of time. It was a portrait of the industry's financial gropings and experiments at the time. As in the case of all experiments, some of them will lead down blind alleys and be abandoned, several already have proved to be successful, others have not yet got off the corporate drawing board, and a few, although not entirely successful, are at least probes in the right direction.

and a toy manufacturer. In each case, these angels have associated with established filmmakers.

Perhaps the most exotic deal was put together by producer Ronnie Lubin. The Jicarilla Apache Tribe financed a $2-million western, *Gunfight*, starring Kirk Douglas and Johnny Cash, which was shot at Columbia Studios and with Cinemobile Systems on location in New Mexico and old Spain.

Paramount then acquired United States and Canadian distribution rights in a rare deal that split film rental grosses between the filmmakers and the distributor from the first dollar, and Lubin took off to Europe to negotiate foreign distribution country-by-country.

In the new Hollywood "system," anything goes, as long at it makes sense, and, of course, its money back.

Robert Radnitz, who made films for 20th-Fox, Universal, Paramount and Cinema Center Films, formed a partnership with Mattel, the toy company, to finance and distribute three feature films a year.

Quaker Oats totally financed Wolper Pictures production of *Willy Wonka and the Chocolate Factory*, the made-in-Germany confection for kids distributed by Paramount, and the Kellogg Company of Battle Creek anted up enough corn flakes to co-finance *Pufnstuf* with Universal.

For Mattel, which was the first toy manufacturer to plunge into heavy TV sponsorship with the *Mickey Mouse Club*, had the license to manufacture and sell Disney tie-ins, and was innovating kidvid of its own, the association with Radnitz was a natural expansion.

Likewise, Kellogg sponsored the *Pufnstuf* program and the tie-in promotion of the feature pic on the back of cereal boxes and point-of-purchase displays made sense as part of an integrated advertising program.

Quaker Oats is considering making and marketing a whole line of new products on *Willy Wonka and the Chocolate Factory*.

A parallel to Mattel Toys expansion, in this case in the field of adult recreation and education, into filmmaking and distribution has already been successfully made by Grove Press, the legal landmark-setting publisher of underground literature, exotica and erotica. Grove's handling of *I Am Curious* (*Yellow*) and Cinema Five's of Z proved that one can have a major boxoffice bonanza without a major distributor.

"You used to have to go to seven guys to get basic financing and distribution," producer-director Robert Aldrich notes. "In a couple of years there'll be 70."

Aldrich, who has made films under every major logo with the exception of Paramount, was unhappy with all of them and stalked off to file a registration statement with the Securities & Exchange Commission to publicly underwrite a $63-million film distribution, production and financing combine. A lot of other film-makers in Hollywood are now carefully perusing the Aldrich prospectus with their lawyers, with their own dreams of going public.

Joe Solomon has done so successfully, although at a considerably more modest level than Aldrich projects. The common stock offering of Solomon's Fanfare Films totaled $1,188,000, which will finance three low-budget summer drive-in programmers to be handled by sub-distributors.

Another source of capital is the currently lucrative record and music business. A & M financed and produced a feature-length rock doc about English soul singer Joe Cocker's national tour without any help from their friends in the studios.

Warner Bros.-Reprise Records underwrote *Rainbow Bridge*, an approximately $400,000 quasi-underground, dramatically improvised, cinema-verité style surfing film. Its primary commercial value on the drawing board was the score written by Jimi Hendrix.

Parent company Warner Brothers' involvement appears to be limited to advice, helping arrange the IATSE and Cinemobile contracts the underground film-makers would work under and possibly to releasing the film, although the latter was on a wait-and-see basis.

Clearly, the studios' function is changing radically.

Some, like Columbia, have aggressively gone into the business of renting space, equipment, crews and even production supervision to independents; other majors, 20th Century-Fox and Metro-Goldwyn-Mayer, sold off equipment to burgeoning independent service and rental companies.

Cinema General Corporation, a rental studio that formerly had been the Paramount-Desilu-Cahuenga Studio, reversed its field and announced the formation of a sub-sid Cinema World Corporation to produce films with the financial assistance of U. S. Steel Finance Corporation.

Cinemobile Systems at any time in 1970 could boast that it was involved in the production of as many feature films as two or three of the majors together, and now Cinemobile president Fouad Said is seeking part of the action by offering to underwrite the below-the-line costs of certain films.

As the established production-distribution companies struggled to work off an inventory of more than $1-billion to generate cash flow for new productions, a series of major companies outside showbiz emerged as potentially significant sources of capital.

The Reader's Digest established an office in Beverly Hills (with Helen M. Strauss as creative head) to develop projects for feature films and TV, drawing on the magazine's rich lode of story material and finances.

Cox Broadcasting and Bing Crosby Productions, after years in

television, moved into feature films with a pact with Cinerama Releasing Corporation for an average of three films for five years.

Bristol-Meyers Co. purchased a majority stock interest in Pal-
omar Pictures, headed by Edgar J. Scherick, and the former American
Broadcasting Company feature film production unit became a division
of a patent-medicine corporate complex.

Even for those working through established studios, there were
new ways of financing that gave the independent filmmaker more
autonomy. Those "Easy Riders," Dennis Hopper and Peter Fonda, went
to the high peaks of the Peruvian Andes and Flatlands of New
Mexico, respectively, to make films on direct bank loans with Universal guaranteeing negative pick-up and distribution of the completed
film.

Producer Al Ruddy, between making *Little Fauss and Big Halsy*
and *The Godfather* at Paramount, spent the summer on location in
Albuquerque making *Making It* with a great deal of assistance from
the state of New Mexico and a Cinemobile System that included a
sound system rented from Columbia on a negative pick-up deal with
20th-Fox.

Although considered revolutionary developments at the beginning of 1970, by midyear they were established ways of doing
business. Hollywood, that wily old magician, had a bagful of new tricks
up its sleeve.

BANKERS AND MOVIE-MAKERS *

A. H. HOWE

*". . . No sane banker can make loans for the production of a
picture where the sole source of payment is revenue from
that picture. . . ."*

To the two sure things in life, death and taxes, there has been
added a third, change. And if the first two are no less sure, the third
is multiplying itself, geometrically increasing its speed, with catastrophic effect on those who do not recognize and ride with it.

During the last two years, this wind of change has blown de-
structively through the motion picture business. It has rocked the
major companies with tremendous losses, has caused grave reductions
in the production of pictures and in distribution facilities, and has
raised serious questions about the splintering of the market for mass
entertainment.

With all this change, a theatrical world market for feature
pictures of some two billion dollars annually still exists. Product for
that market will somehow be made and distributed. If the changes
are well enough understood, this can well be a profitable process.

In 1965 *The Journal* published my article called "A Banker Looks

A. H. HOWE is Vice President of the National Division of the Los Angeles
Headquarters of the Bank of America, with which he has been associated
since 1942. He has been identified with motion picture credit activity for
nearly 20 years, and has been in charge of this activity for his bank since
1959.

* Reprinted from the *Journal* of The Producers Guild of America, June, 1971.

at the Picture Business." It was designed to eliminate some of the misconceptions about the business side of motion pictures and to help the independent producer understand the process of financing them. The change in the last two years has altered at least the emphasis on some of the items in that article, though some basic truths and techniques remain valid. Here follows a banker's look at the picture business in 1971.

It is divided into four parts and an exhibit: (1) Myths about Financing that Just Aren't So; (2) Risk, Risk-Takers and the Need of Change; (3) Spreading the Risk and How the Banks Can Help; (4) Is Producing Abroad Really a Solution? and the exhibit: How to Finance a Picture.

1. *Myths about Financing that Just Aren't So:*

There are two principal myths that I would like to bury so deeply that they can never be heard from again. They are "bankable stars," people who supposedly insure bank credit because of their appearance in a cast, and "control of the industry by the bankers." Neither has any basis in fact.

In the years of change it has been proven again and again, coldly and unhappily, that no combination of actor, actress, writer, director or producer, regardless of past records, hits or awards, can assure success. This cold proof has greatly reduced pay scales for most creative people (except, of course, the fellow who had a hit the last time out) and has greatly increased the deals where the star takes no money from the budget but instead depends on profits, if any.

Bankers try hard to be associated with success, like every mortal man. But the banker's job is to make loans that are repaid, at rates that yield a fair return considering the risk involved. When a customer's business does not go well, and losses occur, the banker tries to determine causes and takes such action as is necessary to protect his loans. Such emergency action sometimes causes the rumor that "the banks have taken over the company." This is an emotional and uninformed judgment from the outside and does not coincide with the facts.

2. *Risks, Risk-Takers and the Need of Change:*

The risk of investment in feature films, which has climbed steadily since divorcement under the consent decrees and the rise of television in the early 1950's, has taken another sharp jump during our two years of change. Ironically, the potential returns from top hits continue to rise also. The odds into which the producer is betting are getting longer, the jackpot bigger.

Each producer with a project in mind still believes, and must believe, that he has the best story, cast, technicians, music, effects; the unique package better than any other; the one which will hit the jackpot.

I can only repeat that over the years I have talked to hundreds of producers, each with the world's best picture, a project where it was impossible to miss, where a hit was absolutely certain, and which would be made so cheaply that to ask any questions was obviously absolutely stupid. The difficulty is, proved over and over again, that these certain hits, when made, are usually lost in the shuffle, and more often than not fail to return their costs. The years of change have continually reiterated this proof.

Pictures are not bankable risks. No sane banker can make loans for the production of a picture where the sole source of payment is revenue from that picture. Producers agree, they won't risk *their* funds in such a project. So for 20 years, it has been the major American motion picture companies who have taken the risk, but there is usually a fast turnover in such characters. There is a whole structure of subsidies abroad designed to provide production money there, to make risk bearable without the backing of the American majors, or to help to reduce the risk if the Americans are involved. Production abroad still fluctuates in direct proportion to the health and activity of these American companies. Even with the subsidies, there has been no real substitute for their risk-taking.

Even before the violent change of the past two years, profitable production and distribution, while bearing the risk, was a chancy thing. A good case can be made that production and distribution of pictures for the theatrical market by the American majors, taken as a single unit for the past 20 years, has been a loser. I can think of no other commercial enterprise where the principal business, the very core, has been unprofitable for such a long period, yet the market survives. So the distributors, who take the risk of the production cost in something like 90% of the total dollars involved, are losing their shirts. Not even the averaging of success with failure, nor the distribution fees and expenses that the producers consider downright dishonest, have enabled them to make ends meet.

The increasing selectivity of the television market, which welcomes successes and pays well for them but tries to bypass the failures, seems to signal the end of the television salvage operation for the dogs. The increasing difference between pictures for theatres and those for television, both in subjects chosen and the treatment of them, makes television values less sure, even for successes. Thus the television market for features, the great bolsterer of picture values for the risk-takers for the last 10 years at least, may have less backstop effect in the future. The risk-takers will probably not be able, even if willing, to take the same sort of risks again.

The banker, then, cannot accept the substantial risk involved where repayment of a loan depends on receipts from the picture created by the loan. For 20 years the banker has had to assume that each new picture financed would not return *any* of its production cost. The banks cannot accept greater risks than they have in the past. In fact, they are human enough to try to tighten down and protect their loans during a convulsive period like the last two years.

The distributor, the American major picture company, who has borne the risk since World War II, has probably lost money over the entire time. Certainly, during the two years of change, those losses have been catastrophic. The television market in the future will probably be less of a stabilizing influence than it has been in the past. The major picture companies must operate profitably or they are doomed to extinction. The risks they accept must be reduced. It appears that some new solution to the problem of making the risk bearable in relation to profits achieved must be found.

3. *Reducing and Spreading the Risk; How the Banks Can Help:*

If you are an independent producer, established or new, you really aren't too much interested in the economics of motion pictures. You just want to make a deal to finance your picture which you are convinced will make a mint, giving away as little of your project as you can. But if you can't find anyone who will provide the money, except in terms much worse than in the past, then perhaps it's time to look at economics and the market.

While statistics in the picture business are unreliable, common assumptions in the business might lead us to:

Annual Worldwide Box Office $2-Billion
Film Rental Share—30% $600-Million
Distribution Fees Deducted—30% $180-Million
                                                   ————

Amount Available for Distribution Costs
    (Prints and Advertising, etc.) and to
    Cover Negative Costs $420-Million
Distribution Costs—30% (of Film Rental) $180-Million
                                                   ————

To Cover Negative Costs $240-Million

Some of the box office and film rental gross is done by foreign companies, indicating a smaller amount available for the American companies. Thus, total returns available to cover production expenditures of about $250-million must be a highly optimistic figure; probably $200-million is closer to the amount produced by the market.

During most of the 1960's, seven major American motion picture companies assumed production risks each year exceeding $50-million each, and all other U. S. companies and risk-takers probably totalled another $50-million, a total of about $400-million. Thus, the expense of making the product exceeded the market return by something like two to one, and something had to give.

The effect of this mismatch was marked by hit pictures in some companies, which enabled them to absorb losses while still showing profits, and by the industry's methods of amortization of costs, which do not relate those costs directly to income received. But these factors served only to delay the day of reckoning, now here; and that day of reckoning is the cause of the great change.

It now seems very apparent that cost of production must be reduced at least by half, just to make ends meet. As always, there will be arguments that the theatre's share is too big, and that distribution costs are highway robbery. But a producer has to live in the world as it is. As a working hypothesis let's assume that costs should be reduced by half. Much of this cost reduction is made possible because of the decline in production during the years of change. Many talented people have been willing to cut their prices substantially, just to get work.

Our overall market look can tell us of a serious pitfall in the current position taken by the risk-taker—"Take little or nothing up front, and I'll be glad to share the profits." This philosophy can be questioned very seriously because it may be removing too much from the overall cash pool devoted to production, thereby increasing the overall risk.

In any year, the $600-million in film rentals postulated above would be generated by about 200 pictures, or an average of $3-million apiece. Some years, one could pick two which would gross $50-million apiece, one-sixth of the total. Profit shares might amount to 20% of that gross, a participation to the lucky recipients of $20 million, about 10% of the total reasonable production pool of funds. Probably total deductions from the cash pool, consisting of distribution proceeds which are not re-risked in other productions, are considerably more than 10%. If you give out participations liberally, put a limit on them, making sure that no one gets more than the limit, which totals perhaps twice what would be paid in cash up front in today's market.

Except for cost reductions resulting from the times and except for reducing cash up front through participations and limiting those participations to reasonable figures, it is hard to find means of reducing the risk. Obviously, such means must either provide equally marketable product at reduced cost, or increase the return from the product without increasing the cost in proportion.

As to reducing cost, it must be mentioned that there seems considerable doubt that there is any correlation between the cost and return of feature pictures professionally made. If your budget is $1,500,000, stand off and look at the philosophy behind it; maybe a different concept will make it for $500,000. Sure, some items won't be there, but are they really important in the marketplace?

As to increasing the return, for over five years I have advocated an attempt at scientific evaluation of the factors which make a picture successful. If a guide could be developed which would reduce the failures and increase the successes by even a small percentage, it would go far to make a viable, healthy industry. And by reducing the risk, it would make the producer's job of financing his picture much easier.

Both reducing cost and improving the batting average are, at the moment, subjective and chancy. Spreading the risk, and hence perhaps making your venture more acceptable to risk-takers, is not.

Commonly, the risk-taker has advanced production cost, or has guaranteed a bank loan equal to the picture's budgeted cost, and has agreed to furnish any over-budget amounts needed to complete. For this risk, he has taken all world rights, including television, and perhaps half of the profits. He usually has some penalty rights if the budget is exceeded, but rarely has used them.

His risks include over-budget costs, often serious; the picture's value in theatrical markets in the United States and in many foreign countries; and the television value in the same markets.

Perhaps the most important risk that can be pulled out of the basic financing and borne separately, is that of completion. Many of the large losses during the years of change were largely from heavy cost over-runs. This has resulted in much attention to this risk, and the probability that you can sell your project more easily at a fixed price, with the completion risk placed elsewhere. This, of course, involves finding some entity satisfactory to the risk-taker and your bank, if one is involved, to guarantee completion. For most of the postwar period, no company making a business of this has been successful in the United States, and only one in England. There are some new ventures in the field, and there is hope that in the future completion guarantees may be easier to come by.

At present, the process of covering the completion risk will probably be a matter itself of spreading the risk. It will often involve contingency funds in and above the budget, contributions by individuals involved in the picture up to or perhaps more than their compensation, and usually traditional strength in the form of outside guarantees. Your banker can help you come up with a plan.

Sometimes even with the completion risk covered elsewhere, the prime risk-taker is unwilling to underwrite the entire budgeted cost. He may question some of the values which you believe are substantial. These separate values are those in the U. S. and foreign markets, theatrical and television, and they can sometimes be sold or contracted to separate entities by region, or country by country, further spreading the risk. There is nothing very new about this—it is a variant of the old States' Rights selling that was general in the early years of the motion picture business. It does, however, permit valuation of certain rights and reduction of the risk on the part of the American major, the prime risk-taker. It can sometimes, as in the following example, reduce his risk to prints and advertising only:

> *Picture*—International adventure, fast action, dialogue unimportant. Network television possible with minor cuts. Probable "GP."
> *Budget*—$1,500,000.
> *Featured Players*—Two known names to facilitate foreign sales. Compensation $25,000 each, plus $100,000 each from profits.
> *Completion*—$150,000 contingency in budget, $150,000 compensation deferred until completion on budget, guarantee of completion by those involved in picture, and whatever outside strength needed.
> *Pre-sales*—Italy, United Kingdom, France, Germany, Spain, Japan and other countries as needed, $750,000.
> *Television Sale*—Network and syndication $500,000.
> *U. S. Distribution*—Major company; producer to receive 40% of film rental from the first dollar. Producer recoups exposure at $625,000 gross.

This is obviously an ideal sharing of risk and one which could be obtained only with a highly desirable package. It is not set out as typical; just as an example of the multiplication of risk-takers which is sometimes possible. Knowledgeable banks can often be helpful in putting together the appropriate arrangements. This is said with some trepidation since such help can often involve much effort and be very time-consuming. When such arrangements result in a loan, the bank must be paid for its help; if closing a loan is questionable, the bank must limit its activity or be paid on some basis.

4. *Is Producing Abroad Really a Solution?*

There is no doubt that wage rates and some other costs abroad are lower than they are in the United States. The subsidies in most European countries help to absorb some of the risk, though they are of greatest value to the successes. Because of the existence of a completion guarantor firm in England with a long history of successfully completed pictures, it is sometimes easier to cover the completion risk abroad than it is at home. It perhaps remains easier to cast a picture abroad, though the reductions in overall production have tended to make creative people more willing to work anywhere.

All of these factors seem to indicate that pictures should be made outside the United States, but the advantage is often more theoretical than real.

Any American producer abroad is doing business in the other fellow's backyard and is at a disadvantage. He must depend on the local people for much technical quality that is almost automatic in Hollywood. The quality of his contractual arrangements with the local people is subject to question; his ability to follow and get good performance is not assured, and legal redress may be nonexistent. Experience with production abroad suggests that production time is longer, control less sure, cost over-runs more likely, and quality of result more questionable.

The sum of these factors is the conclusion that production abroad increases the risk. If we look at a domestic production deal twice to determine its chances, we look at a foreign one four times.

After the two years of catastrophic change, it is more than ever up to the producer to make marketable pictures at less risk to the distributor. To do this he must be a businessman, fast on his feet in the complex financial end of the business. We, his bankers, are here to help.

Exhibit—How to Finance a Picture

The credit available from a bank depends on the credit standing of the risk-taker or takers who back your project. If a number of risk-takers are involved, the loan becomes too complex to describe here, though its main features are the same as those described below.

Assume that you have one of the major motion picture companies backing your project with its credit resources which are unquestionably good for the amount involved. That company may guarantee your loan at once, in which case the pattern of the loan you can get, principally the rate and the percentage of budget which you can borrow, depends almost solely on your backer's credit. Probably you will be able to borrow your entire budget, and the rate will be somewhere within 1½% above the prime lending rate of commercial banks, which on May 5, 1971, was 5½%.

If your guarantor has difficulty qualifying as sufficiently strong to repay the bank's loan if necessary, putting together the loan becomes more complicated. Sometimes a pledge of assets other than the picture may be required. These assets sometimes may be bonds or stocks, interests in pictures, or any kind of personal property which it is possible to value. Usually, real estate is not satisfactory security and it is never satisfactory if it is mortgaged and all that is available for pledge is the equity left after a first lien.

Your risk-taker may tell you that he likes your project and

will give you a pick-up, agreeing to pay your budgeted costs upon delivery of a satisfactory picture to him. He thereby avoids the completion risk and you will have to arrange a completion guarantee, which will guarantee delivery of your picture in accordance with your contract with the distributor.

If a pick-up arrangment involves a completion guarantor whose assets are substantial but whose liquidity is limited, the bank may require a cash completion fund to cover the most likely over-budget amounts, say up to 15% of the budget. Such a fund might be the equivalent of cash: bonds or marketable securities which could be liquidated readily to provide cash if required to complete the picture.

When granted, your loan will be patterned to permit borrowing of funds from the bank for production as needed and repayment from the producer's share of distribution proceeds, assuming the picture is successful. This usually means a loan maturity of two years after the first borrowing, which will occur approximately at the beginning of principal photography. It is expected that release will occur six months thereafter and that the loan will be repaid 18 months following release. The loan arrangments will also include an outside maturity date so that delay in starting production or delay in release cannot postpone the final maturity beyond a certain fixed time.

The loan will then be organized as follows:

1. The producer will furnish to the bank:
   a) Story documents showing the chain of title by which the production entity acquired ownership. These will include clearances from publishers and others to whom rights may have been granted in the past, and proper assignments from all writers employed on the screenplay. This is necessary because ownership of the picture follows ownership of the literary property.
   b) An itemized budget for the picture which should also indicate how all funds shown in the budget are to be furnished. Copies of all agreements covering deferments and profit interests must also be included.
   c) Copies of agreements with the distributor providing for distribution and guarantee of recoupment of production costs, and with the completion guarantor, if that is to be other than the distributor.
   d) Financial statements of any risk-takers (guarantors) other than major motion picture companies whose financial conditions are of public record.
2. Based upon the information furnished, the bank will draw up documents as follows:
   a) A Security Agreement. This will constitute a first lien

on not only the physical properties and literary material on which the picture is based, but on the producer's share of receipts from all sources.

b) A Distributor's Agreement under which the distributor agrees to pay the producer's share of receipts to the bank and which usually limits print and advertising expenses to some agreed-upon figure. The distributor usually will agree to pay the bank loan at its maturity (if the distributor is the risk-taker) and agree to give up distribution rights to the picture at some agreed-upon time if the loan is not so paid.

c) Agreements with those whose compensation is deferred or who hold a share in the profits of the picture, agreeing that their rights to picture income are subordinated to the bank's rights under the Security Agreement. This is necessary to put the bank in an unquestioned first lien position.

d) Unless the distributor agrees to act as pledgeholder for the bank, the bank will also draw a Laboratory Pledgeholder's Agreement whereby the laboratory which has actual custody of the physical properties agrees to hold these properties for the bank's account.

e) If the distributor is not also the completion guarantor, a separate completion guarantee will be required. This may involve the pledge of liquid assets in support of that guarantee.

f) A Loan Agreement between the producing entity, be it corporation or joint venture, and the bank, outlining the terms of the loan and setting forth the various acts required by each party during the life of the loan. This will provide for certain reports which enable the bank to follow the course of production and distribution.

3. Based on the documentation, the loan will be determined as follows:

a) Advances of money by bank will be made periodically, usually weekly, based on amounts spent on production, plus estimated amounts necessary during the following week. Each request for a loan is to be accompanied by cost reports to date, showing each budgeted item.

b) After bank loan funds have been advanced, cost reports are to continue until final cost report is available. Release plans, the general release date, and the print and advertising budget are to be reported.

c) Reports of distribution are to come directly from the

distributor monthly, showing gross, deductions and producer's share. The latter is to be paid directly to the bank by distributor's check.

d) If this income is not sufficient to pay the loan at maturity, the risk-taker pays the balance at that time.

The loan outlined above is a rather simple transaction, but such loans often breed extreme complexities as they progress. Obviously, over-budget expenditures require action by the completion guarantor and, if the excess costs are serious enough, will sometimes result in takeover of control of production by representatives of the risk-taker.

If distribution results are unfavorable, the distributor will be asked to furnish estimates of future returns, and if these are insufficient to pay the loan, additional payments, even before maturity, may be required.

FOREIGN FILM SUBSIDIES *

ROBERT W. GILBERT

". . . With the exception of the United States, almost every single film-producing country of the world subsidizes the production of motion pictures within its borders in one way or another. . . ."

An American lawyer seeking to obtain the advantages of foreign film subsidies or other foreign governmental aid for his producer client must recognize at the outset that his task is, for the most part, non-legal in character and requires the use of professional skills not ordinarily employed in his domestic practice.

Not only will he find indispensable the assistance and close cooperation of a foreign lawyer who is a specialist in the laws relating to the entertainment industry of a particular country, but in most cases he will need to consult foreign bankers, accountants, business consultants and government officials who can acquaint him with the specific steps to be taken and the most favorable methods for carrying out these steps in order to qualify for foreign subsidization.

While his professional ability to analyze over-all business matters

ROBERT W. GILBERT is a Hollywood film attorney who has specialized in labor law all of his professional life. Mr. Gilbert has written articles for such publications as the *American Bar Association Journal,* C. C. H. *Labor Law Journal, Law and Contemporary Problems,* and leading University Law Journals.

* Reprinted from the *Journal* of The Producers Guild of America, September, 1968.

will be helpful, American counsel can provide his producer client with sound legal advice for considering or planning production abroad only if he has an awareness of the specific difficulties to be encountered because of the foreign aspects of the problem.

As pointed out by one of the vice-presidents in charge of the Foreign Service of the Motion Picture Export Association of America, film subsidy plans in other nations "have been designed to leave a good deal of administrative flexibility and interpretative responsibility in the hands of officials who administer them." The lawyer for American producers interested in securing subsidy benefits cannot safely assume, without expert advice from foreign law specialists, that subsidies will be forthcoming merely on the basis of "compliance with what appears on the surface to be the meaning of the written rules."

Moreover, diligent study of the statutes or decrees and regulations containing the film subsidy plans of other countries will not familiarize the American practitioner with the complexities of the many foreign laws relating to corporations, contracts, commercial practices, taxes, labor and business regulation which must be considered in conjunction with such statutes.

Thus, as in other international business transactions, the role of American counsel in obtaining foreign film subsidy advantages for their producer clients is primarily that of interpreter and intermediary between foreign law specialists and those clients.

With the exception of the United States, almost every significant film-producing country of the world subsidizes the production of motion pictures within its borders in one way or another.

Apart from the Soviet Union, Yugoslavia, Czechoslovakia and other Communist countries which completely subsidize their government-owned film industry, there are at least 20 important film-producing nations which offer cash subsidies or other forms of state aid to the independent producer or private company making a motion picture locally under prescribed conditions.

In theory, subsidies, screen-time quotas and prizes are established by the foreign governments, (along with import quotas, import duties, release taxes, remittance restrictions and other trade barriers in certain instances), to protect and support their unprofitable local film industries against the competition of American-made motion pictures.

In practice, many American producers have been able to hurdle or circumvent these barriers to free competition by meeting the conditions for production or co-production of motion pictures laid down by the foreign government, and have become qualified to participate

in subsidy payments or other economic advantages and greatly reduce
their financial risks.

Among the principal forms of state financial aid for national
films of the situs country which can be enjoyed by American producers
making pictures abroad through foreign subsidiaries, co-production
agreements or other business arrangements with foreign film interests,
are the following: (1) cash subsidies; (2) low-interest or no-interest
governmental loans; (3) private loan guarantees; (4) advances of partial
production costs; (5) admission tax rebates; (6) cash prizes.

The tremendous financial incentives for foreign film production
activities by American producers range from an insurance against loss
of up to 80% of the cost in one country to outright payment of
30% to 50% of the cost in other countries. Within recent years, the
United Kingdom, France and Italy have entered into international
agreements to pool film subsidies under conditions which have permitted some American producers to secure tri-national subsidies
amounting to as much as 80% of the cost of a single picture made
in co-production with British, French and Italian film interests.

The complex nature of the various types of co-production,
"split-distribution" and co-financing arrangements which characterize
American-interest foreign film production, and the understandable
unwillingness of the participants to disclose their business confidences,
make it difficult, in many cases, to determine whether a particular
motion picture has been financed and produced jointly by United
States and foreign interests so as to qualify for subsidy benefits.

It is undisputed, however, that the heavy cash subsidies available in countries like the United Kingdom, France and Italy have
been a determining factor in influencing some American producers
to make pictures there. In 1962, one year for which the figures are
available, United States motion picture producers received $5,250,000
in subsidy funds from the three countries just named. More recent
figures would unquestionably show much larger subsidy payments in
favor of American companies.

The best known, most sophisticated and by far the most effective system of foreign film subsidies is that administered by the
British Film Fund Agency and the Board of Trade, established by
the Cinematograph Films Act, 1957. This mandatory statutory system
is still popularly known as the "Eady Plan" after its predecessor, a
voluntary semi-private subsidy pool negotiated by Sir Wilfred Eady
of the British Treasury with four trade associations representing
film producers, distributors and exhibitors in the United Kingdom.
The voluntary plan was in effect from September, 1950 until October,
1957. By passage of the Films Act, 1966, Parliament extended until
the end of 1970 a number of related statutory provisions designed to

foster and encourage the production and exhibition of British films, including the 1957 Act providing for the so-called "Eady Plan." *

Briefly summarized, these British film laws, as amended in 1966, do the following: (1) require that exhibitors devote a prescribed percentage of their screening time to the showing of registered British quota films; (2) authorize the making of loans by the National Film Finance Corporation to private persons for the purpose of financing the production and distribution of films, and provide for loan funds to be advanced to the N. F. F. C. by the Board of Trade; (3) provide financial incentives for British filmmaking by authorizing the British Film Fund Agency to distribute payments to makers of eligible "British" films out of the proceeds of a box-office admissions levy on exhibitors.

The maker of an eligible film (or his assignee under a general assignment or limited assignment as to which notice has been given the British Film Fund Agency), upon presenting a timely claim properly verified and supported and further information relating thereto as required, is entitled to payments in accordance with the "Distribution of Levy Regulations."

As defined by Section 50 (1) of the 1960 Act, the maker of a film is "the person by whom the arrangements necessary for the making of the film are undertaken." While a film may be registered as a "British Film" and a "quota film" when its maker is a British or Irish non-resident of the United Kingdom or a company incorporated in another Commonwealth country or the Republic of Ireland, only a United Kingdom resident or a United Kingdom company can qualify for Eady Plan subsidy payments as "the maker of an eligible film."

The Board of Trade has stated that a United Kingdom company may qualify as "the maker of an eligible film" even though all or a substantial part of the financing came from non-British interests; even though the United Kingdom company is a subsidiary of a non-British company or partly controlled by a non-British company; and even though non-British interests have been given rights in the ownership or distribution of the film. While an American producer can thus indirectly secure the advantages of Eady Plan benefits through a variety of business relationships, such as forming a British subsidiary or making a co-production or "split-distribution" deal with an independent British company, care must be taken that the United Kingdom company makes all the arrangements and enters into all the

* EDITORS' NOTE: In the Cinematograph Films Act of 1970 the Eady Plan was extended until 1980. The subsidy is supplied from an admissions tax on all pictures exhibited in British theatres, but is divided among qualifying pictures only.

contracts necessary for financing, making and distributing the film.

Payments from available moneys in the British Film Fund are made by the Agency to the maker of each eligible film on a pro rata basis, in the same proportion that the total film rental earnings of that film during the distribution period bears to the grand total of the film rental earnings of all eligible films for that same period; except that in making the computation of earnings, weighting takes place in favor of Section 39 newsreels at twice their total earnings and in favor of low cost films and short films at two and a half times their total earnings.

In France, government subsidies, no-interest loans or advances against future box-office receipts are available to producers of French films and some co-productions made under international agreements.

To qualify as a French film for state aid purposes, the original version must be in the French language, technicians and leading players must be French citizens, and the processing and editing must take place in French laboratories and studios.

Funds for French film subsidies and loans or advances vary from year to year as determined by the Ministry of Cultural Affairs, and are made up of revenues derived from admission taxes, release taxes, and reimbursements from prior loans or advances to French producers.

Unlike the British and Italian subsidies, those available through the Centre National de la Cinematographic Française do not result in unconditional payments, but rather in accumulated credits against which the producer may draw when he produces a new picture or sells the production company.

American production companies usually avail themselves of French governmental financial assistance for the production of French films through foreign subsidiaries or co-production arrangements. Since the company producing a French film eligible for aid must have French officers and directors and mostly French executives, this had not proved too satisfactory. It has been estimated that American producers have obtained from France only half the amount of subsidy funds received from Italy and perhaps one-fourth the amount of Eady funds received in the United Kingdom.

While France's higher release tax applies to French films as well as imports, the revenues produced are used to subsidize local producers alone in 80% of the cases.

Under the Italian Film Law, a feature film producer of that nationality is entitled to a governmental subsidy if the film is originally produced in Italian or has an Italian version where several versions exist, provided also that it is made mainly in Italy with predominantly Italian personnel.

Italian subsidy funds are derived from admission taxes, and subsidy payments have been paid in recent years at a rate of 13% to 16% of the total box-office gross of the film in Italy (before deduction of any taxes) for the first five years of exhibition.

Besides these cash subsidies, substantial cash prizes or awards are made annually for "unusual merit" to a significant number of Italian features and short subjects as well as a lesser number of Common Market features and shorts. Italian producers also may secure low-interest credit loans from the Banca del Lavoro.

While only Italian citizens may participate in Italy's subsidy payments, even where the film is a co-production, Italian film interests have shown remarkable ingenuity in working out multinational co-production arrangements under which subsidies have been secured for a single film from two and sometimes three countries.

It is estimated that in a single year, the Italian film aid program produced as much as $32-million in subsidies and $6-million in prizes.

Eighteen foreign countries, including many of the most important overseas markets for American producers, maintain mandatory screen-time quotas established by legislation or government decree that require motion picture theatres within their respective boundaries to devote a prescribed portion of their screen-time to the showing of national films.

The basic objective of these screen-time quotas, which take a variety of forms from country to country, is to increase the potential earnings of national films by forcing the particular nation's exhibitors to give such pictures a specified amount of playing time, while reducing the available playing time and earning capacity of foreign films.

Screen-time quotas are a form of indirect financial subsidy favoring productions made abroad over American-interest motion pictures made in the United States. In Italy, the screen-time quotas are reinforced by a supplementary incentive for playing national films in the form of a rebate of a substantial percentage of admissions tax collections to exhibitors during periods when they show Italian feature films in their theatres, and a smaller percentage of rebate when they show Italian short films.

To the extent that American producers have been able to work out complex business arrangements for production abroad to take advantage of direct cash subsidies by qualifying pictures in which they have a financial stake as national films, they have likewise been able to take advantage of the indirect subsidization of screen-time quotas and so have increased their earning capacity in foreign countries as an aid to financing production costs.

While film import quotas have been eliminated in most countries, this has not been the case with screen-time quotas. In European countries like the United Kingdom, France, Greece, Italy, the Nether-lands and Spain, where cash subsidies and screen-time quotas go hand in hand in favoring national films, there appears to be reasonable prospect for eliminating either of these two types of local film produc-tion inducement. Particularly in those countries, American producers have been able to take advantage of cash subsidies or their direct state financial aid and to benefit from the screen-time quota at the same time.

While there are many reasons for the phenomenal increase in the annual number of American-interest feature pictures being made in other countries during the last two decades, the availability of foreign subsidies and other state aid has been one of the primary motivations.

Since the end of World War II, the foreign market for American-interest feature motion pictures has grown tremendously. United States film production and distribution companies estimate that 53 cents out of every dollar earned by American motion pictures comes from abroad. In view of the admitted shrinkage of domestic film produc-tion during this same period, it is noteworthy that the three European countries from which the largest portion of the 53% foreign earnings is derived—namely, the United Kingdom, Italy and France—offer the heaviest production subsidies and together account for nearly half the so-called "runaway production."

Within the American film industry, the sharp increase in the exodus of United States producers to subsidizing countries has produced equally sharp debates among spokesmen for the various components over (1) semantics and (2) statistics.

The semantic argument over the accuracy of the term "runaway" as applied to American-interest foreign film production is merely a reflection of the conflicting views regarding the merits or economic wisdom of going abroad. Whether the immediate short-range financial advantages to be gained by American producers from foreign subsidies, screen-time quotas and prizes justifies the long-range economic losses at home in terms of mounting unemployment, reduced local business expenditures, declining federal, state and local tax revenues, and erosion of the domestic filmmaking capabilities, is an issue to be settled in some other forum.

Likewise, the statistical controversy as to which of the various sources within the American film industry has most accurately esti-mated the precise number of American-interest pictures made in the principal subsidizing countries during any given year cannot be reconciled in this setting.

It is sufficient for our purpose of generally assessing the impact of foreign financial inducements on the planning of American motion picture production, to observe that in the last eight years the proportion of so-called "runaway" films to the total output of United States producers has increased from approximately 35% to 60%, according to most reliable sources of information, and that American motion picture interests are currently investing over $100-million annually in films outside the United States.

BUDGET ESTIMATING AND PLANNING

MARSHALL GREEN and TIM DONAHUE

". . . It is not a matter of cutting a budget down to a given figure, but rather, an attempt to come up with an intelligent plan which, by spending money intelligently, will produce a good product. . . ."

A studio production budget is a precise and detailed breakdown of the total cost of a film, beginning with acquisition of the property and ending with completion of the production. Although studios vary in the details of the format they use, the basic budgetary ingredients are similar. An examination of budgeting procedures at our studio, therefore, should give a representative example of what a film production budget is and how it is prepared.

A pretty good way to get a concise summary of a budget which *in toto* might run well over 100 pages, is to examine the so-called *topsheet*. As the illustration shows, it is an outline of the major accounts that make up the budget, and it summarizes on a single page the total funds allocated to the various aspects of production. The topsheet is followed by pages of detailed breakdown for each

MARSHALL GREEN is Vice President and Executive Production Manager for Universal Pictures at Universal City, California.

TIM DONAHUE is now in budget estimating at Twentieth Century-Fox Film Corporation. He has been in the motion picture industry since 1952, serving as Budget Department head at Universal Pictures, Inc., Budget Department head of Republic Pictures, and Production Location assistant for Ziv Television.

76

B&W COLOR RATIO

UNIVERSAL PICTURES
PRODUCTION BUDGET

PICT. NO.

TITLE _____

PRODUCER _____

_____

DIRECTOR _____

START DATE _____

FINISH DATE _____

PRODUCTION DAYS _____

_____

PRINCIPAL PLAYERS _____

ACCT. NO.	DESCRIPTION	PAGE NO.	BUDGET		REMARKS
801	Story & Other Rights	1			
803	Writing	1			
805	Producer & Staff	2			
807	Director & Staff	3			
809	Talent	4			
810	Supplemental Labor	5			
	TOTAL ABOVE THE LINE				
811	Production Staff	6			
813	Camera	7			
815–A	Art Department	8			
815–B	Set Construction & Striking	8			
817	Set Operations	9			
819	Electrical	10			
821	Set Dressing	11			
823	Action Props	12			
827	Special Photography	13			
831	Wardrobe	14			
833	Makeup & Hairdressing	15			
835	Sound (Production)	16			
837	Locations (Local & Distant)	17			
839	Transportation (Studio)	18			
841	Film (Production)	19			
845	Sundry & Tests (Other than Cast)	19			
	TOTAL SHOOTING PERIOD				
851	Editing & Projection	20			
853	Music	21			
855	Sound (Post–Production)	22			
857	Film & Stock Shots (Post–Production)	23			
859	Titles, Opticals & Inserts	24			
	TOTAL COMPLETION PERIOD				
861	Insurance	24			
863	Supplemental Labor	24			
866	Unit Publicist & Stillman	25			
867	General Expenses	26			
	TOTAL OTHER				
	DIRECT TOTAL				
	STUDIO OVERHEAD				
	GRAND TOTAL				

major account. Depending upon the specific production, a given account may be elaborated through several pages, perhaps involving
as many as 15 or 20 work papers behind the recapitulated account.
In some cases, if these detailed papers are not needed at a higher
level, they may not be reproduced for distribution with the final
budget.

As the topsheet indicates, each account within a budget has its
own official number and page designation. Uniformity in basic format
streamlines and clarifies the content, facilitating communication in
moving from one budget to another, whether it be in connection with
several possible budgets for a single property or a number of different
budgets for a number of different properties. Account 801, for instance,
deals with *Story and Other Rights* and is located on page 1. Account
817 designates *Set Operations* and is found on page 9. *Wardrobe* is
Account 831, page 14; *Music* is Account 853, page 21. Should the
breakdown for a given account run more than one page, then the
number is repeated followed by A, B, C, and so forth, to the extent
needed. In other words, if the *Music* account needs additional pages,
the second page is numbered 21-A; the third 21-B, and so forth.

The topsheet has two main sections: the so-called "above-the-
line" costs and the so-called "below-the-line" costs. Those funds
designated as above-the-line are concerned with contractual agreements fixed before filming gets underway and involve such people as
author, producer, director and acting talent. The items below-the-line
are further organized into the "Shooting Period," the "Completion
Period," and a little section at the bottom called "Other."

A quick survey of the various accounts listed on the topsheet
will provide a good introduction to what a film production budget is.
Following, then, is a brief description of the various accounts, organized to match the format of the budget itself, beginning with
above-the-line costs.

Story and Other Rights includes the cost of buying the property;
Writing covers any additional preparation involved in readying the
property for the screen. If the original is already in the form of a
screenplay, there may be little additional writing cost. If, however,
the property is a novel or merely an outline or screen treatment,
then this additional writing expense can be considerable.

The next two accounts are labeled *Producer and Staff* and *Director and Staff.* The producer is usually covered by contract. A large
studio may have staff producers on an annual salary. Should the
producer be one of these, then a certain amount is charged by the
studio against the budget of the production. The producer's staff
consists of various associates and secretaries. The director, too, is
contractually engaged. His staff includes such individuals as his as-

sistant director, his secretary for the production and perhaps a dialogue coach, if he works with one.

Talent involves the name people in the cast. There may also be some studio people on annual salary. Here, again, if studio actors are used, there will be an allocation for them included. *Supplemental Labor* includes such items as the fringe benefits, vacation, holidays, provision for raises. This completes the list of expenses above-the-line. It covers accounts from 801 through 810 and runs from pages 1 through 5 in the budget. At this point, a *Total Above-The-Line* is entered as a summary of funds for this section.

When someone claims to have made a film for a modest $600,000, he is usually talking only about below-the-line costs. Under such circumstances, probably most of the above-the-line salaries have been deferred or worked out in percentage deals based on production profits. Because the costs above-the-line are all contractual, they are fixed. Once the contracts have been signed, the budget for this part of the production is set and may not be adjusted by the budgeting department. The only variable parts, then, are those elements appearing below-the-line. These are the areas that might be cut or juggled in an effort to come up with a workable plan for production.

The first account below-the-line is 811, the *Production Staff*. This group consists of the unit manager and his assistants, assistant directors, auditors and script supervisors, and is covered almost entirely by contract with the Directors Guild or script supervisor's local. Many of these people are staff employees on the lot in permanent jobs. Within the *Camera* account, some individuals are under contract and some are not. The director of photography, for example, is a matter of individual negotiation through an agent. This person can range in price anywhere from scale—about $1,000 per week—up to $3,000, depending upon who he is. Others on his crew include the operator, the assistant cameraman and the technicians. Depending upon the film, there may also be a fee for rental of special cameras. A Panavision film, for example, would involve such an allotment.

This topsheet format divides the *Art Department* account into two areas, 815-A and 815-B. First there is the basic labor: the art director or production designer, the sketch artists, the draftsmen. Then there is the actual cost of building the setting and taking it down. Here again, different studios have different methods. Under this particular system, a percentage of the cost of the set is assigned to striking it. Sometimes, if the stage isn't needed, a given set is left up for a television production to move into and revamp after the film is through. *Set Operations* covers grips, greensmen, carpenters, plumbers, painters, special effects men, crane rentals, crane operators. In sum, this budget includes everything needed to operate the set except for things electrical. The *Electrical* budget is entered separately and includes such people as the gaffer, the best boy, lamp operators, generator operators. All electrical equipment and supplies and rental fees come under this account as well.

Set Dressing and *Action Props* include the manufacture or rental of set dressing and hand props plus labor of such staff as set decorator, propmaster and their crews. Vehicles (cars, trains, planes, boats, *etc.*) and livestock (horses, cattle, *etc.*) are also included under *Action Props*.

If a production involves special photography such as rear or front projection, matte shots, trick printing, miniature, all of these costs are included under Account 827, *Special Photography*. The next several accounts are self-explanatory: *Wardrobe, Makeup* and *Hairdressing*, and *Sound*. These accounts can vary greatly from film to film, depending upon how large the cast is and whether or not it is a period piece or involves special wardrobe such as uniforms.

Another very significant budgetary item is *Locations* (*Local and Distant*)—where the film is shot. A budget can be greatly modified by shifting the location of production from the back lot to another place, perhaps even a foreign country. This particular account can be one of the most variable in the whole budget. It is an area in which money may be saved or costs may go sky high. A large studio operation may have as many as six or eight films being shot on location simultaneously, ranging from one as nearby as Carmel or San Francisco, to others as remote as Washington, D. C. or Mexico or Africa. This account includes transporting the company—car, bus, plane—and providing room, board and local transportation. It also covers rental fees on property and equipment used on location. Clearly, it can be one of the biggest accounts in a given budget.

Transportation (*Studio*) is the cost of vehicles and drivers for production on the studio lot as opposed to location. Then there is the cost of *Film* and its processing. Also on page 19 is an account called *Sundry and Tests* (*Other than Cast*). Telephone, telegraph, postage and the like fall under this account, plus costs for film, processing and labor involved in tests for wardrobe or makeup or any other aspect except casting.

All of these accounts, from number 811 on page 6 through number 845 on page 19, add up to the nuts and bolts of the *Total Shooting Period*. A sum of the expenses of this section is entered here. It is this part of the below-the-line budget that is the most variable and, therefore, the most controllable. It is in this area that those responsible for the budget can say, "We can cut here," or "We need to spend more there." Very rarely does someone already contracted above-the-line offer to take a cut in order that a film might be made.

The next segment of the budget follows the completion of principal photography and involves such accounts as *Editing and Projection*—film editor and his assistant and negative cutters who actually put the film together, plus projectionists. The *Music* account involves composers, arrangers, conductors, coaches and other musicians, as well as fees for clearance and royalties. Then there is another account for *Sound*, but this one has to do with post-production activities such as dubbing. *Film and Stock Shots*, again, have to do with the post-production schedule as opposed to the negative used in production. Finally, there is the cost of *Titles, Opticals and Inserts*, followed by a summary of the cost of the *Total Completion Period*.

The final section of the costs below-the-line is labeled *Other* and includes *Insurance* against sickness and injury for six people on every feature film, including usually the director and major talent. *Supplemental Labor* is similar to that listed above-the-line. In this instance, it covers the people below-the-line and adds up to a big hunk of money. It is figured by formula based on percentage.

Account number 866 is the cost of the *Unit Publicist and Stillman*. It is the budget to cover their salaries and expenses during the production. It is not involved in the exploitation of the film after production. Advertising cost for exploiting a film after it is made is not included in the production budget. Although it is one of the studio's expenses in releasing the film, the money is not allocated by those responsible for the production budget. The final account in this segment, vaguely labeled *General Expenses*, covers the cost of such items as the Production Code Administration Seal, and various special fees and royalties. The funds for the whole section are then summarized and entered under *Total Other*.

The DIRECT TOTAL is the sum of the total budget above and below-the-line. To this is added the STUDIO OVERHEAD, to complete the GRAND TOTAL for the production.

It is sometimes claimed that one of the reasons for the trend away from production inside a big studio is that the overhead is so great. Actually, however, there is no clear-cut conclusion possible in this regard. It is no doubt true that if there were not a lot of television production going on in the studio area, there would not be a need for so great a plant. There are, however, certain kinds of films that simply cannot be made properly except in the large studio facilities. *The Andromeda Strain*, for example, had to be produced in a place large enough to hold a huge and complicated set that could not be found anywhere in the real world. The studio not only offered the space but the know-how to construct such a tricky project.

Furthermore, there is a tremendous amount of equipment in a large studio that the small company could never afford to own. This equipment is available to any company working within studio facilities without additional charge beyond the overhead. There are also services involving legal fees, accounting, payroll, and the like, that are provided by the studio. Taking into account all of the equipment and services that a company may need for a given production, the overhead can be a very good deal. Currently, television production makes up a large part of the activity, with two or three features also usually in production at any given time. The fact that a big studio can remain busy and full is further proof of the need for such an arrangement.

A great many details are recorded on the breakdown sheets which back up the topsheet. For as accurate a budget as possible, every aspect must be pinpointed as specifically as possible. Each account, then, has numerous subdivisions. While it would be pointless and tedious to duplicate a budget format in its entirety, a sample breakdown of one account from above-the-line and one account from below-the-line will serve to illustrate the general set-up and great detail of the basic format. On page 4, for example, is located Account 809 *Talent*, an above-the-line cost. This account might include any or all of the following sub-accounts:

> Talent—Contract (Term or Series)
> Talent Freelance (Daily or Weekly)
> Specialty Acts
> Stunts
> Loops, Wild Lines, Recall
> Coaching (Voice, Stunt Coordinator, *etc.*)
> Cast Travel and Living Expenses (Los Angeles only)
> Extra Talent Outside Studio Zone

Page 4-A continues:

> Extra Talent—Studio Zone
> Sideline Musicians
> Teachers—Welfare Workers
> Extras Fittings and Interviews
> Extras Casting Service Fee
> Casting Tests—Talent
> Casting Tests—Operating Labor
> Casting Tests—Material, Transportation
> Casting Tests—Film and Processing
> Cast Insurance Exams and Medical Expense
> Miscellaneous Expense

There is a *Total Talent* entry at the end of this account that would give the sum of all funds allocated to it.

Account 817 *Set Operations*, located on page 9, has the following basic breakdown in terms of weeks, rate, amount and total cost:

> First Company Grip
> Second Company Grip
> Company Grips
> Crane and Dolly Crew
> Grips—Other (Resetting Walls, Tarping, etc.)
> Craft Service—Company

Page 9-A continues:

> Craft Service—Cleanup, Move Equipment
> Special Effects—Company
> Greensman—Company
> Greensman—Water, Refurbish, Reset
> Studio Hospital and First Aid Man (other than location)
> Other Crafts (Carpenters, Plumbers)
> Staff Shop
> Standby Painters
> Heating and Ventilation
> Drapery

Page 9-B continues:

> Set Watchmen, Firemen and Whistlemen
> Maintenance—Grip Equipment
> Dressing Rooms—Rentals—Revamp and Maintenance
> Load and Unload—Locations
> Special Effects—Purchases (incl. explosives and ammo.)
> Materials and Purchases (other than special effects)
> Special Effects—Rentals
> Rentals—Cranes
>> Drivers
>> Insert Car
>> Driver
>> Dollies
>> Camera Boats
>> Camera Planes
> Rental—Other Equipment
> Miscellaneous Expenses

Again, there is an entry for *Total Set Operations* at the end of the account, indicating the sum of all funds allocated to this account within the budget.

Each account in turn is similarly broken down throughout the entire budget, with the topsheet remaining a concise over-view of all budgeted accounts and the money assigned to each.

One of the earliest assignments regarding the financial records for a property the studio is considering for production is to check it out as thoroughly as possible in various studio files. There might be a number of memos on it. There would be a record of financial costs to date. Depending upon how long the property has been around and how many areas have taken a look at it, a property could have several identifying numbers. Each of these is searched thoroughly to provide a complete record of what work has been done with it, how much interest there has been in it, and how much money has already been spent on it. The information gathered is put into a kind of pre-budget or profile sheet. All of this information is gathered before any kind of production budget is projected. Those responsible for the budget need to know what costs are already charged against the property before they begin to work with it.

As soon as a copy of a script comes to the budgeting department, six or seven Xerox copies are made and distributed to pre-production departments for breakdown. The preliminary budget is made as soon as possible. Sometimes it is made for just a screen treatment or a novel under consideration. This preliminary budget is often prepared before many of the important ingredients are even known.

Hundreds of scripts come in and receive a preliminary budgeting. Most of them, of course, are never made into films. Assessing what it will cost to make a given film is one aspect that helps the studio head to decide whether to undertake production. The studio knows ahead of time approximately how many pictures it will make in an up-coming year. Information is often supplied with a script as to about how much the studio wants to budget for it. Then the production department will come up with a picture plan within the general area of the figure suggested. It is not a matter of cutting a budget down to a given figure, but rather, an attempt to come up with an intelligent plan which will produce a good product. There is only loss, not gain, in saving money by not doing justice to the property. If the estimate turns out to be within the amount suggested, then the studio decides whether to go ahead with production. If it is over the suggested amount, then the studio head has to decide whether to abandon the property or pledge the extra money to produce it. It is not unusual to work up several possible budgets for a given property, contingent on various elements that might be modified to cut costs. There might be, for example, one budget based on a studio production, one based on filming on location, one based on a foreign location, one with a certain combination of director and actor and another with a different combination. The possibilities for modification can be many and quite varied.

The initial attempt at a budget for a property is an effort to come up with a reasonable figure that allows for the needs of the property. If there is a request to try to cut costs even further, one of the first areas to examine is the time schedule. Time is obviously money. There is a limit beyond which one cannot go without jeopardizing the production unless something is cut out of the script. This does not mean just cutting the dialogue to shorten the script by a few pages; it means eliminating something physical that is expensive to supply. Perhaps, for example, rain can be cut from a scene, or a night sequence can be changed to a day sequence, or a location shooting can be moved from Bangkok to someplace less remote. Perhaps one setting can be revamped to serve double duty for a saving of $10,000 or $12,000. If a whole setting can be eliminated, one can save not only dollars from Account 815, but also funds allocated for set dressing, props and electrical equipment, plus a couple of days off the production schedule. This cut in schedule would reduce costs of wages, fringe benefits and overhead charges for the two days. Taking all of these items together, quite a hunk of budget can be cut from total production costs by eliminating a setting. Another area where considerable savings can be made is in the number of extras used for a film. Sometimes extras are picked up on location with a consequent saving in transportation and room and board expenses. One argument against this practice is, of course, that the professional extra is experienced and will give a better day's work than will the geen extra picked up on location. If time is a factor, it may be better economics to go with the professionals.

There is no attempt to pad a budget in anticipation of requests to cut it later. There is not even an allowance for possible complications arising from bad weather or illness. It is assumed when the budget is made up that conditions will be ideal and everything will happen according to plan. Even construction is budgeted on ideal conditions. It is not assumed that there will be night crew constructing, which could involve permit men who may not be quite so efficient as number one men. Nor is it considered that the crew might be working on a stage with a red light that will go on periodically to signal the crew to cease noisy activities while a company next door is shooting. Even in location shooting, it is assumed that everything will proceed smoothly and there will be no unanticipated expenses, such as building or repaving roads or getting stuck in the mud and having to bring in heavy equipment for a rescue operation.

Certainly a lot of the success of those who are responsible for budgets lies in their ability, not just to add and subtract, but to estimate accurately. While some of this ability is intuitive, it is certainly developed and improved through experience. It isn't just a matter of looking in a book and discovering that a grip costs so many dollars a day. It is a matter of knowing the job can be done with two grips rather than three, or that four will be needed instead of three.

One of the major challenges in estimate budgeting is judging the time schedule, not only for the whole production but for each of the various aspects of production. Each area needs a certain amount of preparation time to get ready for shooting. And some individuals within a given area will work more days than others in that area. This applies to talent as well as production crews. A certain cast member may not report until the twelfth day of production, while another may be on call throughout shooting. Extras are brought in and taken out as needed. If the film involves some shooting on location, there may be one or two scouting trips required for such people as the director and the unit manager plus others who may need to seek out and study the area. Being as accurate as possible in estimating all of the various contingencies of the time-table can be very crucial to the validity of the budget. Preliminary to firming up the budget, those in charge will have had extensive meetings with the producer, the director, the unit manager and perhaps the author, during which many questions will have been asked and answered to the best of the ability of all involved. Additionally, every key production man will have been informed as to exactly what is expected of him.

The seemingly endless jungle of considerations facing those responsible for a workable production budget somehow eventually begins to take order and a pattern begins to emerge dictated by the desire to create a reasonable plan that will realize the potentials of the property. The success of a budget is not measured only in dollars spent or saved, but more importantly in how well it served the property by providing a plan which could produce a good product.

PART THREE

Film
Company
Management

As in other industries, film companies are responsible for profit-and-loss statements, re-payment of bank loans and favorable reports to stockholders. There is, however, no guaranteed supply-and-demand factor, and acceptance of new product can be traced only after production. While the need to make a full commitment before being certain that a commercial art product is marketable is not unique to motion picture companies, the degree of investment—which usually exceeds $1-million in negative cost per picture—can be unnerving. Further, depreciation of product can be rapid indeed, a circumstance which accounts for the urgent pressure of time throughout all stages of production and post-production activity.

Before considering the business problems involved in actual production, however, special attention must be devoted to working procedures of the key decision-makers who guide motion picture companies. These men must begin with a philosophy rooted in financial practicalities, and must work out the strategy which will keep their companies in effective competition for the market. In the section to follow, three major-company executives consider the finer points of establishing such a philosophy as well as practical details of its implementation. Industry veteran Richard Lederer *sets forth some guidelines which he feels management must observe if it is to meet today's challenges, and United Artists' President* David V. Picker *describes in detail how the "profits pie" is divided—with slices to the exhibitor, distributor and producer. Finally, the problems of initiating a motion picture company destined to achieve near-overnight growth into full competition with the "majors" are detailed by* Gordon Stulberg, *founding President of CBS' Cinema Center Films.*

A recent flurry of land and studio-property sale by oldline movie companies indicates that the re-structuring of the traditional studio concept in accordance with new economic demands is having some effect upon studio physical plant operations. Nevertheless, these vast centralized studio plants—actually created for another era in film industry history—continue to serve essential needs of today's movie-makers. Gordon Forbes *and* Roger Mayer *consider the contemporary operation of the studio in the final essays of this section. Their discussions range over the practical problems of maintaining a giant physical plant as well as the theoretical problems involved in anticipating future production needs.*

MANAGEMENT: OLD GAME—NEW RULES

RICHARD LEDERER

". . . Movies are, as one old-timer put it—not an industry, but a disease . . ."

The industry is changing, but only to the degree that it has always evolved throughout its history. It has never been static, but has always reacted in one way or another to various conditions. It has never stood still as a communication form, as an entertainment form or—to lesser degree—as an art form.

Yet it is too easy to assume that some violent upheaval has taken place—that a "new art form," a new "now" audience, and a whole new set of business rules are at hand. We must in fact observe that pictures are made today—some of which are the most successful films we have at the moment—that conceivably could have been made in exactly the same way 35 years ago. They are traditional motion pictures in a real sense, and they are very successful. This suggests that not all the rules have changed.

While it should not detract from the expression of social concern or the aesthetic possibilities inherent in any film, major companies who have economic interest in the business must continue to regard movies primarily as an escape entertainment form. The management of such publicly-owned companies must show a responsibility to shareholders and, consequently, to profit-and-loss statements. These are the realities a major studio must observe, and it therefore follows

RICHARD LEDERER is presently Vice-President in charge of Advertising and Publicity for Warner Brothers Inc. He served as Vice President, Production at Warner's Studio before assuming his present responsibilities.

that they will be making pretty much the same kind of film they have always made. But this hardly implies that a slow evolution is not constantly in the making. Taste is more advanced and technique is more sophisticated than in the past. The nation has matured with regard to what it will accept and what it will tolerate in the arts and literature. Audiences have accepted, for example, a far more candid and explicit screen exploration of sexual relations. Essentially, however, the movies are simply dealing with human problems in a more realistic fashion, and the degree of realism and detail should not suggest a trend away from the basic escape-entertainment appeals.

We must not confuse, however, *what* is going to be made with *how* it is made. Having said, in effect, that there is a great deal of stability in the fundamental nature of movies, I must now turn to the factors which set motion pictures apart from other businesses—and one of the greatest of these is the uncertainty of the marketplace. Many other industries can have accurate indications of what their market will be when they set out each year. The automobile industry can judge its potential sales and make sound business decisions regarding styles and models, the number of cars to make, and other factors. Unfortunately, the movie business has not enjoyed having that degree of predictability in over 20 years. Before the consent decree,* a major company owned its own theatres, and consequently knew where its marketplace was. It knew how many films it could make in a year, and that those films would be exposed in regular fashion. There are old-time exhibitors today who privately confess their wish that perhaps the legal action which forced the split of production companies and theatres should never have been taken, because one important consequence became the lack of orderly production at any of the studios. Since the studios no longer knew with certainty where the market was—and whether their films would indeed get booked—they were unable to make judgments about how many films to make and how much money to commit to production, and the number of films made fell off drastically.

A second major factor which distinguishes motion pictures from all other businesses arises from the enormous impact of in-

* EDITORS' NOTE: Prior to 1948, it was an industry standard for most studios to own major interests in theatre chains, thereby controlling production, distribution and exhibition. The Justice Department deemed this triple involvement to be anti-competitive, and began litigation against the companies. The majors— but not other companies involved—agreed to the entry of a "consent decree," in which they consented to divorce themselves of theatre ownership, in accordance with the Justice Department's anti-trust position. Thereafter, the landmark Supreme Court decision in 1948 (*U.S. v. Paramount, et. al.*) compelled *all* companies to divest themselves of theatre ownership, while retaining production and distribution. The result of the 1948 decision has been the emergence of many new theatre chains and small production entities, which now comfortably compete with the majors.

dividual creative talent upon production cost and upon market success. Evaluation of what the audience will accept is difficult at best and unfathomable at worst. This is a major aspect of the "Old Game," and new rules are not really changing it. The only business that comes rather close to it, I should think, would be fashion, where trying to judge what women will buy next year—how to tailor an inventory, how much cloth to buy, how much to cut and so forth—would be a bit of a guessing game. But movies are the super, number-one guessing game. They are, as one old-timer put it, "not an industry, but a disease."

Let's consider the role of talent in this game. Ultimately, <u>movies are a product, and that product comes in a package</u> which <u>can be more important</u> than what it contains. It can be more or less attractive, depending on the names that are associated with it. A producer who has a fairly good action script, for example, can make the film for $2-million with one actor, and $2.5-million with a "top" actor. That extra cost is something he must begin to think about in terms of actual return. Is it worth the extra $500,000? Will the film do $2-million more in business as a result of over-investment in this actor? There are, after all, only a few actors who seem capable of delivering a larger audience than the ordinary actor, and a good deal of that happens overseas. It is a fact that a good western with one of five names attached to it will do 40% more business than the same picture without those names in it outside the United States. It is in that type of film that the industry seems willing to spend extra money for one of the "super-actors." Clint Eastwood is one of them, Steve McQueen another, Burt Lancaster might be still another. Lee Marvin works very well overseas, as does Paul Newman. That kind of name is attractive in the western, or outdoor adventure package. Escapist entertainment is still the number one attraction around the world, and although the "star system" is supposed to be on the wane in America, many a picture is made only because a certain actor will commit to do it. The industry still goes to the bank on names of people.

To some degree, the contemporary audience dictates the type of film Hollywood will produce. It is sad but true that <u>movies have always been an imitative—not an innovative—industry.</u> Miscalculation abounds. Everyone reads the new demographics, and learns that we have a very young audience—that 70% of our regular patrons are under 24 years old. Their immediate reaction is to plan and make films that are geared to the tastes and interests of young people. This in turn results in all kinds of unsuccessful films. It has always been that way, and I don't suspect will ever change. If students in this country begin to revolt against the establishment, and we have a thing known as student unrest, or political activism, 40 movies about campus unrest are made, and by the time they come out, no one is really interested in them. It is a fact that the industry, in its frantic efforts to analyze audience wants, seizes upon what they feel is the only "evidence" available, and they deny the history of movie entertainment as well as their own instincts by jumping on the topical bandwagon. Management's alternative, if there is any single approach to planning successful pictures, is to try to make an interesting film without regard, necessarily, to whether it really is geared to a certain type of audience. A major studio committed to doing 20 to 25 films a year should be trying to make marvelous stories—films that are interesting, different, special. Films need not necessarily be off-beat or entirely youth-oriented—concerned solely with problems that deal with how young boys and girls confront today's world. If a classic Alfred Hitchcock thriller came along, well-directed with a tight story, it would be a tremendous success. Even if I knew it wouldn't be ready for a year, I'd bank on it.

The evidence is there; it's always worked that way. Successful films have always been well-directed, well-written, well-made films about something that a majority of the people can relate to or empathize with. It has always been that way, and it will always be that way. But this does not mean management should avoid taking risks on what is new, fresh and has a specialized appeal. *Woodstock* was a gamble that worked for us. When we first committed to making the film, no one believed that it would be as successful as it ultimately became. No one was sure the event itself would come off the way it did. We take pride in the fact that at least two of us in the company sensed that something special was going to happen at this place. We didn't know what it was going to be. We didn't know how well it would take off. No one thought the event would take on the significance —the aura—that it did, and, of course, we hardly realized how accomplished Michael Wadleigh would be. His brilliant concepts about how he was going to edit that film, and the multiple-image ideas that he had were unknowns and too difficult to forsee at that time. I would say that we made a good, educated guess. But I also consider it to be an accident in a sense, one we cannot learn much from. To try to make another would be a big mistake.

The *Woodstock* type of film is not the only area, however, in which imitative management can suffer from miscalculation. *The Sound of Music* is another true accident. For some reason it touched the audience nerve, perhaps more than any other film in history, and it earned an enormous amount of money. Seeing the fantastic return for invested capital, many industry leaders saw a whole new potential. The theory became the fact—the exception the rule—and it was assumed that nearly impossible sums could be invested wisely and safely in negative cost. All this, of course, was based on an expectation of great revenue returns. In a way, this assumption nearly led the industry into extinction. The industry was weakened,—especially three companies—as a result of false expectations derived from the success of *The Sound of Music*. It was a rude awakening for many when it became obvious that investing $20-million in a film did *not* assure success.

Miscalculations are possible, of course, under the best of circumstances, but I think they are even more likely to occur because of new industry developments—particularly the new controls upon management which conglomerate take-overs introduce. In such cases there are predictable changes, and my guess is that they usually are for the worst. We must remember that until a very few years ago the industry was still in the hands of the so-called "pioneers." Good, bad, indifferent, right or wrong, they were a unique breed of men in American business life. Their backgrounds were dissimilar. None of them came out of film schools. Many were immigrants—barely teenagers when they arrived in this country. With no scholastic training, they went into various businesses, and somehow happened to be around when movies were born. All had an innate sense of showmanship, an instinct about this country, and a prescience about the entertainment form that the movie would become.

These men were very special people. When their kind passed on, new management or ownership replaced them and some significant things happened. In nearly every case where the new management was a conglomerate, the company became overly business-oriented. This new breed, in the best American tradition, were well-trained business management graduates who were used to systemized and highly-structured business organizations. They knew everything on the business side of how to run a company, and after one look at a movie company they found it to be amorphous in form and seemingly running amok. They were aghast. Their strict sense of business training was offended by this, and their impulse was to systematize and structure it, to make it, in their terms, "make sense"—and this has literally put many companies close to bankruptcy.

Unfortunately, movies are not a business in that strict sense of the word. Studios demand unique talent and unique understanding if they are to be be run effectively. The successful major motion picture studio of the future will be the one that manages the following: 1) a reorganization of its outdated physical structure to bring production overheads down to reasonable scales; 2) development within its creative manpower of a "sure nose" for potential motion picture material; 3) The ability and know-how to attract the proper talent in the industry to these various projects; 4) the diplomatic skill needed to cope understandingly with the creative excesses and temperaments of these gifted producers, directors, writers and stars while at the same time imposing upon them realistic and responsible fiscal controls. Utopia? Maybe. Admittedly a nearly impossible set of conditions—but a challenge that I feel can and will be met.

THE FILM COMPANY AS FINANCIER/DISTRIBUTOR

DAVID V. PICKER

". . . We don't have a gigantic studio mouth to feed—a situation which can force you to make pictures just to keep the studio busy instead of making pictures because they are the kind you should make at a given time and place. . . ."

Since 1950 those major studios established in earlier years have had to seek new roles and functions for themselves within a changing industry. My own company, United Artists, created what may in many ways be regarded as a guideline for film companies who sought to combine an already-existing enterprise with the skills of successful financing and distributing of motion pictures.

In order to understand how this new identity was established we need to begin when Arthur Krim and Robert Benjamin bought control of United Artists from Charles Chaplin and Mary Pickford in 1951. By late 1952 the company, which had been losing money, was in the black, and Krim and Benjamin were in a position to consider financing their own productions. Their plan was to finance pictures by dealing directly with the creative forces who make them. Their initial concept involved the extension of creative autonomy and a per-

DAVID V. PICKER is President, Chief Operations Officer and a member of the Board of Directors of United Artists Corporation. Educated at Andover and at Dartmouth, where he received his B.A. in 1953, Mr. Picker joined United Artists in 1956, and served in a variety of executive posts before his election as President in June, 1969.

centage of the profits to a filmmaker. The company's interest was to secure all distribution rights and a share of the profit in the film. This *modus operandi* clearly was contradictory to the policy of the major studios, who owned all their films and—by keeping editing powers to themselves—did not relinquish creative control to individual filmmakers.

This idea could not be given any real test, of course, until United Artists could build a strong financial base. But as a result of a succession of good pictures, the concept which Krim and Benjamin had conceived and initiated became a way of life for the company. Such early successes as *High Noon, The African Queen* and *Moulin Rouge* resulted from deals with filmmakers. By the mid-50's we had also initiated production programs with various film companies, one of which was Hecht-Hill-Lancaster—and this resulted in such remarkable films as the Academy Award-winning *Marty, Trapeze* and *Sweet Smell of Success*. Later, we established a relationship with the Mirisch Company which is now some 60 pictures old.

Throughout our history, the mangement of United Artists has given creative filmmakers the right—within various approved frameworks of budget, script, cast and director—to make films as they wanted to make them. We did not look at rushes. The finished picture was delivered to us without *caveat* on our part, if it fulfilled budget obligations. Stanley Kramer, with whom we had a multiple picture deal, is one of the filmmakers who never showed us a foot until his picture was completed. In exchange for that right, which was revolutionary for Hollywood, we were able to attract many of the top filmmakers in the world.

Other companies eventually caught on, because there is nothing essentially unique in what we offer—with the exception of our own mangement techniques. Some aspects of the approach have changed, of course. Initially, we offered a profit percentage in exchange for higher salaries. Faced with industry competition we now not only have to give up a greater share of the profits but have to pay the "risk-money" in front. Nevertheless, it was the Krim-Benjamin philosophy of extending creative freedom to the filmmaker as early as 1952, which led to the general industry approach of today.

It may be informative for me now to consider in some detail the way this philosophy has been translated into operational realities at United Artists. We can usefully examine what happens to a dollar that comes in at the theatre box-office window, following its course backward from there in order to see where we get the money for financing.

Let us assume that we have arranged a 50% deal with the theatre—which means that $.50 of each dollar is retained by the exhibitor and $.50 is turned over to us as distributor of the film. We do not share in the receipts from concessions in the theatre—which are exclusively the exhibitor's. The $.50 which comes to United Artists represents 100% of our film rental. We are now operating with the money—defined as "film rental"—which is turned over to us by the theatre owners of the world. When we say a picture has "done $20-million," that does not mean it's box-office gross is $20-million, but that the film rental earned by the distributor is $20-million. The figure in fact represents—depending on various deals in various theatres throughout the world—the sum which comes to United Artists as the distributor.

We charge a percentage of this money for distributing our film. It may vary in other companies, but United Artists has set a standard of 30% of the gross for the United States and Canada. In other words, 30% of the money which comes to us is retained by us in order to operate our business. Out of each dollar of film rental paid to United Artists, $.30 is retained by United Artists as its distribution fee. In addition, we deduct our distribution costs, which include prints, advertising, and interest as well as other expenses. From the "film rental dollar" then, $.30 is taken as distribution cost, and another $.20 is taken to cover prints, advertising, interest, taxes, distribution expenses. (These figures are approximate.) What is left is known as the *net producer's share*—which is used to pay off the loan we secured to pay the negative cost of the picture.

We finance each picture with a bank loan, and we borrow from banks all over the world. Each loan is guaranteed by United Artists Corporation. The bank has the picture as collateral, of course —but more importantly—it has the guarantee of United Artists Corporation. The latter is significant, because, unfortunately, every picture does not show a profit. If there is a shortage, United Artists has to make up the difference between what we have earned from the net producer's share, and what the actual cost of the picture is. If we assume that a picture cost $1-million, then when those $.50 returns which constitute the net producer's share add up to $1-million, the picture has broken even.

At this point, all profits are split. The typical deal at United Artists is equal-share—50/50. The producer and creative entities will get 50% of the balance, and we will retain 50% of the balance. This is an oversimplification, however, because deals do get much more complicated. Quite often, there are multiple-profit participants. Occasionally, gross participants get money "off the top," without any concern for what actual profits are. A particular actor might be given "$100,000 cash against 10% of the gross." In this case, "gross" is the distributor's film rental, not the theatre gross. If the film rental on the picture totals $5-million, that actor will have received $100,000 in advance against the total $500,000 he will earn on the film without regard to distribution costs, prints, advertising or any other costs. A *percentage of the gross* deal, it might well be said, is a favorable deal if a picture does well.

If the net producer's share always equals the cost of the film, then there are never any loss pictures. Of course it does not always work out that way. Some pictures make a lot of money and a lot of pictures make no money. Where does the distribution/financing company look for money to repay loans if films cannot gross enough? The only available source is the distribution fee. We get that 30% of the gross as our distribution fee, and we have to maintain our business with proceeds from that. Some measure of profit also has to be built into that 30%, simply to assure our survival. We have to use the profit built into that distribution fee to pay off bank loans on pictures that do not independently earn money.

To summarize: If the entire net producer's share equals the amount of overall production risk, the company is in good shape. If it falls short and losses can be recouped from the distribution fee without threatening a basic financial position strong enough to carry on our organization, then we are also in good shape. Where we can get into trouble is when we have a motion picture which costs a great deal of money and grosses nothing at all. This is why it is so dangerous for any company to sink an enormous amount of money into one picture. If the picture fails, they not only have lost the distribution fee which keeps their establishment going, but also have no distribution fee profit to pay off the loan against the picture. And, of course, they lose the net producer's share as well. That is why companies, including United Artists, have been nervous about making any additional commitments in high-cost pictures.

Before considering a number of operating principles and procedures which United Artists management has adopted and observed over the years, I should review my position vis-a-vis the "conglomerate take-over" which some in our industry regard as near-fatal. United Artists has recently become a part of a large parent company—The Transamerica Corporation—and my observations may be germane to the discussion.

In looking around for businesses, most large multi-level companies look for leisure-time activities because—clearly—they are the businesses of the future. In United Artists, Transamerica evidently found what they considered a well-managed company where they could make the right kind of financial arrangements. Since the move gives United Artists an umbrella of enormous importance, the deal was negotiated. Transamerica is not involved in the operation of our company. It does not guarantee our bank loans. We are not operating any differently. Yet, the psychological impact of the fact that United Artists is now part of a corporation with over a billion dollars in assets is of great importance.

It is not a one-sided proposition by any means, however. United Artists is a strong independent addition to Transamerica. We are in many ancillary businesses. We have the largest film library in the world through our ownership of the pre-1948 Warner Brothers library.

We market films to television—both Warner and United Artists films. We handle short subjects, and we are in the broadcasting business with two TV stations—one in Puerto Rico and one in Cleveland. We have a very large sheet music publishing and record company and we are planning for active video-cassette distribution, which is clearly of enormous residual value.

In considering the various principles and practices we have established, I should begin by saying that acquiring a film is just a business negotiation. The greater question is one of evaluating what you think it is worth. If there is a demand for his work, the filmmaker is going to get the best deal he can. If there is no demand—and only one financier is prepared to take a chance—then the creator has to decide whether he is prepared to make the deal. If you are a businessman in a business involving art, there has got to be a point beyond which you are not prepared to go, in any given deal. This is a first principle we must observe.

In practice, we face the same basic dilemma which confronts any financier or distributor. What an audience is going to want to see, how they will respond to a given motion picture, and all the variables that take place while a picture is in production—these factors are beyond analysis. One difficulty we meet in this regard is the lag between the time when we make the decision to finance a script or go into production, and the time the picture is released. In addition, there has been a polarization in taste. More people are going to *certain* movies than ever before, but less people are going to movies generally—so the audience is shrinking. In practice, this fact means that the successful picture is more successful than ever before, but the unsuccessful picture is more unsuccessful. There used to be a base audience, and you knew you could count on certain numbers for almost every picture. That audience simply does not exist anymore. How can we know that the $3-million or $800,000 we are going to spend is going into a product the mass audience will want to see a year hence?

Once we agree to finance a picture new questions arise. Since we have distribution offices all over the world, we must market our films to each individual country according to our beliefs about the way each will react to the film. Since our business is to distribute films throughout the world—and since we have offices and manpower capable of doing it—our problems lie not in logistics, but in knowing what pictures to make.

Our philosophy is never to be burdened with the operating overhead of a studio. Our producers have the right to make their films at any studio they want, and in practice to secure the best individual studio rental deal for any film. We don't have a gigantic studio mouth to feed—a situation which can force you to make pictures just to keep the studio busy instead of making pictures because they are the kind you *should* make at a given time and place.

In closing, I might say that we are in a time that is more precarious, but at the same time more exciting, than ever before. Audiences are extremely unpredictable and their decisions often have nothing to do with a film's merit. When you have to risk millions in an effort to choose those few pictures that audiences will decide to see, it can become a pretty scary business. The trouble with our business is that nobody trusts anybody in it. The distributor doesn't trust the exhibitor. The exhibitor doesn't trust the distributor. The producer doesn't trust the distributor. The distributor doesn't trust the creator. The creator is sure the distributor is putting in invalid charges against his picture. The financier is positive that the creator has spent 43 unnecessary days in shooting the picture. Despite all this, somehow or other, we wind up with films that sometimes people go to see.

THE ESTABLISHMENT OF A FILM COMPANY

GORDON STULBERG

". . . The curious fact is that almost every criterion we established for viability has been adopted by every major studio in the last three years. . . ."

In the mid-'60's the Columbia Broadcasting System began to consider the possibility of establishing a Division devoted to the production and distribution of motion pictures. In 1967, after considerable research, Cinema Center Films was formed for that purpose. Their estimate was that there would be an opportunity for independent companies to come into the market and—provided they were creative and careful about their costs—turn the production and distribution of movies into a profitable venture.

This concept fit into CBS, Inc. expansion plans because in its' diversifying role it has traditionally sought to grow in areas where it has had some previous experience and a core of knowledgeability. The production of entertainment films was such an area and so, in the

GORDON STULBERG was Vice President and Chief Administration Officer of Columbia Pictures before becoming President of Cinema Center Films— the theatrical film division of The Columbia Broadcasting System—in 1967. Just after completing this essay, Mr. Stulberg was elected (in September, 1971) as President and Chief Operating Officer of Twentieth Century-Fox Film Corporation. Mr. Stulberg is a member of the New York State and California Bar.

spring of 1967, CBS invited the author to join the organization and, in effect, develop the new division.

The *precis* which was prepared at the time outlined certain basic courses to pursue.

First, it was recommended that Cinema Center Films not own a studio or operate a studio but rather rent studio space when necessary. Since the network owns CBS Studio Center, it was assumed that the new division could probably utilize it for in-studio production and in-studio post-principal photography. In the same context it was also recommended that we should not attempt to develop a distribution company, but instead engage specialized executives who would supervise distribution. If such a group chose the most knowledgeable and experienced local distributors in all territories in the world and made deals with them—it was reasoned—there would be no major continuing annual overhead for distribution. The supervisory executives would plan the pattern of release, arrange the terms and let the local distributor actually execute sales policy.

Finally, it was suggested that a company with limited production, distribution and advertising operations should not attempt to supervise more than 10 films in a year. It was estimated that the average negative cost would be in the area of $3-million and the cost history of the first 22 pictures confirmed the accuracy of the estimate. Negative cost actually averaged $2,960,000.

The above—all spelled out in the *precis*—summarizes our essential, continuing operating philosophy some four years later. We intended to enter the market with a desire to finance the kind of picture that would let the industry know we were serious and to test out long-held theories with respect to the elimination of large-scale fixed overhead in production and distribution. We also hoped to apply some of the more sophisticated management and financial tools which for too long had been ignored by the industry.

We began, in May, 1967, adding executives somewhat more rapidly at production level than at distribution. We moved slowly, however, bearing in mind that we were going to have only a skeleton production operation and would deal mostly with independent producers. We developed a small nucleus of highly-motivated production, distribution, and sales and advertising executives. We opened sales and advertising offices in New York, and a production office and a European sales and advertising department in London. Subsequently, we engaged representatives to supervise at the local level distributors in such major territories as Japan, Italy, France, West Germany, Spain and Australia-New Zealand as a combined entity. The key distribution executives who were first brought in made agreements with distributors throughout the world. For United States and Canada distribution, we turned to National General Corporation which had formed a company to distribute pictures they were producing.

Essentially, that is the organizational history of the company. The tradition of CBS has always been to see their ventures through, and it backed us in whatever project we felt had economic viability —including permission to build up an inventory of unproduced material in full knowledge that on the basis of industry experience two-thirds of it ultimately would have to be written off as abandoned material.

Once we were under way we naturally devoted a major portion of our time to the acquisition of properties. The rule we adhered to was to avoid obviously distasteful material—either sexually erotic or excessively violent properties. At that time the market was showing strength in the *I Am Curious (Yellow)* type of film as well as Italian westerns, which were in some cases excessively gratuitous in their violence. Many exhibitors were taking on that type of product, but we did not feel we wanted to go that way.

For one thing, a quick dollar would not help us if it offended the corporation and tarnished the traditionally sound CBS image. Conversely, we went after *Boys In The Band* because we also wished to make it clear to all that we had authority from CBS to acquire and to bring controversial material to the screen as long as it had other than prurient reasons for being produced. We felt *Boys In The Band* met that definition. Beyond that, we established no guidelines other than to try to develop a line of product that would bring us into the market at the rate of about 10 films a year.

Several major business problems confronted us almost from the outset. First, we were entering at the top of the seller's market, just about the time that the million-dollar player was becoming fashionable. Everyone was scrambling for Paul Newman, Steve McQueen and John Wayne. If we were to become a viable company, we were going to have to meet, but not exceed, prices then being established by every company in town. That was a major problem at that time because we had to translate those prices to CBS in terms of investment.

Second, in light of the number of buyers in the market in those years, the agents—with the notable exception of William Morris Agency—were somewhat reluctant to break their traditional lines of communication in order to deal with us. Our legal status was apparently still under examination by the Justice Department, and we had not really announced our plans for world-wide distribution—because we did not have our local distributors lined up until we were in business for well over a year. So it took some courage and faith on the agent's part to sell their clients to us for films and for packages when they might have gotten the same deals with more traditional companies. We were very thankful that the William Morris office led off in that direction because the first major deal we made was with Jack Lemmon. After that we used Steve McQueen and others of his stature, and established our credibility as a major film company.

Our next major decision involved selection of a U. S. distributor. We have been asked why we selected a new company like National General. The answer, of course, is that our choice was the best of those options which were available to us. We could have set up a distribution system of our own, to which we were opposed from the outset. We could have gone with a major distributor, which was not advisable because the majors were then making 20 to 25 pictures of their own each year and we did not want our product lost among their films. The only logical choice, then, was to go with an independent distributor. Among available companies were the "States Righters"—companies which handled franchise product from American International, whose background and tradition was to sell exploitation pictures. There were also a few companies with five or six exchanges operating out of New York, but these would have to expand operations to handle the type of pictures we were going to make. And then there were National General and Cinerama. Since the latter already had a contract with ABC, and was therefore unavailable, when National General went into the distribution business, we engaged them. We were aware, of course, that NGC managed a theatre operation intelligently and still was in that business. (See pp. 214-20). We felt that if NGC was going into distribution it would know whom to hire. Their own theatre managers and their management would tell them who were the best distributor salesmen in the various regions and those were certainly men that NGC would be going after as they set up their own distribution company. In effect, then, we were buying their expertise with regard to the kind of salesmen who could best sell our films.

Nor did we have to make any guarantees to NGC. We did state at the outset that we planned to feed only about 10 films a year into the market—something less than a major has traditionally offered. We helped them ease this problem by offering a deal in which the percentage of the gross that NGC collected for its distribution fee would be larger at the front end, and then would—on an annual basis—drop down as more product was introduced. In other words, even though we might give NGC only two or three pictures, the distribution fee on those would be high enough to help defray a reasonable proportion of the expenses of their distribution organization. Then, of course, if we supplied more, the incremental cost of servicing additional pictures would not be very much. That is the deal we worked out, and it continues in force. For our purpose, it was excellent because if we produced for distribution even a reasonable number of pictures—less than ten, but perhaps five or six—our distribution cost would be far less than it would be had we gone with one of the major distributors. There would really be no basis for comparison.

It would be well at this point to dwell on those general decisions which can have great influence upon whether the company turns a profit or not. This is, after all, an all-encompassing concern of management. My entire experience in the motion picture business convinced me that our company was not going to survive without some great fiscal orthodoxy and some more imaginative approaches to controls in the field of sales, advertising and production, and indeed in our relationship to CBS, which is a highly sophisticated financial operation. Even the most imaginative managerial techniques, however, must be grounded in hard facts of our business. We must know how our various pictures are doing around the world before we can develop those cost control patterns which can be applied not only to a specific picture at a given time, but to the entire annual output as it affects—or is affected by—the success or failure of that single picture.

Such knowledge comes to us first through NGC which gives us a weekly report of domestic film rentals during the previous week. Similarly, each local distributor in a foreign country reports distribution income either to our local representative in the territory or directly to London or New York. The major territories are reported on a weekly basis and the smaller territories bi-weekly or monthly. Major territories include Japan, the United Kingdom, France, Italy and West Germany. Reports come in as quicky as the local distributor can send them on. Thus we have a fair estimate every week of how our pictures are doing all over the world—an important body of information with which we begin "tracking" our successes and failures.

As tracking begins, we can read early warning signs. If the picture opens poorly, we are in difficulty because it is a rare picture that opens badly and then builds. This building has become even less possible in recent years, simply because more people are going to theatres as a result of word-of-mouth publicity. If word-of-mouth on a picture is not good when it opens, it is unlikely that it will improve. There are exceptions, of course—primarily among large extravaganzas that open well because of their size and pre-sell. Even though word-of-mouth is not good on them, the mere fact that they are big and have attracted a lot of publicity will hold them in theatres for a number of weeks on exclusive runs.

But those are decidedly the exception. Once a typical picture has played for from four to eight weeks, the dimensions of the problem or the prospects are clear. The "tracking" procedure then helps us to deal with the upside or downside limits. Any picture, for example, could open big in New York and then let down badly everywhere else in the country. Still, if we open exclusively in New York, Los Angeles, Washington, Dallas—say seven or eight geographic areas—and uniformly perform either very well or very badly in the earliest weeks, we know a great deal about what will happen elsewhere.

The guessing process with respect to "estimates" now must begin, particularly once we report on revisions in full year budgets on a monthly basis. We track the picture as its future opens both here and in foreign, since what happens abroad is a key factor. Sometimes the difference between success and failure lies in foreign reaction. A western might barely turn costs on the basis of domestic returns, but it can go through the roof abroad. And unlike domestic tracking, where eight or nine local engagements may tell the story, the foreign projection must wait until reaction in at least three of five major territories has been reported—Italy, Japan, West Germany, France and the U.K. We may do spectacularly well in Japan and fail elsewhere—or succeed in Japan and Italy and fail in the U.K., France and West Germany—and still wind up in the red. If your picture is good enough to become—as did, for example, *A Man Called Horse*—a runaway success in four out of five of these territories, you know you have a successful picture abroad. Then we begin to track on a basis of comparison with other pictures that have played those territories at approximately the same time of year and in the same theatres, and under the same terms—and that is how, by using an historical track, we can come up with what we think the picture ultimately will do.

But all we really have established thus far is how we determine the parameters of success or failure. One might ask, where do all the financial controls fit in? If everything is boom or bust, why are we so preoccupied with management skills and techniques in controlling sales? The answer is that skilled financial management applied to three out of every ten pictures made can minimize the effect of boom or bust. What is important is to concentrate upon the fact that there are pictures whose losses can be dramatically minimized and pictures whose success can also be maximized.

If the difference between being in the red and the black on an annual divisional accounting can turn on a swing of as little as $100,000 a picture, management must ask itself—what factors in handling each film can we control so as to effect the divisional statement in this manner? Where can we save costs or stimulate the added business which can so impact the P & L statement?

First, we keep under constant scrutiny our annual operating overhead. The number of people kept on production, sales and advertising staffs on a year-round basis must be constantly reviewed. Since we attribute a portion of our annual costs to each picture, the smaller that portion is the less, in the aggregate, the total cost of the film will be.

Next, we examine our pre-production and preparation costs. How much is spent on development deals? If we assume that over half of development money never results in a picture, then obviously we must do as much as we can to avoid this expense and more aggressively seek "packages." If a script, a budget and a producer already exist, the chance of a film's not being made are reduced. Our Business Affairs Department keeps close track of the costs of acquiring and developing material and expresses these costs as incurred rather than permitting them to be carried in inventory. In addition, we submit a budget for development expenses in advance of each year and require production to track its costs against that budget every month.

Another area of costs protection lies in a constant review of spending on the picture while it is in production. We exert pressure to budget realistically in advance to keep cast costs down, to reduce location moves, and eliminate "protection" personnel and equipment. The same thing holds true in the post-principal photography stage. The longer we hold onto the picture while it is being edited the longer we must pay interest. The money is tied up. The sooner we get the film into release, the sooner we return our investment and the less the interest charges will be against capital we have frozen in production.

Assume we trim production, post-principal photography, and project development costs on any picture by $100,000—or 5% of a $2-million picture. Multiply that $100,000 by seven or eight pictures and we are suddenly considering a $750,000 item in our annual profit and loss statement.

Management can also initiate savings in the sales area, especially in terms of advertising dollar commitments. An early decision to foreclose advertising if it looks as if the picture is not going to perform can save a great deal. Shifting media expenditures or trimming the size of the advertising buy if it looks as though the picture is going soft can effect real savings. In this connection we insist that *advertising is a function of sales* and the amount of expenditures must be directly responsive to sales estimates of the potential revenue from any engagement.

Finally, we try to negotiate better distribution deals as we go along. We try to neutralize the exhibitor's bargaining strengths by negotiating for advantages that will ultimately keep more of the theatrical income in the hands of the financing-distribution companies. These relationships have a long way to go but, up until 1950, the exhibitor was also the distributor and the contract between exhibition and distribution was just a matter of bookkeeping. Since divorcement, however, we have had to establish arm's-length negotiations between distributor and theatre owner, and we must continue to rid the industry of practices that grew up when the left hand was negotiating with the right hand.

These are the major areas film company management must concentrate upon if it is to swing the pendulum from loss to profit. We believe that we have really made the "new economics" of motion pictures work for us at Cinema Center. We have, on occasion, paid some penalty for our small overhead, but our concept has come to life for us. The curious fact is that almost every criterion we established for viability has been adopted by almost every major studio in the last three years. They have eliminated the studio; they have tried to eliminate large production staffs; they have sought as small a distribution overhead as possible; they have contracted advertising campaigns out—which we did from the start—thereby eliminating an in-house advertising overhead ranging in the millions of dollars. We could be a great deal more sanguine about what we are doing if we judged our success in terms of the emulation that takes place. Other companies are now coming to where we were three years ago. But we cannot sit still because we know that there are other problems in the production and sale of movies which have yet to be solved if the industry is to be economically viable.

STUDIO OPERATIONS

GORDON B. FORBES
ROGER L. MAYER

MR. FORBES — *MCA Universal City Studios*

"*. . . Part of the success of a large studio operation is undoubtedly due to an excellent modern physical plant that allows for a steady, efficient flow of production. . . .*"

Universal City Studios is a modern facility with up-to-date equipment. When MCA bought the physical plant in 1959, it undertook strategic improvements which updated the property and insured its future growth. At a time when other big studios have been selling off parts of their lots and property and consolidating operations in other ways, Universal, with its expansion into television, has been relatively successful in keeping the studio running at near capacity. This is not to say that Universal has not felt the economic pinch that has affected the industry as a whole. It has. Relatively speaking, however, it has managed to do better than some of the others. Part of the success of a large studio operation is undoubtedly

---

GORDON B. FORBES served as Assistant Production Manager at Republic Pictures and as Unit Production Manager for John Wayne's Batjac Productions before taking up his current tasks as Vice President/Studio Operations Manager at Universal TV.

ROGER L. MAYER is Vice President, MGM Laboratories, Inc. and Assistant Secretary, Metro-Goldwyn-Mayer, Inc. He served in a number of positions at Columbia Pictures Corporation and MGM before being named to his present position.

due to an excellent, modern physical plant that allows for a steady, efficient flow of production.

With strong financial backing, the parent company, MCA, bought the studio plant at a time when other studios were cutting back operations to economize. This purchase enabled the studio to modernize and expand its facilities just as television production began rapid growth. Thus the studio was ready and able to adapt to the demands of the future. While other studios have been tightening up, Universal has actually been expanding its complex. Good judgment has resulted in successful films produced within reasonable budgets, and a strong sales force has managed to sell the product. It has all added up to a basic faith in the business despite an occasional set-back.

Typical pre-production as well as in-production demands on studio operations include such areas as camera, sound, lighting, greens, setting, wardrobe, makeup, hairdressing, transportation. Post-production operations add areas concerned with editing, sound effects, music, dubbing. Besides all of the usual production concerns within the studio itself, shooting on location poses additional assignments. Transportation must be provided for cast and crew; the location setting has to be prepared; hotel and meal accommodations must be established; perhaps the daily rushes need to be screened by the producer and the director, entailing further technical arrangements.

Added to the plant itself, then, is a fine technical staff of permanent studio employees available whenever they are needed. The large studio has a labor relations department to handle employees' problems that arise. Since most employees are union members, such a department might require a staff of several full-time people. As soon as a complaint is made, it is immediately turned over to the labor relations department. Contracts are very complicated. While a studio tries to operate carefully within them, problems do arise. The wise management assigns staff to work out minor problems before they become major ones. This way, good relations exist and there is a mutual feeling that everyone is at least trying to live within the agreements. The top quality of these permanent employees, these "below-the-line" people, is really evident in difficult productions like *Airport*—one of the biggest box-office grosses the studio has ever had, and *The Andromeda Strain*—one of the most challenging technical settings the studio has ever undertaken.

With a feature production, studio operations has quite a bit of "lead" time; that is, time in advance of production for organizing and scheduling everything. A good producer who knows what he is doing will manage several weeks of lead time in working things out with studio operations so that everyone has adequate warning and can get ready to meet each day's schedule in advance. His biggest problem might be a complication regarding some of his cast, who are available only on certain dates. Their schedules can determine when shooting must start and/or end. But generally, there is adequate lead time on features. For television, however, with the quantity that must be turned out in barely a week of shooting, there is usually little lead time. The television schedule of necessity is fast-paced. It demands professional technical crews who really know what they are doing and give an honest day's work for an honest day's pay.

The major difference between maintaining a motion picture schedule and maintaining a television schedule is that of speed. The typical six-day schedule for television is quite different from the typical 40-day schedule for a feature film. Once the television director falls behind, it is difficult for him to catch up. Because of this pressure, there may well be a change in directors before the next segment in shot. Things really get tense when a group is running behind on a stage that has been promised to another group in back-to-back timing. Studio operations, and particularly the unit managers, really sweat it out, sometimes switching around as many as four or five companies to help out the company that is in trouble. There is usually a period of three or four months each year when production is so heavy that studio facilities are taxed beyond the point of comfortable operation. Most of the time, however, problems can be worked out relatively easily through a little cooperative juggling.

Once a project is approved and a date is set to start, the logistics begin for studio operations to service the production, supplying the needed crews, the people who work behind the cameras. Even before shooting actually starts, various departments in the studio get involved. The art department checks out stage allocations and space in conjunction with requirements of set construction. Studio employees provide the manpower and tools necessary to do the job according to the budget. Tight controls are kept on this aspect so that the studio knows every morning by 11:00 a.m. where it stands financially in relation to where it was the previous evening when the company shut down.

While the unit manager has to solve the problems of meeting the day-to-day schedule and keeping people happily working together, the studio operations manager worries about the factory problems of making sure what is needed is available on time and in good repair. This responsibility does not entail the artistic aspects of production, but rather those elements that have to do with the physical plant of the studio: the equipment that the studio makes available to any production operating within its facilities. There are always spare parts and technicians on the job to repair, or even replace equipment. If the company is shooting at the studio, assistance is only five minutes away. If they are out on location, the studio will usually send along a back-up piece of equipment on an item that might be troublesome.

All departments have preventive maintenance programs the year round. Then, when there is a slow period, certain pieces of equipment receive a major overhaul. A studio like Universal may have close to 900 pieces of rolling stock in transportation alone. One of the ways that the studio keeps track of maintenance is through an electronic data processor. This computer provides, for example, printouts on vehicle maintenance, including a summary of all vehicles owned, which ones have received preventive maintenance and what costs were involved in labor and materials. It prints out all costs on all pictures in production each day. In fact, all jobs involved with studio operations are included, even those not specifically connected with production. For instance, information on refurbishing dressing rooms, replacing heat pumps, maintaining the studio buildings, researching uses of new equipment in all of these elements of operations are checked through the computer. In addition to specific needs, an EDP (Electronic Data Process) report comes out each week, giving the studio operations excellent control of the facilities.

Operations departments are always working to improve the quality of their service. This intent often means improving a piece of equipment so that it is more efficient in some way. There is, for instance, a great variety of kinds of cameras used. Recently, the sound department and the camera department discovered a way to silence a new reflex camera called the SPR. Since this camera is the most popular one in use today, the studio has completed the modification on all its reflex cameras. All studio cameras are now "cordless," a feature which has eliminated the need for all the wires that used to run between camera and sound. The mechanics of it are synchronized through radio waves.

Sound equipment is now fully automated with a cartridge of tape for each reel of film. The operation is fully self-contained in a carton that houses the recording equipment. It was, incidentally, another "first" for Universal, whose sound department invented it. The studio now owns seven self-contained production truck units, each of which is capable of going out and handling a company.

A continuing technical problem is that of heat on the set from the lights. Perhaps it is always going to be there. But in some of the newer lights, the heat is dissipated faster than it used to be despite the fact that the lamp is in a smaller housing. An even greater problem in the lighting was the tremendous weight of the instruments. Now the manufacturers have come up with Xenon globes with very lightweight casings. The lens for this instrument has not yet been perfected and, therefore, limits its usefulness at the moment. Researchers are working on it, however, and think they are only a year or so away from a solution. This development will be a tremendous technical advance.

A variety of special effects machines is available to companies using the studio: machines to make rain, snow, frost, ice, fog, cobwebs, waves. If a company needs something out of the ordinary, special effects people will work it out, as in the effects for *Airport*. The machine may be very funny looking, but it will do the job.

The most intricate set the studio has ever built—and no doubt one of the most intricate ever built for any film—is that for *The Andromeda Strain*. Constructed on Stage 12, which allows a height of 50 feet, the set also extends into a pit that was dug 16 feet deep. And to complicate the challenge even further, the structure had to be round. It was a most difficult task.

Airport is another recent production that posed some problems for studio operations to handle. Airport facilities had to be acquired for certain runway scenes. For example, the shots of the plane that had to be moved from the runway were made at Milwaukee Airport, except for the close-ups, which were made on the back lot. It is just about impossible to tell which scenes were shot in Milwaukee and which are the studio shots. Another even more difficult scene involves an explosion that makes a hole in a plane in flight. The effect consists of imitating what really happens as the air pressure in the plane changes and then corrects itself. There is a combination of a sucking-out of the contents of the plane and a fogging of the interior. One of the biggest problems was to accomplish the sucking effect without sucking the fog out too quickly. Both effects happen at once and the fogging needed to stay in the plane up to 15 or 20 seconds. The special effects supervisor, who is a veteran of his trade, had to work it all out so that it was authentic in its representation. He did such a good job that airlines have actually requested this segment in a film clip to show to their personnel as part of their training program.

Although some of the big studios have temporarily fallen on hard times, within the next five years the demand for tapes and films for cassettes and pay-television is going to grow to such an extent that studio soundstages and other facilities are again going to be very valuable property. With this increase in production, the future of the big studio operation once more looks very bright indeed.

MR. MAYER — *Metro-Goldwyn-Mayer, Inc.*

> *". . . If the industry makes more and more product for more and more sources—and the predictions seem to point toward such a likelihood—the big studio will not only survive, it will be more important than ever. . . ."*

In only the last 10 years, the below-the-line cost of producing a film in the United States has risen at least 50%. Of course, costs of production have risen in many industries besides films. But the important factor here is that the increase in costs in the motion picture industry has not been offset by an increase in box-office receipts. There has been an overall decrease in gross receipts. An individual picture might gross a great deal more than in the past, but this is the exception, not the rule.

Studio "overhead" charges that are added to a production budget are frequently cited as contributing to this sharp rise in the cost of making films. The term "overhead," however, is a widely misunderstood concept. Many people believe that overhead is not actual cost. They somehow have the notion that it is a charge just tacked onto a budget to give the studio a little more income at the expense of the production. In fact, it does represent the actual cost of innumerable studio operations. These services are varied and sometimes not easily identifiable. Therefore, instead of trying to figure out what part of what cost is applicable to a particular production, the overhead is figured on a percentage of the total production costs. This amount is then charged by the studio against that film. It covers studio services that are available for any production working within its facilities, all the way from simple janitorial services to maintenance and the use of complicated special effects equipment. It even includes such services as preparing legal contracts, researching copyrights, making out payroll and accounting for production and distribution costs. Most studios also provide cameras, lights, grip equipment, editorial equipment and projection equipment. While some may charge a separate fee for use of these facilities, others do not. In either case, the cost of acquiring and maintaining the equipment is chargeable to overhead. All of the commissaries, a necessary service to production, run at a loss. There is a need for police protection, plant engineering, plumbing, air conditioning, mailroom, messengers, telephones, salaries for department heads involved in running the studio, and an overall planning department in the production area. All of these services and more are provided by the studio from income it receives through overhead. This brief survey should provide more than ample evidence of the justification for such a charge.

All of the people involved in corporate affairs, beginning with the initiation of a deal to make a film and going right on through the execution of the deal and the implementation of the deal once the film is made, have to have some kind of headquarters of operation. The most organized and economical way to keep them working together efficiently is to house them in a central location. A studio plant already owned by the company, seems a very logical solution. Actually, the actors and directors and other talent that the public usually thinks of as making up the studio, are really a very small percentage of the people who work there. With a production schedule of approximately 20 feature pictures and from two to five television series a year, MGM as a studio varies in its employment from about 800 to 3,000 people, depending upon the number and scope of the productions going on at a given time.

When people talk about the studio as obsolete, what they really mean is that it is not necessary to have a studio in order to make a motion picture. This is true. But it is necessary to have some kind of facility. There needs to be some kind of corporate headquarters for activities involved in financing and distributing. There is surely a need for some kind of post-production headquarters. And to some degree at least, there needs to be some kind of facility for production headquarters. All of these needs add up to the feasibility of the studio as a central physical plant. Despite the fact that many changes have occurred in the operation of the studio, it still serves very well the individual needs of individual productions as they arise.

MGM studio facilities in Culver City include 27 working sound stages and extensive pre-production and post-production facilities such as a full motion picture production and release laboratory. In the 1930's and '40's, on a given day the plant population would consist of a large number of writers, directors and producers on a year-round weekly salary. They would be working on stories for a potential production schedule of between 30 and 50 feature pictures a year. Some of the stories would be based on purchased material, some of them would be original. A great volume of scripts would be turned out, from which would be selected the material for production. There would be four to six pictures in active pre-production, involved in such aspects as budgeting, location scouting, scheduling and casting. Another three to six would be in actual photography. Six to 15 films would be in post-production activities, such as editing, re-recording and scoring.

Most motion pictures are now shot on the actual location of

the story. Consequently, utilization of studio stages for theatrical motion pictures is not very extensive. This does not mean that studios are not used on occasion, particularly for films of a period nature or with special physical effects in them. But in the main, the utilization of studio stages depends upon the amount of television production the company handles in a particular year. A typical day at MGM currently, in contrast to the one described for the 1930's and '40's, would show four stages being used for photography and several stages being prepared through construction for future use. Unless a company really needs to use a particular stage, the tendency is to leave the set standing after a production has finished with it. Construction costs are so high that television films cannot be made economically unless they take advantage of using a set that is basically already up. While stages are used less often, they do play an important role, particularly in television production, in that they can house basic sets that can be used again and again with modification.

Because it has become more and more desirable to shoot pictures on location rather than in a simulated environment on the studio back lots, MGM is selling most of these back-lot facilities and eliminating the traditional standing out-door set. As the land upon which these sets stand has grown more and more valuable over the years, the utilization has grown less and less frequent. This combination of factors, unless there is a tremendous volume of television production using exterior sets, renders it economically unsound to keep them. Both the creative talents and the audiences prefer actual location shooting. Perhaps the studio could force the producers to use the back lots more than they do. But with little difference in overall cost and with modern portable and economical ways of shooting on location, it does not seem reasonable to force a method on a production just for the sake of using studio lots. The main expenses added to location shooting are transportation, room and board for cast and crew involved. These expenses can sometimes be offset by the fact that it is not necessary to build elaborate expensive sets. Construction costs have risen so much in the past ten years that often the kind of set required would not be feasible to build in any event.

The additional development of the technique of front-projection has also added to the popularity of location shooting. In this instance, background film of the location is shot by a small camera crew. Then, using front-projection on whatever size screen is desired, the action can be shot in the studio with cast and crew. The combined results are so good that this kind of photography is practically interchangeable with that shot completely on location. And the savings are substantial.

The most important activity that goes on in a studio is still the preparation of motion pictures and the post-production handling of them. Post-production facilities are available outside the studio, but since a major studio has a volume of productions that it finances and releases each year, it can support post-production facilities economically and has the finest equipment available for the job. No matter where a picture is made, therefore, unless it is a foreign project that requires post-production in the foreign country in order to qualify for a subsidy, the major company makes every effort to have post-production carried out at its studio. These activities—including such areas as re-recording, dubbing, scoring, opticals, superimposed titles for foreign distribution, and other laboratory work —are carried on under strict studio supervision and provide another important reason for the existence of the studio.

Added to post-production are other activities connected with making motion pictures that can take advantage of the centralized studio location. Estimating and budget control, accounting, payroll —all of the financial aspects of production—are conveniently handled in studio facilities. Union agreements have grown more and more complicated as they involve residual payment not only for television films but for theatrical motion pictures as well when they are shown on television. A studio computer helps to keep track of an extensive financial operation.

Feeling that there must be some kind of library collection of all of the films it has had an interest in, whether a feature film or a short or a cartoon, MGM has spent a good five years and many millions of dollars preserving its library. Prior to 1952, most pictures were made on nitrate stock, which disintegrates with time. Since that date, pictures have been made on durable safety stock. Fortunately, it was possible for the nitrate negatives to be converted to the safety negatives, thus preserving the most important asset a motion picture company has: a record of its production. In addition to insuring this heritage through a studio library collection, the company has a second copy of everything stored in underground vaults in Kansas with ideal temperature and humidity controls, thus giving double protection should a disaster occur at one location.

There has been a tendency to read too much significance into an activity such as the recent auction by MGM of a vast supply of properties and wardrobe accumulated from the past 30 or 40 years. Those convinced that the big studio is dead read such news as confirmation of the grimness of the studio's situation. Actually, the auction was a relatively minor economic move, geared more to updating the facilities than to making a lot of money. It was discovered that most of these items were period pieces, used so rarely that it was not worth the expense of storage, upkeep and personnel needed to care for them. Also, similar items are easily available from outside sources at modest rental fees on the rare occasion they are needed. Held in storage, the intrinsic value of the materials was negligible, whereas public interest in bidding on the things as memorabilia put a value on them. Considering all factors involved, an auction seemed sensible as one more way to modernize the plant and cut operating expenses. It did not, however, have a substantial effect on the overall method of operating the studio. It should not, therefore, be considered a major change in studio operations.

Since there is no reason why the big studio cannot continue to streamline its operations and manage to operate within current economic conditions, its future would seem to depend upon the future of the motion picture business itself. If the industry makes more and more product for more and more sources—and the predictions regarding CATV, cassettes and the world market seem to point toward such a likelihood—then the big studio will not only survive, it will be more important than ever.

PART FOUR

Production—
Preliminaries

Readying a screenplay and drawing up budgets are critical activities in development of a motion picture project, but their completion by no means sets the stage for actual shooting. Still to be conducted are a variety of preliminary tasks, including often subtle negotiations for talent.

As the literary agent provides a necessary service in representing the seller/writer of a screenplay in negotiations with the buyer/producer, so the talent agent represents his creative clients in the open market of producers and production companies. Barry Weitz *reviews the structure of the agency and the special responsibilities of the talent agent, while the elusive art of negotiating a deal for a client is considered in greater detail by agent* Don Kopaloff. Saul Rittenberg *offers a summary of basic legal matters which will arise in this phase of production, with special attention to producer-union relations, and—in a thoughtful review of the history of the Screen Actors Guild—*Charlton Heston *provides insight into why talent has formed its own collective bargaining organizations.*

While the completion of all negotiations will normally permit principal photography of a film to get under way, the logistics of production must still be attended to before personnel and equipment are committed and the complex, tightly-scheduled process of actual shooting begins. Ivan Volkman *offers some indication of the awesome amount of preliminary homework involved in preproduction. His examples from Stanley Kramer's 1971 production,* Bless The Beasts And Children, *illustrate how paperwork related to personnel and facilities required for one scene in the screenplay proceeds through stages of continuity breakdown, shooting schedule, call sheet and production report. Still another vital element of pre-shooting planning is the scheduling of facilities and equipment required for location shooting.* Fouad Said, *founder of Cinemobile Systems in Los Angeles, describes the services of his company in this field.*

THE TALENT AGENT

BARRY J. WEITZ

". . . Agents are diplomats, negotiators, salesmen, friends, and a very real part of the performer's life. . . ."

The strength of a talented individual lies in his ability to continue to create. Whether it be a performance, a book or a screenplay, creating is where the strengths and energies are. More frequently than not, creators do not desire to cope with business decisions, or in fact, career guidance. An individual who must sell himself, or in fact negotiate terms in his own behalf, might well be less successful than if another individual were taking care of these matters for him. Therefore, the commission that is paid to an agent—10% or 15%—is often the best investment that an individual can make in his career. An agent generally receives 10% of the gross fee that an actor receives. For instance, if an actor is to receive $100,000 for a role, the agent will receive 10% of that fee, or $10,000.

In the triangle of buyer, seller and agent, the agent obviously performs two important functions. First, he sets up a very clear delineation between the buyer and the seller, and second, he gives the buyer a professional person to deal with on a consistent basis and in a business atmosphere. Thus a freedom from emotion is

BARRY J. WEITZ graduated from New York University in 1962. He joined the William Morris Agency the following year, and worked in the public appearance department from 1963 to 1968. He is currently a member of the motion picture department in the Beverly Hills office of William Morris.

established, allowing the parties to cut to the core of the negotiation and agree upon what each party considers as essential. The presence of an agent is certainly a great aid to the buyer, since he does not have to become too closely involved with the artist during the negotiations. The buyer can deal with the artist on a creative level, and with the agent on a purely business and career level. For these reasons, the talent agency is a very real part of the entertainment business. Indeed, it is essential to it.

At the William Morris Agency, I deal mostly in the motion picture and television areas. In these areas, the creative people who have agents to assist them include screenwriters, producers, directors, actors, actresses, costume designers, choreographers, and perhaps cameramen. William Morris, being a very large and all-encompassing agency, is fortunate to have departments to serve the client in all areas of the business, including separate departments of *motion picture* and of *television*. The latter includes television variety programs (like those of Dean Martin and Glen Campbell), and dramatic television (which deals with shows like *Marcus Welby, M.D.*, various motion pictures for TV, Aaron Spelling-produced shows, and others). We also have a *television packaging* department, which involves itself mainly with the creative assembling of shows for sale to networks. Our *literary department* addresses itself to working with authors, manuscripts and related matters. There is also a *personal appearance department*, which deals with talent for night clubs, concerts, college tours and the like. Our *dramatic stage department* covers summer stock, touring shows and Broadway, and our *commercial department* services our clients for the various commercials and advertisements in all media. It is clear that the entertainment business is quite thoroughly covered by the services of such an agency.

Although there is size and stature to the William Morris Agency, we tend to keep the agent-to-client ratio very low. In the motion picture area there are 13 agents in Beverly Hills—the base of our operations—six agents in New York, and agents in London, Paris, Madrid, Rome and Munich. Here in California, we hold staff meetings two days each week in which we review either current casting of films or general activities in the business. The meetings help us to determine what we can do to effect changes in our clients' careers, and serve as a clearing house for communications, helping each agent to be more knowledgeable about what is going on in everyone else's respective area and in the industry as a whole. All agents are fully aware of every motion picture being made in the United States as well as international productions. They know what the scripts are and they know the product that is being planned. In fact, many make a point of reading the scripts that are in production and that are planned so that they can familiarize themselves with various personnel needs of the project—directors, actresses, actors, cameramen, costume designers and others.

There are two ways for a talent agent to obtain clients. He can, through his connections or aggressiveness, bring the individual client to the agency on his own. He may also be assigned a specific client because of his experience, seniority, or a personality which complements the client's. Because human lives and livelihoods are so closely involved, the goal is to find the right kind of combination between agent and client. It is obviously most important to us that the client be satisfied with his specific link to the business world, the individual who must communicate his thoughts and aspirations to the rest of us.

When the Agency takes on a new client he is required to sign an authorization contract with our company. This contract calls for the agency to represent him in all areas for a stated period of years. Depending on the stature of the client, the agent will plan different approaches to potential buyers. If he is representing a relatively young, less-experienced actor, the agent may feel it necessary to have him meet casting directors and other individuals who are active on a day-to-day basis in casting films and television roles. The agent has a fairly good idea of what his new client's abilities are, but he may decide to move him into the area of dramatic television for the purpose of getting a certain type of role which will show a young actor in a certain light. Of course, he may make the same decision merely in order to get the actor to work immediately. There are a great many more employment opportunities in the TV episodic drama area than in the feature film area. An agent may feel that it is best to move into the TV area at the outset—assuming that if the venture is successful the agent and his client will be provided with the type of film that can be shown to other producers and directors, both in the feature film and television areas.

Dealing with a new young client obviously requires a certain experience. The agent must take maximum advantage of the client's talents and expose them effectively in a fair atmosphere with proper sense of direction. The agent's plan should be to move the actor along to various important roles while increasing his salary to the point where he is making steady advances in both areas. For instance, if an actor earns $750 a week in a supporting role for which he achieves proper acclaim and notice, the agent is then able to move him further along—perhaps to a co-starring role where he may make as much as $25,000. If this level is successfully mastered, the agent may well have a young talent who will—as few actors can—move into major starring roles. Either because of lack of opportunity, improper combination of role and actor, or various other indefinables, these ideal situations may never present themselves. In any event, assuming success along the line, the agent may have an actor who can move from $450 a week up to a very high six-figure category which also involves percentages of profits, or percentages of gross on a given film.

An agent must be very cautious with an actor, however, and move properly to keep him working at good roles. Continuity of employment is an extremely important aspect of client development. The creative lives of many performers are generally not as long as those of other professionals such as lawyers or doctors. The best-earning years of their careers may be very few, and certainly during that time they have every right to try to make the most of their talent. The agent has the obligation to try to extend their creative life.

Contract negotiating is probably the most time-consuming as well as important aspect of an agent's work day. Some agents like to think that there are certain secret methods that enhance their ability to negotiate, but there is no standardized formula or check list that can be relied upon. Each negotiation is individual and unique. The aim of all negotiations is, of course, to secure the best possible deal for the client—to persuade the studio, network or buyer to make the best arrangement. Every agent, I am sure, has walked out of a negotiation assuming he has secured the absolute last penny only to later discover that the buyer was prepared to offer more than was finally paid. Our business affairs department is brought in on negotiations to assist the agent in specifying the requirements that the client will be making, and what will be required of his services. This is specially handled, and there is no room for haphazard or careless thinking.

There are times in an agent's life when he is working with an actor who is "hot"—one who is in demand throughout the industry because his popularity in earlier films indicates that his presence in a film will probably insure a degree of potential success from the outset. The agent's responsibility in this situation is one of exercising great care in analysis of screenplays that are being submitted to him. He must choose scripts that will have an important influence in the film business in the next year or so, thus exposing his client in a well-rounded fashion that will insure greater career longevity for him. This, of course, is the ideal situation, but even in these moments of great demand, great care must be taken by the agent in resisting any tendency to overplay his position. Work and creative contribution are still the most important aspects in the performer's life.

If a client is not an "in-demand" actor, the agent must go out and strongly "hustle" for his sales. If the talent is there, and if various reviews have not overlooked that talent, then the agent has some sort of "hook" to use in selling his client. If, however, the performer has little motion picture ability—if he had the opportunity but has not been able to prove himself—then the agent must re-evaluate his client's career. There are many clients, for example, who have not been able to succeed in features but have ended up starring in their own television series—or even directing television shows, since these are two entirely different markets. There are also clients who have not been able to succeed in either motion pictures or tele-vision, but have become major stage performers. A great deal depends upon the talent finding his own media. The agent certainly should assist in the search, and give proper guidance to a client in this endeavor.

If, for any reason, the client should not be satisfied with the progress he is making in the agency—or if he is simply not happy with the way he is being represented—he can discharge the agency. The unions and guilds generally allow a period of 90 days after he signs a contract, or 90 days from the time that he has received his last offer, in which he is able to terminate his agency relationship. The client is always able to discharge his agency, but if he is not able to show cause, then he is obligated to pay the commission to the agency until the termination of the agreement.

I like to think that if we had the enthusiasm to sign a person it is because we believe in his career—believe in his potential and genuinely want to do our best for him. Under these circumstances I think that we would be able to convince him of this desire, either in meetings with him, or in obvious work results.

On a more personal level, there are major differences in dealing with women in this business. They seem to be more goal-oriented, and their thinking really revolves around establishing a predetermined career. They do not generally wish to be dealt with as one might deal with a woman outside of the business. They want to be dealt with as performers—as people who are looking for a specific career and not just as bits of feminine fluff. Men should be dealt with in a very level-headed way, straight-on and honest as one would deal with any man of business.

There are many clients who do not want their agents to become too involved in much of their lives. They prefer to keep things on a very non-emotional, business-like basis. For many people this can work very successfully. Over the long term, however, I think it is almost impossible for a client and an agent not to become involved with one another and interest themselves in things other than the day-to-day business. If a client is so inclined, an agent can be a major support in the client's life with respect to what he is doing with his career and where he wants to be going in the next years. The client may feel that money is not even a primary consideration—that popularity, doing good things, or making a contribution to his art are more important sources of satisfaction.

Along with the popularity, of course, usually comes some degree of remuneration, and as an agency we are very much interested in proper remunerations. But often, the business-oriented studio types do not concern themselves with a creative environment for the client. They may be more concerned with getting the project out or just the return on the dollars. The agent's problem may very well start, then, after the deal has been made and the buyer and seller start to "live" together. Keeping the relationship alive and viable—and keeping the creative juices flowing—may be the most important aspects of the agent's work, and thus some of the services an agent renders often begin only after the deal is made.

After he has closed the negotiation and the contracts have been signed a different phase of the work actually begins. An agent must now live with his deals, and not expect someone else to follow up. I think if an agent does not emerge from behind his desk his relationships with his clients are going to fall apart and his relationships with buyers, producers, directors and studios are going to deteriorate. The studio looks to the agent to be there at times to help in solving his client's various problems. The agent, of course, may have to walk a thin line between asserting himself in his client's behalf and meddling in matters in which he really should not be involved. Generally, however, the studio is open and receptive to the agent. They feel his behavior and presence will, in the final analysis, be of help in easing difficulties.

One can easily see that a good agent will raise a business relationship to a human relationship—a circumstance that is difficult to find in any industry outside the entertainment business. The relationship can be a very personal, intimate one. Agents are diplomats, negotiators, salesmen, friends, and a very real part of the performer's life. Being a part of any person's life obviously creates a new and very important responsibility, the execution of which demands careful shaping of the client's career, sound negotiating for the right kind of deal, awareness of what the trends in the market are, and the ability to anticipate what the market will be like after a film has been completed. It is difficult, however, for an agent to generalize to a client about this responsibility. He can put his finger on it only after he is able to find the right type of project, after he has been successful in bringing that project to his client's attention, and after he has negotiated a deal with a studio for X amount of dollars for the client to perform a specific role. When the performer is paid for his performance, the agent is then in a position to say, "I have performed a function for you by negotiating a deal for which you have been paid, and from which we have both made money. Now we are prepared to go on to the next step."

The agency will always be an integral part of the motion picture business because there will always be a need for the creative middleman—the buffer—who is constantly in touch with a changing business and new concepts in the media, and who can bring together various creative and business elements for the mutual satisfaction and reward of those who participate.

NEGOTIATING FOR TALENT

DONALD I. KOPALOFF

*". . . Negotiating is a competition, like a game. The nego-
tiator must treat it as such. If he loses his sense of humor
and enjoyment, he should look for another job. . . ."*

What first prompts a producer to want to do a film is his
desire to see a particular piece of work transposed to the screen.
Before he is ready to approach a studio or another production company with the hope that they will finance the production, he is likely
to work out several preliminary steps toward a plan of execution.

Perhaps the property is a book, and not a best-seller. He con-
tacts the author's agent and negotiates with the agent for the exclusive
dramatic rights to his book—i. e., motion picture rights, television
rights, theatre rights. This negotiation takes the form of an option:
a payment of monies to be charged against the total payment for the
purchase of that book, as a down payment for a period of time which
again is negotiated—six months, a year. This is the time during
which the producer has to try to set his project in motion. Once
he has the rights, he then tries to build a package. He finds the most
suitable writer and/or director. Assuming that he does not want to

DONALD I. KOPALOFF is a motion picture agent in the Los Angeles office of
International Famous Agency. In the past Mr. Kopaloff has served as Vice-
President in charge of Production at Avco-Embassy Pictures, as Vice-President
of Creative Management Associates, Ltd., and as President of Donburry Management, Ltd.

lay out the money himself, he then takes the director and the writer —who have made a commitment to the material—and goes to the source of financing, which can be either a major studio or an independent group of financiers. This first step in interim financing can be negotiated by the producer himself, his agent or his attorney. The writer is ready to write. The financier agrees to put up the first portion of the writer's money, with the rest to be spread out in payments extending to the start of production. The financier also puts up a portion of the director's fee in order to secure his services on a non-exclusive basis during the writing of the screenplay, so that he can work with the writer. During this period, the producer may negotiate for himself as well, to receive a portion of his fee in advance, to be paid during the course of the writing of the screenplay.

From the time the producer attracts a buyer, the negotiating stage requires considerable talent. A good negotiator must be imaginative. He can lose a deal by being too rigid, by not bending with the current pressures of the industry. When the screenplay is finished, woe to the studio executive who has not finished his negotiations on all of the elements to that point. If the screenplay happens to be very good, and he has not completed his deals, the producer, director and writer now have a very saleable piece of material, and know it. If the financier does not come up with particular deal points which are demanded, they may reject the financier, return the money, and set up a deal elsewhere.

An example: On a budget of $1.5-million and more, it is reasonable to estimate that the producer's fee is $100,000; the director's fee is $150,000; and the writer's fee comes to a total of $100,000. The man who receives the lion's share of the money in advance is the writer, because his is the first of the services which are put to use. The financing company's obligation might be to pay two-thirds of the writer's fee during the writing of the first draft of the screenplay, or roughly $65,000. The producer in today's market often receives no advance during the writing. If, however, he has a very good agent or is a very strong producer, he may be able to secure 5% to 10% of his fee during the course of the writing. The financier's investment is now substantial. The director, who will receive $150,000 plus whatever his participation might be, may be paid $25,000 during the writing stage. Under such a plan, the financier (or studio) invests $100,000 before even knowing whether there is a chance to produce the motion picture.

After the deals are set and the screenplay is turned in and the green light is given on the project, a whole series of new negotiations begins for the principal members of the cast, crew, production facilities and laboratory. If the producer is to make the picture with a studio, there are always set charges which he will have little chance of negotiating: i. e., overhead (for the use of the studio) and lab costs, which are usually covered by deals previously set up by the studio. If he is operating independently, the producer can negotiate all of his own deals.

A picture made a few years ago for a budget of about $650,000 on the Eady Plan in England is a classic example of shrewd negotiating. The director/writer took a profit participation of 33⅓% and no salary; just living expenses. Thirty-three and a third percent of the profit on a picture that cost $650,000 and grosses over $18-million is a lot of money. He had negotiated his deal very shrewdly, except that he did not receive the dollars coming in up front. He had to wait until the picture grossed roughly $3.5-million before he started to see any money. Instead of salary and profits participation, the star decided to take 10% of the gross from first dollar. He knew the picture would have to earn at least $1-million worldwide for him to come out with $100,000. The picture grossed $18-million; the star's share was $1.8-million. Once the money started to come in, it poured in so abundantly that the director's profits participation of 33⅓% far exceeded the actor's 10% gross participation.

In any deal-making, a negotiator must know his strength. If he has a commodity that everyone wants, he has strength; if he has something buyers are ambivalent about, he has no strength. In that case, it is really his selling ability, rather than his negotiating ability, that is tested. Negotiating ability comes into play when neither side will move. Negotiating is a competition, like a game. The negotiator must treat it as such. If he loses his sense of humor and enjoyment, he should look for another job.

Going into a session, the negotiator knows what the ground rules are. He knows exactly how far he can go and how much he can give up. This flexibility always depends upon the relationship he has with his client. He has worked out a plan covering certain factors. His client has a salary structure, a deal structure. The opposition knows that he is going to ask for X dollars, X benefits, X deferred compensation, and X profits participation, or X gross participation. In almost every case, his client has an established, current deal. When the client is new, the negotiator is starting from scratch. That is an enjoyable situation, because he tries to get as much as he can.

The man on the other side of the desk works for the studio. He is a hired negotiator, looking to conserve studio dollars. Unfortunately, today very few negotiators have the right to say "yes" or "no." They have certain guidelines, and if anything falls within these, they're permitted to say "O.K." Anything that falls beyond the guidelines has to be left an open point, and the parties must have another meeting.

If a negotiator starts to lose, he should take care not to lose his client's job. Keeping the job and maintaining salary terms and compensation are key points in any successful negotiation.

For his client's protection, every good negotiator should have a checklist, which includes the deal points from whatever prior deal his client has made. Points include compensation, employment period, services to be rendered, contingent compensation if any, expenses, and others. The man negotiating for the purchaser has a checklist too. Obviously, it is very helpful if he forgets certain points; as long as they are not mentioned, they cannot be included in any agreement. Strengths and weaknesses of the negotiator's position and his imagination really determine the outcome.

After everything is agreed upon, a deal memo is composed and exchanged, and there are comments made: "No, we did not agree to that"; "Yes, we did agree to that, but we asked that this be changed." Once the negotiators get past the basic points, the contract is prepared. Because the language used in elaborating all the points can alter the deal, the contract stage can go on for months. It is at this point that lawyers enter and fight out the problems among themselves. They actually draw up the contracts after the basic deal points have been worked out by the negotiators.

PRODUCTION:
GENERAL LEGAL CONSIDERATIONS

SAUL RITTENBERG *

*". . . In a sense, the industry lives on honor;
mostly it works, sometimes it doesn't. . . ."*

When production gets under way, any producing organization
—whether a major studio or a small independent—faces a variety
of similar problems which require legal expertise. Contractual arrangements at all levels within the production team must be drawn up.
Negotiations must be conducted at various steps along the way. The
producer will therefore do well to be familiar with all areas in production where continuing legal attention is necessary.

To begin with, there will be a need for continuing relationships with the various craft unions and creative guilds. I have already
touched upon the contract with the Writers Guild of America in my
earlier discussion (see page 33), and there are other such organizations which play a key role in production (see Appendix II). Among
the major craft organizations with which the producer inevitably will
deal is the International Alliance of Theatrical Stage Employees
—know as IATSE. This Alliance—affiliated with AFL-CIO—is constituted of various unions which serve a variety of motion picture
workers ranging from studio grips to art directors. Some 24 locals
can be found in Hollywood alone. (See p. 350 for full listing of
West Coast locals of IATSE member unions). IATSE and the MPMO
—or Motion Picture Machine Operators—have a common standard
basic agreement. Simply put, this means that if a producer breaks
contractual agreements with the Make-up Artist local in Hollywood

---

* For a biographical note about Mr. Rittenberg, see page 30.

he could find himself in difficulties with the other craft unions.

It is necessary to be aware of and respect the jurisdictional claims of individual unions. A Chicago local of the Photographers Union, for example, may not allow a Los Angeles-based cameraman to shoot in their area without special arrangements. Further, a contract drawn with the Hollywood local must be considered when drawing contracts with the same union in another city. Normally, locals will want different contracts, and too-generous terms for one local might only result in difficulties when negotiating terms of contracts with another. It is essential that someone connected with the producing company be aware of what contracts are in effect, and what those contracts stipulate, and be prepared to answer—in behalf of the company—any claims of violation of contracts.

Another significant area of legal negotiation is film music. Music, of course, makes a major contribution to the force and beauty of a film. Once the picture is shot, music will be added, and this presents a whole new field of legal implications. Problems of copyright arise at once. If any kind of published or already-exploited music is used the producer will need to deal with the publishers, and must have his lawyer negotiate a license and work out a form of license agreement. Composers engaged to write background scores normally will be members either of The American Society of Composers, Authors and Publishers (ASCAP) or of Broadcast Music, Incorporated, (BMI). Each organization has its own arrangements with its members, which will require special handling in negotiating the individual contract with the composer. If a team of composers is used, one of them may be BMI and the other might belong to ASCAP. That will introduce further complications in drawing up contracts.

One might ask why ASCAP or BMI is involved when one is really simply paying a composer directly for his services. The answer is that when a producer employs a composer, the matter of public performance rights must be specially treated because the composer will expect to derive additional revenue from that source. The right to perform is a separate right which arises as a result of a peculiarity in the copyright law. Performance rights in the United States are administered by performance societies—ASCAP, BMI and others— and they have "treaties" with similar performance societies all over the world. Such rights are a source of additional income for the composer since the foreign theatres which play the pictures in which his music is performed have to pay a fee to the performance rights society in their own country, and that society in turn pays a part of that money to ASCAP or BMI. The situation is similar with respect to broadcast rights in this country, where theatres do not pay a performance fee, but television stations do. When a feature goes on television, NBC, for example, will pay ASCAP for the privilege of performing the music in the ASCAP catalogue. The ASCAP formula for division of that money is extremely complicated, and BMI's is no less so. The point, however, is that the composer is entitled to revenue from performance of his work, and licensing societies like ASCAP and BMI undertake the collecting function—hence they must be dealt with.

Arrangements with composers also take various forms. Usually they are engaged on "flat-price" contracts—a certain fee per score. Sometimes the producer may contract with a composer to deliver an already-recorded score—an arrangement wherein the composer becomes an independent contractor who takes responsibility for all the costs. The legal complications increase if songs are included. Arrangements must be made if singing groups are included. Such contracts are fairly complicated. Sometimes music may be taken from a record and put directly into the picture. In this case the phonograph company must be paid. The musicians who recorded the phonograph record did not record for pictures, and so agreement must be reached with the American Federation of Musicians and additional fees paid. The composer—usually through his publisher—will be paid something and—of course—the performer must be recompensed. A picture with 15 or 20 different songs in it may involve many legal complications.

In addition to the special legal problems of negotiation in the major creative fields, the producer will also need to understand various precedents related to "below-the-line" union laborers who are normally not under contract. In this area one will find that certain practices are "observed." I will not say "understood" because that suggests a contract. It is more or less the practice, for example, that a crew is retained throughout the production. If a man is on as an editor, he can feel fairly certain that he will work until the picture is finished—unless, of course, he gets sick or does not perform his job properly. A certain amount of tenure is established, therefore, but only through practice—not by written contract. A contract may often be written with a cameraman, however, and sometimes with a production designer and costume designer, and in the latter case terms may be set forth related to such questions as ownership of sketches, for example, or the right to manufacture clothing for retail sale based upon the designs. Matters of credit also may be spelled out in contracts, but for the most part, below-the-line work is not covered by written contract.

These considerations lead us to the often sensitive and complex area of oral agreement. An oral agreement, within certain legal limits, is a valid agreement. The problem, of course, is that a written agreement is there for all to see, but oral agreements are based in human memory—where all things lose precision. For example, was there really an agreement or simply a preliminary discussion? If there was an agreement, what were its terms? Despite these uncertainties, a great deal of the activity in the industry is based on agreements that are not in writing. They are usually intended to be in writing but are not reduced to writing for any number of valid reasons. For one thing, time is too short. Most agreements are voluminous, there are many of them, and there are only so many hours in the day. Sometimes it is very difficult just to go through the physical work of getting them ready—especially when time pressures are involved. Second, every agreement is scrutinized very carefully by each party. Typically, an agreement is prepared by the producing company and submitted to the employee. The employee may have an agent, an attorney, a tax lawyer, a business manager, and a wife—and they all take a crack at it. You might submit a 10- or 12-page contract and receive an equal number of pages of requests for changes which vary from major deal points to the most trivial kind of comma snatching. By the time all these details are worked out, the picture may be finished and nobody cares any longer. So it is typical of the industry that contracts are often never written in a complete form until after the fact. Efforts have been made to solve this problem; one involves use of *memorandum agreements*, another is the use of a *letter of intent* or a *preliminary agreement*. These have a certain value, but they often leave many items to be negotiated in the future, and it is those items that may create problems. There has been some litigation—with varying results—involving deals that have not been reduced to writing. In some cases the courts have enforced the oral agreement of the parties, and in other cases they have ruled that the parties never did get together, and there was no agreement to enforce.

There is no real cure. The industry just lives with the situation, and in the vast majority of cases, there is never a problem. Many of the agreements in the industry are handshake deals—never even intended to be reduced to writing. In the case of free-lance actors—the under $25,000 group—the Producer-Screen Actors Guild Agreement requires writing, but in that case a simple form is used. The stipulations in it (other than money, dates and credits) are set by the collective bargaining agreement and it is quite simple to fill out. Such contracts are almost always signed. The other Guilds have tried to develop similar contracts but with limited exceptions have not been successful because the deals and the requirements of the individual companies vary too much, and the use of uniform contracts with very substantial people and large sums of money is too difficult. And so, in a sense, the industry lives on honor; mostly it works, sometimes it doesn't.

ACTORS AS UNION MEN *

CHARLTON HESTON

*". . . We look forward to a rejuvenated and resurgent film in-
dustry . . . and to the part the actor will play in this pattern.
If things go as they are, maybe someday you'll even let your
daughter marry one! . . ."*

Acting is only the second oldest profession, but society has
always looked on both trades with equal suspicion. In the eyes of
the average citizen, actors are generally labelled as deadbeats, drunks
and wife-stealers. In the last decade or so, the actor has become
slightly more respectable, but there are still clubs and hotels from
which his profession bars him, just as it marks him as a target for
higher insurance rates and other forms of economic discrimination.
It could be argued that actors constitute the oldest minority group
in the world, with a list of grievances dating back further in history
than Jews or Negroes, or even Chicanos. Oddly enough, actors seemed
almost to enjoy their exclusion from the comfortable company of
Us, confident that their parties back of the barn were more fun
than the fancy doings up at the big house, anyway.

All actors love the story of the violinist, Ysaye, quoting a fee
of $2,000 to perform at a very grand ball to be given by one of the

---

CHARLTON HESTON is a major figure in the performing arts who has a'so
extended his energy and stature in service of various social and professional
concerns. He was Film Chairman of the National Arthritis Foundation during
the '60's and has served as a member of the National Council on the Arts
since 1967. He was President of the Screen Actors Guild from 1966-1969.

* Originally prepared as guest column for Victor Reisel (July, 1970). Reprinted
courtesy of Mr. Reisel.

Comstock heiresses. The fee was acceptable to the lady, she said, and so was Ysaye—as a performer. "Naturally," she added, "you will not be expected to mingle with the guests." "Ah, in that case, madam," said Ysaye, "the fee will be only $1,000." No actor doubts for a second that the pleasure of the put-down was worth the $1,000 to him.

Wedded to a profession that literally marked him as an outcast until well into our own century, and trying to earn his bread in the most insecure of all trades, the actor would seem an unlikely candidate for a trade union. But the barbarously unfair conditions of the theatre at the turn of the century made change inevitable. Desperate at the necessity of rehearsing long weeks for no pay at all and, if a play closed on the road, of being abandoned penniless in unfriendly towns, actors began to talk of union. In 1914 a group of actors calling themselves, oddly, the White Rats achieved a charter, but no recognition from the stubbornly hostile producers.

Finally, in 1919, the actors struck, darkening every theatre on Broadway, and the producers at last surrendered. For the first time in history a performers' union was contractually recognized as a legitimate bargaining agent for the profession. This was Actor's Equity, which still has jurisdiction over all stage work, and whose example served as both model and inspiration for the efforts of actors determined to organize unions in other media.

Among the most bitter of these struggles, and perhaps the most significant in terms of its final results in shaping the industry it depended upon, were the years of passionate effort spent in the formation of the Screen Actors Guild. In 1933, when actors began meeting furtively in one another's homes to talk desperately, hopefully, of the union they knew they needed, the profession shared the economic distress that gripped the nation. Fifteen dollars for a day's work of unlimited length and indeterminate working conditions was a standard wage; there was no provision for overtime or meal periods, travel time or rehearsal calls. Even including the salaries earned by the stars on whom the industry depended, actors as a group only got a little more than a penny out of each dollar taken at the box-office.

When the studios to which almost all working performers were then contracted imposed on this unfortunate minority a 50% salary cut, actors read the grim writing on the wall. In July, 1933, the first official Guild meeting was held, with the total membership of 15 actors in attendance. One of these brave souls, Leon Ames, later served as president and is still a member of the Board of Directors. The early action of stars of the stature of Gary Cooper, Spencer Tracy, Fredric March, Groucho Marx, James Cagney, and Boris Karloff in joining the infant organization was as decisive as it was courageous. By allying themselves with a group dedicated, as the Guild remains to this day, not to the needs of the star but the requirements of the ordinary professional actor, these men demonstrated the basic justice of the actors' cause. Four years of harsh struggle lay ahead, but the end was clear. In the spring of 1937, in a Hollywood boxing arena, President Robert Montgomery read the scribbled message of agreement which averted the strike that many feared inevitable, and spelled success for the Guild. The studios, however reluctantly, capitulated, and soon reached agreement on the first of the basic contracts under which all actors work in American films.

From those modest and difficult beginnings, the Screen Actors Guild has grown mightily. While small compared to some of the big industrial unions, it has nearly 23,000 members in eight branches, headquartered still, of course, in Hollywood. It is perhaps the most influential labor organization in the film industry, and the largest performers' union in the world. One of our members, Fred O'Neal, is a national vice-president of the AFL-CIO and a member of their executive committee.

The wages and working conditions achieved by Guild negotiating teams over the past 30 years afford American film actors more protections and higher minimums than any other performers in the world; the same claim can be made for SAG's pension and welfare plan, which has since 1960 allowed older actors the dignity of a decent retirement.

For the past several years, the Guild has been active in opening channels of communication with foreign unions, a step American labor has historically been reluctant to take. Since our contracts represent concrete achievements in areas still only dreamed of by actors' unions in other countries, we have repeatedly sent teams to counsel those unions in their negotiations. Admittedly, our motives are not solely altruistic. Our members, along with all American filmmakers, suffer desperately from the competition made possible in foreign countries by the lower wage scales that prevail there. One of the best ways to meet this challenge is to help filmmakers in those countries achieve the wage scales that we enjoy here.

The Guild possesses a power surely unique in all of organized labor: it can close down an industry without even manning a picket line. If the actors do not report for work, obviously no filming can be done. Happily, the Guild has by and large regarded this nuclear muscle as a deterrent force rather than a ready weapon against the studios. In 1960, to gain for the actors a small share in the income even then flooding in from the sale of old movies to television, the Guild struck for the first and only time against the studios making theatrical films. No members manned picket lines, but the studios closed, of course, and filming stopped for several weeks. Then agreement was reached, the cameras turned again, and today old actors in retirement enjoy recurring stipends from the exhibition of all those old movies you see on the late show.

Of course the widely held concept of a movie actor as a tanned deity in sunglasses, lolling around a fur-lined swimming pool with a naked starlet in one hand and his agent's heart on a fork in the other, is totally false. The average film actor is a serious professional trying desperately to make a living in one of the most depressed industries in the American economy.

In the 1940's, the peak period of movie-going in this country, nearly 80 million admissions a week were sold. Last year, with our population all but doubled since those years, the weekly total had dropped to 15 million. From this source in those peak years, SAG members (only 8,000 of them then) divided up about $40-million a year. Last year the sum was $25-million—divided among more than 20,000 members. When you consider the difference in the purchasing power of the dollar in those two periods, and the difference in the tax structure, that picture of the movie actor as a wealthy idler begins to fray a little, doesn't it? To clarify the point further, only one third of the Guild's total membership last year made as much as $3,500—for the year!

Nevertheless, though the picture seems bleak compared to the rosy fantasies of the fan magazines, the future has light in it. The possibilities of the tape cassettes which will make it possible before long for you to rent your own movie to show on your own TV set spell golden opportunities for the actor; so does the future of subscription television. Just as it will afford the viewer a wider choice of what to watch, so the actors will have more parts from which to choose.

Meanwhile, the Guild is leading in the fight to stimulate more film production here in the United States. Along with the technical unions under Richard Walsh, we've made real progress in actually reducing production costs with a special contract designed to encourage production here. Under this contract producers have shot 19 films since February that either would not have been made at all, or would have been made out of the United States.

The Guild is proud of its responsibility as a moderating and reasonable force in the film community. We do not feel, as old-line union thinking used to hold, that what's bad for management is good for labor. We feel the health of a union depends on the health of the industry it serves. We look forward to a rejuvenated and resurgent film industry, responding to the increasing importance of film in the world's culture, and to the part the actor will play in this pattern. If things go as they are, maybe some day you'll even let your daughter marry one!

PRODUCTION MANAGEMENT— PRE-PLANNING

IVAN VOLKMAN

The pre-production work involved on any picture is consistent with the type of picture, its technical difficulties, as well as the overall budgetary considerations. A simple, easy low-budget picture might require as little as two or three weeks preparation. In other cases, pre-production planning might require as much as six to nine months.

Script or Screenplay *

The schedule and budget of a motion picture begins, of course, with the screenplay or script. The script is read and, at the same time, the important ingredients are underlined so that this information can later be transferred, in the second step, to the continuity break-down page. The actors, bit players, number of extras, the set, day or night shooting, props, special effects, are just some of the factors which are considered.

IVAN VOLKMAN was Assistant Director at Stanley Kramer Productions before being named Production Manager.

* The example in this case has been provided from a scene in Mac Benoff's screenplay for *Bless The Beasts And Children*, a Stanley Kramer production from Columbia Pictures (from the novel, © by Glendon Swarthout, published by Doubleday & Co.), classified as Scenes 109, 110, 111 and 117.

FIRST REVISION 7/14/70 #8990

108

CUT TO:

109 INTERIOR BEANERY - DAY   *109*

A seedy place. America's contribution to fine cuisine.
Thousands of them all along similar roads, all working for
Alka-Seltzer. A row of turning stools along a bar being
served by a tired, mean Mom. Backed against the wall, the
usual griddle and old cash register, hardly ever used beyond
the $2 key. Above the register and under the Coca-Cola
supplied, concave, missing-letters menu, is a sign:

> HELP THE OPPRESSED ~~MINORITY~~
> MAJORITY

The boys enter.

> SHECKER
> (to the boys)
> Eat at Joe's. One million flies
> can't be wrong.

3/4

But the boys are so hungry they have piled onto their seats
and are ordering. The lady eyes them suspiciously.

> BOYS
> Double hamburgers with everything.

> LALLY 1
> And the biggest milkshakes you
> can make.

> LADY
> Let's see your money.

They quickly go through pockets to produce evidence.
Goodenow puts a coin in the juke box.

> SHECKER
> We're on Master charge.

110 Lady gives him a look, notices the money and proceeds to   *110*
work up the orders. From the back of the place come two
twenty-year-olds wearing long sideburns and tight jeans, who
immediately swagger up as olders when they see the kids at
the bar. They have been playing a pool table,

FIRST REVISION - 7/14/70 #8990

110 Cont.   110

which takes coins in a slot. From the juke box comes
the music of a rock group. The pool hustlers hold a
can of beer each. (Cotton is surprised; he had not
seen them.)

                    HUSTLER #1
               (exaggerated drawl for
                the boys; showing off)
          We need more quarters.

                    LADY
               (without looking at them)
          I gave you four. Where's my
          dollar?

                    HUSTLER #2
               (motions to pool table)
          In that there cotton-pickin' pool
          table. Ten minutes for a quarter
          ain't enough time to scratch your
          cuestick.

They both laugh their dumb haw-haw laughs and elbow
each other at this sort of dirty joke.

                    LADY
          Well, that's all you're getting.
          You'll have to find some somewhere
          else.

This ragging is the only way they can be friendly.

                    HUSTLER # 1
          Oh, hell...
               (pouts; then, to boys)
          Say, you milk drinkers wouldn't
          have some spare quarters, would you?

                    SHECKER
          Yeah, we got some. Only they're
          not spare, they're round.

Cotton, anxious to avoid any dialogue, quickly covers.

                    COTTON
               (to Lady)
          Whatever you got for those hamburgers
          is fine. We're hungry.

                    HUSTLER # 2
               (about Shecker)
          He sure don't look hungry...
          What are you?

FIRST REVISION 7/14/70 #8990

110 Cont .(1)   110

                              SHECKER
              We're musicians.
                      (points to juke box)
              Like that group. Going to L.A.

                              COTTON
              Can it, Shecker.

                              HUSTLER #2
              What's your name?

                              SHECKER
              Group Therapy.

The boys laugh, as Cotton gives him a look to stop.

                              HUSTLER #1
              What are you, wise guys?

                              SHECKER
              No, I told you - we're musicians.

The boys giggle, and Shecker is on.

                              SHECKER
              I'm Ringo, that's Ono Ookoo.

They howl as the lady hands them the milkshakes. They
grab them and begin to guzzle.

                              HUSTLER #2
                      (getting mean)
              Okay. You got a real name.

                              TEFT
                      (gets bugged fast)
              He told you. Fact is it used to
              be Group Therapy. Now we changed
              it to The Before Christ.

                              HUSTLER #1
              Before Christ?

                              TEFT
              Dig our backs, man.

144

Production—Preliminaries

FIRST REVISION 7/14/70 #8990

0 Cont (2)   110

He shows them the B.C. on the shirts.

>   HUSTLER #1
>   (to his friend)
>   I think it's a put on.

>   HUSTLER #2
>   And I don't like it.

>   TEFT
>   I don't like being bugged for
>   quarters.

>   HUSTLER #1
>   What are you guys doing this way?

>   LADY
>   (to the bowlers)
>   Mind your own business.

She starts putting the burgers on the counter.

>   HUSTLER #1
>   Shut up, Mom... Okay, smart
>   asses. What you up to?

>   COTTON
>   (to the boys)
>   Just eat.

>   HUSTLER #1
>   (is now mean; to
>   Teft)
>   I asked you a question.

                                                                              ///
Jc: /// He pours beer from his can down the straw of Teft's milkshake.

>   HUSTLER #1
>   If there's anything I can't abide
>   it's a driplip dude kid... Well,
>   you gonna talk....?

When he says the next speech, it is mouthed by him, but it
is the voice of the C.D. that we hear:

>   CUT TO:

                                                                              112

FIRST REVISION 7/14/70 #8990

/17 <u>INTERIOR BEANERY - DAY</u>   //7

SAME AS PREVIOUS SHOT
as HUstler #1, having poured some beer into Teft's milkshake,
looks at him.

> TEFT
> (deliberately)
> In the West everything sticks,
> stings, or stinks!

The Hustlers react.

> LADY
> (enjoying that)
> You can say that again, sonny.
> (to the Hustlers)
> You let these boys be, you hear
> me, you pool hustlers?

> HUSTLER #1
> Aw, shut up, Mom... Digger, let's
> get some of the other fellas.

> COTTON
> (worriedly; to boys)
> Okay, you guys. Let's go, we're
> late.

> LALLY 2
> But I'm hungry.

> COTTON
> Take it with you...
> (hands a bill to
> the Lady)
> Thank you, Ma'am. We really have
> to go...

> LADY
> (to HUSTbrs)
> You boys'll be the death of me yet.

The six take their things, using both hands, and exit
worriedly, passing Cotton.

> COTTON
> (whispering)
> Walk and don't run into that truck
> and let's roll. Don't look back,
> act natural and keep going.

CUT TO:

CONTINUITY BREAKDOWN

Title: Bless the Beasts and Children	B.D.Page No. 36
	Sequence 16
Prod. No. Director Stanley Kramer	Day or Night D
Set Int Beanery	Script Pages 4 3/4

Scene No. 109-110-111-117

Synopsis: 109-Boys enter and order food. Lady asks to see their ~~her~~ money.

      110-Lady starts cooking. Bowlers enter and asks for money. Shecker wises off

      111- Bowler pours beer in Tefts milkshake.

      117- Bowlers continue harassment. Cotton tells boys to leave. As they leave Cotton tells them to walk slowly and not look back.

Cast	Cos. No.	Atmosphere	Props

Cotton
Teft
Schecker
Lally 1
Lally 2
Goodenow
Bowler 1
Bowler 2
			6 Transistors
			Menu on wall
			SIGN- Help the oppressed
			  minor & majority
			Juke Box
			SIGN- We reserve the
			  right to feed anyone.
			Money, change, bills
			Mechanical bowling
			  alley
			Cans of beer
			Hamburgers
			Milkshakes

			Vehicles and Livestock
Bits		Special Effects	Truck outside
Lady Bit Scn 109		Sound Muted Juke box	
		Music Off stage music from juke box.	

Special Note: At~~#~~ end of Scn 111- Bowler #1 talks with camp directors loud voice. Pre-record Camp Directors voice here.   Time _____

Continuity Breakdown

The continuity breakdown contains all the necessary technical information which is eventually transferred to the breakdown board and the schedule. All the scene numbers contained in this sequence are indicated, as well as the cast, props, bits and other information. Any time a new set occurs, another breakdown page is used.

Breakdown Board

Upon completion of all the continuity breakdown sheets, this information is then transferred to the breakdown board, a large headboard where all the cast and various requirements are listed. And to the right on individual colored strips, all the sets are listed along with the breakdown page, sequence, day or night, number of pages, set numbers, actors who work in that particular set, along with extras, bit players, and other requirements listed on the continuity breakdown. Then, the strips are juggled in a manner which is most convenient for shooting, as well as to hold the actors' shooting time to an absolute minimum. By way of example, an actor might work in the beginning of the picture and not again until the very end. It should also be considered that excessive overtime is costly and anything over 12 hours a day amounts to double time. It is also important to the director that as much continuity as possible be retained in the final result. Upon completion of the breakdown board, a meeting is then set up with the director and/or producer so that he is aware of what he must accomplish each day. After the director has approved the breakdown board, the information we have now gathered is incorporated into a shooting schedule.

Shooting Schedule

The shooting schedule (see p. 148) indicates exactly what must be done on each given day. The number of days required to shoot a picture varies from as little as 8 or 10 days to as many as 150 days depending upon the physical difficulties, the importance of the project and the overall budgetary limitations. In a studio, each department head is given a schedule so that all the various problems can be solved in advance: sets must be built, wardrobe manufactured, properties collected and special effects organized.

SHOOTING SCHEDULE - #8990 - BLESS THE BEASTS & CHILDREN   13

19TH,20TH,21ST DAYS - MONDAY,TUESDAY,WEDNESDAY 8-24&8-25 & 8-26 (CONTINUED)

	PGS	D/N	SCS:	CAST	PROPS
EXT. CITY & BEANERY (35)	5/8	D	4	1. COTTON	22 rifle
				2. TEFT	6 transistors
SC: 107 Pickup turns in-Cotton				3. SHECKER	Lally #2 pillow
runs to door				4. LALLY #1	SC: 118: Boys bring out
SC: 108 and tells everyone it is OK				5. LALLY #2	hamburgers,milkshakes
to go in(2/8)				6. GOODENOW	
SC: 118,119 Boys out of beanery with				9. BOWLER #1(119)	
hamburgers,etc.- get into truck				10. BOWLER #2(119)	
& drive off.Bowlers exit beanery					VEHICLES:
& see them go(3/8)					Truck

NOTE:
Natural background

- -

INT. BEANERY (36)		D	4	1. COTTON	BIT
				2. TEFT	LADY
SC: 109 Boys enter & order food-				3. SHECKER	
Lady asks to see their money				4. LALLY #1	PROPS
SC: 110 Lady starts cooking-bowlers enter				5. LALLY #2	6 transistors
-ask for money-Shecker wises off				6. GOODENOW	Menu on wall
SC: 111 Bowler pours beer into Teft's				9. BOWLER #1	Sign "Help the oppressed
milkshake				10. BOWLER #2	minority & majority"
SC: 117 Bowlers continue harassment-Cotton					Juke box
tells boys to leave.As they leave					Sign: "We reserve the
Cotton tells them to walk slowly					Right to Feed Anyone"
& not to look back					Money,change & bills

Mechanical bowling alley
Cans of beer
Hamburgers
Milkshakes

Note: At end of sc 111 - Bowler #1 talks with
Camp Director's loud voice.Pre-record
Camp D rector's voice & playback here

VEHICLES
Truck outside

SOUND
Set Juke box to play
without sound

MUSIC:
OS Music from juke box

NOTE:
Natural background

END OF 19TH,20TH,21ST DAYS-TOTAL PAGES: 7-3/8
SUMMARY: BIT: Lady,ATMOS: 10 drivers,6 doubles for boys,
ACTION PROPS: Picture truck-boys,10 nd cars

22ND,23RD & 24TH DAYS, THURSDAY,FRIDAY,SATURDAY 8-27,8-28 & 8-29(PRESCOTT,ARIZONA)

	PGS	D/N	SCS	CAST	ATMOSPHERE
EXT. TRUCK ON ROAD(JUST OUTSIDE OF	1/8	D	-	1. COTTON	3 drivers
CITY)(MOVING SHOT) (40)				2. TEFT	
				3. SHECKER	PROPS
120-part - Establishing				4. LALLY #1	22 rifle
				5. LALLY #2	Pillow
				6. GOODENOW	Transistors
NOTE: THIS COULD BE A CAMERA CAR SHOT					
					VEHICLES
					3 nd cars
CONTINUED ON NEXT PAGE					Truck

- -

Call Sheets (Shooting Call)

A call sheet is issued each day to the cast and crew for the following day's shooting. This information includes the times the actors must report to hairdressing, makeup, wardrobe, and be ready on the set. This applies to the bit players as well as the extras and all the technical requirements which are necessary. The call sheet is prepared first by the second assistant director, then approved or changed by the first assistant director, who must discuss and secure approval from the director for the following day's work. The production manager is then responsible for the final approval. The call sheet represents the total work to be done on the given day.

A sample call sheet (front and back) is shown on the following pages.

COLUMBIA PICTURES CORPORATION

__44th__ DAY OF SHOOTING   **SHOOTING CALL**

PICTURE __BLESS THE BEASTS AND CHILDREN_____ NO._8990_ DIRECTOR _STANLEY KRAMER_____

SHOOTING CALL _____9:00 AM_____ DATE _MONDAY, 9/28/70_____
SET AND
SCENE NO.   INT. BEANERY 109 THRU 111, 117 - DAY   STAGE #15

CONDITIONS: COVER SET:

CAST AND BITS	CHARACTER AND WARDROBE	HAIRDRESSING	MAKEUP	ON SET
BARRY ROBINS	COTTON			8:30 AM
BILLY MUMY (Minor)	TEFT			8:30 AM
MILES CHAPIN (Minor)	SHECKER			8:30 AM
BOB KRAMER (Minor)	LALLY #1			8:30 AM
MARC VAHANIAN (Minor)	LALLY #2			8:30 AM
DAREL GLASER (Minor)	GOODENOW			8:30 AM
WAYNE SUTHERLIN	HUSTLER			8:30 AM
BRUCE GLOVER	HUSTLER	WARD 8 AM	READY	8:30 AM
KEN SWOFFORD	WHEATIES HOLD	WARD 8 AM	READY	8:30 AM
(NEW) JUNE C. ELLIS	MOM	WARD 8 AM	READY	8:30 AM
(Come made up and hair fixed)				

ATMOSPHERE AND STAND-INS INDEPENDENT CASTING	THRU GATE	REPORT TO	READY ON SET
6 STANDINS		REPORT STAGE 15	8 AM
1 STANDIN (for June Ellis)		REPORT STAGE 15	8 AM
1 MAN AS COOK		REPORT STAGE 15	8 AM
RICHARD WICKLUND - WELFARE WORKER (WEEKLY) - AS RECALLED	8:30	STAGE 15	

TOTAL: MAKEUP: SEASON:

SPECIAL INSTRUCTIONS:
                          ADVANCE SCHEDULE
TUES., 9/29/70

     INT. BEANERY - CONTINUE SC. 109 THRU 111, 117   STAGE #15

WED., 9/30/70
THURS., 10/1/70
FRI., 10/2/70

     INT. BOYS' CABIN - SC. 158, 71, 72, 73 (DAY)   STAGE #15
     INT. BOYS' CABIN - SC. 3, 4, 92-96, 101, 185 (NIGHT)   STAGE #15
     INT. ANOTHER CABIN (REDRESS) - SC. 55 (NIGHT)   STAGE #15

SCHRAGER/KUNODY/POER   IVAN VOLKMAN
     ASSISTANT DIRECTOR   UNIT MANAGER   APPROVED

COLUMBIA PICTURES   PRODUCTION REQUIREMENTS – PICTURE BLESS THE BEASTS & CHILDREN

DIRECTOR _STANLEY KRAMER_   PICTURE NO. _8990_ SHOOTING TIME _9 AM_   DATE _MON., 9/28/70_

SET #	·INT. BEANERY	LOCATION STAGE #15	PHONE
SET #	·	LOCATION	PHONE
SET #	·	LOCATION	PHONE
SET #	·	LOCATION	PHONE
SET #	·	LOCATION	PHONE

No.	CAMERA	Time	No.	MAKEUP	Time	No.	RESTAURANT	Time
1	BNC | R | NC | Standard	7:30A		Makeup Artist			Breakfast For:	
	Arri-Zoom | MK II - Zoom			Extra MU				
	Zoom For:			Extra MU			Lunches	
	Lenses:			Body MU			Dinners	
1	Cameraman:	7:30A		Hairstylist			Suppers	
1	Operator:	7:30A		Extra Hair		5	Gals Coffee	7:15 A
2	Assistant:	7:30A		Extra Hair		3	Doz. Donuts	7:15 A
	SPECIAL PHOTOGRAPHIC			WARDROBE		3	Gals Coffee	2 PM
	Cameraman – Process		1	Wardrobe Man	7:30A		POLICE	
	Matte Supervisor			Extra Ward Men			Flagman	
	Port. Proj.			Ward Girl			Set Watchman	
	Moviola			Extra Ward Girl			Night Watchman	
	Grip			SOUND			Lockerman	
	Electrician		1	Mixer	7:30A		Matron	
	1/2/3 Head Proj.			Recorder			Uniformed Police	
	Projectionist		2	Mikeman	7:30A		Studio Fireman	
	Stereo Mach./Proj.			Cableman				
			x	System	7:30A		HOSPITAL	
				Playback Mach./Oper.			1st Aid Man	
	TECHNICAL			Batteries/Hookup			MUSIC	
x	Key & 2nd Grip	7:30A		Radio/Oper.			Piano/Player	
2	Co Grips	7:30A					Sync Man	
	Crane #						Sideline Musicians	
1	Crane Oper.	7:30A		Walkie Talkie			LOCATION	
x	Crab Dolly			Electric Megaphone			Permits:	
	Greensman		x	Wigwags/Phone			Police	
1	C.S.E.	7 AM		Records			Firewarden	
	Painter			Nagra/Sync Pulse			San Wagon # Drms.	
	Plumber			STILL				
	Propmaker Constr.		1	Still Man/Still Equip.	8:30A		TRANSPORTATION	
	Special Effects			EDITORAL			Phone Car·	
	Effects			Film Editor/NEC Film			Standby Car	
	KD Dress Bus			PROPERTY				
1	Drs. Rm.(2 people) out-		1	Property Master			Buses	
	side Stage #15	6:30A	1	Asst. Prop Man				
7	Sing. Dr. Rm. outside			Lead Man				
	Stage #15	6:30A		Swing Gang			Stretchout	
				Draper				
1	~~Dxx Maxdrax Trixed~~	out-	1	Set Dresser (M.	7:30A		Grip Trk/Trlr	
	and hangers			Hoffman)			Prop Trk/Trlr	
1	Wardrobe Racks Fot # 25	6:30A					Ward Trk/Trlr	
x	Schoolroom For # 5 Stg. 15		1	M/up Tables Lighted-	7 AM		Sound Trk	
	~~Xxxx Axx xxx xxxx Dxx xxXX~~			Ready			Elec. Trk/Trlr	
	~~xx xx xx xxxx5~~			AHA Representative			Generator Trk/Trlr	
1	Office Dr. Rm. with			Animal Handler			Goose	
	phones on Stg. #15 as			Wranglers			Utility Trk	
	discussed for Mr. Kramer			Live Stock/Picture Cars			Water Wagon	
	ELECTRICAL	6:30A					Power Wagon	
X	Gaffer & Best Boy	7:30A					Insert Car/Lights/Gen.	
4	Lamp Opers.	7:30A	1	Art Director	7:30A	1	Driver (Bruce	7:30 A
	Generator			(L. Wheeler)			ND Driver Petty)	
	Gen. Operator					1	Prod. Van #1	
	Wind Mach.					1	Prod. Van #2	
	Wind Mach. Oper.							
	Battery Man						Above trucks to be parked	
	Batteries						near Stage #15	
	Camera Mechanic							
	Air Conditioning							
	Booster Lights							
x	Work Lights	6 AM						
			1	Script Supvr.				

DEPARTMENT	MISCELLANEOUS & SPECIAL INSTRUCTIONS

NOTE: Requirements for all depts. as per Page 13 original shooting schedule.

ASS'T. DIRECTOR	UNIT MANAGER	APPROVED

NOTE: Dressing rooms lighted and ready 6:30 AM
School room lighted, etc., Stage #15 - Ready 7 ~!

Production Report

The production report represents what has been accomplished: the time of the first shot; the number of scenes completed; the number of pages completed; the finishing time of the cast; the total length of time the cast has worked, the extras and the bit players, and the total length of time each crew member has worked. The production report also shows the amount of film consumed, the number of prints made, the number of minutes shot as well as the number of camera set-ups. The production report also serves to point out the progress of the shooting company in terms of the schedule. For example, a company might be two days behind schedule or a day-and-a-half ahead of schedule. In this way, close observation is possible in terms of the overall budget. In a studio, copies of the production report are distributed to all the department heads and executives concerned with that particular production.

A sample production report (front and back) is shown on the following pages.

COLUMBIA PICTURES

DAILY PRODUCTION REPORT

		SHOOTING SCHEDULE AND STATUS									FOR REMARKS AND DELAYS SEE REVERSE SIDE		NUMBER OF DAYS ON PICTURE INCLUDING TODAY								
	1ST UNIT	REHEARS-AL	PRE-PROD.	TRAV-EL	HOLI-DAYS	LAY-OFF	RE-TAKES	IDLE UN.T	POST PROD.	BEHIND		SHOOT-ING	REHEARS-AL	PRE-PROD.	TRAV-EL	HOLI-DAYS	LAY-OFF	RE-TAKES	2ND UNIT	POST PROD.	IDLE
1. DAYS SCHEDULED	39			1	1							44			1	1					1
2. DAYS REVISED							1			13											

Date **MONDAY 9-28-70**

Producer **STANLEY KRAMER** Director **STANLEY KRAMER** Unit Director _____

Working Title **BLESS THE BEASTS & CHILDREN** Prod. No. **8990**

Picture Started **8-4-70 (CORRECTED)** Finish Date Scheduled **9-21-70** As Revised **10-7-70**

Sets (Set No.) **INT. BEANERY**

Location **STAGE #15 COLUMBIA STUDIOS**

Crew Call **7:30am** Shooting Call **9am** First Shot **11:15a** till Lunch **12:54** till **1:54pm** Dinner ___ till ___ Last Shot **6:25pm**

Company Dismissed: At Studio ___ On Location ___ At Headquarters ___

SCRIPT SCENES AND PAGES			MINUTES		SETUPS	ADDED SCENES	RETAKES			STILLS		
	SCENES	PAGES	PREV.	91:05	PREV. 435	PREV.	PAGES	SCENES		PREV.	PROD.	PUBLICITY
ORIG. SCRIPT	264	120 6/8	TODAY	2:40	TODAY 9	TODAY 9	TODAY			TODAY		
NET REVISED TOTAL			TOTAL	93:45	TOTAL 444	TOTAL	TOTAL			TOTAL		
TAKEN PREV.	199	87 7/8	SCENE NO. STARTED 109-110									
TAKEN TODAY	0	2										
TOTAL TO DATE	199	89 7/8	ADDED SCENES									
TO BE TAKEN	65	30 7/8	RETAKES				SOUND TRACKS					

Picture Negative Budgeted ___ Color-B & W

Picture Negative Used to Date ___

PRINTED		WASTE		
Previous	118,530	Previous	10,770	
Today	2,820	Today	180	
2nd Unit		2nd Unit		
Total to Date	121,350	Total to Date	10,950	

NOTE: FOOTAGE CORRECTED THRU 9-28-70

SHOOTING HOURS BUDGET ACTUAL	
Sch. Pgs.	
Previous	Shot
Today	Sch. Scenes
Total to Date	Shot

EXTRAS USED		
NO.	5	
RATE	32.65	
ADJ.		
O. T.	1/4	
MISC.		
NO.	1	
RATE	32.65	
ADJ.	11.00	
O. T.	1/4	
MISC.		

PLAYERS – CAST – WEEKLY – DAILY Start-S Worked-W Finished-F Hold-H Rehearsed-R Test-T Travel-TV Brkf'st Served-B		TIME IN	SET CALL	TIME ON SET	TIME DIS-MISSED	ARRIVE STUDIO	LOOPED TO	B	EXTRAS	
1	BARRY ROBINS	W	8:30am	8:30a	8:30a	6:25pm				NO.
2	BILL MUMY (M)	W	"	"	"	5:30pm				NO. 1
3	*MILES CHAPIN (M)	W	"	"	"	"				RATE 32.65
4	BOB KRAMER (M)	W	"	"	"	"				ADJ. 11.00
5	MARC VAHANIAN (M)	W	"	"	"	"				O. T. 1/4
6	*DAREL GLASER (M)	W	"	"	"	"				MISC.
7	KEN SWOFFORD	H								NO.
8	WAYNE SUTHERLIN	W	8am	8:30a	8:30a	6:20pm				RATE
9	BRUCE GLOVER	W	"	"	"	"				ADJ.
10	JUNE ELLIS	SW	8am	8:30am	8:30am	6:25pm				O. T.
11										MISC.
12										NO.
13										RATE
14										ADJ.
15										O. T.
16										MISC.
17	*WITH GUARDIANS: MRS. GLASER, H CHAPIN									NO.
18										RATE
19										ADJ.
20										O. T.
21										MISC.
22										NO.
23										RATE
24										ADJ.
25										O. T.
26										MISC.
27										TOTAL 1 STANDINS 6
28										TOTAL ADJUSTMENTS 2
29										1ST MEAL 12:54-1:54pm
30										2ND MEAL
31										REMARKS
32										
33	SIDELINE MUSICIANS									

J. VEITCH / PRODUCTION MANAGER   ASST. PRODUCTION MANAGER   IVAN VOLKMAN / UNIT MANAGER   SCHRAGER/KUNODY/POER / ASSISTANT DIRECTOR

COMMENTS — DELAYS (EXPLANATION) — CAST, STAFF, AND CREW ABSENCE
MONDAY 9-28-70

NOTE: CREW LUNCH - 12:45-1:45pm
GRIPS, ELECTRICIANS 1/2 HOUR LUNCH

Shooting Units Working Today _____ 1 _____   Directors _STANLEY KRAMER_

STAFF AND CREW		SET OPERATIONS LABOR		EQUIPMENT	
Director	KRAMER	Grips	2		1-2-3 Head Projectors
Unit Manager	VOLKMAN	Crane Crew	1	1	Cameras BNC NC R
Asst. Director	SCHRAGER	Craft Service Man	1		
2nd Assistants	KUNODY, POER	Greens Man			Camera Pickup Truck
Script Supervisor	SCHLOM	Painters			Generator Truck Trlr.
Camerman	HUGO	Propmakers			Electric Truck; Trlr.
Operator	SHEARMAN, JR	Electricians	4	x	Sound System
2 Asst. Camerman	FENNEL, KING	Generator Operator			Passenger Car S.B.
Still Man	MONTE	Wind Machine Operator			Stretchout
1st Grip	LIVESLEY	Ladies' Costumer			Passenger Cars
2nd Grip	RABUSE	Men's Costumer			Picture Cars
Gaffer	MCCARTHY	Makeup Artists			Truck
Best Boy	HODGINS	Body Makeup			Bus
1st Prop Man	FRANKEL	Hair Stylists			Moviola. Oper.
Asst. Prop Man	P CALHOUN	Public Address Operator			Crane
Standby Effects	ANDERSON	Playback Operator		5	XXXXXXXXX DOZ TON
Ladies' Costumer		Prop Men		13	XXXXXXK GAL COFFE
Men's Costumer	BANKS	A.H.A. Representative			Dinners
Makeup Artists		Wranglers			Wagons
Hair Stylists		Animal Handlers			
Mixer	FRESHOLTZ	Flagman			Horses
Recorder		Watchmen		1	PROD VAN
2 Mike Man	SALMON, HOGUEL	Policemen			Animals
Cable Man		Fireman			Water Wagon
Art Director		Drapery Man			Drivers
Set Decorator		Sync. Men			Knock Down Dr. Rms.
Film Editor		Rehearsal Pianist			
Assistant Film Editor		First Aid Man			
Dialogue Coach		Welfare Worker WICKLUND		7	Single Dr. Rm. Trlr.
Technical Advisors		Projectionist			Triple Dr. Rm. Trlr.
Choreographer		Drivers	1		
Livestock Man					
Cashier		**SET OPERATIONS LABOR** — per verbal orders		1	School Room Setup
Timekeeper				x	Air Conditioner
Coordinator				x	Wig Wags Phone
1 Publicity	FISHER				Teleprompter Oper.
Driver Captain					Honey Wagon - Dr. Rms.
					Stage Heat
SPECIAL STAFF AND CREW				1	DR RM (KRAMER)
				1	DBL DR RM

	Hours	SPECIAL EQUIPMENT & LIVESTOCK	Hours			Hours
CRAB DOLLY						
PICTURE EQUIP: 1 WEAPONS CARRIER						

CINEMOBILE SYSTEMS

FOUAD SAID

". . . Motion picture location work has been increasing every year. . . . It is more realistic, cheaper, faster and really the only way to go. . . ."

The argument for location filming goes back to the audience: they sense and appreciate actual locations, and reject a phony one. Motion picture location work has been increasing every year. *Easy Rider* was all done out on location, as were *Joe* and *Thumb Tripping*. Previously, film-makers used to ask, "Why go out on location?" Today, they ask, "Why go into the studio? Why build an $80,000 set?"

Location work previously demanded a caravan of trucks, with each truck for an element of the soundstage: lighting, electricity, grip, sound, camera, generator. When we were doing *I Spy*, we were traveling all over the world. After the first location in Hong Kong, I came up with the idea of having one truck combine all elements. We built one in a hurry and worked it for 3½ years all over the world. Since we could put it into any commercial cargo airplane like a 707 or DC-8, the mobility of the company increased tremendously. We worked with a small crew and this truck, which was later dubbed the Cinemobile. It included the generators, cameras, sound,

FOUAD SAID is the originator and President of Cinemobile Systems. Since 1967 he has been innovative in the area of "on location" shooting for which he developed the Cinemobile (mobile studios) concept. Before going into business with Cinemobile Systems, Mr. Said was director of photography of many television and motion picture releases, including the television series, *I Spy*.

electrical equipment, everything needed. The resulting demand was so tremendous that we started building more, and finally went into business as Cinemobile Systems.

Motion picture equipment is changing fast. The lighter, more mobile equipment increases the daily output, reduces the manpower, and produces pictures for a cheaper dollar. To keep up with all developments, one man in our organization travels constantly, doing three things: first, looking at the other available systems, observing how the studios go out and shoot with their 10-truck caravans; second, observing the efficiency of our Cinemobile on location; and third, traveling throughout Europe and Japan, looking for new and more modern equipment to include in our new models.

When Cinemobile is hired by producers to service a film, the minute they hire their cameraman, soundman and production manager, we have a meeting with them all. For example, on *Thumb Tripping* I went with the producer to the location and reviewed with the cameraman exactly what equipment would be needed for the production. Then, I came back and equipped the Cinemobile to their needs. Every production is tailor-made that way. We then set a daily price based on the equipment needed.

When the film starts, generally we send a maintenance man, who drives the Cinemobile and also maintains the equipment personally. The first week out, we also give them a camera mechanic, full-time on our company charge, just in case the cameraman wants to change any equipment. Then, we watch closely their day-to-day shooting schedule, following them from our home office in Hollywood. This check is very important to us in scheduling Cinemobiles. A Mark V unit costs $700,000. Scheduling a piece of equipment like that has to be very tight; otherwise, we lose a lot of money. When one of them is out on location, it is important to keep tight control over when it will return, so that it can be booked. It is like an airplane: our turn-around must be minimal so that we can make our maximum profit, or flying time.

Actually, the rental of a Cinemobile is very cheap. A Cinemobile Mark I rents for $400 a day, which includes the generators, cameras, sound, grip, electrical, communications, and the vehicle itself. The fee can go up to $1,200 to $1,500 a day, depending upon what kind of vehicle and equipment is needed. The average cost for a feature picture now is $20,000 to $40,000 a day, and if that Cinemobile ever stops, the company is out of business. It is, therefore, no small task to keep it functioning on location. If anything happens, our driver picks up the mobile phone immediately and calls us. In addition, each system in the Cinemobile has a back-up. For example, we never equip them with only one Nagra; we always provide two. There are two generators in a Cinemobile so that a back-up is available. We have been operating since 1964 and we have never stopped a company so far.

In 1967, there was one Cinemobile. In 1968, the supply jumped from one Cinemobile to five. There are plans to double the number almost every year. Since one can generate only so much cash, it becomes impossible to have that kind of progress internally. The only way to move very fast is with some fresh capital, and with projection of outside money. Our business consultant advised us that we could go two ways: either go over-the-counter, or merge with some other company. We were doing both at the same time, and the minute it was announced that we were up for merger, we received many offers. Since the Taft Broadcasting people were the most sound financially, we merged with them. They believe in our operation and are leaving us alone.

The best kind of merger is that in which a big company acquires a small company, and then gives the man who owns the small company X number of dollars. This is the greatest incentive for the management of the smaller company to generate as much profit as possible and still have the feeling that they really own the company. Our merger deal was one in which I got X dollars up front, and seven years during which I share profit with the parent company, which is a very big part of the net profits of our division. As a result, I do not feel as though I have been "acquired" by anybody; the harder I work, the more money I make. And because of this incentive the parent company does not worry at all. If I don't make money for them, I don't make money for myself.

The arrangement with Taft is called *earn-out*. The principle behind it says that the more we earn, the more we keep. If we make $10 net after taxes as profit to the parent company, we keep four or five. Often when a big company acquires a smaller one it purchases the small one as a *buy-out*. In this arrangement, because the smaller company does not get big incentives or a share in the profits, they feel as if they have retired. I have never felt any control from Taft at all. Normally, when one does a job well, nobody bothers him. He gets into trouble only when he ceases running his division well.

Most of the money for productions today is financed money. There is no one single man who personally finances pictures. Most of the money comes from big corporations, insurance companies, finance companies and banks. These people are not going to invest in a picture because they love Hollywood; rather, they do it because they have shareholders, and responsibilities to their investors. If a picture is cheaper to do in England or in Spain, they will film it in England or Spain. Since many producers today are hired producers, they will get the package together, obtain the money from the financial sources, and film it wherever they can make it more cheaply. We have had several Cinemobiles working overseas. No one has a monopoly on motion picture production; the industry must be competitive. Our duty in Hollywood—the studio's duty, the union's duty, the duty of anyone earning a living from this industry—is to make the Hollywood industry more competitive with the European, the Japanese, or any other foreign industry.

As for the future of our company, we are continuing to double the number of Cinemobiles we have every year. A Mark IV Cinemobile is $500,000, and a Mark V or Mark VI Cinemobile costs about $700,000 each. Because building half a dozen of these is very expensive, we are making a big feasibility study. The increase of location production on features and television encourages us to keep building. I see more and more pictures being shot on actual locations. It is more realistic, cheaper, faster, and really the only way to go.

PART FIVE

Production: The Creative Functions

Both sympathy and respect must be accorded those who bear the awesome burdens of creative responsibility for producing a theatrical motion picture. The budgets are immense, the logistical details are overwhelming, and the intensity of those human interrelationships inherently involved in such a creative venture is an item to ponder.

Yet someone must carry all or a goodly share of final, decision-making authority throughout the process of planning and bringing the film to readiness for exhibition, and at no time can that person make any decision which is entirely free of economic consequence. For the most part, the full responsibility falls upon the man who is identified as the film's "producer," but the functions of producer, director and writer are often so closely related that roles frequently tend to merge and blend within single personalities. Hence the emergence of such designations as "Producer-Director," "Writer-Director," "Writter-Producer" and other hyphenated variations.

The experiences and opinions of these men who assume creative authority over major films are considered below. Stanley Kramer *reviews some of the distinctions between the two roles he has assumed—producer and director—while* Sydney Pollack *analyzes the economic pressures upon the director.* Bud Yorkin and Norman Lear *reflect upon how a writer-producer team can logically share creative responsibilities—to the ultimate benefit of both.* Stirling Silliphant *describes how he became a producer in order to protect his writing interests, and* Russ Meyer *discusses in some detail how a producer with a limited budget can achieve some creative satisfactions and still do quite well at the box office.*

THE PRODUCER/DIRECTOR

STANLEY KRAMER

". . . I think anybody who is not a creative producer has no business even being called a producer. Because somebody has to have the dream, and has to participate every inch of the way—from story to release—and that is quite different from being strictly a financial man. . . ."

My original production group was formed after World War II with a company of people who came together in a community of interests and donated their services for later benefit. What we wanted most was to be *independent*. Our pictures were financed by United Artists, and included *So This Is New York*, which was a failure we survived, and then *Champion, Home of the Brave, Cyrano, The Men* and *High Noon*. Although I wanted to be a director, I signed a deal for a limit of three years at Columbia to make 12 pictures, which put me in the category of an executive in charge of production. The reason—to intrude the idea of independence into the major studio operation. We made *Death of a Salesman, Member of the Wedding, Happy Time, My Six Convicts* and *The Wild One*—which may have been a little bit ahead of its time—and finally, *The Caine Mutiny*. By that time all my partners had left for political, social or economic reasons. The experience through failure at the box-office had not been

STANLEY KRAMER, one of the motion picture industry's most respected producer/directors, began his career as a producer with Columbia Pictures and United Artists. Among his major films are *Cyrano, Member of the Wedding* and *High Noon*. His more recent accomplishments include *It's a Mad, Mad, Mad, Mad World* and *Bless the Beasts and Children*.

a happy one. I decided to return to my original ambition—one film at a time—as a director. I left Columbia and went back to United Artists in 1956—and that's when I started to direct.

Usually a director who achieves sufficient stature will also become the producer in order to control what he does. Through force of circumstances, I had reversed the order. I became a producer to make the kind of pictures I wanted to make, and promoted money in exchange for a large part of the receipts. I became a director after that—a producer/director with the Stanley Kramer Corporation.

My independent company is based with Columbia Pictures, which does the complete financing of the films. I draw whatever salary is commensurate with the picture in question, plus the profits and/or gross—whichever applies by certain formulae—in terms of the picture's success. Our agreements are usually made on a picture-by-picture basis. On *Bless The Beasts and Children*, for example, I wanted very much to use just six unknown kids in the cast. I did not take any salary on the picture, deferred everything, and made the picture as reasonably as I could.

One does not deliberately divide the responsibilities of a producer from those of a director even though he wears both hats. By managing whatever is going through my mind creatively as a director, I may be able to shoot three days less at a location and save $100,000. At the same time, as a producer, I might be using a pencil—trying to shave a little bit off the property budget, a little bit off the electrical budget, or wherever possible. I think anybody who is not a creative producer has no business even being called a producer, because somebody has to have the dream, and has to participate every inch of the way—from story to release—and that is quite different from being strictly a financial man.

For any picture, the first move is to acquire the property. And when you do acquire it you ought to have in mind how you will handle it and who will write it—and whether you can work together as a director-writer team. If you are working in a studio and releasing through the company, they will have a production department with all the machinery necessary to make estimates of what a property will cost to produce. You have your own man, usually, who makes a breakdown. He makes a day-to-day schedule, in a production budget. You will usually get a budget approximation even before a book is in final script form. Then, you start to write.

The minute you start putting pen to paper perhaps $200,000 in overhead charges will go up in the left-hand column. As long as I'm working at Columbia, I have to pay for social security, obligations, retroactive pay—things which will never come to the screen. Overhead is one of the reasons why so many young filmmakers have broken away from the studio. On the other hand, a studio is helpful to the producer if he cannot achieve financing other than by giving private investors more than their fair share. A studio charges overhead to keep going, but in exchange it may take only 20% of the profits. If you go to an oil man he may want 50% of the profits.

To continue—now the property is being scripted. The next person brought in after the writer may well be a production designer (or art director) because he is concerned with creating the sets and planning the picture—with establishing the nature and the feel of it. I will usually also bring in a cameraman on a consultation basis with the art director.

When the second draft script is completed, it is distributed to all the departments and each begins to make a budget. The first time specific figures have any meaning is when that preliminary budget is estimated on the actual material you are going to shoot. Next there are meetings on how fast—and where—you are going to shoot it. Sometimes you have to look for locations, and this involves a big expense.

Then you fix a starting date. The longer the delay until your starting date, the more the picture will cost—because the money that has been going out is borrowed money. I stress this aspect because the inflationary spiral is so great that it is really not propitious to make a picture with the overhead prices that are now being charged. Change has to come. The way things are now, you undergo terrible mental and moral stress when you attempt to cut costs on these pictures. I grew up during the years when there were no unions, for example, and we fought like hell just to get union minimum, social security, retroactive pay and vacations. We finally got these rights into contracts. And yet when you make up budgets in this inflationary time, the cost of labor murders you. You are loathe to relinquish any of it or duck it—because it was a fight of blood to raise the standard and give the working man in the film industry a dignity and a position. In recent years the unions have agreed to help meet the problem by making adjustments for low-budget pictures.

When I begin to select the cast for a picture, I negotiate with talent agents only in terms of what I'm willing to pay. Once we get to the details of the contracts, the work is done by the lawyers. I don't think I ever started a film with all the contracts signed. Sometimes they were not signed until it was finished.

As producer/director, you have no way of telling whether a decision to spend an extra sum—say $10,000 or $20,000—will, in the final analysis, make a difference to an audience. More importantly, does it make any difference to *you*—as the director? When making *The Defiant Ones* we had to manufacture rain for a scene which took place on a highway in the middle of the night. In one shot, a truck was supposed to go off the road and then we were to pan up from the truck to the road. What I wanted to see when we came up from this ditch was the distortion of the police car lights. We did it eight times and when I saw the dailies, the police cars were perfectly clear. There was no distortion in the lens. We had missed the setting. I knew that it cost $25,000 for shooting that night—including all the people, the trick stuff and the crash. I had to ask myself whether I should go back—purely on the basis of my creative directorial urge to have that shot—and spend another $25,000. I decided against it—not because I wanted to water down the creativity, but because there is a point at which it is just as creative to save that $25,000 as to spend it. As producer, I have to live with all the detailed costs. Creativity has "czar" attached to it. There is a reason for this arrogance, I think, because decisions on money, budget and time are all related. What is involved is a sense of responsibility—an understanding of what you are doing and what it is costing to do it.

When the shooting is over and we have isolated the dailies, I do all the editing. You can have a film editor who is quick, fast and bright, which helps, but I edit every frame of the picture, and ultimately get a final print. And well before I finish, the advertising and publicity and exploitation budgets have to be drawn up. Every picture is in a different advertising category. A film like *It's a Mad, Mad, Mad, Mad World*, required tremendous advertising in all media. So much money is tied up in that kind of picture that you must reach for the greatest possible audience. A picture like *Bless the Beasts and Children*, on the other hand, is designed to play to a film festival and to be shown to opinion makers who—one hopes—will spread the good word slowly but surely.

I would say in conclusion that one thing which will continue to change in the motion picture industry is basic approach. The attempts to rectify and revolutionize the framework in which this medium operates have been effective, and this has stregthened movies as an art form. Such changes as the elimination of the old-time mass-producing studio structure—along with the evils that went with it —are to the good. Personal talent, individual initiative, now dominate the picture-making scene, and this personal control of creative destinies is taking basic approaches to where they belong.

THE DIRECTOR

SYDNEY POLLACK

". . . Economics is probably the most inhibiting factor for a director making a film . . . Every time the director says, 'Let's try it this way,' and not 'Let's do it this way,' he is spending money at enormous rates. . . ."

It is only in rare instances that one realizes money from a percentage deal. Although I do not speak from personal experience here, it is my understanding through a general consensus in the business, that this is the area where people run into problems. When a picture is made for $2-million it should, theoretically, begin to pay off when it has grossed $4.5-million. When the picture has grossed $6-million without paying any profit money and someone asks why, he is shown an array of figures, probably all accurate, that have to do with costs of distribution, advertising, prints, overhead, executive entertainment, and so on, all added onto the negative cost. On a big-grossing picture, it *is* possible to make money with a percentage deal, but even here it takes months and sometimes years. Most of the time there is no percentage return. But then most often the people involved were paid up front anyway.

SYDNEY POLLACK has earned distinction as a director in motion pictures and television. Among his several theatrical-screen credits are *They Shoot Horses, Don't They?*, for which he was nominated for Oustanding Directorial Achievement awards by the Motion Picture Academy and the Directors Guild. Mr. Pollack also has directed numerous episodes for various major TV series, and was awarded an Emmy by the TV Academy for his direction of "The Game"—a teleplay produced for *Bob Hope Presents The Chrysler Theatre*. He is a partner, with Mark Rydell, in Sanford Productions.

Economics is probably the most inhibiting factor for a director making a film. Almost every creative person in the world, with the exception of actors and directors, creates alone and in silence. With actors and directors it's a little like taking your clothes off in front of a mob of people. There are hundreds of technicians; if we are on a street, there are horns honking; the clock is ticking away. Every time the director says. "Let's *try* it this way," and not, "Let's *do* it this way," he is spending money at enormous rates. The average Hollywood studio company, when it is out on location, spends anywhere between $20,000 and $28,000 a day. Breaking that down into 8-hour segments, it is $3-4,000 an hour. So, if the director wants to take an hour to play with a scene, and try it two or three ways, that is $3-4,000 added to the cost of production. That's why there is such a necessity for the director to do his homework.

The economic pressures funnel backward from an assistant director; this is his job. He is being leaned on by a unit manager; the unit manager is being leaned on by a production manager; the production manager is being leaned on by a producer; the producer is being leaned on by the studio. And so on. A director does not *want* to have a reputation for being wasteful because that is harmful to his career. People generally know how much money he spends. I have had the reputation of being an expensive director, and it has always bothered me. I know that when I was signed for a picture at a studio, there were usually certain creative people who were happy, but the production department was depressed as hell. When you shoot a scene ten or twelve times looking for some special expression from an actor you are always vulnerable to production office criticism. Is Take Ten *really* better than Take One? How much better is better? $1,000 better? $2,000 better? No one can decide that except the director. He must try ultimately to be intransigent, while hoping that everything he is doing is contributing to making a better picture and is, therefore, not wasteful.

The first thing usually asked a director when he is signed is, "How much do you think it will cost?" Sometimes it is difficult to know in the beginning, but I usually make a wild guess. Then I work with an assistant director and a production manager to make what is called a "breakdown," which simply means a scene-by-scene itemization of what will be required: how many extras; should a set be rented or built; will we be on location or in a studio; how much will living expenses be; how many days will it take; how large a crew; will we need multiple cameras; how much action will there be; how many sequences involve large numbers of people; what will the weather be like? And so on. With sequences involving large numbers of people will we be outside the 300-mile Hollywood range so that we can get

unemployed local personnel for extras, or do we have to pay Hollywood rates to the extras? If we have 100 people and they get the
Hollywood rate of $35 per day, that is a considerable sum of money.
In *They Shoot Horses, Don't They?* we had between 700 and 1,000 extras a day.

Finally, we see that we have a 75-day shooting schedule and
that the picture is going to cost, let's say, $3-million below-the-line.
This price does not include above-the-line costs, which cover all the
creative people—the salaries of the writer, the producer, the director,
the actors. The studio then says, "We can't spend that much money;
we must cut it down to $2-million." So we start to cut.

Instead of building a detailed log-cabin for a certain scene, we
erect only a frame and perhaps cover it with canvas. That savings
is knocked off the budget. We forget the 300 extras in Scene 10 and
do it with 100 well-spaced extras. Instead of carrying a crane and the
two additional men required to operate it for ten weeks, which would
cost some $30,000 dollars, including transportation, room and board,
and fringe benefits for these men, I might agree to group all the
crane shots into a two-week period, if I can. This change saves us
some $27,000. But nothing saves money on a film compared to cutting
days off the schedule. Every other change becomes relatively minor.
When we have finally worked out the shooting schedule the production
department makes a budget. It is usually higher than the studio
wants to go and more cutting or discussion takes place until finally
we have a schedule and budget that is approved by everyone.

The choice of crew is next and obviously extremely important.
Not only do their various creative and mechanical abilities contribute
to the final effect of the film, but every moment they save you is
an extra moment that you can spend creatively. Every director re-
searches the background of a tentative crew religiously. What pictures
have they done; how fast are they; do they get on well with other
crew members.

The early stages of production depend upon the nature of the
individual picture. If it requires an enormous amount of set construction, for example, then the art director is one of the first people
hired. He has a practical problem: he has to build a town; that will
take two-and-a-half months to construct, and we are three months
from shooting. I start thinking about a cinematographer from the
first day I come on the picture. But we usually cannot afford to
hire one until a couple of weeks before we start shooting. I sometimes sit down with a cinematographer two months before shooting,
just to talk to him. We may have hired him, but his start date
could be two months later. He may be finishing another picture,
but we get together for a couple of evenings, run two or three pic-

tures together, talk about an effect, a concept, or a way of working: how to desaturate the color, how to make it look hot, how to make it look cold, how to work with the lenses wide open so that we don't have really sharp focus all the time, or we don't have a lot of depth-of-field, and so on.

Photography has been an avocation of mine, so I like to become as deeply involved as possible in the photographic techniques to the film. I like to choose the lens, discuss the *f*-stop, the light level, the color level, what the focus will be like. These aspects of production are all part of the vocabulary of the director. It's possible to shoot a scene twice, doing the *same* thing with the *same* actors and if they are photographed in two different days, they will be entirely different in mood and emotional effect. A famous example occurs in *Sweet Smell Of Success*, in which they reversed the normal shooting concept. They shot almost every master shot with long-focus lenses, from very far away, in order to pack the buildings and the street in tightly behind the people. Then they shot their close-ups with wide-angle lenses, to keep the background in focus and, again, an awareness of the buildings. These techniques create an over-all effect, in which the lay movie-goer feels oppressed by the city, by the sense of the city's closing in, without necessarily understanding why.

One of the first problems I had with *They Shoot Horses* is a common problem in films shot in color: how to make it look unglamorous. Color film tends to glamorize and enrich. We finally did two things: since we were shooting the entire picture on one set, I needed to have the freedom to shoot 360-degrees for purposes of variety. That meant no standing lights—otherwise they would be photographed. Lighting people from above, from over their heads, is usually ugly; it casts hard shadows. Well, that happened to be perfect for the film. The second thing we did was to force-develop everything. In other words, we underexposed the film and kept it in the developer a few minutes longer, making it grainier, milkier, and taking some of the glamorous texture off it. In the picture *This Property Is Condemned*, which I did with James Wong Howe, we made tests to try to desaturate the color for the same reason—it was a 1930's picture, a poverty picture. We took a gray shirtboard and set it up in front of the camera. We photographed the gray shirt cardboard, filling the frame, but with perhaps one-tenth of the proper amount of exposure. Then, we wound the film back and shot the scene with nine-tenths of the exposure, so that it was pre-fogged a little bit. This process took some of the color out of it. One cannot underestimate the technical end—it is a technical medium, like architecture.

I do not usually believe much in rehearsal; it is a concept that comes from the theatre. In a film, because we do not have the luxury of time, I try to catch a performance before it starts to become aware of what it is doing. Just before each new scene, I do some rehearsing, but very little. It depends, of course, on the scene. Some of the scenes in *Horses* between Fonda and Sarrazin were three and four pages long, and I rehearsed them for maybe 20 minutes. There were many critical shots in that picture in which people had perhaps a tenth-of-an-inch of movement possible, because I was shooting through 40 people, out of focus. Instead of cutting in to a close-up, we tried to make the focus work like a close-up, so that we would not lose a sense of the environment. The frame covered perhaps 20 couples, but there was only one pair of heads sharply visible in the center of it.

During principal photography, I view the dailies each day with the editor, pointing out to him which take I like best. We might, for instance, use the first part of Take One, and the third part of Take Two. The editor makes a note each time. After shooting, I see a first assembly, and then begin work on a first cut. The assembly means that the editor has simply put together all the film chosen from the rushes. Seeing it is usually a disaster for me. But then we start from the beginning to trim, rearrange, accent, find the rhythms and moods.

Somewhere along the way we bring in a sound-effects man. Probably by this time we already have a musician. I have a few meetings with him and then show him the final cut. Then we have a *spotting session* where we sit together with a footage counter and I might say, "Start the music when she turns her head there, and go to the point where he walks out the door." Now he knows that he has 130 feet there which he has to fill with music.

Next, there is optical work to do. We figure out where the dissolves are going to be. Then a title man comes in, and we space the titles out, figuring how many feet they are going to run.

If the sound quality is poor, or does not match from scene to scene, *looping* must be done. During a master shot, for instance, an airplane goes overhead and when the close-up is shot there is no airplane there. Since the two cannot be intercut, it is necessary to loop the whole master. This process involves lip-syncing, which is always a problem. It is boring, difficult work, and usually has a very artificial sound. It is worth great pains to get good original sound tracks.

With the final cut made, the film is ready for music *scoring,* which has been anticipated in advance, according to the budget. Then, we take the film into a dubbing room, where three or four men control audio mixing channels. There may be as many as 25 channels: one has all the men's dialogue; another has all the women's dialogue; another the looped, post-sync lines, because they have to be treated. Since they are done in a canned room, they have to be made to sound as if they are coming from the outside. The director spends days in this room, supervising the delicate mixing of all the available sound with the picture, and into the final soundtrack.

The next step is to look at what is called a *mute answer print* at the lab. It has no sound on it, because until now we have been working with magnetic sound, on a separate strip of film. The sound is not on the picture itself; this merger will eventually happen in a printing process. There is no dialogue. This is a dead silent print, but we look at it for the colors. Invariably, it is not right the first try, and the lab makes corrections. When it is approved, we are ready to add the sound, which has been transferred to an *optical negative.* It is just a bunch of squiggly black lines which will become squiggly white lines on the positive, that an exciter lamp will pick up on a projector and translate into sound. This negative, which is made in the studio, is then sent to the laboratory. The laboratory takes all of the technical data from the viewing of the mute answer print, puts the sound negative with it, and strikes the first, final, viewing *answer print.* From there, all the other prints are made.

It's difficult to account for the success of certain films while others, which might seem to some to be quite good, fail. I think that for a long time one of the essential ingredients in a successful picture was the distance felt between the spectator's life and the life he was viewing on the screen. When audiences watched Bogart in the fog in his trenchcoat in *Casablanca,* it was not *like* their lives and that is *why* they loved it. Today, quite often it is the shock of recognition of their own lives that makes an audience respond to a film. Today the smallest event can be made into a successful motion picture. The trend seems to be toward making pictures about the audience, about the people who go to see pictures.

TEAM PRODUCERS

BUD YORKIN
NORMAN LEAR

". . . The first thing that can break up a partnership is ego. . . . We do not have any kind of ego thing; we all work for our company. . . A lot of gratification comes from that. . . ."

MR. YORKIN

We got together originally when we were both involved in television. We felt that the combination would work well in the sense that Norman was primarily a writer at the time and I was primarily a director, and both of us had produced television shows. It seemed that the combination of ability to write, produce and direct a show would be a self-encompassing entity, and very helpful for us. For many years we had both wanted to be in motion pictures. This now seemed the thing to do. The first picture we did was for Paramount, *Come Blow Your Horn* (1963), for which we had the rights. Norman wrote the script and I directed the picture; we co-produced it.

The financial aspects of production are probably more reward-

BUD YORKIN holds four Emmy awards, and Peabody, Sylvania, *Look* and Directors Guild Awards for his producing and directing accomplishments. Among his motion picture credits are *Come Blow Your Horn* and *Start The Revolution Without Me* (produced and directed); *Divorce, American Style, Inspector Clouseau* and *Never Too Late* (directed).

NORMAN LEAR was nominated for an Oscar for his screenplay for *Divorce, American Style* and developed and produced the Emmy-award winning *All In The Family.* He produced *Come Blow Your Horn* and *The Night They Raided Minsky's,* and wrote, produced and directed *Cold Turkey.*

ing in television than in motion pictures. When one has a series that he owns a portion of on for two or three years, he is dealing in profits from the very first day. In motion pictures, since there is not a great deal of front money, he does it much more out of passion, love. Everyone hopes that the picture will go into profit, but the number of pictures that really do is infinitesimal compared to the number made per year.

We do not finance our pictures. We invest our money in acquiring the rights to a property. We take an option on a book, hire a writer for the screenplay if Norman is not doing it, but that is as far as we go financially. We make deals with major distributor/financiers, who put up the money.

MR. LEAR

We just develop to a point; we do the creative development. Then we go to a distributor and negotiate with him to put up the money it will cost to make the picture, in exchange for distribution rights. In our distribution deals, we get 50% of net profits. On subsequent deals, we split 50% with the distributor. *Cold Turkey* was an exception because we had a partner, Dick Van Dyke, who was also the star in the picture. Our company and his company together took 75% of the net profits. This is the kind of deal that has been frequent in the recent history of the business, because the distributors in these harder times have been less willing to pay important money up front, and more willing to pay greater profits later.

MR. YORKIN

The rule of thumb is that in order to see any profits, a picture has to realize for the studio roughly 2.6 times its negative cost. On a film that cost $1-million, then, the studio would have to earn in return $2.6-million to cover expenses. We did *Divorce, American Style*, which cost roughly $2.5-million, and we started realizing profits after it went over the $6-million figure.

A production company such as ours deals in net profits. Even if we get into profit, we realize that the distribution company is taking 35% off the top right away, and the exhibitor is taking another 20% percent. By the time we have a net profit, we are dealing with perhaps only 40 cents out of the dollar. If we own 50% of the net profits, we are down to 20 cents out of a dollar. As you can see, it is difficult to see profit even when you own 50% of the profits.

In the motion pictures we have done, we have never prepared a property that did not take at least four years from the day we started on it, until it came out on the screen—four years from the time we started to work on the script. Our average time in pre-pro-

duction, until we are ready to shoot, is anywhere from 18 months to two years; add another year of shooting and post-production, and then six months or so until it is released.

We have found that we really cannot put all our efforts into one project exclusively for four years and keep a company going. The ideal way for us to work is to be totally aware of the kinds of things we each want to do. I may like a property better than Norman does and prefer to do that one; and he may like one that I do not fully see. This way, we can double the number of projects in the works, and complete more than if we work together on one project, as we did in the old days.

MR. LEAR

The way we divide our responsibilities varies. On *Come Blow Your Horn*, I wrote the screenplay and Bud was the director. Since we were partners, while I was writing, he was very much there as the director, conferring with me. Usually, this situation does not occur, because the director is off doing something else, and comes in on the project after the screenplay is completed. When we went into production, as he began to direct, I was on hand. And so the collaboration was constant, from the minute we had a deal to advance what was a Broadway play. We followed it through that way —I writing, he directing, both of us producing—until the picture was completed.

On *Divorce, American Style* (1967), I wrote the original screenplay, while we divided other responsibilities. During the *Come Blow Your Horn* period, for example, we put an Andy Williams series on the air, serving as executive producers. During the *Divorce, American Style* period, we did a couple of other TV specials. Bud directed *Divorce, American Style* and I produced it; then we started to vary it. We next developed two properties together—*The Night They Raided Minsky's* and *Start The Revolution Without Me*. We had two screenplays, both ready to go at the same time. Bud took *Start The Revolution* to Europe, and produced and directed it, while I acted as executive producer. I took another director, Bill Friedkin, and *The Night They Raided Minsky's* to New York and made it, and we had two pictures going for Tandem Productions. As I was editing *Minsky's* I developed the first pilot of *All In The Family* for ABC. This was the show that sold three years later to CBS, and is currently on that network. In that period I also began to write the screenplay for *Cold Turkey* and a deal began to develop with United Artists who eventually agreed to go ahead with it. Since Bud was not back from France, I decided, with their agreement, to direct and also produce this one. We are set up now to work in any combination.

The minute a distributor says "yes," or even beforehand, we

may have a script broken down on paper by a professional production man, budget item for budget item, to see how much the picture will cost. With this breakdown, we can go into a studio and say, "We can make it for $1.8-million." When the distributor approves, one of the first members of our personnel to go to work on the project is a production manager and/or first assistant director, who breaks the budget down into a daily shooting schedule.

MR. YORKIN

But if the distributor says, "We don't want to spend that kind of money; we can spend only $1.7-million," we confer with the production manager to see where we can reduce the budget. Then we return to the same studio and say, "Here is where we trimmed $400,000 by rewriting, changing, and dropping that scene totally." Once we have the go-ahead, we become further involved, because all the deals have to be negotiated through us. We negotiate for all the key people: actors, cameraman, costume designer, musical director. By this time we are involved in the day-to-day economics beyond and above the "below-the-line" of the budget.

Today, many companies have what they call a "penalty factor." They might say, "All right, you can spend up to $2.3-million. If you go over budget by $200,000, you have to pick up $100,000 of that deficit." This way, the brunt of responsibility falls upon us very heavily, in dollars and cents as well as in the creative end of the picture.

When we are through with principal photography, we go into editing the film. When we did *Cold Turkey*, Norman was with United Artists. Since they don't have a studio, he cut the picture over at MGM in rented space. *Start The Revolution* was at Warners, and I did the editing over there. We edit and score the film, then go out and preview it. After all this we hand the final print over to the studio.

MR. LEAR

Advertising depends on a relationship, and our working relationships have always been good. With United Artists, where *Cold Turkey* is concerned, they had complete control, but they never finished anything off without flying it out here and laying it all out for us. They did not make a final decision on any aspect of advertising without talking to us. Long before tearsheets, they did not accept artwork without our approval.

MR. YORKIN

In selecting a distribution pattern, we really lean on their experience. They consult with us and say, "We think this picture, in-

stead of opening in one city, ought to open in eight cities." We may say, "No, we'd like it to play New York first for the reviews," and usually we come to an agreement.

The biggest advantage that Norman and I have—and I think it's the secret to any kind of partnership—is that we respect each other. Many times, we will disagree on a scene, or the movement of a script, or casting, or some other element. Out of that difference, something very good usually happens. If nothing else, it gives us food for thought, even though we may not come to any total agreement on the point. The first thing that can break up a partnership is ego. If one is worried about the other's getting more publicity, no partnership can last. We do not have any kind of ego thing; we all work for our company. If our company does well, Norman and I benefit; if it does poorly, we suffer. It is a cold world out here for a company. This is not a situation in which somebody hires us and we work. We have our offices, our secretaries, our invested money, our law firm— we are supporting a lot of people, and we have to put aside our own personal egos for the good of the company. A lot of gratification comes from that.

We believe that the industry is going to be bigger than ever. Something has to fill all those cartridges and cables and new theatres. It will be good, certainly for independent producers with companies like ours.

THE WRITER/PRODUCER

STIRLING SILLIPHANT

". . . I regard producing only as a protective adjunct to writing. . . ."

I actually began my motion picture career as a publicity man, then became a producer, and worked my way up to being a writer. I regard producing as only a protective adjunct to writing. I had spent 14 years as publicity director at 20th Century-Fox in New York. After learning that aspect of the business, I felt stifled creatively because we were given many films to sell which I regarded as abominations. So I resigned to do a film of my own and then moved to Cuba because it was an inexpensive place to live. While there, I wrote a novel called *Maracaibo*. The novel sold to Universal, then Columbia offered me a deal to write and produce a film, so I followed the money to Hollywood and settled down, saying, "Now I shall become a writer."

When I finished my Columbia script, I was virtually told that now I might as well go home—the studio machinery would "produce" the film—my function as producer was virtually titular, nothing

STIRLING SILLIPHANT is a successful screen and television writer-producer who won an Oscar for his screenplay of *In The Heat of The Night* (1967). He was a principal writer for the series *Naked City*, and wrote 71 hour-teleplays for *Route 66*, the TV series of which he was also co-creator. He is creator, writer and Executive Producer for a new Paramount Television series, *Longstreet*. Among current motion picture projects and recent releases of his production company (Pingree Productions) are *The Silent Flute, Shaft, Murphy's War* and *The New Centurions*.

more. It occurred to me the only dignity to be found anywhere in the film industry was in writing, so for the next ten years, which brings us up to the more recent years, I remained a writer resolutely, despite many offers to write and produce.

Then I became intrigued by what was happening in Europe, where the *auteur* new wave of French filmmakers was evolving. These men began as critics and ended up directing films, some of which were handsome and moving works of art. It occurred to me I was really deceiving myself—that I was creating films only to turn over the blueprints to people who subverted my intentions. It seemed to me I had better go back to the business of protecting that which I seemed able to create. What this came to was the formation of Pingree Productions. Before that, roughly from 1958-1964, I was in partnership with Herbert B. Leonard on the *Naked City* and *Route 66* television series. He was producer and I was supervising writer and partner. It was in television, really, that I learned my craft as a professional filmwriter.

One of the problems today in the film industry is that the old methods of raising capital, or of making distribution deals, or of selling a property which you create, have for the most part vanished. As an example, I formed Pingree when I found a slim book—*A Walk in the Spring Rain* by Rachel Maddox. I bought the film rights with my own money, and took it to Ingrid Bergman, who said if she liked the screenplay, she would commit to act in it. I then took the property to Columbia and made a deal to finance the production. Instead of getting my usual fee for screenwriting, I received only 25% of it to write and produce the film. In return for that concession on my part, however, I was given 50% of the film's profits. I was also given total creative freedom by Columbia. The risk was to go in with very little money up front, which is the pattern of deals today, but with maximum ownership or participation in the profits if there are any—and risks in the losses, if there are any. Since that time, almost everything I have done has been in the risk area, some rewarding, some not.

When a playwright creates a play and it's in rehearsal, he has total control over the material. Nobody, including the director and actors, can change one word of dialogue unless he agrees. If, on the other hand, someone comes to a screenwriter and says, "I want to hire you to write a screenplay for me from this book I've bought," he really is hiring only that much of a man—his writing ability—and if the writer is stubborn, or reluctant to follow instructions, then the writer quite logically can be replaced. If a writer wants to control his material, he must be willing to write without payment—until such time as he sells it directly to someone who wishes to finance his project, rather than to a producer.

In any event, as I began looking for properties I believed in, I discovered a strange thing—I was more concerned about my feeling toward the property as an artist than I was about its ultimate commerical success. Here is what I intend to do with a project called *The Teachings of Don Juan, A Yaqui Way of Knowledge*, by Carlos Castenada. It tells the story of the five years a young anthropologist spent in the desert with a Yaqui *brujo*, or sorceror. It deals essentially with metaphysics and this fascinates me. It was apparent from the beginning that this project had to be privately financed. We are in the process of trying to get together $300,000, and to help finance the film we are going to theatre exhibitors around the country.

In its first year of existence as a picture, I want the film to be seen only by college audiences. We plan to take the film to Boston first, since it has a large college population from several universities. Assuming that we draw only 2% of them and charge $2.50 for admission, we will have raised a good sum. We feel that we can take over $100,000 out of each of four university situations around the country. Since we have no distribution charges aside from minimal costs for advertising and personnel, we do not have the "2.6 formula," to deal with. This formula states that if you do a film for a studio that costs $1-million, you have to earn back $2.6-million before they let you get into profits. That $2-6-million pays off all the studio expenses, interest, overhead and departmental charges. On *Don Juan*, our figure will be an actual cost figure, so if we can take $100,000 each in four situations—Boston, Berkeley, Chicago/Wisconsin and New York—we will already be into profits. If that works, we will extend the idea to foreign universities as well. I would want to keep the film out of the regular theatres as long as possible in order to create a mystique for the property. Assuming that all this operates properly, our partners, the tough theatre exhibitors who put up the cash, will now have their money back. We will then go into the next phase, with the film in art houses. Then, it will be a question of what the picture can achieve on its own in the regular consumer market.

I do all pre-production financing myself, and it has taken me a long time to reach that point—ten years of writing other people's movies, of saving and investing. I have probably invested close to $50,000 in *Don Juan* at this point. But the film is now ready to be shot. We have a shooting script; the locations are set, and we have no deal. We do not want one. We know what we need is $225,000, which will bring us to the end of shooting. Post-production will cost an additional $50,000. We can go to exhibitors, real estate developers, any number of people interested in supplying the growing need for a product which the studios, because of their own financial failures, cannot fill.

THE LOW-BUDGET PRODUCER

RUSS MEYER

". . . Once you sign with one union, it begets another. . . ."

I have had considerable success in making what are called sex-ploitation movies—ranging from earlier films like *The Immoral Mr. Teas* to a recent picture called *Beyond the Valley of the Dolls* for 20th Century-Fox. Part of the success can be attributed to my own background in magazine photography and industrial film. I developed my particular genre of sexploitation film inexpensively. *Lorna,* for example, was made for $37,000. I distributed it myself and made a very substantial profit.

The market was pretty much mine for a while—until the majors decided to produce this kind of film. Two years ago, a hard-core kind of material began to come in from Denmark. As a result, I was hard pressed to compete in the area that I had been playing—which is a kind of spoofing of sex. Nevertheless, my name continues to sell my pictures. However, the inexpensive "sexploitation" film has become a glut on the market. More and more the attitude of "if you've seen one, you've seen them all" seems to prevail. One possible future lies in more expensive and extensive kind of production which takes a

RUSS MEYER began his career in magazine photography and industrial film. An expert in the area of low-budget filming, Mr. Meyer is a forerunner among the independent filmmakers handling both the production and distribution elements of films. His most recently-released film is *Seven Minutes.*

179

tongue-in-cheek look at sex and violence. I joined Twentieth Century-Fox because Richard Zanuck and others sensed this trend, and made the decision to hire me to do *Beyond The Valley of the Dolls*—happily one of the five top-grossing films of 1970. My discussion here, however, relates primarily to my low-budget experience.

The budgetary formula applied in my earlier films was simple. I would hit upon an idea, and then impose strict limitations upon myself before even considering budget. I knew we had to have a villain, a hero, a heroine, perhaps two fallen women, and another kind of villain who is a victim of circumstance. With just a thin outline in mind, we would try to find a location. Then and there, I would know how to build my story. It is like putting the cart before the horse but, instead of getting caught in a story requiring locations in Yuma, Reno or Las Vegas, we could work with what we had at a given place— with a four- or five-man crew operating without outside interference. *Vixen*—a film which has grossed over $10-million—was shot on a six-acre ranch. We lived in the cabin and shot the footage on a creek that rambled through the property. Except for the airport scenes, which we filmed for four days, the entire film was shot within the six-acre location. This is an example of finding a location and making your story fit that location, most successfully.

I was the producer, director, cameraman, camera operator and gaffer. I also cooked, if we were camping out. I had an assistant cameraman who was responsible for loading the magazines, following focus, and hustling the camera around. I handled the exposures and rigged the lights. A lone grip handled the reflectors, and a sound-man rounded out the crew. There were no problems with unions, because I was not a signatory to any agreements. I hired good, journeyman actors and paid them at least scale or above. Once you sign with one union, it begets another. I am not opposed to unions, but if you have only $70,000 to make a film, there is no point in signing with even one local, for what was once $70,000 can become $750,000.

My budgets were kept low through direct economies during production and post-production. I was always conscious of the simple fact that film cost $.14 a foot, and how much it cost to process it. I was aware of cast scheduling. In my situation, for example, we could not afford the luxury of an actor working the first day and not working again until the third week. He still had to be paid every week. In post-production, I did all the cutting with my soundman—who is also my sound-effects cutter—working alongside me. Formerly, I had employed film cutters to cut sequences, but was never completely satisfied with anyone. In *Beyond the Valley of the Dolls* I re-cut the whole picture even though I had two picture editors, and it took three months to recut it. Editing is the most important creative contribution one can make to a film.

Although it is possible to effect savings in nearly every area, laboratory costs must remain a fixed item. Of the total $72,000 budget for *Vixen*, laboratory costs—including the answer print, interpositive, titles, opticals—came to $32,000, which was a large percentage of the total. The picture was made in five or six weeks, and acting budget was not over $5,000, with the crew approximately the same. The balance went for logistics—food, gasoline, car and plane rental. Because most of the crew members were also friends, I paid their overtime off in partial shares of the picture. They got a flat $500 a week and did, in effect, invest their overtime pay in the production. Some of these investors in *Vixen* have received over $20,000 for their overtime in the last year. I've used some of the same people since I began, and we have often had this participation kind of arrangement.

Importantly, I took the time to establish my own distribution representatives around the country—19 local distributors who also handle other independently-produced pictures. I know each and every one of them personally. When I make a picture, I know that at the end of the first week it plays in theatres I'll get a check. I do not wait six months, and that is an advantage that few filmmakers have.

My distribution network is broken down into exchange areas. This system was devised many years ago by the majors in order that no one would try to sell in another person's territory. In distribution, I believe you have to get people who are real shirt-sleeve salesmen. They go out and sell in the sticks, and that is where my films have done so well—in the breadbasket of the country—the midwest, south, and southwest. You can go into Lima, Ohio and come out of a weekend with $3,700 film rental. That same weekend you might go into a theatre in Chicago and get only $300. The reason for the big Lima gross is that it has a big drive-in theatre, and the young adults have little to do but to go to that drive-in. The major distributors play the keys and sub-keys, and then often forget about this lucrative area.

The majors are becoming more aware, however, of these lesser communities. They used to send a film out and get $100 back, with the theatre owner banking $4,000 on Monday morning. The independents have shown the majors the real value of these small communities by going in there with a percentage deal. An independent will not sell you the picture on flat terms, but will ask for as much as a 50% deal, shared advertising, and a sliding scale. *Joe*, released by Cannon, is a good example. (see pp. 196-99) My distributor in Kansas City told me that he finally had a film that everybody wanted—every exhibitor in the area. Happily, *Joe* demanded a "50% floor"—meaning that in the first week, whether the theatre takes in $100 or $5,000, the distributor would get half of what is grossed, and a split of all advertising costs.

To me, it is always reassuring to know there are 19 people out there waiting for a can of film of mine. Any independent can have his can of film, but if he lacks a good distribution set-up he may not be able to do much with it. Perhaps his last quarter is in it, and he has bills and lab charges due. He may then be forced to go to someone who will offer him a $5,000 advance, and a 50/50 split of rental, or even more—a bad deal, created by someone who is taking advantage of a man who has worked hard to make a picture. In the past, many independents accepted it—ending up with a lot of accounting forms and perhaps little money, while the real take went to the exhibitor and to the distributor. The independent may have heard excuses like, "Well, we didn't do too well. It rained." "A lot of opposition." "Walt Disney was here," and all that mumbo-jumbo. Everything but film rental. Having a completed film of good commercial value is hardly enough—an independent filmmaker requires a good reliable distribution facility.

PART SIX

Distribution
and
Exhibition

Whatever the merits of a film, little is accomplished if it does not get seen. It is for this reason that distributors and exhibitors are essential to the existence of the theatrical film industry. They control the delivery system and collect the money which is paid at the box office by the viewing public. If the total of net receipts is large enough, a return on invested capital is assured to all who have participated. No other fact holds much meaning in the film business.

Within the tri-partite division of industry power, the producer relies on the strength of the distributor's sales force and upon the exhibitor's presentation to the public. The distributor, on the other hand, relies on the commercial appeal of the producer's work, on cooperative advertising, and upon an accurate division of box office receipts provided by the exhibitor. The exhibitor, in turn, relies on the drawing power of the producer's picture, on favorable exhibition terms, and on the national advertising and publicity campaign designed by the distributor

The essays in the following section serve to explain this system, with considerable elaboration upon how it works—and where it is faltering. Paul Lazarus *and* Don Carle Gillette *describe some of the strengths and weaknesses of current distribution practices, suggesting that general changes within the industry have not always been incorporated into distributor practices.* Walter Reade, Jr. *and* Dennis Friedland *discuss the origins and practices of their own distribution companies. The services provided by the distributor's sales force are explained by* M. J. E. McCarthy, *and* Benjamin Solomon *outlines the steps by which useful and accurate accounting procedures are developed.*

The final essays in this section are devoted to the work of the exhibitor. Michael Mayer *argues first that there is need for drastic revision of contractual procedures if exhibition agreements are to have any legal meaning to others in the industry. Finally, two leading figures in the exhibition field,* Nat Fellman *and* Stanley Durwood, *offer useful descriptions of contemporary practices and procedures as observed in their respective companies.*

DISTRIBUTION: THE CHANGES TO COME *

PAUL N. LAZARUS
DON CARLE GILLETTE

MR. LAZARUS

Opening Litany

So why pay some cruddy major company 30% of the gross—
all right, maybe you get a deal at 27½%; who says that's such
a bargain when you can practically distribute the picture your-
self? All you need is a phone and a credit card. 70%—that's
what the smartasses say—70% of the domestic gross is in the
first thousand dates. You can wrap those in with a couple
dozen phone calls. You call Nat Fellman, Bernie Myerson, Salah
Hassanein, Larry Lapidus, and you're home free. Who needs a
cruddy high-priced sales manager and a million branches?
We'll do it ourselves. . . .

Let us begin by conceding two given things: first, that there
have been major changes in the distribution system of the motion

---

PAUL N. LAZARUS has served at executive levels in various film advertising
and promotional assignments for nearly four decades—beginning with a
stint at Warner Brothers from 1933 to 1942. He served, successively, with
United Artists, Columbia Pictures Corporation, Samuel Bronstein Productions
and the Landau Company before becoming Executive Vice-President of National Screen Service Corporation in 1965. A Cornell graduate, Mr. Lazarus
has served a great many industry and civic organizations.

DON CARLE GILLETTE has written for and edited amusement industry papers,
general magazines and newspapers for over 50 years. He edited *The Billboard*
in the 1920's when it covered all-around show business, then successively
edited *The Film Daily*, *Radio Daily* and *The Hollywood Reporter*. His articles
have appeared in *Esquire*, *Coronet*, *Barron's Financial Weekly*, Sunday *New
York Times*, and other publications.

* Reprinted from the *Journal* of The Producers Guild of America, December, 1970.

picture industry in the last year or so and, second, that these changes are long overdue and unquestionably for the general good.

The shrinking in the number of branch offices, for example, has been an obvious need since the advent of jet transportation and high-speed roadways. It is difficult to understand how the companies could ever justify the maintenance of four branches within today's commuting distance of New York. But there they sat like the monoliths at Stonehenge—fully-staffed offices in Boston, New Haven, Albany and Philadelphia.

One reason given was that the routes of the film truckers dictated the limits of the areas served. A second argument was: "How can I close an office when my competition stays open? If the other companies would close, we would." After that, the traditional clincher was: "We've always done it that way and it seems to have worked pretty well." None of the arguments stands close examination.

The combining of foreign operations has been an equally obvious move. Until the recent Universal-Paramount amalgamation, however, each company operated in costly but proud independent form throughout the world. "We don't want to mix our product with any other company's," they said. Now, the combining of officers is blessedly becoming the "in" thing for management.

It's about time.

Three other major changes of distribution technique at present in process or impending are not so readily apparent, and yet they probably are more far-reaching in their significance to both producer and to exhibitor.

First, the default of the major companies and the resultant burgeoning growth of the "mini-major" and the independent distributor. To define our terms, the mini-majors are companies like National General, Cinerama, Avco-Embassy and AIP, which have continuing flow of product and have developed a distribution facility with its own network of 10 to 15 branch offices to handle film. The independent distributor is more likely to work on a picture-to-picture basis, distributing through local franchises or "state righters," as they were formerly known. Many of the indepedents are actually just that, moving their prints from city to city, area to area, setting their deals themselves. Their names are New Era, International Film Enterprises, Headliner, Fanfare, Crown International, Cine World and dozens of other world-encompassing examples of cinematic humility.

Midway between these two groups there has recently cropped up a third bustling breed of indies like Cinemation, Cannon and U-M. They have a line-up of films and the energy to make them work. Also five or six branches.

National Screen Service, which handles the distribution of trailers and accessories for distributors in all three categories, says that the bookings of major company trailers in the first six months of 1970 were off by 25% from the previous year. Not surprisingly, the trailer bookings of the mini-majors and independents were up by almost exactly the same percentage.

Second, a revolutionary development in the mystical world of distribution is its recent willingness to admit that some pictures don't have it, can't make it and we'd better forget it, Charlie. David Picker, president of United Artists, is quoted as saying, "It is sometimes pointless to pursue additional bookings beyond a picture's intital engagements—and sometimes unwise to open it at all." Such a statement was heretical and treasonous in other times and other places. "Liquidation" was the password. "Playdate drives" were commonplace; whether the picture played profitably was unimportant. The important thing was to get 'em played even if all concerned went broke in the process. Today, a bomb is a bomb is a bomb.

The sales manager of a major company recently told me, "We don't really try to sell the flat rental situations any more. After the percentage towns are sold—maybe as many as 5,000 bookings on a top film—it doesn't pay us to go after the rest."

Where this leaves the producer and investor does not appear to be distribution's immediate concern. Nor do they appear to be distraught over the plight of the exhibitor in the little town of Resume Speed, Oklahoma, who can't really afford to pay more than $25 flat film rental but is most anxious to pay that to someone.

This development in the area of what the trade calls "tail-end selling," leads us logically into what I believe will be the next major development in distribution.

Third, at any moment the companies will take the plunge into mail-order selling of flat rental accounts and computerized billing and collection of film rental. Say it fast and it sounds easy. Actually, it means the elimination of the motion picture salesman (a vanishing breed) and the complete re-education of the small exhibitor to an order-by-mail-pay-in-advance buyer.

As a matter of fact, the progressive and forward-thinking young sales manager of 20th-Fox, Peter Myers, is already experimenting in one branch with a mail order operation. Two of the bustling young independent organizations, Cannon Films and Maron Films, have announced their affiliations with Cybernetics, a computer film service.

It must come. The distributors must cease competing in noncompetitive areas. The selling, billing and collection of small accounts must be handled with the smallest involvement of manpower and the greatest use of automation to make it a viable operation. The limited number of field sales executives should be used on circuit deals where they can earn their keep rather than in working the less lucrative down-state situations. It means an expensive conversion and a painful dislocation. But it means the future.

Another less basic but equally significant change in distribution: In the halcyon days, attending a national sales meeting combined the best features of a revival meeting, a six-day bike race, a saturnalia and a college reunion. The all-day sessions alternated between being inspirational and somnolent; the all-night activities gave you a simple choice of booze, broads or table-stakes poker. It was not unusual, as an example, for a great sales manager like the late Grad Sears to give a branch manager a substantial raise in salary at the morning session and take the entire next year's increment back across the poker table that night. But the conventions had a character, a color, an effectiveness and a memorability about them.

Today's convention is streamlined, telegraphic, computerized and impersonal. It enables the sales manager to make his pitch just once instead of to each branch manager separately. It enables the company to screen upcoming product and pray that the field force becomes enthused. It enables everyone to attach faces to the names they see on the bottom of countless letters of instruction and complaint. It enables the data processing section to pass out print-outs which tell each manager how bad his performance is. The man in charge of arrangements usually sets up a hospitality suite with one bottle of scotch, one bottle of bourbon and six dozen packs of gin rummy cards. The conventions are sterile, forgettable and dull.

Closing Litany

> Jeez, Max, I can't tell you why they played only 836 dates on your picture. O' course a major company should play more bookings—maybe six, seven, eight thousand. So they quit on it. They gave up. They stink. They should go back to selling Pearl White serials. So what can you do, Max, fight the Establishment? Maybe when you release *Velma's Venereal Victory* we'll handle it ourselves. Or maybe we'll give it to some little distributor who gives you, fuhcrissakes, a chance to live.

MR. GILLETTE

*". . . If cooperatives are practical in film buying, why not
cooperative film distribution?. . . ."*

In the various moves under way to improve the industry's distribution machinery, not much if any attention is being given to a
chronic ailment—one that often means the difference between profit
and loss for a picture.

This has to do with film buying and playdating.

In terms of film rentals, the film buying for about 90% of U.S.
theatres now is done by cooperatives and circuits, and it is a common
complaint of house managers that on countless occasions they do
not receive notice about their bookings, nor are they supplied publicity material and advertising accessories until too late to give the
films proper promotion. So a lot of box-office revenue is lost because a
large percentage of potential customers don't learn about pictures
until after they have come and gone.

Many of the delays are caused by the bidding for films, as required by the government, and the inevitable dickering between
competitive exhibitors for a fair split of the product. Distributors also
can lose substantial income when a film is rejected by a cooperative
buyer who picks product for 100 to 200 or more theatres.

In any event, the situation seems to indicate one thing: Despite
repeated assertions that every film today must be given individual
merchandising, distributors have failed to develop a most obvious essential for the efficient marketing of their releases. Since first-run
houses get the generally well-publicized initial playdates of new pictures while the subsequent runs do not play the films until weeks or
months later, it seems this should allow ample time to set the subsequent dates and get the local campaign started far enough in advance to achieve maximum penetration. So why isn't it done? Why do
even some first-runs complain about late information on their bookings? No satisfactory explanations are obtainable. Theatre managers
can only take what they get when it is presented to them, so there
is more playing-by-ear than long-range procedure in marketing movies.

Economy drives having resulted in the reduction of the number
of release prints for each film, more time now will elapse between the
first-run showings and all subsequent runs or return bookings. This
should allow plenty of time to set and promote these dates if theatres
get the information and promotional materials they need in time.

Cooperative Distribution

If cooperatives are practical in film buying, why not cooperative film distribution? That's a question being asked in some distribution quarters. In the marketing of food and merchandise of many

kinds there are jobbers who handle the output of different standard brands. Centralized receiving film warehouses, servicing retailers in their respective areas, have proved serviceable for decades, particularly in supplying small accounts on which film companies usually lose money. Perhaps the same system would work in film distribution.

Movies are a product like any other manufactured article. They require individual salesmanship and showmanship, of course, and can keep getting them—and even more of the same—with the physical distribution handled by one set of centralized exchanges serving all producers, just as jobbers handle the refrigerators, TV sets, kitchenware, toys or what-have-you of six or a dozen different factories.

It's about time the men who set policies for the film business started practicing what they preach. They keep saying every picture must be sold individually, yet a large percentage of films receive only token advertising and promotion. Full-blown campaigns are given to only a few high-budget pictures. So a lot of attractions come to theatres as totally unknown quantities. House managers have neither the data nor the enthusiasm to exploit them to their patrons.

For the past dozen years, American companies—major and independents alike—have released a combined average of little more than 450 films annually, and the indications are that this average will not be changed much at the end of this year. To handle these 450 features in the U. S. there were, until recent months, 180 major and independent distributors with an aggregate of 492 films exchanges listed in a total of 47 cities. That averages out at less than three films per distributor. There also are 74 film exchanges in seven Canadian cities and 380 non-theatrical film distributors in the U. S.

It may not be fair to bunch all these distributors and exchanges without a lot of explanations and a separation of the majors from the independents, but the simple enormity of the present machinery in relation to the amount of product handled certainly suggests that the facilities could be compressed into fewer branches which would result in substantial savings, some of which could be utilized in promotion to increase attendance. Perhaps a setup such as the one operated by the Clark physical distribution service, which has branches in several cities, could be developed on a national scale. There could be separate units for the majors and the independents, and even one to handle imported films.

Fundamental Problems

Current drives by major distributors to reduce the number of branch offices from 30 or more to 20 or less, eliminating a lot of salesmen, dividing the territory into fewer divisions, computerizing and centralizing accounting systems and so forth, may bring some benefits, but there still remain some fundamental problems which will multiply with the increase in smaller theatres designed to draw special audiences to their respective types of films. Among these problems are: (1) getting playdate notices and promotional materials to theatre managers earlier; (2) giving a good campaign to every release, instead of only the hopeful blockbusters and kicking aside pictures merely because they don't please the New York critics or aren't a box-office sensation in a few isolated test-runs; (3) supplying exhibitors with an even flow of good product instead of holding back top attractions for holiday periods; (4) maintaining an adequate force of field men for the multiple purpose of exploiting current playdates, stirring up enthusiasm of theatre managers in coming attractions, promoting general public relations, and making realistic audience research reports; and (5) releasing films as soon as possible after completion, not only to save interest charges on inventories but also to get pictures out while the publicity generated during production is still alive.

Archaic Advertising

Since advertising of films is among the functions of the distribution department, it may not be out of order to say something about the shortage of ingenuity in ads designed to sell pictures to the public as well as to exhibitors. Film advertising seems to have become a lost art, and this probably accounts in part for the lack of exhibitor enthusiasm over coming product. Gunplay, violence and sex continue to be the main themes in press and TV advertising of films. This is particularly true of the TV spots, which are so crammed with physical violence, shooting, brutality, killing, destruction, ugly faces and other unpleasant matter, that viewers are left dizzy, horrified and bewildered —enough so to frighten them away from such films.

More ingenuity and finesse are needed in the creation of ads that will stir up "want-to-see" among today's sophisticated movie fans. Injection of mystery and a provocative teaser would seem preferable to archaic gimmicks and scaring people with blasts of brutality.

Mini-Theatre Trend

The mini-theatre and twin-theatre trend is another factor in favor of more compact and centralized distribution facilities, to make it easier for exhibitors to shop for the particular types of films for their clienteles. With smaller cinemas—some seating as few as 200 and others up to 400 and 500—there will be more catering to special audiences, and this not only calls for special product appealing to the different groups but also will require promotion designed to reach these particular fans. Again, it will be imperative for theatre managers to know about their bookings well in advance of opening dates.

Films produced in or by foreign countries—which in the past

decade have accounted for 65% or more of the annual releases in the
U. S.—will continue to dominate the schedules of both major companies and independents, according to all present signs. Of the 185
films that went before the cameras in the first eight months of 1970
under the banners of American companies, some 95 were on foreign
locations. This does not include films made by foreign producers that
eventually will be released in the U. S.

Except for the notorious sex films that receive a lot of sensational publicity, few imported movies are able to make much money
over here because of the high marketing costs facing distributors of
a very small number of pictures. Every season there are about 30
companies that distribute no more than two or three foreign films
each—and at least a dozen distributors with a single release. So
here once more is a situation that could benefit from a cooperative
setup for the handling of product.

Because of unstable political regimes that can affect film imports,
exports, taxes, censorship, co-production and other matters, the foreign
distribution offices of American companies have had to maintain a
flexible position at all times. The Motion Picture Export Association
of America always has kept a close watch on the overall situation
and has done a generally good trouble-shooting job. On the economic
level, a few American distributors have found it advantageous to
combine their offices in some countries, and also to take over the
distribution of native productions. This has enabled most U. S. firms
to avoid burdensome overheads in their foreign departments.

Industry Round Table

Since product is the lifeblood of the industry—and since supply
usually follows demand—the burgeoning of smaller cinemas in the
U. S., Great Britain and other countries eventually should bring
about a flow of films suitable for these houses. This process could
be hastened if the distributors—now that they are again holding
more national sales conventions—would invite some representative
filmmakers and exhibitors to participate in at least one good round-
table discussion at every sales meeting.

The different branches of the industry never seem to have been
able to establish regular communication with each other in order
to develop guidelines and implement procedures that will lead to
mutual prosperity through a better understanding of public tastes
in entertainment. This is a sad commentary on the industry's leadership. Playing it by ear does not promote stability. And it's about
time this industry stopped carrying on internecine strife, taking
potshots at each other and providing its enemies with ammunition
to downgrade movies in the eyes of the world.

THE DISTRIBUTORS:
A SOUND OF DIFFERENT DRUMMERS

WALTER READE, JR.
DENNIS FRIEDLAND

MR. READE — *The Walter Reade Organization*

". . . So we made our first investment on a lease of a small second-run unit and started to get property around the key area of 59th Street and Third Avenue. The rest is history. . . ."

The Walter Reade Organization is structured as a totally integrated communications organization. At this stage we are not distributors/producers of feature films in the commercial market, but are still acquiring feature films for our 16mm division, *Walter Reade*

WALTER READE, JR. is President and Board Chairman of the Walter Reade Organization, Inc., a dynamic force in motion picture production, distribution and exhibition. The company he built can exhibit films in nearly 80 theatres, and also has developed a major 16mm distribution division, *Walter Reade 16,* and an educational film and film-strip distribution unit, Sterling Educational Films. Mr. Reade is past president of the Theatre Owners of America.

DENNIS FRIEDLAND is the Chairman of the Board and founder of The Cannon Group, Inc. He graduated *cum laude* from Harvard University, and from Columbia University Law School with a J.D. During his last term at law school he conceived of an entertainment corporation specializing in the production and distribution of motion pictures. The Cannon Group was incorporated for that purpose in August, 1967.

'hich sells to colleges, schools, churches and similar organiza-
We are still producing for our educational branch, the Sterling
ltional Division, where we now have over 500 titles.

Our company was originally among the leaders in distribution
of foreign films to the United States. Shortly after World War II,
we carved a niche for ourselves in foreign distribution because the
majors were not then in that business. Our record included such
films as those of Jacques Tati, English comedies from the Rank
Organisation, our own *Room At The Top*, and more recently *Ulysses*.
We created a formula which worked with *Room At The Top*, a wholly
British-made film. We invested 25% to 50% of the total budget, for
which we took a similar equity position in the negative. For example,
let us say the film cost about $900,000 and we invested about 30%
or $300,000. In addition to that, we took Western Hemisphere distribu-
tion rights at an agreed figure of around 35%. After all investors
recovered investments, we shared profits in the world in direct proportion to our equity investment. That formula kept changing as we
received more competition from the majors, and more recently has
resulted in a 50% investment, which is the formula generally used
today.

Lord of The Flies is an example of a film that ran the gamut.
It was produced by an American-English group in the Bahamas, and
we invested in the film's distribution. We put it in general release
in 35mm through our then-Continental Distributing Division in our
own theatres and theatres throughout the country. It was quite
successful, and we then sold it to television through our TV distribution organization. Simultaneously with the sale to television, we released it through *Walter Reade 16*, where it has been one of the top
titles in colleges. The release date for TV and educational distribution
is after the film exhausts itself in commercial theatres. Because of
the classic penetration of the book, *Lord of The Flies* is still being
shown commercially in theatres.

Sterling Educational Division functions primarily for secondary
schools, some grammar schools and colleges. Demand for our product
is at the high school level—public and private—and in most states.
These states operate on a tight, well-managed budget and that part
of state funds for education which filters down into the school systems
is augmented by national funds from Washington. Each year, for
example, the state of California sets aside so many millions to buy
films for the various school systems. There has to be a marriage
between the curriculum and the amount of money made available to
buy films for the schools. It is at that level that we begin to negotiate
in order to determine what the demand for a certain series of films

—rather than an individual title—might be. One of our most successful series at this time is on sex education, covering levels from grammar school through to college. Not every school system will buy the total series, of course. One may want it only at the grammar school level and another only at the high school level.

Once a series of films goes into production, we know there is a market for it. Whether it will be a large enough market to warrant our total investment can be difficult to project, but we are assured of at least a nucleus of interest before entering production. While we do operate on speculation, it is rather modest compared to the overall speculation of creating a feature film. The average educational film will probably not be more than seven or eight minutes long, and may be part of a series of films which may run for a total of only an hour. The individual parts of the series would be used daily in the classroom, scattered throughout the whole curriculum.

Our educational distribution is done primarily by direct call on the school system and through mailing pieces. Above all, we have a very substantial catalogue, distributed by mail, with ordering done by return mail.

Each division of the Walter Reade Organization operates on a very carefully planned annual budget. The head of Sterling Educational submits a budget for approval which projects anticipated profits on new investments during the coming year and beyond. Production money spent in 1972 will not get into release until 1973, and then three years of amortization must be allowed—years in which no income other than just modest distribution profits are expected. The management group must also be apprised of additional areas of income which might be realized from films—particularly the potentials in adaptation to tapes, discs or cassettes. Finally, the foreign market should be estimated.

While these general projections are mandatory, we must recognize that it is difficult to suggest the cost of a film series. Generally, every ten minutes of educational film involves actual production costs somewhere in the $10,000 range. This is a very rough rule of thumb.

The educational film field is burgeoning, and is still in its infancy. It is always going to be a business where, like textbook publishing, one can minimize one's loss and look forward to modest profits. There is no big return on invested capital as one could find in the feature film market. The risk, however, is minimal as compared to feature production.*

In exhibition, our nucleus is northern New Jersey and New York City. Historically, the exhibition business always had its "haves" and "have nots." The "haves" were those exhibitors like ourselves,

* For a discussion of the "industrial" or "sponsored" film business, see Appendix I.

who had a territory—northern New Jersey in our case—where we were the boss. After the consent decree the independents, who were the "have nots," began to build. We determined that we wanted to be in the downtown urban areas of the United States—territories that were hard to penetrate and easier to protect. That is where we have made our investment, and in recent years some of our most substantial profits. We are partially responsible, for example, for the growth of Third Avenue on the east side of New York City. I had thought that Third Avenue would be the most logical place for business to spread, and knew that the El would ultimately come down. So we made our first investment in a lease of a small second-run unit and started to get property around the key area of 59th Street and Third Avenue. The rest is history.

In our first-run houses we operate under what is known as the "90/10 deal," which exists primarily in New York City and one or two other major markets in the United States. In this 90/10 situation—where the distributor is having to support or launch his film—the advertising expense is so large that it can not properly be allocated to an engagement in one or more houses. It means that all profits above house expenses are divide 90% to the distributor and 10% to the exhibitor. It is accepted practice in the industry, however, that the exhibitor does have some built-in profit in the overhead. Conventional deals exist in virtually all of our other theatres—where the division is between 35% and 60%, depending upon the attraction and number of weeks. We hope to re-negotiate with the distributor if the run is not successful.

MR. FRIEDLAND — *The Cannon Group*

> "... *It's probably the only industry in the world where a contract just gives you the right to argue.* ..."

The Cannon Group was begun by Chris Dewey and me, and at the beginning we were less interested in attempting any very ambitious project than in simply selling ourselves as people who could analyze a market and make a commercially successful picture. The first picture we made was a Swedish exploitation movie called *Inga*. In analyzing its chances we spent a great deal of time on New York City's 42nd Street and in some of the art houses looking at films like *I, A Woman* and others that were playing at the time. Luckily, *Inga* was a success both for its backers and for the company. We were not committed to exploitation, of course, although some good talent comes out of that market and a great deal can be learned about making low-budget films from being involved in an exploitation movie. But that is how we started the company. By financing—from outside sources—a number of pictures of this type we gained a modicum of success, and with that leverage we went on to more ambitious films.

Our financing came primarily from friends at first and then from anybody we met who wanted to take a $1,000 flier in a partnership that was going to produce a movie. As the company got bigger, we began to think that some cheap stock might serve as the equity kicker to a production fund. This would preserve the principle that the company would be earning producers' fees by making movies, the cost for some of which would equal our overhead in a given year, and that the company would never have money in the riskiest aspect of the film business—the production cost itself. This way, we could use a little bit of our stock as the equity kicker to a fund for the purpose of producing low-budget films. When we hit upon this method of financing, we found interested parties from some of the finest Wall Street brokerage houses, and that's where our principal financing still comes from.

A distribution company is successful for three reasons. First, there is a first-rate sales force—namely the general sales manager and the key salesmen. They are motivated by high pay. Next, the company must have reasonable assurance of some flow of product, which serves two purposes: first, it enables the company to project income to cover sales overhead; and second, it gives the company additional credibility in the marketplace if exhibitors can expect a fair number of films each year. This can help any distributor when he is dealing on something other than a smash winner. Finally, the third and probably most important element in successful distribution is to have the odds with you. If you can have a winner every now and then you have some security.

We started our company in the same way every independent begins distributing—by doing business with local sales representatives who work on a percentage. They are called sub-distributors, "states-righters," or franchise holders in the industry. It is a difficult way to go, because these people handle product from competing companies, and the more successful of them have made film investments themselves. Some of them own films for their own territory, so they are never pushing your product as much as they could. It is more likely that they are looking for a quick dollar. But it is still the only way to get started without a seven-figure bankroll behind you. Film companies that have started with a lot of money have lost it by setting up a sales force before they had the product to occupy it. We have chosen to stick with the sub-distributors until we have a considerably larger and more successful inventory than most independents have had in the past.

Our attempts to insure collection and a fair count have taken a form which is a bit different from what most independents have done. Although we have remained with sub-distributors, we deal and collect our money from the home office, and we submit our permissions to the sub-distributor from there. A computer service provides us with billing information on a weekly basis. We hold sub-distributors' commissions, which are remitted monthly, in order to give them some incentive to follow instructions from the home office.

Cannon has staked its reputation and committed itself to making relatively low-budget films. You have to *want* to make a commercially successful, quality, low-budget film. In your search for properties and for talent, you have to be conscious of the need and excited by the challenge of bringing in a quality movie for a price. You do not make low-budget films by taking a script someone else budgeted and cutting the numbers in half. Then you make a lousy movie. Films that have messages, redeeming social value, and are commercial can be done extremely well, with no compromises, for $300,000 to $400,000 tops.

Like all companies, we spend a lot of time and money looking for properties. We are constantly discussing story ideas and scripts. My personal feeling is that the best way to find a script for a low-budget film is to look for original ideas and treatments that can be developed under the supervision of a story editor and the production managers so they can be budgeted almost as they are. We go through a number of formal and technical procedures in budget control before and during production. All our staff get weekly and daily production reports and revised production budgets for each picture. It is not an easy thing to ask your director to listen patiently while you review the problems of running over budget. Yet you must work with him —and the screenwriter—in eliminating or consolidating scenes during the shooting of the picture in such a way that no impact will be lost. If you want your picture back on schedule and on budget it must be done.

The terms under which we distribute pictures we produce are part of the investor's agreement. When the financing is arranged, the terms of distribution are set forth in the agreement. People who have been in the industry for a time know the effect of cooperative advertising. They have some idea of the cost of prints and how many prints are needed on a successful picture; they know whether these recoveries come off the top or off somebody else's side; and they know what percentage of the take they will end up with regardless of the formula. That is why so many distribution deals are made with independent producers in which they do not stand a chance no matter how successful their film is going to be. The deals that one should get from an exhibitor—90/10 over a house nut, a sliding scale, 90/10 with a floor, or something even more imaginative—really just depend on your bargaining power. If you have a winner, you will want one deal; if you have a loser, you will be happy to get the date. Regardless of what the initial terms are, everything is subject to settlement, readjustment and negotiation. It is probably the only industry in the world where a contract just gives you the right to argue.

Exhibitors like to know the distributor had enough confidence in his film to spend the money it takes to open in New York City. We spent around $60,000 the week we first opened *Joe*, and between our first run and our flagship dates in New York on *Joe*, we spent almost $300,000 in advertising. If you do not believe in your film, you have no business opening in New York City.

Cannon is in the happy position of being a growing, successful company in a time when many other companies are having difficulties. Until recently, I believe, there has been a fundamental absence of sound business thinking—of the elimination of ego—in motion pictures generally. Huge amounts of money are involved in making small efforts. An advertising campaign, for example, may cost from $5,000 to $10,000. If you decide you do not like it and want to change it, that will cost an additional $5,000 to $10,000, and you may not like it then. The size of the numbers you deal with in this business can be frightening. The cost of one film, which is just one shot to a film company, is all the capital needed to go into a great many other businesses. In movies, the risks are very high. The problem is that you get involved in the huge costs in sales, distribution, advertising, production. In order to exploit the rights that you have created you need a vast overhead and sometimes these things get out of balance. It is almost like running a supermarket, where the profit margins are pretty slim if you just consider return on capital. If more people were aware of that in this business, the difference between success and failure would lie in running a movie company the way you have to run a supermarket—just to break even.

DISTRIBUTION: THE SALESMAN'S ROLE

M. J. E. McCARTHY

". . . A motion picture is the only commodity that does not carry an established price tag. . . ."

The Avco Embassy sales organization is constituted of 13 branches—called exchanges—and a number of smaller sub-branches. The Boston main branch, for example, operates a Buffalo sub-branch. Kansas City operates in the same fashion, with the branch manager in St. Louis taking care of both territories. The Los Angeles market includes salesmen who cover Denver and Salt Lake City. San Francisco also covers the Portland and Seattle territories, with the branch manager of San Francisco being the only representative covering those two areas in the northwest. The entire organization is under the direction of the general sales manager, who is also a vice-president, based in New York. Three division managers function as assistants to him.

The initial information covering any picture to be made by the company is provided in press notices announcing the purchase of a propetry. This usually occurs 18 months to two years in advance

M. J. E. McCARTHY entered motion picture distribution with Pathé Exchange in June, 1923 in Butte, Montana. He migrated to Los Angeles in 1925 and served in a variety of positions with Pathé, Tiffany, Columbia, Gaumont British, Educational, Fox and Republic before becoming a branch manager of Monogram-Allied Artists in 1948. He joined Embassy Pictures as assistant to Duke Douglyn in May, 1965.

of actual release date of the picture. The sales department advises the men in the field by way of inter-office memos and general press hand-outs regarding the progress of the picture. Stories covered include casting, production dates, and finally, the fact that the film is completed and has been screened by home office executives. Around two months after that, the first release prints are sent to the various branches, and screenings are set up for the press, exhibitors and, of course, exchange personnel. Prior to screening we are usually advised of the company's appraisal of the value of the picture.

If the home office advises us after their screening that this picture requires special handling, we are instructed to find a market for it in the most productive theatre in our exchange area. In Los Angeles, for example, we look to placing it in a top theatre in Westwood or an exclusive house in Hollywood. The exhibitors generally are aware of the product, since part of their job is to gain some knowledge of the value of pictures being released by Avco Embassy and all other companies.

After screening the picture for all important exhibitors in our area, we hold follow-up discussions with those who indicate the greater amount of interest or those who represent the houses we want most to play this particular picture. The negotiation can take place quite rapidly—assuming a set of acceptable terms. Usually, a sales policy stipulating the basis on which the film is to be sold is set forth by our general sales manager. We then negotiate acceptance of those terms with the interested exhibitor. The various terms relate to: (1) guaranteed film rental to the distributor; (2) the length of the engagement; and (3) the minimum terms for each particular week. These terms are usually on a descending scale of minimums in anticipation of a lower return in each succeeding week as the picture goes through its run. The advertising is agreed upon and a date for the opening of the picture is set. All of these items are then incorporated into a standard exhibition contract, and all of the negotiations take final shape in this document. The signed contract is then forwarded to our New York office. Once the general sales manager places his stamp of approval on it, a copy is returned to the exhibitor and the contract becomes binding.

The rental of a motion picture involves so many considerations and ramifications that it cannot carry a fixed price tag. Each individual sale of a picture is usually conducted through the barter system, with the exhibitor trying to secure the lowest possible terms consistent with his particular operation. The distributor's representative, on the other hand—the salesman—seeks to make the most lucrative deal for the company commensurate with extensive production-distribution and advertising costs.

In reviewing some of the specifics of the contract, let us assume a multiple-release in Los Angeles. In this case, terms for a picture are invariably identical for each theatre in the engagement. The overall amount of advertising is agreed upon with our home office, and the distributor usually absorbs 50% of the cost of the ad campaign. The remaining 50% is equally divided among the theatres participating in the engagement. If 20 theatres participate and the campaign cost is $15,000, the distributor would pay $7,500 and each of the theatres would pay 5% of the remaining $7,500, or $375.

With a tremendously important picture such as *The Graduate*, *M*A*S*H**, or *The Lion in Winter*, the distributor establishes minimum terms acceptable on a competitive bid. It cannot, however, be an auction bid. The bids that are received by the stipulated deadline are evaluated and a picture is simply awarded to the "best bid by the numbers." The distributor is, however, entitled to evaluate the variances in the potential grosses of the theatres involved, and decide —if he wishes—that an ostensibly low bid will result in greater returns than a better-looking "numbers" bid. For example, a 400-seat house may offer $10,000 as a guarantee on the film, and certain favorable terms. A theatre with 1,200 seats, on the other hand, may offer no front money, but might produce greater revenue at the same percentage terms because of its capacity. In this case the distributor will analyze his accumulated records of average weekly grosses before making a decision. The general sales manager is the final authority in awarding bids in any given area, and he receives a copy of every invitation to bid that goes out to the trade, regardless of quality or importance of the picture.

Following initial runs and some subsequent runs on percentage, subsequent terms are eventually flat. The salesman gets the best flat rental terms he can secure for the distributor, who lets the picture play as a supporting feature. The days when an exhibitor bought a second feature outright because it was cheaper are coming to an end. The exhibitor's aim is always to have two block-busters on every program.

Let me now review various details of operations in which the sales office involves itself. Once a date is set, delivery of the actual print to the theatre is a very simple matter. In Los Angeles, our shipping is handled by the Gilboy Film Company, and we maintain an inventory of prints at their film depot. The distributor's responsibility for delivery is discharged when the print is labeled for the theatre at our film depot in time for shipment, usually by truck, to the theatre involved. The trucker is an agent of the theatre, and the exhibitor is responsible for the safety of the film in transit, at the theatre, and on the return trip to the depot. The exhibitor has his own contract with the trucking company.

The physical advertising material—mattes, trailers, one-sheets, three-sheets, six-sheets, and other exploitation material—is handled by National Screen Service Corporation (see pp. 234-36). They have a national contract with all major distributors, in which they agree to stock adequate supplies of these items in their branches so that they can service the exhibitor with the material he needs to dress up his theatre front and place newspaper ads, and otherwise exploit an attraction.

When a theatre runs a percentage picture, the exhibitor fills in a form, supplied by us, which lists each day's grosses. Ticket numbers for each admission price are entered, and the box-office statement has to agree with the number of tickets known as being issued during the engagement on a daily basis. A high level of stealing on percentage engagements is suspected throughout the industry today —especially since theatres are no longer obligated to report ticket sales to the federal government. Further, checking box-office grosses is a hit-or-miss operation because of the expense of employing professional checkers. It is very difficult to check a theatre for a week at a cost less than $200.

A frequent problem for us is inconsistency between contract terms and actual theatre gross. A daily box-office receipt from a theatre in our area, for example, shows a gross of $1,267.75 on a given picture for a week. In this case, the film was sold at 50% of the gross receipts, and the gross for that theatre simply did not warrant those terms. Our job then is to work out a reasonable adjustment of terms with the exhibitor. The clerical department then reduces the box-office statement to an actual billing. The invoice is based on the box-office figures, reflecting the adjusted terms, and is mailed to the exhibitor, and—theoretically—he immediately mails us a check.

In sum, an important job of any exchange—any film distribution office—ostensibly is to obtain money for the film and services. Actually, however, our most important function is to secure the maximum number of playdates for each picture the company places in our hands for distribution. The amount of sales effort required to handle a picture decreases in direct proportion to the value and importance of the picture. Conversely, when the picture is devoid of apparent value, the amount of sales effort going into it rises. For a film like *The Graduate* or *The Lion in Winter*, the exchange is beset with paper-work, and when a picture doesn't move, the paperwork becomes negligible. The single greatest problem for a salesman is to move a picture that has no great box-office value. Yet competent sales people who know the trade are able to help their companies realize—if not a profit—at least the greatest possible income from film rentals which can be obtained under the circumstances. Despite opinions to the contrary expressed by top echelon people in the industry in recent years, the enterprising and resourceful film salesman can be the difference between profit and loss in the handling of motion pictures of marginal quality.

DISTRIBUTION: THE ACCOUNTANT'S ROLE*

BENJAMIN W. SOLOMON

". . . It would be advisable to have a provision specifying which books and records may be examined. . . ."

Agreement over methods of accounting between producer and distributor is perhaps one of the most important aspects of their business relationship—one with which both sides might well be familiar. Some of the more important ways in which agreement is achieved—or broken—are detailed below.

With reference first to double bills—where two pictures are sold as a package for one price or one percentage of the box-office receipts—the producer should have a voice as to method of allocation. The gross receipts of any outside picture should be made available to the producer so that he or his representative may be in a position to determine the fairness of the allocation. In one case where this was provided for in the contract, another provision in the same contract actually gave the distributor the right to make the allocations at his own discretion.

In the matter of foreign gross receipts the following informa-

---

BENJAMIN W. SOLOMON, a Certified Public Accountant, is senior partner in the accounting firm of Solomon & Finger, specializing in motion picture and television auditing. His article here is a condensation of a talk given by Mr. Solomon at the invitation of the Beverly Hills Bar Association to a symposium on Entertainment Law conducted by the University of Southern California School of Law.

* Reprinted from the *Journal* of The Producers Guild of America, September, 1968.

tion may be useful to the producer whose participation is determined by a percentage of these receipts. First of all, in order to prevent the participant from claiming his commission on any foreign receipts that may be blocked or frozen, gross receipts are frequently defined as "the actual United States dollars received in the United States." The distributor never gets the full foreign gross receipts in dollars in the United States—even though the currency in any given country may be entirely free—because there is a distribution fee allowed to the foreign subsidiary to cover the expenses of operation. Situations have been found where the distributor interpreted this clause to mean that in accounting to the producer only the net amounts received from abroad were included in the gross receipts. Sometimes even costs of prints, advertising and other items—as well as the distribution fees charged by the distributor's own subsidiary—were also deducted.

Therefore, if it is the intent of the parties that the producer receive his percentage on the full gross receipts, such intent should be clearly stipulated. Further, in the case of net monies received from the liquidation of blocked currency, such monies should be translated to their equivalent in gross receipts. For example, the receipt of $5,000 from the liquidation of currency previously blocked may represent the "de-blocking" of $10,000 in foreign gross receipts.

Another area in which accord must be sought is in handling income from television, which has grown tremendously in recent years. Sales to networks run as high as $2-million for a single picture, and in many cases a distributor will sell a large number of pictures for a lump-sum price, a transaction which poses a problem of allocation. Sometimes the total is divided equally among all the features, although any large group must contain a number of inferior pictures. It should be stipulated that the distributor make available to the producer, his representative, or auditor all the data necessary to determine the fairness of the allocation. A distribution fee of 10% is adequate for a network sale, 25% for syndication sales.

Satisfactory agreement should also be established in provisions for participation in miscellaneous sources of revenue, such as music royalties, income from merchandising, 16mm non-theatrical rights, soundtrack recordings, radio, serialization and book rights—usually pocket books. The distribution fee for this type of revenue generally is 10% of the net revenue derived. Where a distributor owns or controls the music company, the participant should receive 50% of the *gross* revenue without any further charge for distribution.

Where expenses of distribution are concerned, some contracts will provide that certain charges be deducted "off-the-top," which means that the gross receipts will be reduced by the amount of such charges before the distribution fees are applied.

Cooperative advertising is another important area where mutual understanding of accounting procedure is essential. It is a project entered into jointly by the distributor and the exhibitor. The arrangement usually provides for advertising the picture to an extent greater than the theatre's usual expenditure, and inasmuch as it is expected that the advertising will result in mutual benefit, agreement is made whereby the two parties share in the additional cost. The exhibitor is generally permitted to deduct the distributor's portion of the cost of cooperative advertising. In more recent years producers have seldom received the benefit of an arrangement, which, in effect, provides that the distribution fee be charged on the net film rental rather than on the amount realized before the deduction. In permitting the distributor to take this deduction entirely from the producer's share, inequities often result. In some engagements, the distributor will collect a substantial distribution fee while the producer's share sustains a loss after absorbing the full advertising cost. Where a producer must allow this deduction entirely against his share, the amount so chargeable should be limited in the contract. Should the parties decide to go above that, at least the additional costs should be off-the-top.

Foreign taxes should be carefully considered. A number of producers do not avail themselves of the privilege which permits them to take—as full credit against their United States income taxes—amounts paid to a foreign country as income taxes. The United States Internal Revenue Department has given a very liberal interpretation to the types of taxes that may be taken as a full credit. Where such privilege is exercised by a corporation, for example, it means that instead of taking the amounts charged as foreign taxes as a deduction and saving approximately 48% thereof, the taxpayer instead received a 100% credit against its United States income tax. There is a limitation to this privilege, the intent of which is to disallow any portion of foreign taxes arising by virtue of the fact that the rate of tax may be higher in any given country than it is in the United States.

The producer should be credited with all discounts and rebates which are taken by the distributor in paying bills for the producer's account. Inasmuch as distribution contracts generally provide that the distributor recoup his advances, it would appear that only the actual amount advanced would be taken into consideration. This is resisted by the distributor on an audit, and it is often a losing battle for the producer. Therefore, it is advisable specifically to provide for this in the contract.

Some producers have permitted a clause which gives the distributor the right to approve the producer's auditor—a surprising generosity that is not at all necessary. Any reputable certified public accountant should be acceptable, and this should be provided for in the distribution contract. Such a provision does exist in many contracts.

The distribution contract should provide that during the first 18 months of the release of a picture the report should be issued monthly—this usually means on the basis of a four-or-five-week period. After the first 18 months, quarterly statements should be adequate. If after 18 months substantial monies are still being realized, a distributor will often agree to continue monthly reports to enable a producer to get his share of these monies more often than once every three months. There often is a limitation as to how far back an audit may go. This period should be no less than two years back from the period covered by the last report issued by the distributor.

The reports should be on a country-by-country basis and all income and expenses definitely should be segregated on this basis. Auditors are usually permitted to examine all reports and accountings submitted to the home office by sub-licensees and subsidiary companies, but it would, nevertheless, be advisable to provide for this in the distribution agreement. It is also advisable to have a provision which permits the auditor to interview officers and employees in connection with all such reports submitted, and to have the right to request that the home office obtain, where necessary, further details or breakdowns of these reports. It is important that box-office returns from key situations in foreign as well as domestic territories be obtained for examination by the producer or his auditor. The question of double-feature allocations in foreign territories is of great importance. Sometimes, a foreign manager will not assess the value of two pictures and arbitrarily allocate the revenue on a basis of 50% to each. This is most unfair where the producer's picture is the big percentage picture.

The reports should indicate which expense items, if any, were charged but not actually paid. This is important because sometimes the liability is settled for less than the amount deducted and sometimes even cancelled altogether. Full details of all blocked currencies should also be a part of the reports submitted by the distributor, indicating the producer's share of such blocked currencies in each foreign territory.

In writing off bad debts, a distributor will often treat the amount of such bad debts as a distribution expense. It is advisable to provide contractually that all bad debts should be written off by reducing the gross receipts; otherwise, the distributor obtains a distribution fee on revenue which was never realized.

In the general matter of accounting on percentage deals, both the producer and his representative or auditor should be permitted to examine all exhibition contracts. This enables them to determine if collection was made on the basis of the original sale. In cases where errors have been discovered, the distributor as well as the producer has benefitted from the correction of these errors. Indeed, where the negative cost of the picture had not yet been recouped, the distributor has received the entire benefit of such additional income. In many cases, however, the failure to collect according to the contract terms is not the result of a mistake in billing, but of a picture's failure to realize the box-office gross which would entitle the distributor to be paid on those terms.

Strictly speaking, all such contract terms can be enforced. Such enforcement might cause the exhibitor to lose on the engagement and—if it became a universal practice—might even put him out of business. The distributors, therefore, have all taken into consideration the amount of business done and have made adjustments. An important producer might obtain a provision requiring that the distributor insist on collecting on the basis of the original contract terms. In such an event, there would be situations where the distributor would have to make up the difference out of his own pocket because he would not desire to antagonize a good customer. Realizing this, the picture might be sold on lower terms than might otherwise be obtainable. An exhibitor will seldom pay on the basis of higher terms than provided for in the contract, although he will insist on an adjustment where the business does not warrant the original terms.

Finally, it would be advisable to have a provision specifying which books and records may be examined. Instances exist where the distributor has not permitted an examination of cash records and the general ledger, yet these records are most important. The books and records made available to an auditor should include:

(1) *All* exhibition contracts.

(2) All theatre box-office reports.

(3) Shipping sheets.

(4) The gross receipts of pictures sharing a double-bill with the picture.

(5) All bills, vouchers, and cancelled checks for charges made against the picture.

(6) Original reports from subsidiaries and licensees.

(7) All documents pertaining to the transfer of foreign currency—for purposes of verifying the rate of exchange used in conversion to U. S. dollars.

(8) All books and records pertaining to the business of the motion picture, including but not limited to the general ledger and cash receipts and disbursements.

(9) All contracts with advertising agencies and distributors of trailers.

(10) Contracts for merchandise tie-ins, music and records in connection with the film.

THE EXHIBITION CONTRACT—
A SCRAP OF PAPER *

MICHAEL F. MAYER

". . . The 'standard' exhibition contract . . . has become little more than a snare and a delusion. . . ."

Producers have a very distinct interest in the terms of the exhibition contract under which their films are licensed by distributors to theatrical customers. They may well want to know how or where their picture is promoted. They may be concerned with its advertising. They may feel the need of a proper showcase for their efforts. Most of all, they may be involved with the financial returns of their film, for they may have a participation in a share of the ultimate net or gross proceeds.

This report will not serve to make such producers happy. For the "standard" exhibition contract in this respect has become little more than a snare and a delusion. In fact, it is a high compliment to call this piece of paper a contract. In brief, as presently construed, it does not bind both sides. It is more in the nature of a one-way

MICHAEL F. MAYER—a partner in Mayer and Bucher, theatrical attorneys— has been attorney, teacher and author practicing in the entertainment field for a quarter-century. From 1959 to 1968 he was Executive Director of the International Film Importers and Distributors of America, Inc. Mr. Mayer published *Foreign Film on American Screens* in 1965, and *What You Should Know About Libel and Slander* in 1968.

* Reprinted from the *Journal* of The Producers Guild of America, September, 1969.

license to exhibit a film or films without any equivalent commitment to pay a definitive sum by the theatrical user.

While the film license covers a multitude of terms, including clearances, advertising, taxes and all the other fine print clauses, its key provisions are in the matter of film rental, i. e., monies paid during or at the end of an engagement. These are the essentials of any proposed deal. In the vast bulk of important engagements across the country, film rental is determined on a percentage-of-gross basis. It may be 30% to 70% of the total gross or even more; it may range on a sliding scale from smaller to greater figures, or it may apply only after a deductible amount for "house" and other expenses. In some instances there is a cash guaranty as against the percentage payable. In any event, the arrangement is relatively elastic in character, with rental usually related to the drawing power of the film in question.

One would think that this flexible formula, arrived at after bargaining and discussion (and occasionally competitive bidding*), would be final and completely binding. After all, in most instances when the gross goes down, the rental goes down; and if the gross goes up, so does the payment to the distributor. In theory, this seems fair to both sides.

But is this the way it works? Nothing of the sort! In practical effect, the vast majority of exhibition contracts have what is known in the trade as a "look"—a second view by the exhibitor after the engagement is concluded to determine whether, in his view, the film rental payable under the contract is reasonable and appropriate. There is little or no written authority for such a "look" in the licensing agreements.

Here's the way it works. If in his fair and unbiased judgment the film's gross has been sufficient to justify the rental provisions, the exhibitor may deign to pay pursuant to contract terms. As any distributor can tell you, this is the rare and unusual situation. In the regular and ordinary (not extraordinary) case, the exhibitor simply determines what would be the proper *reduced* rental and pays accordingly. Although logic might counsel a contrary result, unknown to the memory of man is the case where the exhibitor finds the gross so substantial that he feels morally obligated to pay the distributor a sum based on a percentage in excess of the agreed contractual terms.

This is the "look" or the "adjustment" which has made the percentage terms of the exhibition contract a dead letter. The financial conditions on which films are licensed in key situations have become

---

* Where bidding is competitive, the exhibitor and distributor face the danger of suit by a losing bidder if contract terms are unilaterally reduced. Hence, the description of practices that follows is generally inapplicable to bid situations.

to a very large extent subject to a unilateral determination by the dominant local exhibitor. It matters not what the distributor thinks or whether the figures objectively call for a reasonable reduction. The judgment involved in determining the ultimate rental is that of the exhibitor and of the exhibitor alone.

This, then, is not a matter of renegotiation of agreements or of mutual understandings to modify harsh or improvident terms or joint consent. If there is discussion, it is *pro forma* in nature to inform the distributor of the reduction. Except in the rarest of cases, a diminution of film rental from terms is imposed. Sometimes the remittance check is kindly endorsed "Payment in Full," just in case a distributor might desire to challenge an arbitrary reduction.

Things have reached such a point that in a recent case the contributor of this article, representing a distributor, was confronted by a defense from an exhibitor that it was now "a custom of the trade" in the film business to reduce rentals from contractual terms and that the distributor therefore had no right to sue on the specified percentage terms of payment. I might add that in this instance, to add insult to injury, the exhibitor had also stopped payment on a belated check for a guaranty against film rental, so there is no assurance even in guaranties unless paid before exhibition.

I know of no parallel situation in any other industry. Contracts may no longer be the sacred documents many of us learned about in law schools, but in general their terms are still enforceable as written. I believe the process of adjustment as here described is *sui generis* to the motion picture business.

How could this condition arise in a self-respecting industry? How could a solemn, binding, and negotiated accord become a mere scrap of parchment, no more enforecable than Sam Goldwyn's famous oral agreement: "Not worth the paper it is written on?" In answering this question, some of the following conditions may seem relevant:

1. There were times when film rental arrangements were imposed by powerful distributors at such injurious and excessive terms that they resulted in unconscionable payments by the exhibitor. I regard a payment as unconscionable if it costs an exhibitor a significant sum while his theatre is actually operating at a substantial loss. Under these circumstances an exhibitor would require a helping hand and, together with the distributor, payments were frequently voluntarily reduced. These situations did not and do not justify unilateral action by the exhibitor. He is not the first person in this world who has ever lost money living up to a contract. In any event, reductions in these situations may have become so habitual with some that exhibitors consider them an established right.

2. Films for which hopes are highest may prove box-office disap-

pointments. Although the percentage formula is the best way of sharing the disappointment between the parties, again the rental may be excessive where an exhibitor suffers a serious loss. A bilateral reduction may be in order. Exhibitors may have so enjoyed justified reductions under this formula that they now continue the practice without bilateral authority.

3. Distributors have tolerated these one-way reductions because they fear they cannot stay in business by constantly suing their customers every time a rental is reduced. They are concerned with having happy customers. A strong picture may be followed by a weak one, and a second license precluded by vigorous enforcement of the first.

4. The consequences of years of anti-trust litigation (both private and public) have been such as to discourage mutual action by distributors helpful in enforcing covenants. Film companies scrupulously avoid joint enforcement activities as possibly contravening the anti-trust laws.

Whatever the background and origins, a grave condition has arisen in our industry. Efforts have been made to curtail or abolish it, but to date they are in vain. The practice of unilateral reduction of film rentals by exhibitors persists in virulent form. This course of conduct denies substantial sums justifiably due to distribution and production. Unless distribution and its allies in production are prepared to act forcefully to enforce their contracts this will continue with predictably dire results for all concerned.

THE EXHIBITORS:
SHOW AND TELLER TIME

NAT D. FELLMAN
STANLEY H. DURWOOD

MR. FELLMAN — *National General Theatres, Inc.*

". . . as experienced showmen we endeavor to present the finest motion picture entertainment with total service and hospitality while maintaining the most economical overhead possible. . . ."

Our parent company, National General Corporation, started as a theatre company—a spin-off from the 20th Century-Fox production, distribution and theatre company (Fox West Coast Theatres)—in 1951 as National Theatres, Inc. In the years since, National General Corporation has evolved into a multiple-faceted company, concentrating in the leisure-time and financial businesses. In addition to National General Theatres, Inc., NGC operates Great American Life Insurance

NAT D. FELLMAN is President of National General Theatres, Inc. and a Vice President of NGT's parent, National General Corporation. Mr. Fellman served with Warner Brothers Theatres/Stanley Warner Theatres from 1928 until he joined NGC in 1968, rising from office boy to Vice-President and General Manager of Stanley Warner Theatres, Inc.

STANLEY H. DURWOOD is President of American Multi-Cinema, Inc., and serves as a Director of the Motion Picture Association of America. A 1943 graduate of Harvard (B.A.), Mr. Durwood is an active leader in the civic and cultural affairs of his native Kansas City.

214

Company (one of the country's largest insurance companies), Bantam Books and Grosset & Dunlap. National General Theatres operates nearly 300 theatres, of which 16 are in Canada.

As exhibitors, we are informed of new film releases either directly by distributing companies and producers or by picking up pertinent data from the various trade magazines and papers. The National Association of Theatre Owners' monthly newspaper also carries a product schedule, listing releases by month and by distributor. *The Hollywood Reporter* and *Daily Variety* list forthcoming pictures and are good sources of information. Finally, the distributors' sales organizations or advertising personnel advise exhibitors in writing, by telephone, or by personal visits about new pictures and their availability and release dates.

In Los Angeles, on most important pictures, the distributor is looking for an *exclusive* run—a one-theatre run. In some cases, it will be the kick-off for nation-wide distribution. In the case of a very important picture, it may be tied in with a glamorous Hollywood premiere with stars and television coverage—with the expectation, of course, of wide publicity. This is a *first-run, exclusive* situation.

There is also a *first multiple run*, where a picture plays for the first time in more than one theatre. The picture may be exhibited on Hollywood Boulevard, along with Westwood or Wilshire Boulevard. It might play in four, five—or as many as 15 theatres located in different areas in the Los Angeles community, plus a large number of drive-ins. This is a *first multiple run*, as compared with an *exclusive first run*.

Following an exclusive run, a distributor may take a *limited multiple run*, playing in six areas or less on a very limited multiple run, after which the picture is generally booked on a *wide sub-run*. The pictures which play a multiple first run—whether in a few theatres or many—then find homes in a *second* multiple run, and then perhaps a *third* multiple run. In a smaller town, a picture will play a first run in one theatre for a week or longer, and if there are other theatres, it may play a second run following the conclusion of the first-run exhibition.

The more subsequent runs a picture plays, the less the financial gaurantees, if any. Percentage terms, however, may be about the same. A company may still insist on its same percentage terms, but for fewer weeks, in a smaller town as compared with a large town. If the company has a policy of 60% on a given film, it may take one or two weeks at 60% in a small town as compared with asking for four or more in a large town at 60%.

The distributor decides which type of run a picture will have. He may be influenced by the producer—and the more important the producer, the greater the tendency to do as the producer wants. In some cases, the distributor may look for a large theatre for a picture that will play to a wide audience. On the other hand, certain pictures will play to a more limited or specialized audience and thus be placed in a small theatre, where overhead is lower, in order that the picture can continue for a longer run and show profit with a smaller box-office gross. Many distributors prefer to play such theatres as the Chinese in Hollywood and Radio City Music Hall in New York because of the glamour, prestige and reputation these fine theatres have.

A *hard-ticket roadshow attraction* implies reserved seats on an exclusive first run. Such a picture usually plays with an intermission and in some ways parallels a legitimate theatre performance. The producer and distributor enter into roadshow policy with the idea of setting up the picture as an extraordinary motion picture. There are extremely large investments in most of these pictures, which are exhibited on large screens in 70mm., Cinerama, D-150, or others. For the exhibitor, a roadshow may mean higher costs for union treasurers instead of regular cashiers, added expense for group sales people, and increased personnel. The scale for projectionists may also be higher than for a traditional run.

There are many instances when an exhibitor, to secure a picture for a theatre, must bid in competition with other theatres. Bidding involves several steps: First, the distributor of a particular picture will send each exhibitor in the same competitive area a letter or a form announcing that his picture is available in this given situation for a playdate, calling for a specific opening date, and requesting that each exhibitor make an offer. The distributor may or may not include his minimum requirements. He may, for example, offer a picture for three-week minimum booking and minimum terms. The terms —the actual cost of film rental—will be spelled out in the distributor's letter in this way: "First week: 60% of the gross receipts; Second week: 50-60%; Third week: 40-60%."

These are minimum requirements. The exhibitor who bids the most will usually get the picture. In bidding, one bids both playing time and terms. If minimum playing time is three weeks, an exhibitor who is anxious to get the picture may bid four to six weeks. He may bid more than 60% even though minimum terms are less. The bid will also ask the *clearance* required by the exhibitor; i.e., the kind of exclusivity he wants in his area. If he wants to play the picture ahead of theatres A, B and C, he must make this clear in his response. Obviously, theatres require clearance as no exhibitor will want to meet these high terms to play the picture if it is to open simultaneously with, or shortly after, the scheduled opening in "a theatre across the street." Accordingly, he may stipulate in his bid that he expects an exclusive run with "x" days' clearance from the conclusion of the run over theatres A, B and C.

The bid request will specify a return due date. If the bid does not reach the distributor's office by this particular date, it is not considered. There is also a standard bid policy which may state that "distribution reserves the right to reject any and all bids by exhibitors for any reason." If, for example, all exhibitors send in offers considered unacceptable, the distributor will accept none, send them back and ask for new bids. If the distributor is still not satisfied, he may negotiate with each individual exhibitor and try to secure the terms he wants. An example from a bid invitation states:

> Exhibitor, please take note of the following bid solicitation. Your bid may be submitted by letter or telegram, and the attached envelope should be used in submitting your bid. Please make sure your offer includes all pertinent details, including playdate. On approval, a regular bid contract will be prepared for signature.

The picture is named, and the availability date is stated. This bid response is due on a specified date. It names the town, and says "First Run." It may stipulate the distributor's share of any approved cooperative advertising expenses as the same percentage as film rental to gross, computed on a weekly basis.

As an additional example, the exhibitor's office may receive the following telegram:

> This wire will serve as an invitation for you to bid on (*Picture* "X"), second run, "XYZ" area, available September 30, 1971. If you care to submit an offer, please do so to arrive at this office no later than Tuesday, September 7.

No minimum terms are mentioned. The exhibitor simply makes an offer.

Here is a more specific example of a bid in which a number of conditions are set forth:

> We invite your written response to bid for a license to exhibit (*Picture* "X"), first-run in "Y" County. The availability date is October 14, 1971; bids must be received in our office no later than Tuesday, September 15. We will accept one conventional and one drive-in run. We will select from the bids received the one which we calculate will produce the most film rental and provide the most adequate exposure for the picture. Since we are not zoning in the area, your offer should stipulate those theatres over which clearances are desired.
>
> No offer will be considered unless it meets the following re-

quirements: an opening date of October 14, 1971, a minimum of ten weeks, a minimum guarantee of film rental . . . [meaning that an exhibitor must guarantee them a dollar amount] . . . to be paid one-half a week prior to the opening, and one-half on or before completion of one-half of the specified playing time.

If the percentage terms for the above bid were 90/10, it would mean the distributor would receive 90% of the gross receipts after the exhibitor had first deducted and retained his specified house expenses. This bid request also demands minimum percentage terms of "half of the specified number of weeks at a minimum floor of 60%; the next half of the specified number of weeks at a minimum floor of 50%." This "minimum floor" arrangement is rather complex. First, the exhibitor guarantees playing time for a number of weeks, hit or miss. Then, he must gamble on the guarantee with dollars. Against this guarantee the distributor is asking as a minimum offer 90% over his house expense. If house expense is $3,000 and the exhibitor takes in $10,000 at the box-office, he has $7,000 over his house expense. The distributor gets 90% of that $7,000, or $6,300. If $8,000 is taken in and the house expenses are still $3,000, only $5,000 is left, of which $4,500 belongs to the distributor. The bid invitation also stipulates that for half of the specified number of weeks, a minimum floor of 60% is established. Under these minimum terms, the house expenses are not considered. With a box-office gross of $8,000, the distributor receives $4,800—$300 more than the 90/10 portion of the contract terms.

Below are excerpts from two additional bid requests. The first involves a *blind bid*, which means the picture has not been screened and the exhibitor must take a calculated risk based on his experience and business judgment in making a bid offer for the picture.

We are listing below guidelines to be followed when submitting bids:

First and second week: 60%
Third and fourth week: 50%
Fifth and sixth week: 40%
All additional play time: 35%

A holdover figure for additional playing time should be included in your bid offer. Unfortunately, we will not have screening prints for quite some time. We are, however, inviting you to bid for this attraction, as we want our exhibitors throughout the country to be able to intelligently plan their important Christmas playing time.

The second request reads in part:

> We enclose our request for your offer and contract forms for your convenience in submitting an offer for the following production. . . . Deadline is 2 P.M. September 22.
> Playing time: 8 weeks minimum
> Suggested guarantees: $50,000
> Suggested terms: 90/10, with the following weekly minimum:

First week:	70%
Second week:	60%
Third week:	50%
Balance:	40%

When an exhibitor guarantees 70% as film rental, it means he must pay all of his other expenses; *e.g.*, rent, light, heat, salaries, advertising—everything involved in running his theatre—from the remaining 30%.

The invitation continues:

> Our contribution to advertising will not exceed final film rental percentage terms earned each week. Procedure for paying of minimum guarantee: minimum payment of $5,000 down upon signing contract, balance to be paid 14 days prior to opening date.

When an exhibitor agrees to pay this money in advance, he must take into consideration the interest costs on such money.

In non-bidding situations, if a theatre's box-office receipts are not commensurate with the terms, it is an industry practice for the distributor to review and adjust the terms of the picture—depending upon the actual gross. He may not hold the exhibitor to the contract unless, in a particular run, the contract specifies that the picture is not subject to any adjustment or review. This does not apply to a bid, however. Once a bid is made, it is binding in every way. In many situations where there is no bidding an exhibitor may split pictures with his competitors—so long as the distributors are aware of it.

Another important phase of the exhibitor's economic decision-making activity lies in the area of how much to charge. Admission prices generally reflect the size of the town or community, the type of run and the economic situation in an area. The inflationary spiral has resulted in an increase in prices generally. The exhibitor must be careful that he does not price himself out of business. All organizations are concerned with doing sufficient business to earn reasonable profits on their investments. Our admission prices are very flexible. We have theatres in certain depressed areas where only $.50

admission is charged. In such a community, we believe more patrons attend our theatre at this price—and this means more concession sales. The concession business is a major factor in theatre operations. If exhibitors did not have their concession business, there would be far fewer theatres operating today.

The film terms mentioned are not the film terms on all pictures. Our average deal will run between 35% and 40% of the box-office gross, which leaves the balance to take care of expenses and turn a profit. And, we have our concession business. For the motion picture business, the peak periods are no-school periods, summer months, and the holidays.

MR. DURWOOD — *American Multi-Cinema, Inc.*

> "... *It is not a policy of our corporation to use commercial advertising for income on our screen. We are selling the public one item—a particular motion picture—and to use the screen for other purposes detracts from this item.* ..."

Durwood Theatres, now known as American Multi-Cinema, was founded in 1920 by Edward D. Durwood. In 1947 the company operated one theatre in Kansas City and 11 others in cities in the Missouri-Kansas area. In 1963 we opened the Parkway Theatres in the Ward Parkway Shopping Center in Kansas City. They were the first twin theatres in the world with a common lobby, box-office, projection booth and concession stand. In 1966, the company opened the world's first four-theatre complex, the Metro Plaza Theatres in Kansas City. In 1969, the first six-theatre complex, the Six West Theatres in Omaha, were opened. Currently, the company operates over 120 theatre screens in nine states and plans to open at least 40 additional screens.

Since American Multi-Cinema has planned its expansion program on the basis of constructing twin-, four- and six-theatre complexes throughout the country, we have established our own marketing department, which analyzes the market potential of cities throughout the United States. Our initial concern is the potential number of movie-goers within a geographic area.

We consider all cities that have a population in excess of about 100,000 as potential locations for a multi-theatre operation. Next, we evaluate the growth potential of each city and the particular future

growth areas within a city. We also attempt to evaluate the population
centers by various economic and demographic considerations, including average age, income, education, and occupation of residents. We
prefer to locate theatres in growing middle-class areas, inhabited by
college-educated families and potentially college-educated young people. These groups are the backbone of the existing motion picture
audience, and our future audience.

Once we have evaluated the market potential of a particular
city, we proceed to find the locations of all the existing theatres and
determine how many additional theatres can be economically supported, in order to set our specific plans for development within a
particular city. As examples, we may determine that in a city the size
of Dallas, we would like to erect between five and eight multi-cinema
locations; in a city like Denver, three; or in a city like Philadelphia,
14 multi-theatre locations.

After our plans are set, the workload shifts to our real estate
department. We locate all our theatres within shopping centers, in
prime retail space. Since we are constructing only multi-theatres in
units of two, four or six, containing between 200 and 400 seats in
each theatre, the design of our theatres is fairly standard. We do not
create a new form for each shopping center; but we construct our
theatres to fit the pattern of the shopping center's motif.

The cost of operating theatre chains can be broken down into
four basic areas: (1) rental cost of the motion picture, (2) advertising
cost for the motion picture, (3) direct cost of operating the theatre
itself, and (4) overhead cost of the entire theatre chain's executive
management.

Each picture released by a particular distributor is licensed to
us in each of our theatres on an individual basis. In some areas, we
license pictures on a competitive basis (*i.e.*, we compete through
bidding with other theatres operated by other exhibitors) while in
other areas, we license our pictures through negotiation, on a noncompetitive basis.

Almost all of our pictures are licensed from distributors on the
basis of a percentage of gross receipts. This might be a straight percentage, such as 50% of the income derived from the exhibition of
a picture over a certain number of weeks. Another form of percentage
license provides that we keep the first amount of dollars to cover our
operating overhead, and the distributor receives 90% of the gross receipts in excess thereof, while we retain the remaining 10%. This is
a *90/10 over-the-house expense* deal. Often, these deals are combined
so that the distributor would receive whichever is higher between a
90/10 over-the-house expense deal, and a direct percentage of the gross
receipts. At times, pictures are licensed on a flat rental basis, but such

deals generally take place on second-feature pictures, and to theatres of minimal grossing potential.

The basic operating cost of a theatre itself includes such elements as salaries to employees, rent to the shopping center, amortization of the cost of the furnishings and fixtures of the theatre, including cost of seats, projection equipment, screen, concession equipment, maintenance costs, cost of concession items, supplies, tickets, and incidental costs. In operating a circuit, we also have management overhead costs, which include the salaries of the film buyers, theatre operation executives, the accounting and financial departments, legal fees, and auditors.

For first-run motion pictures, advertising is generally shared on a cooperative basis between distributor and exhibitor, in accordance with the percentage of film rental earned on a motion picture. If the deal is a 90/10 over-house expense, the distributor will pay 90% of the advertising.

On the first sub-run break of motion pictures in major cities, the advertising is divided on a different basis. The picture is licensed to a certain number of theatres in one area—as determined by the distributor—and each theatre is asked to contribute a set proportion of dollars (i.e., $50, $100, $150) over the theatre's normal advertising budget for the sub-run campaign. The distributor, in turn, will contribute a certain proportion to the amount financed by the theatres. Although advertising costs vary with pictures, we estimate that an average of 6% to 8% of the theatres' box-office grosses are expended in advertising dollars. It is not a policy of our corporation to use commercial advertising for income in any of our theatres. We are selling the public one item—a particular motion picture—and to use the screen for other purposes detracts from this item.

The general policy of our corporation is not to use double-bills in indoor theatres. They are used only to bring back two successful pictures as one show. It is our opinion that people most often want to see just one particular picture, and do not care for a second feature. The drive-in public, on the other hand, has come to expect a bargain of two or more pictures for their evening's entertainment. The combination of *A Man Called Horse* and *Cheyenne Social Club*, or two of the James Bond pictures, are pair-ups that achieved great success. With respect to shorts and cartoons, these are used only as fill-ins for time schedules. Often, when a picture runs an hour and a half, the time schedule may be on a two-hour basis, so a 10-or 15-minute short or cartoon is used to fill out the program.

Our theatres must be booked differently, of course. In Lansing, Michigan, we cater to a large number of students from Michigan State University, and their movie-going fare differs greatly from theatres located in upper-income, conservative, middle-class areas. Our theatre in St. Petersburg, Florida, attracts audiences of older people who are not interested in the provocative problems of the day and for whom a film like *Getting Straight* has no appeal. We must cater to their tastes by showing musicals like *Funny Girl* and *Hello, Dolly! Easy Rider,* which had such great success throughout the country, should not be exhibited in our theatres in St. Petersburg. On the other hand, I would not recommend playing *Hello, Dolly!* on a third or fourth run in Lansing, Michigan. I could, however, bring *Easy Rider* back to Lansing. I suspect there will always be an audience for that picture in that town.

We are the originators of the multiple-theatre complex, and are continuing to build theatres on that basis. In essence, variety is the key to the multiple-theatre operation. Adults may attend a picture with adult appeal, while their children are in the adjacent theatre attending a film specifically designed for children. Certainly, some pictures are held over, but if you are operating four or six theatres in a complex, at least one or two new pictures are added to the films each week.

Economically, the multiple-theatre operation benefits the distributor. A theatre operator who has one large theatre within an area has a higher overhead than a theatre operated as part of a multiple-theatre complex. With this high overhead, the exhibitor cannot hold a picture for a long period of time. Once the picture falls below a certain gross, the exhibitor must put in a new picture. In a multiple-theatre operation, the house expense of a particular screen is much less, so the picture can be held in that theatre at a lower gross. This gives the distributor the benefit of having his picture before the public for a longer period of time. A short run, in my opinion, deprives the distributor of income to which he is entitled.

We are convinced that the multi-theatre concept is economically right for our form of operation and the motion picture distributor, and that it will play a large part in the future of the motion picture industry.

PART SEVEN

Building
Film
Audiences

Money, time and creative energy now have been committed on a large scale. A vast, world-wide machinery, established solely for the purpose of getting both film and viewer to the same place at the same time, is set in motion. But who will come to see the movie? Why? When? What approaches to bringing the public to the box office are tried and tested? Which are the most important, and how are these implemented by the industry?

Many will agree that the most effective form of advertising and publicity for any film is word-of-mouth—that kind of positive, person-to-person communication which takes place after a smaller number of people have seen and liked a film, and go forth to spread its praises to ever-widening circles of potential viewers. But even this kind of help can occur only after the initial audiences have been secured, and in a media-drenched world the industry has little choice in this effort but to fall back upon the conventional devices and methods for building an audience. Advertising and publicity campaigns must be mounted, and the very media which so effectively compete for the movie audience must be employed to help build it up again.

In essays here, David Lipton *considers the resources which are available to publicity-campaign planners, and evaluates the strengths and weaknesses of various media-utilization plans in building "momentum" for varying types of films.* Paul Lazarus *next reviews a few of the basic services which have been developed by his company to supply media and in-theatre advertising supporting materials.*

Finally, although many are quite willing to minimize the influence of motion picture critics upon the size of today's audiences, few are willing to dismiss their long-range staying power and their salutary influence in general upon the motion picture art. The role of the critic vis-a-vis *the box office success of any film deserves a patient and reflective overview, and such is provided here in* Charles Steinberg's *scholarly appraisal of the critical art of criticizing.*

ADVERTISING AND PUBLICITY

DAVID A. LIPTON

". . . We have found through many years of effort that the public cannot tell you in advance what their tastes will be. . . ."

talk about film in General

There is no such thing as one motion picture audience; there are many motion picture audiences. An advertising and publicity campaign for a film is generally tailored to the audience which seems most likely to be attracted to it: a mass audience, a young audience, a small-town audience, or some other group. The major effort is concentrated on the point of sale. Despite many years of experimenting with presale advertising through the national media with long-range publicity campaigns, the present trend is to concentrate specifically at the time that a picture is released in a given city.

There are two pieces of information that are important in order to attract your audience: when the picture is going to open and where it will be shown. Unlike other products that are nationally advertised and available at the point where the advertising occurs, a film is a very perishable product, available only in certain theatres at certain times, and not necessarily simultaneously throughout the United States. We concentrate on the campaign, therefore, immediately prior to the opening of the picture in a given situation.

DAVID A. LIPTON is Vice-President, Universal Pictures. A veteran in the field of motion picture advertising and publicity, Mr. Lipton began his career with Balaban & Katz Theatres of Chicago in 1923 and served in various executive positions over the years with Columbia Pictures Corporation and Universal Studios.

Another reason that the first ad appears just shortly before a picture opens is that the cost of advertising has gone so high that we are limited insofar as our advertising dollar will carry us. The principal media rates are going up all the time. Our prime medium is newspaper advertising, for which motion picture rates are substantially higher than those of other kinds of advertising. This circumstance goes back to the days when all theatrical advertising was at a higher rate, because of the losses sustained when itinerant companies placed advertising and left town without paying for it. Today the newspapers argue that motion pictures, unlike other products, receive a great deal of publicity through feature columns, and syndicate services, and, therefore, should pay a higher rate.

Their only real basis for claiming that film rates should be higher than retail rates is that film ads are classified: all industry advertising has to run on the same page or pages. Ordinary advertising is placed on what is known as "run of paper," which means that the newspaper has the option of placing an ad wherever it is convenient in the make-up of the newspaper. An ad on a specific page or in a specific position on a page involves extra costs.

Rates generally keep going up each year, as all the costs of publishing go up. The same situation prevails in the two other major forms of film advertising, radio and television. The newspaper is the only medium available in virtually every home, every day. Since motion picture bookings change very rapidly, the newspaper is the prime medium for advertising.

A newspaper ad can be as large or as small as one chooses. A budget covering advertising is generally set up between the distributing company and the theatre. The advertising budget for an opening in Los Angeles, for example, might be $10,000. Of that budget, $6,000 is for newspaper advertising. The size of the ad is important only in relation to all other ads. What was formerly an opening day ad of 1,000 lines is now down to 600 lines.

Because it is graphic, television is a very effective medium for motion picture advertising. It is also an extremely expensive one, particularly in prime time. In almost any major city, a very good-sized motion picture ad is available in any newspaper for the price of one 30-second television spot. Not all pictures, however, lend themselves to TV advertising. *Airport*, for example, with a cast of 10 stars, could not be presented adequately in the 20-to-30-second TV spot commercial. The practice is to make a rough cut of a set of television commercials, and then determine whether they do the job of selling. If they are effective, we may concentrate on television instead of radio.

Although in some cases we divide our funds evenly between

radio and TV, generally we concentrate on one or the other, depending upon which does the better selling job. We do considerably better
on musicals, for instance, through radio advertising. It is difficult
to get the feel of a good musical score on a 30-second television commercial; whereas on radio, we can buy 60 seconds. Radio has an additional advantage of a great deal more flexibility in reaching specific
audiences. Since surveys show that most daytime radio listeners are
women going about their housework, when a picture has an enormous
interest for women, we buy daytime radio spots. For a picture that
is particularly youth-oriented we rarely go to television, because
statistics show that young people generally do not watch television.
They do, however, listen to radio, particularly rock stations. If it is
a picture in which we have a simple message to get across we take
what is a very effective time slot for radio—rush-hour drive time—
from 7 to 9 a.m. and 4 to 7 p.m. Almost every city has a variety of
radio stations geared to different audiences. We buy certain stations
according to the audience who will be reached for a specific picture.

At one time magazine advertising was widely used. For several
reasons this situation has changed. Magazine ads were most effective
at the time when pictures were released on the same date throughout
the country. Then the ad appeared in the magazine simultaneously
with the release of the picture. In those days, pictures were booked
specifically on certain dates and ran for a certain number of stipulated weeks. That practice slowly came to an end as theatres began
running pictures not on specific booking dates, but in sequence. For
example, a picture now opens and there is no date for the start of
the next one! If it happens to be successful, a picture can run 6, 12,
40 weeks first-run, holding up the release for the rest of the city. There
is no longer a simultaneous opening nationwide. We know what pictures will open in Los Angeles and what pictures they follow, but
we do not know the specific opening and closing dates. In Los Angeles,
for example, we were set to go in following a picture which we knew
nothing about, called Z. We wound up waiting six months, and eventually moved our picture to another theatre. In view of these facts,
it is no longer possible to make an impact with magazine advertising.
Even without these problems, magazine advertising is so costly that
there is reluctance to use it without some indication of the picture's
acceptance with first-run audiences.

Huge, outdoor displays can be found only on the Sunset Strip
in Los Angeles and on Broadway in New York—nowhere else in the
United States. A company must be practical in separating that which
is done with legitimate advertising reasoning from that which is done
to satisfy the egos of particular producers, stars, or others involved
in the picture. The Sunset Strip line of boards has no practical pur-

pose, and their cost is out of proportion in relation to their effect on movie-going. The Broadway boards are not as frequent as they used to be; they are coming down pretty fast now, because they are so costly and because most of the picture-makers are in Los Angeles. There is still outdoor advertising, in that there are materials prepared on every picture: one-sheets, three-sheets, six-sheets, sometimes 24-sheets, and a certain amount of posting throughout the country on a local level.

Whereas a successful motion picture may play as many as 10,000 engagements in the United States, only the first-run and the first multiples (a film playing in more than one theatre in an area) are supported by distributor advertising. The vast majority of all theatres do their own advertising with their own money, and with material provided by the National Screen Service. Since we do not participate in that advertising, we do not have a voice in its selection or in the use of media, except in the early engagements in the principal cities. In major cities—perhaps 100 at most—we may start in the first engagements with a substantial campaign, phase it out if the picture does not perform, or continue if the picture is successful.

With the possible exception of certain times of the year, release schedules are flexible. First-runs may open over a period of two or three months, in various cities around the country, depending upon the availability of the right theatres and the right deals. The only time we actually lock up a date is for Christmas/New Year's; otherwise, we play pictures according to the previously-playing picture. The best playing time is in the summer, and the very peak of attendance at motion pictures is about the second week in August, when the 4,000 drive-in theatres are attracting a larger attendance than the 10,000 conventional theatres.

Part of the function of the distributor's advertising department is to deal with cooperative advertising—the determination of how much money to spend for a given picture in each city and the use of media and specific ads. We communicate with the theatre circuit involved, and we negotiate with them about the amount of money to be spent. In most cases, the theatre has a fixed amount of money to spend, beyond which we have to pay the difference. Certain theatres contend that their capacity and record of business indicate that they can put up only $1,000 for the first week of advertising. We may, however, want to spend more than that. Because we may be establishing that picture for the entire city and area, we are willing to spend substantially more than the theatre. We negotiate the exact terms with the advertising head of the theatres, or with the theatre managers. The process is called cooperative advertising, or participatory advertising.

It is similar to that cooperative advertising in retail stores which is arranged with the manufacturer of a product, who puts up a large part of the cost.

Many pictures frequently have multiple first runs. A given picture could be playing in three or even ten theatres in one city and involve us in participatory advertising. While exclusive first-run advertising is relatively simple, the multiple is a little more complicated because each theatre participates in it with various amounts of money. Someone has to prepare the advertising for all the theatres, many of which are under different managements. Someone is designated in almost every city to place the ads, break down the costs, and bill each theatre for its share.

In the second multiple run, we frequently participate in advertising as well. In Los Angeles, for example, where the number of theatres that play simultaneously varies from around nine to 28, we may have as many as 28 theatres each putting up $200. This sum is a pretty good start on the ad campaign. We then put up the difference. The least we would contribute in a campaign would be 50% of the total cost, and sometimes substantially more, depending on the prospects of the picture.

Another deal is one in which the distributing company shares in advertising on the same percentage that it receives for film rental, particularly if the film is rented on a sliding scale. In a sliding scale, the percentage of film rental will be determined by the gross of the picture. As the gross increases, so does the rental. For example, if the distributor asks a film rental of no less than 25% and the theatre grosses $5,000, the film rental is 25%. If it grosses $6,000, we get 30%; if it grosses $7,000,—35%; $8,000,—40%. This kind of deal generally runs from a minimum of 25% to a maximum of as high as 60%, or 70% of the gross to the distributor. For our major pictures, we are making deals whereby we pay the same percentage of advertising as percentage of film rental. For example, at the end of a week, if our film rental, on a sliding scale, runs as high as 70%, we pay 70% of the advertising, and the exhibitor pays 30%. If it is a 60% film rental, we pay 60% of advertising, with a minimum of 50% on our share. The percentage is actually in proportion to the film rental we are earning.

After a certain point, the picture plays in theatres where participation is not involved, because it isn't worth the accounting. This arrangement is called flat rental. A very popular picture can play 12,000 dates, of which there can be around 5,000 theatres where the income is so small that it does not merit a percentage agreement. In these theatres the picture is rented at a single, flat price, generally determined by the house record of annual earnings. The rental can be as low as $50 in some cases, and we still pay the cost to service the print and deliver it.

The campaign for a picture really begins at the point when the company decides to make it. An announcement of the project is handled through publicity in movie columns. Next, prior to production, we announce where it is going to be shot, who is in the cast, and other details. The major publicity material is gathered during production. Since this is the only time that the entire cast is together, the publicist assigned to the picture prepares the material. The advertising department's first contact with the picture is in the preparation of a list of suggested still photographs that they will need for the eventual advertising and publicity campaign. The script indicates the basic approach. The advertising department sees the still proofs daily to make sure they are getting all proper material. At this time, too, stories are gathered for the press book, and for the publicity that is held until the time of release of the picture.

The next step occurs about the time that the rough cut of the picture is available. The art department and the copywriters view a rough cut and discuss the general approach. In many cases, we also confer with the producer and the director. Next we prepare the "rough layouts," which run the whole gamut of the possible ways to sell the picture. The copy is frequently submitted in advance for discussion and editing. It is then a process of elimination until we come up with an advertising format that is finally approved. It then goes to art work.

After the rough cut is screened, other things get underway: the trailer department begins making up their trailers; television commercials are made; the advertising department starts on its radio spots. An ad campaign may have two or three different approaches. Because half our business comes from overseas, we also prepare the components for foreign ads. Overseas, the emphasis in advertising is far more visual than it is textual, and tends to stress action and sex.

If there is such a thing as a philosophy about today's market, it is to gear all efforts to getting the audience into the theatre at the earliest openings, which now rarely happen concurrently in more than two places. Once the picture has been exposed, what takes over as the major factor is word-of-mouth—audience reaction word-of-mouth. After that, the amount of advertising makes little difference. There are instances in which very costly campaigns have been used without success. On the other hand, there are pictures with very little advertising which have caught on instantly. The industry has spent millions of dollars on surveys and polls, and we still do not know how the audiences know specifically what they want to see before a picture opens. But they know. Sometimes, we have a back-up ad campaign ready in case the first campaign fails, and sometimes even a third. It comforts the exhibitor down the line who knows that the advertising used in the initial campaign did not succeed, and feels that he has a right to a different campaign. But it rarely makes a difference. The difficulties arise from the fact that one is dealing with something very intangible: the public interest at a given moment. We have found through many years of effort that the public cannot tell you in advance what their tastes will be.

NATIONAL SCREEN SERVICE CORPORATION

PAUL N. LAZARUS

National Screen Service is the only national distributor of trailers and accessories with a network of branches in the United States. It is a publicly-held company which grosses approximately $15-million annually for its services. It maintains 18 branch offices in the U.S. and an office in London. The office in London ships to exhibitors throughout England.

NSS does not have branches in either Canada or Latin America. In Canada, the distribution of posters is handled by an associated company utilizing NSS material, named Consolidated Theatre Services, in Toronto. The individual companies handle their own trailers in Canada. In Latin America, the distributors handle their own posters and trailers, usually reprinting them in Spanish.

Here, NSS ships 20,000 trailers per week to aproximately 13,000 theatres in the U.S. After about three years of storing material, the NSS distribution centers substantially reduce their inventories and send representative sample copies to Kansas City for indefinite storage.

Exhibitors provide NSS with a booking schedule and NSS delivers material substantially prior to the date that the feature will be shown. NSS pays all freight costs to its branches. The exhibitor pays freight only from the NSS branch to a theatre and back. Local trucking

* First published in *Motion Picture Industry Management Services*—a brochure distributed by International Automated Controls, Ltd. Sept.-Oct., 1970.
For a biographical note about Mr. Lazarus, see page 185.

facilities are used. Two trailer prints are usually made by NSS for each feature print made by the distributor. The average length of a regular trailer ranges from 150 feet to 275 feet. The exhibitor pays NSS from $5 to $50 a week, depending upon theatre location and grossing potential, for servicing them with all trailer requirements.

In addition, National Screen supplies exhibitors with teaser trailers. These are 90 ft. (60 seconds) advance trailers designed to run a week ahead of the regular trailer. They are given free to the exhibitor. Prints are supplied by the distributor. NSS charges $1 for each shipment it makes, and it insists on return of the print a full week prior to playdate.

The price paid by exhibitors for accessories is based upon a published rate card.

Standard advertising accessories:

1. Posters called "one-sheets" (27" x 41"), price $.75 each; three-sheets (41" x 78"), price $1.75; six-sheets (79" x 80"), price $3.60; 24-sheets (231" x 103"), price $15.00. NSS discourages the use of six-sheets and 24-sheets because they were principally designed for the days of "walk past" trade, which for all practical purposes does not exist today.

2. Still photographs, 8" x 10", price $.35 each (black & white), $.48 (color); 11" x 14", price $2.50 per set; 14" x 36", price $1.35 each; 22" x 28", price $1.45.

3. Window cards, for placing in store windows and other locations, price $.35 each.

4. Mats. A mat is an embossed piece of cardboard used by newspapers to reproduce ads and stills, price $.40 per column.

All of the foregoing are considered "standard accessories" because they were the poster sizes supplied by all the film companies. Most frames in theatre lobbies are in these sizes.

Specialty accessories:

1. Posters, 40" x 60", price $7.50 each; 30" x 40", price $5.00.

2. Title displays, 24" x 82", price $5.00; 24" x 60", price $5.00.

3. Hi-rise standees, which are silhouetted cut-out displays mounted on a stand and a pole, price $9.95.

All accessories are the property of National Screen Service and are licensed to theatres for use only in connection with the exhibition of the pictures for which they were designed. Licensee agrees not to trade, sell or give them away, or permit others to use them, nor shall licensee be entitled to any credit upon return of such accessories. All accessories must be either returned or destroyed immediately after use.

NSS also maintains an inventory of radio transcriptions and television spot announcements.

The terms of contracts made with major producers differ from those contained in contracts with independent producers. The reason for this is that the majors may have 20 to 40 pictures in release every year; therefore, NSS's risk of incurring a loss is not nearly as great as when only one or two pictures are serviced for an independent producer.

THE SIGNIFICANCE OF FILM REVIEWS

CHARLES S. STEINBERG

". . . What is important for all motion picture criticism, journalistic or academic, is that the critic function not only to inform, but also to provide a direction-finder for the viewer. . . ."

In the Age of Reason, when criticism of literature in particular and the arts in general assumed academic and social respectability, the adversarial position of creative artist versus critic was established. There were those, a century later, who were to chafe under the stringent "rules" of the neo-classical tradition, but the development of criticism as a serious endeavor in England was primarily structured to lay down guidelines for the poet or essayist from which deviation was considered a departure from orthodoxy. Yet, even then, the critic was satirized by no less a person than Pope, whose lines are familiar to every student of English literature. Of critics, Pope said that they:

> Damn with faint praise
> Assent with civil leer
> And without sneering, teach the rest to sneer

Some 200 years after the development of criticism in the so-called classical tradition, the position of the critic *vis a vis* the creative

CHARLES S. STEINBERG is Vice President, Public Information, CBS-TV. He holds the Ph. D. degree, and has taught and lectured at several schools, including New York University and The New School. He is the author of *Mass Communication, Mass Media and Communication*, and *The Communicative Arts—An Introduction to Mass Media*.

novelist, poet, composer or painter is still adversarial. A search among scholarly critiques or literature reveals no end of world-renowned critics—Edmund Wilson, Alfred Kazin and many others. And the literary output of serious writers of this century has been dissected to the unfortunate degree where easy familiarity with Twentieth Century novelists comes often not by direct perception but through the filter of the critical article or biography. Hence, it is common to hear Faulkner, Hemingway and Fitzgerald discussed by those who have read *about* them, not of them at first hand. An unfortunate situation, surely, and emphasized to a point where those who are critical of critics paraphrase Bernard Shaw's comments on writers and teachers by observing that those who can, write creatively; those who can't, become critics.

In this era, when approaches to serious criticism have embraced Freudian psychology, anthropology, political science, Marxian dialectic and various theories of sociology, the critic of the art forms has been all at once, the most respected and reviled, the most praised and calumnied, the most feared and the most intrepid of people. Indeed, there are those who, particularly in the popular arts of movies and television (and to some extent theatre), denigrate the work of the critic to a point where the professional appraiser is denied any social status at all—although the newspaper journalist whose responsibility it is to review the various lively arts is thought of as a "professional critic" as opposed to the academic scholar whose function is not daily, ephemeral opinion but aesthetic judgment from historical perspective.

In any period, however, the chasm between creative artist and critic is wide and deep. Good creative writers are not usually good critics, although there are notable exceptions. Nor, conversely, does the aptitude for criticism—particularly in the field of music and perhaps less in literature where evaluative judgments are required—demand that the critic write with the inspired touch of the poet. Critics themselves are not respected for their creative prowess, but for their ability to see a work whole and to render a valid aesthetic judgment. But critics are not all of a piece. The journalistic critic who must meet a daily deadline does not use the same parameters, nor does he have the same responsibilities as the scholar. And the capsule reviewers— those who condense content and criticism of movies and television programs into a few brief lines for the masses—have none of the obligations of the scholar or the newspaper critic but, ironically, probably carry greater weight than both with the purveyors of popular culture and with the audience.

The Role of the Critic

Throughout the flamboyant, frequently bizarre and always unpredictable history of the movies, the role of the critic never has been clearly defined. Erratic at its best, and deplorable at its worst, criticism of the motion picture—like criticism of the television program—has not enjoyed the prestigious position, either with industry entrepreneurs, press or public, accorded the critic of theatre, books, music or fine arts. No responsible newspaper editor would normally select an art critic or a book or music critic from shipping news, city desk or sports. But few television critics and equally few movie reviewers can lay claim to either special training in, or knowledge of, broadcast or film media. This is less true of motion pictures in recent years than it is of television. Paradoxically, the erosion of the movie public since the advent of television, the age of tribulation for the Hollywood moviemakers, has seen a curious phenomenon in the appearance of a group of controversial, intellectually able and well-trained critics of contemporary cinema. Indeed, students of serious criticism of the arts incline to look with passive but superior good humor at the posturings of some of the more tendentious cinema critics and at the controversy that swirls around such concepts as the *auteur* theory of motion picture criticism.

Yet, while movie criticism may never attain the status of music or theatre criticism, film has more journalistic practitioners than both and, along with the television column, the movie review column is a fundamental part of most of the large daily newspapers in this country. The impact, however, may be in inverse ratio to size and numbers. It is no secret that the anguished nightmare of theatre producers is that one bad notice in the *New York Times* which means success or failure of a new play. And the feverish hope of every book publisher is for that one favorable review in the Sunday *Times Book Review* and the few other newspapers that run daily book columns or Sunday book supplements.

Not so in the movies. Films on which were bestowed brilliant reviews may fail dismally at the box-office, while the popular imagination may be titillated by a movie that suffers nothing but slings and arrows from the critics. All of which raises several interesting questions, the most fundamental of which is precisely how effective is the motion picture critic? How much impact does his review have on the newspaper reader and moviegoer? Do audiences go to movies because of, or in spite of, good or bad reviews? Does the formidable press agentry, promotion, advertising and exploitation which producers and studios put behind movies carry greater weight with the public than critical judgment? Corollary to these fundamental questions, which relate to the effect of motion picture criticism on audience motivation and behavior, are considerations of the attitudes and motivations of those whose calling it is to render judgment on movies. What makes a movie critic? Is there any preparation, academic or vocational, that is required in order to attain professional status as a journalistic or scholarly critic of film? What are the essential differences, despite areas of mutuality of intent, between academic and professional (or journalistic) motion picture critics?

Unfortunately, there are few studies of genuine significance which answer with any quantitative certitude many of these fundamental areas of legitimate inquiry. The evidence is both empirical and subjective, based partly on observation and studies of professional criticism, partly on subjective comments from producers, critics themselves, newspaper and magazine editors and students of cinema courses in various colleges and universities. It is clear that the difference between the effect of motion picture and television criticism and criticism of books, theatre, music and the fine arts is both qualitative and quantitative. Newspaper editors do not seem to demand the same preparation and training for movie and television reviewers as they do for critics of the other arts. The difference, the academic critics would say, is between "high culture" and "popular art." Nor is the effect on the public the same. More people see a popular movie and watch one high-rated television program than those who could conceivably fill all of the Broadway theatres over a very long period of time. Audiences for theatre, music and books are different, too. They are apt to be selective, they pay a great deal more (the TV viewer pays no more than a long-term investment in the receiver) and they are inclined to respond seriously to the judgment of critics. True, there are occasions when plays succeed in spite of poor notices, when a novel which is badly mauled by book reviewers (such as *Valley of the Dolls* or *Love Story*) becomes a phenomenal success as both book and movie, but these are exceptions that tend to underscore the conviction that newspaper reviewers of movies and television have far less impact on audience behavior than do critics of books, theatre, music or painting. And it is certainly true that the publicity ballyhoo attendant on movie and television premieres tends to draw audiences without any relation to the reviews.

Curiously, however, as the motion picture industry changed its ways, so, too, did film criticism and the public's reaction to it. Prior to the advent of television, Hollywood was grinding out picture after picture—and only the major, superproductions were previewed seriously for the movie critics. An important spread in *Life* or *Look* at a time when these magazines commanded formidable readership was an important factor in abetting the launching of a new picture. And excerpts of reviews by the newspaper critics were touted in the press, on billboards and posters and on radio spots. Many of these, however, were comments taken out of context and, indeed, historians of the era of wonderful Hollywood nonsense recall more than one occasion when the major studios threatened to cancel lucrative daily advertising in retaliation for a bad notice from the movie critic.

Effects of Television

The activation of commercial television in 1948 and the Consent Decree of the Department of Justice, which divorced motion picture production and distribution from exhibition, wrought far-reaching changes both in the economic and cultural aspects of the film industry, and these results were to be reflected eventually in subtle changes in the style and effect of motion picture criticism. Hollywood's new image after television was revolutionary. The number of films produced each year became fewer with each passing season of successful television production. Tax advantages and high costs drove many producers and stars into independent production, with the result that the great studios of Hollywood's halcyon days, such as MGM and Warner Brothers, contracted and took desperate moves to survive, even to the extent of selling off property. And all of the major studios, along with several smaller enterprises, became heavily involved in the production of film for television. At the same time, after unsuccessful experiments in gimmickry, such as three-dimensional pictures, the Hollywood product of the late 1960's turned more and more to themes of sexual license. Language and action went beyond realism to a naturalistic depiction of human biological behavior never dreamed of by those who, in the '20's, considered Hollywood lewd and licentious and structured the so-called Motion Picture Code—a maneuver which, to many observers, simply drew the line at negative behavior without emphasizing anything constructive or positive in the way of creative cinema. In the 1960's, too, the Motion Picture Association drew up a new code which rated pictures—basically on their sexual overtones— on a scale from "X" (adults only) through "R" (restricted to those under 17), to "GP" (parental guidance suggested), and finally to a "G" rating, where all were invited without restriction or reservation.

As Hollywood changed, other movie makers began experimenting with film techniques—a development that was greatly to influence motion picture critics and criticism. Apart from the so-called "camp" movement, exemplified by the Warhol films, there came about a most stimulating proliferation of experimental filmmaking in the colleges and universities, along with the introduction of courses in film techniques in major educational institutions. Film now became a phenomenon apart from Hollywood product. It began to be thought of, once again, as an art form. Film criticism, professional and academic, took on a new importance. But a formidable question remained to be answered: Did the newspaper critics, most of whom had no training in serious film evaluation and most of whom were essentially chosen to report on conventional Hollywood pictures, have the inclination, background and training to render judgment on these films? The answer was forthcoming in the appearance of a small group of critics, each

controversial, fiercely independent and even antagonistic to one another, who were qualified by training and experience to write mean-
ingfully of the experience of cinema as a genuine art form. There is
developing, in the special magazines and in the publication of many
fine volumes, a literature of film; and the medium, once compared to
television as trivial and popular "low culture," has taken on an un-
characteristic aesthetic significance.

It is true, of course, that the journalists and the serious critics
still must deal with product intended for mass theatre audiences and,
eventually, for an edited version on the television screen. But, at the
same time, there continues to develop a group of serious filmmakers
in the colleges who are interested in experimenting not only with
photography but with story content and direction as well. The serious
Twentieth Century critics—the late James Agee, Dwight MacDonald,
Penelope Gilliatt, Andrew Sarris, John Simon and others—have
abetted this thrust toward more significant filmmaking, although Mac-
Donald gave up reviewing in despair because, he wrote, there was
simply nothing worth reviewing. But the newer concepts of film as art
form cannot be anything but a healthy development. Students of the
motion picture are producing a spate of useful books on film criticism,
techniques, history and sociology. The *auteur* critics have raised an
issue which many consider pure absurdity, but they have stimulated
interest in and discussion of film. And the healthiest aspects are, first,
the distinction between Hollywood product for theatres and television
and films which are frankly experimental; and second, a need for
better trained professional critics of both popular and art films.

The Harris Study

Who are the journalist critics and how do they view their calling? One of the few evaluations on the nature and direction of motion
picture criticism was a major part of a research study conducted under the auspices of Louis Harris and Associates for the Office of Communication of the United Church of Christ. The basic thrust of the research was the assumption that the substance and quality of American
life can be gauged to a great extent not only on the quality of the
media, but on the quality of criticism of the media. For example, does
criticism of the mass media degenerate into mere "puffery" designed
to lure audiences to the box-office? Are some critics too vindictive? Are
there critics who, true to the best tradition of a serious profession,
have a genuine talent and integrity for aesthetic evaluation and judgment? Free from government interference with a responsible press,
criticism of any aspect of American society by such media as press
and broadcasting is healthy, necessary and effective, provided that the
critics bring to their function a combination of adequate education,

training, high ethical standards and, above all, the aptitude to make normative judgments.

Several hundred critics, most of them newspaper journalists, participated in the Harris study—one of the first objective efforts to study criticism of the communicative arts in this country. The position of the movie critic assumes an interesting relationship to critics of other mass media. As one might expect, the daily newspapers employ many more critics than do magazines or radio and television stations. 95% of the newspapers have critical columns on the arts, as compared to 30% for magazines and television stations and 25% for radio stations. And, most significantly, 75% of the nation's newspapers print critical reports on movies—second only to theatre criticism. The newspaper critics do not consider themselves scholars of the arts. They are content to call themselves journalists and to assert that the profession of writing criticism for print journalism probably should not require a training program with professional standards comparable to medicine or law. Nor are there any educational pre-requisites for the making of a movie critic. More than three-fourths of those who responded indicated that they had completed an academic degree, albeit most with no specific training in criticism. About half majored in English and slightly more than a fourth majored in journalism. Most did not set out to become motion picture critics and, indeed, worked in other areas before being assigned to the movie "beat." Most did not seek the job. The job sought them. And most had no academic courses in cinema arts.

Those movie critics, who characterize themselves as working press, have specific answers to specific questions. They do not write for an intellectual elite or for a cultivated minority. Their comments on motion pictures, printed in the daily newspaper, are intended for that amorphous audience which may be termed "the general public." But, significantly, on most newspapers the motion picture critic's job is not a full-time one, with the exception of newspapers in very large metropolitan areas such as New York, Chicago, Philadelphia and Los Angeles. Almost 80% of those who review movies undertake other journalistic assignments as well—a most significant variation from the major journalistic critics such as Vincent Canby, Judith Crist and certainly from the major magazine critics mentioned earlier. Indeed, half of those journalists writing motion picture criticism look upon this assignment as only part of their responsibility in an over-all news reporting job. Equally significant, however, is the finding that 50% of those writing motion picture criticism believe that their absorption with film should call for *all*, not part, of their energies. And many are journalistic critics for still another reason. As do many television critics, they write not only reviews of the new pictures, but also cover so-called "hard" news of the motion picture industry and occasionally are called upon to write color stories and interviews with screen personalities. As the Harris report points out, "Criticism is journalism, but with a difference." The difference is that the journalistic critic finds that his responsibility to editor and reader calls not only for a critique, but a journalistic or news report as well. Daily critics, particularly of motion pictures and television, differ from the reviewers for the major magazines—particularly such publications as *Saturday Review*, *The New Yorker*, *Harpers* and *Atlantic*—in that they are expected to be reporters first and to render aesthetic judgment second.

Nevertheless, the majority of newspaper critics, particularly those who write for newspapers in large metropolitan cities, do try to set high standards of critical performance. They assert first that the critic must set forth a clear and succinct exposition not only of what he thinks about the film, but also that he define the basis for his judgment. And the critic must, in any case, explain with honest conviction whether, in his opinion, the film is "good" or "bad," along with an equally clear exposition of what makes it inherently good or bad. It is true, as at least a fourth of the critics agree, that totally objective criticism is almost invariably impossible to achieve. Nor, it might be added parenthetically, is total objectivity always desirable. Alexander Woollcott's dance in the streets after seeing a fine play was a purely subjective, affective judgment, and many of the great literary and drama critics have conveyed the quality of contagious enthusiasm for a work, not only because of its objective merits but because of its emotional impact as well.

But newspaper critics believe, also, that criticism of the arts should be something more than capable journalism. Almost three-fourths believe that it is possible—and desirable—for the critic to make some contribution to scholarship. Film critics, interestingly enough, generally agree that a movie review should have a purpose beyond informing and entertaining the reader. They are convinced, probably against the better judgment not only of their editors but also of the producers and studio entrepreneurs, that criticism should have a serious purpose and that the public can—and frequently does —react affirmatively to criticism which is thoughtful and responsible. There is a general consensus that the motion picture audience responds to criticism as a barometer of quality and as a guide of what to see and what to avoid. The motion picture critic believes, too, that the reading of criticism cannot avoid an effect on the reader's social and political, as well as aesthetic, attitudes. And there is little doubt that, on any basis—subjective or empirical—the film critics are correct in their conviction that they have greater influence on the public than do television critics. One factor here, however, may be the tendency of most television critics to review an offering after it has been on the air, although there has been increasing opportunity in the past two seasons for television critics to pre-review programs and thereby give the viewer an opportunity to know something in advance about what he might be viewing on the home screen.

In summary, the Harris study concludes that movie critics believe that they, as well as critics of other arts, do play an "indispensable role" in modern society. They are proud of their status and believe their work is prestigious. They look upon themselves as journalists who must write clearly and for the general public; they are convinced that their work is educational; and, while they do not believe that critics should be licensed as are doctors or lawyers, they would welcome an opportunity to take academic courses which might serve as a spur to better critical performance. Most significantly, the motion picture critics admit that they, like drama critics, are subjected to a variety of pressures to write favorable reviews.

The Auteur *Theory*

These findings are, of course, general opinions, culled from a study of critics of varying tastes and backgrounds and writing for a variety of newspapers throughout the country. The most prestigious of journalistic critics, however, work mainly in New York and Los Angeles and in the major cities across the country. And the scholarly critics write mainly for the major literary magazines and for such journals as *Film Quarterly* and *Partisan Review*. It is from this group that anything resembling a theory of motion picture criticism has emerged. And the theory around which considerable controversy has swirled is not so much a method of criticism, but a kind of aesthetic dialectic by which film is to be confronted. In 1957, in a Parisian monthly magazine called *Cahiers du Cinema*, the famed French cinematographer, Francois Truffaut, outlined what was to become one of the most hotly-debated issues in the arena of serious motion picture criticism. Truffaut postulated what has become known in the United States as the *auteur* theory of motion picture criticism. The theory is uncomplicated. Indeed its adversaries—and they are many—believe it is ludicrous and simplistic. According to the *auteur* theory, the critic is to confine his judgment of film solely with the work of the director. The producer, the writer and the stars are of no consequence. As Marshall McLuhan believes the medium is the message, the proponents of the *auteur* theory believe that the medium is the director and that only certain directors are worthy of being *auteurs*. The director, then, is viewed by critics who accept the *auteur* theory—Andrew Sarris in particular in this country—as the one and only, the true creative force in the making of a film. Fortunate, indeed, are these directors who are deemed worthy of achieving the enviable status of being selected by Sarris as *auteurs*.

The *auteur* theory of cinema criticism has taken up a good deal of space in *Film Quarterly* and other publications—probably more than it deserves. In the pages of these scholarly publications, Sarris and his adversaries, such as Pauline Kael and John Simon, flay at each other with acerbic bite and frequently with considerable venomous disdain. Sarris insists his position on the *auteur* theory is one of "defense in depth" and concludes that the *auteur* theory is by any standard "the most efficient method of classifying the cinema, past, present and future." It is a method that is neither mysterious, esoteric nor snobbish, but is rather a sensible way of communicating effectively about film. The *auteur* theory presents no fixed ideas, but is flexible and malleable. The theory is notable, however, for its fixation on the director, and the critical evaluation of film is not on the script or the performance or even the photography, but on the director's technique. The critic, in evaluating film, is a communicator, a catalyst between the director and the public and the *auteur* theory is a method by which the critic may most effectively explain style and meaning to the reader.

But the *auteur* proponents are not immune to demurrers from other able critics. In the first place, many of Sarris' contemporaries would take issue with the selection of those directors who, in terms of the *auteur* theory, are outstanding. Sarris' adversaries believe, for example, that such choices as Otto Preminger or Howard Hughes as outstanding are absurd choices. In his review of Sarris' book *Confessions of a Cultist: On Cinema, 1955–69*, Richard Gilman scores Sarris' views on several counts. Admittedly, Sarris has made a provocative contribution to serious motion picture criticism. But Gilman and others believe that the *auteur* theory leads to the selection of second rate movies and inferior directors. In other words, the *auteur* theorists apply a high seriousness of approach, not to genuine work of art but to "kitsch." Motion picture criticism departs so radically from the journalistic approach that it becomes immersed in cultism and in an existentialist philosophy which has little relevance to the meaning of what audiences actually see on the screen. The movies, in fact, are as a rule neither high culture nor "kitsch," but fall somewhere in between these polarities. And the best critics combine not only good journalism, but a sense of aesthetics and sound scholarship as well. Since motion pictures are a visual art form, there is no denying the importance of the director. But the *auteur* theory leads to a *reductio ad absurdum* because of its total disregard of story or script. If, in McLuhan, the medium is the message and content is, therefore, of no consequence, in the *auteur* theory the director is the film. The plot, or narrative values, may be disregarded entirely. Surely, an untenable method of criticism of any art form.

The *auteur* theory, above all, denigrates the screenwriter and makes of film a hybrid art. Hollis Alpert, a gifted observer of motion pictures, asked rhetorically in an article in the *Saturday Review*, "but who wrote the movie?" The point is clear. The making of movies becomes a kind of *pastiche*, with the director selecting at random and, in effect, improvising the script as the film progresses. It is this non-creative, medium-as-message viewpoint which has downgraded the creative writer and which, in Alpert's opinion, may have contributed to the unhealthy state of affairs in Hollywood today. From a critic's point of view, the elevation of the director above that of creative writer tends to make cinema a second-rate art. And, ironically, the two factors responsible for the deification of directors would seem to be antagonistic, rather than cooperative forces. The *auteur* theory critics believe that genuine motion picture creativity flows from the director. At the same time, the entrepreneurs in the industry business offices traditionally have publicized the director, both in blazing on-screen credits and in national advertising and publicity. In other arts, such as the theatre, it is the writer who assumes primary importance. But few movie-goers—or critics—will readily recall the screenwriters who were responsible for Hollywood's finest pictures. Indeed, one of the most discerning of movie critics, Dwight MacDonald, elected to give up reviewing film because he was convinced that every new film which appeared already had been reviewed under another title. Only in a business that deprecates the contribution of the serious creative writer can such a situation prevail.

Much of contemporary motion picture criticism, on the other hand, tends to look upon motion pictures as a very serious art form. Reviews lean increasingly toward a concern—real or imagined—with the relationship between cinema and society. Characters are dissected from the vantage point of various psychologies, and movie-going is looked upon not only as entertainment, but as a significant sociological and psychological experience. But movies are more than that. Like television, they are primarily a mass entertainment phenomenon. More importantly, to the bankers who run much of the industry, they are a business enterprise. This viewpoint considers picture-making not an aesthetic endeavor, but in terms of integers on a calculating machine that comes up with figures of profit or loss. And between the esoteric *auteur* theory and the relentless demands of the box-office, how is the contemporary critic to judge film? What is he to look for?

Pragmatic vs. Academic Criticism

These questions come to the heart of what film criticism should be and what it should offer the potential movie-goer. And they underscore the differences between the pragmatic and the academic critics, between critics such as Bosley Crowther, Judith Crist and Pauline Kael and Andrew Sarris and John Simon who, despite their enormous differences, can hardly be termed journalistic critics. The most respected of motion picture critics during his many years of tenure on the *New York Times*, Bosley Crowther, was succeeded by Renata Adler who, presumably met the *Times'* curious new standard of what the "new criticism" ought to be. But Renata Adler's tenure was short-lived. According to some sources, conflict between Miss Adler and her editors over questions of style forced a showdown. This may or may not be true. Miss Adler had her advocates and her detractors, and many felt that she was not writing for the general reader but for a select few who might appreciate her extraordinary sensitivity and her taut style. As one Adler advocate put it, she came to motion pictures as a fresh experience and "in her ignorance managed to say more interesting things about movies in a year . . . than most critics would manage if they lasted 27 years."

Journalistic criticism of film has its own self-styled exponent in Judith Crist who, in an interview in *Film Quarterly* (Fall, 1968) called herself essentially a "mass medium person." Journalistic criticism of film, Judith Crist believes, functions to inform the public and to recommend or steer people away from seeing the film. In a communicative sense, this is an exemplification of the sheer informational use of language. In addition, and because most movies are *not* art, Miss Crist believes that movies must be recognized not as an esoteric aesthetic phenomenon, but as a medium of mass communication. Nevertheless, because plot or content *is* important, those who subscribe to the *auteur* theory are wrong, because emphasis on the director inhibits that free-flowing expressive communication which makes movies a mass medium. The journalistic critic believes clearly that most people who go to the movies want journalistic reports, not aesthetic judgment. But a nagging question arises. Is it not possible to combine good journalism with sound aesthetic judgment in motion picture criticism? Many students of film believe that a critic such as Bosley Crowther and the late James Agee each accomplished this in quite different ways. And to many, Pauline Kael does so today. To write such criticism requires an understanding of the simple fact that most contemporary motion pictures do not issue from Hollywood with the stamp of everlasting greatness. Most pictures are quite ordinary and conventional entertainment. Many, in recent years, have sought to increase the box-office lure by an attempt to attract public attention to erotic, or "blue," themes and dialogue. Nor are most movies either "camp" or high culture. Film is a combination of many diverse arts including writing, music, cinematography and even dance.

And the technical proficiency of even the most capable of directors should not always be confused with art.

From all this, it is clear that there are wide and deep differences among the motion picture critics, depending upon the audiences each critic sets out to reach. There have even come to be subtle semantic distinctions between "motion pictures" (popular Hollywood entertainment), cinema (the *auteur* theorists) and film (the experimentalists on the college campuses). But all pictures, from a critical point of view, are communication. Indeed, the motion picture uniquely combines the qualities of both verbal and non-verbal communication. What is important for *all* motion picture criticism, journalistic or academic, is that the critic function not only to inform, but also to provide a direction-finder for the viewer, to attempt to help the movie-goer perceive what is excellent and what is meretricious, perhaps to help, too, in seeing what is not so easily perceivable on the surface. The best critics, in all the arts, have communicated an enthusiasm for what is excellent, both in popular entertainment and in serious art. And the best critics, above all, have had the great virtue of incorruptible, ruthless honesty.

PART EIGHT

The
New
Technology

An industry founded upon advances in the physical sciences and the concomitant revolution in communications technology which they have generated can ill afford to underestimate the potential impact of new technological advances. Wilton Holm of the Motion Picture Research Center in Hollywood describes some of the imminent technical changes which may influence industry procedure, while Peter Guber analyzes the effects which the videocassete may have upon movie business practices in the future.

It is inevitable, of course, that any conjecture in the rapidly-changing field of communications technology is in risk of being outdated within weeks or even days of its initial expression. It should be stressed, therefore, that neither Mr. Holm nor Mr. Guber has had opportunity to record significant changes in the field during the several months between the original date of composition and the publication of his essay here.

MANAGEMENT LOOKS AT THE FUTURE *

WILTON R. HOLM

". . . The motion picture industry must consider its product in the broader context of the nature of the social environment it creates—and stress the values and experiences that people need, and are willing to pay for. . . ."

In predicting the technological future of film, one thing seems fairly certain: Motion pictures will persist and evolve whether they are recorded on film, magnetic tape, or something else; whether viewed on a projection screen, a cathode ray tube, or something else; and whether they are made by today's creative artists and technicians, or by someone else. At our Research Center, our ultimate concern is with the best and most effective devices and techniques to record, store, playback and view time-sequential action and happenings. These may involve humans, animals, nature, animated objects and beings, even abstract phenomena, all enhanced by sound, stereo sound, stereo vision, color, smell, or any other attribute that helps to better satisfy society's leisure-time wants and needs.

WILTON R. HOLM is a Vice-President of the Association of Motion Picture & Television Producers, Inc. and the Executive Director of the Motion Picture & Television Research Center in Hollywood. Prior to becoming Director of the Research Center, Mr. Holm was a motion picture specialist and technical administrator with the E. I. DuPont Company for 15 years. A physicist, Mr. Holm graduated from St. Ambrose College, and did graduate work at the University of Iowa. He is the author of numerous works dealing with physical optics, photography, color motion pictures and color television.

* Reprinted from the *Journal* of The Producers Guild of America, September, 1970.

253

Our technological concern with motion pictures for theatres and for TV is divided into two basic categories: the motion picture product and tools for producing the product.

Under product, we list image quality, sound quality, standardization, and, in my judgment by far the most important, the marketability of that product—especially films made for theatre release. It has been said by members of our production community that only 30% of the pictures made today actually make money; most of the others have not been attractive at the box-office. The Research Center has a statistical study in the feasibility stage, the purpose of which is to isolate—and assign weighting factors—to a number of emotional response elements in a picture, so that audience appeal can be judged with reasonable accuracy before a picture is made. It may seem incredible that something so subjective would respond to the methods of modern statistical technology; but our results to date, using recent pictures, are showing some definite correlations with their box-office earnings.

Under tools we list two main categories: A Studio-Stage System and a Location System. For theatrical pictures, location shooting is strongly in the ascendency. This trend has been greatly enhanced by the Cinemobile and by such other factors as (1), the new filmmakers' disinclination to work in studios, (2), the fact that films shot on stages look unreal, and (3), that it costs less to shoot on location. There is an interesting anomaly here—namely that TV shows are shot as much as possible in studios because it costs less to shoot them there.

There is considerable truth, however, to the claim that much stage photography looks unreal today. But it need not—and it will not—when the Studio-Stage System becomes as viable a system as the Location System has become. I predict at least one new studio-stage complex will exist in Hollywood within the next two to three years. This complex will feature stages which will have high utilization factors—that is, which can be used for production 80% to 100% of the time as compared with today's stages, which are used to build sets for about 35% of the time, striking sets for another 35% of the time, for production photography only about 30% of the time. The facilities of these new stages will include workable front projection, an electric traveling matte system which permits viewing a composite scene as it is shot, and provision for viewing next-day dailies. With the exception of outdoor long shots, photography on these stages will be indistinguishable from location photography. The viewer, of course, does not care whether the picture on the screen is of a real location; he merely wants it to look real, so verisimilitude becomes the name of the game.

There will be other interesting sub-systems in the new stages. Smaller, lighter, remotely-controlled cameras will be included, as well as radio microphones no larger than a large capsule which can be made to sound any desired distance from the camera. New, high-definition varifocal-zoom lenses, self-synchronizing camera motors, laser and electronic systems—all will be standard elements of the new studio-stages. Many of these will also be inputs to the Location System.

Theatres of the immediate future will continue to present pictures on film, primarily because a good projector which will accept electronic information and present it as a theatre-size picture is not available today. The Eidophor type projector is not adequate, and electoluminescent screens of sufficient definition are not yet possible. A scanning laser projector might become a possibility, and if it does we may see the beginning of the end of the release-print system as we know it—at least in the United States. The scanning-laser projector pictures could be sent to theatres electronically via co-axial cable or microwave relay systems. This would reduce the number of release prints from 400 or more per picture to about 25. Eventually distribution could be by satellite, and the number of prints could be reduced to one or two per picture. The CATV and home video-cassette makers will create a great demand for entertainment motion pictures, whether they involve the EVR system, the RCA system, the magnetic tape system or some other mechanism. It is probable that the CATV and the home video-cassette markets will double our present demand for product. To be sure, theatres will not disappear. New housing and apartment complexes will all build theatres, just as shopping centers are building them today. All these facilities will provide a baby-sitting service, so young married as well as young unmarried will go to the movies.

TV will prosper too. In perhaps ten years all TV is likely to come into the home via cable—even "free" TV—because all homes will be wired. The air space occupied by present TV channels will be needed for other communication needs of society. There will probably be commercials on pay-TV, but only at the beginning and end of a show, and perhaps at natural intermissions—not every seven minutes.

Quality of entertainment will be much better, not only in theatres, but on TV as well. Using Jack Valenti's words: "Tomorrow's audiences will demand entertainment which enters deeply into their lives, speaks *to* them and *of* them and their times. But they will also demand the preservation of the past and an insight into the future." I see no reason to disagree with that. Psychologists and sociologists with whom we have worked say that we are on the leading edge of a new wave of spirituality, even though many theatres report good business for "X"-rated films, and poor business for "G"-rated ones. The old "G" pictures on TV are very high in the Neilsen ratings. This apparent dichotomy may be telling us something. Theodore Roszak, author of *The Making Of A Counter-Culture*, claims that this is what today's disaffiliation of youth is all about—that ". . . they want desperately to stop being the children of even a reformed and humanized Dr. Frankenstein, and become the children of God. Literally. Experientially. Miraculously." Whether Roszak is correct or not, his thought leads me to consider the new industrial revolution, and the opportunity I believe it offers the motion picture industry.

Alert managements are already feeling the stirrings of this new industrial revolution. They recognize that their industries—and ours is no exception—will soon have to be concerned with fulfilling basic human needs; they will have to concern themselves with finding out what people really want during that short time they spend on earth. In an affluent society, human needs tend to move up a scale from material goods toward the desire for self-realization. Even the most avid consumer can use only so many TV sets or so many cars. Thus, if a corporation is to continue to serve a useful function, it must redefine its role in terms of delivery of human value. It will have to create that quality in life that people really seek.

The motion picture industry must also consider its product in the broader context of the nature of the social environment it creates —and stress the values and experiences that people need, and are willing to pay for. Despite the different emphasis, this is still what the marketing process is all about. People want more and more to feel a sense of hope and meaning. Motion pictures can provide them with this feeling of self-fulfillment and self-realization by establishing an empathic response to people in pictures which solve social problems the way society should solve them—the way society will have to solve them ultimately. I believe that movies can and should lead the way. We should ask: "What sort of critical life-experiences do humans feel they ought to have? What does it take to make a person feel he belongs to a worthwhile group?" We should provide real heroes, not anti-heroes.

The industry needs to conduct market research directed toward finding out what people want in life. This does not mean product research, or the Dichter-type motivation research. We do have a way of measuring how well our pictures fulfill the human needs of our audiences—the box-office. We hear much about segregated audiences, but every now and then a picture comes along that has broad appeal —*The Sound of Music, Gone With The Wind, The Graduate, Guess Who's Coming To Dinner, Dr. Zhivago, Mary Poppins, The Love Bug, True Grit*. Each is different, but all share a charisma, a mystique. Why? Has the box-office been telling us something that we have continued to ignore? This is part of what the Research Center wants to learn from its research project based upon box-office receipts. If we succeed, we can learn how to make pictures that make a profit, true. But modern management today recognizes profit as a by-product, not an end in itself. It can be a genuine measure of how well an organization is serving society.

THE CARTRIDGE REVOLUTION *

PETER GUBER

". . . When one considers the enormous television market together with the vast quantities of programming TV devours, and then combines those with the market for the record, tape, publishing and exhibition industries, the audio-visual cartridge market begins to take shape. . . . Its potential is limitless. . . ."

In 1948, the motion picture industry faced a monumental crisis. The enemy was a 10-inch picture of flickering quality and tinny sound. Giant motion picture studio complexes (later to reap the benefits of this technological innovation) reacted to the fledgling by burying their heads and refusing to believe anything could shake the dynasty. As a consequence, television networks and their production arms entered a market devoid of competition from the single source best equipped to take a prominent position in the emerging empire. The motion picture houses' negative attitude aided and abetted the recession that plagued the theatrical business for years. Yet it was television that rescued the motion picture industry by purchasing its vast film libraries —thus infusing millions of dollars of capital into the coffers of the faltering giants.

Today the industry once again seems imperiled by technological

PETER GUBER is Production Vice-President for Columbia Pictures. A graduate of Syracuse, he holds a J.D. degree from the NYU School of Law, and is now pursuing graduate study at the University of Southern California. He is a member of the bar in New York, California and District of Columbia.

* Reprinted by permission of the author, from *Cinema*, May 2, 1970. (Supplemental Edition)

innovation, yet the question remains—has experience given it the wisdom to approach the current crisis in some positive way? The answer appears to be no. Because of a cost crush and shrinking profits, Hollywood's majors are rushing to rid themselves of stages, equipment, craft services and back lots, together with personnel and executive management necessary to run those complex facilities which are capable of churning out vast quantities of product. A clouded future seems darkened further by a growing disenchantment among young filmmakers—who are now being turned out of cinema schools in droves, and are unable to find their way into an ever-shrinking industry. Unions, forced to face runaway production costs and a greater cost consciousness on the part of major financiers, have also failed effectively to face the situation.

What all elements within the industry fail to realize is that a fomenting revolution in technology will solve all of those problems which now appear so insoluble. As a result of this new innovation and its impact, studios will run on three shifts—24 hours a day—with the need for product being so enormous that executive studio personnel will once more be steeped in supervision and development of product on a wholesale basis. Independent production will flower. There will be room for all in the industry of the future. Union problems will disappear with full employment, and opportunity will abound. Not only will studio film libraries again be revalued upward—as assets on their financial statements—but the immense catalogues of unproduced properties heretofore abandoned or written off will be reactivated to meet the almost insatiable need for product.

This revolution will assuredly occur. Battle lines are drawn, combatants are armed and well-defined, and the stakes are enormous for both victims and victors. The technological development underlying this upheaval is a small, mass-produced plastic cartridge capable of reproducing high-quality sound and color picture through a normal color television receiver. The emerging medium will make the word "television" an anachronism. Electronic home-entertainment hardware may well become the country's most widely owned durable good, eventually surpassing even automobiles as our national product. The impending revolution will have an impact in virtually every area of American culture, making the home the focal point for entertainment, education and spiritual enrichment—and providing one answer for a burgeoning population's needs.

THE COMBATANTS

The entertainment and electronic complexes and their allied industries have long recognized the culturally acquisitive nature of Americans—their voracious appetite for records, taped music, books, movies and television. A study of consumer habits reveals not only preferences for new things to hear, see, read or attend—but significant information about when people choose to expose themselves to the messages. Clearly, if films—via television or theatrical exhibition—could be controlled by the individual, a greater audience could be achieved —with more product and at greater profits. This entrepreneurial principle was evident to CBS, RCA, Sony and others who invested heavily in research and development of the audio-visual cartridge medium. Now four essential hardware situations seem to be evolving: the CBS EVR system; RCA's holographic system; Super-8mm systems; and videotape recorder playback units. Whether one or more will win the day is not yet evident. The fact that these and other emerging systems are entirely incompatible magnifies the stakes. A schematic description of each is essential to a basic comprehension of the issues which are involved.

Videotape

Sony Company of Japan is manufacturing the Videocorder. Though this system has been on the market for quite some time it has not stirred great consumer interest. Unlike the other three, the Videocorder has a record and playback capability which allows the consumer not only to view programming, but to produce and create his own home product. Sony markets—for approximately $350—a portable black-and-white TV camera which records right into the Video-corder. The recording factor in the Videocorder (aside from the legal problems) allows the home entertainment buff to tape any pro-grams or films from free or pay TV, thus building his home library at no greater cost than raw stock. Legal implications with respect to piracy and copyright infringement in the *modus operandi* are enormous. Earlier Videocorders had their own built-in small screen TV monitor through which the programming was viewed. By simple adaptor, programming can now be piped into any standard black-and-white or color TV, but in black-and-white form only.

In November 1969, Sony officials unveiled their entry into the cartridge/cassette market—a Videocassette player which will provide color programming. Ostensibly, the cassettes will run 100 minutes and will cost $20 in raw form. A shotgun of differing press releases from Sony indicates that they have no clear-cut strategy to capture a specific segment of the market. Great confusion surrounds its expected price, announced at $350 but later quoted by Sony as being closer to $400. Private research firms investigating the equipment estimate the price tag may be as high as $750. The Sony system utilizes half-inch magnetic videotape much the same as that used commonly by the television networks for programming and "instant replay." It is packaged in plastic cassettes the size of a book. The video cassette is compatible with either color or black-and-white TV sets, and the size of the unit is comparable to present audio tape decks. Another advantage of the Videocorder is that the tape is erasable, and thus initial investment for raw stock cartridge has broader potential. Furthermore, it could mean that one might buy a number of raw stock cartridges, go to a distribution center and there have the master unit record a program onto the individually owned cassettes for a minimum charge of between $3 to $5. Thus, by utilizing the "refillable soda-bottle" concept, one could reach the broadest market at the best price. Each video cassette might have a built-in counter that could indicate the frequency of plays and charges could be made accordingly.

Perhaps the most exciting breakthrough is the proposed marketing by Cartridge TV, Inc.—a division of AVCO—of a self-contained, fully integrated unit which combines a regular TV set with a videotape cartridge player. The set appears as any normal TV set would except that it has an intake slot on its side for the insertion of continuous loop cartridges. The system uses normal half-inch magnetic audio tape with a playing time of two hours. The consumer will have his choice of pre-recorded color and sound programming, or will be able to record his own shows directly off free TV. The software price with or without programming has not yet been determined; but since the raw stock is merely audio tape as used in home tape recorders, it will undoubtedly be far less expensive than videotape. The hardware unit is priced at $895 complete. Avco is making its initial entry directly into the home consumer market and unveiled its breakthrough at a trade show in New York in June, 1970. This system undoubtedly thrusts the videotape situation into a prominent position. Furthermore, videotape, unlike either the RCA or CBS systems, is an originating process. Thus, one can create programs directly on videotape and this may, in the future, be an advantage in a cost-conscious, highly competitive market. George Gould, President of Teletronics International, feels video tape will eventually take the place of film in most production areas. He claims 25% can be saved on a TV series over film and perhaps up to 40% on feature films. One of the impediments to tape acceptance is the absence of top creative talent, now beginning to gravitate toward the medium.

Avco plans to market their cassettes under the name Cartrivision. They will be released to chain stores for an annual fee of $50 per feature, and the rental cost should be about $5 per use. Avco also plans to market short subjects in a 30-minute package that will be sold directly to the public. Avco recently announced competitive retail prices for its software units. Suggested costs for pre-recorded cartridges will range from $7.98 to $24.98. Blank cartridges of four different playing lengths will cost about $10 for 15 minutes of playing time, and up to $25 for the maximum two-hour cartridge. Rental prices for pre-recorded material begins at $3. No average rental price has been indicated. Other blank cartridge prices are 30 minutes for $12.98, and one hour for $16.98.

Ampex, the originator of videotape, made its bid early in September, 1970 for the leadership in the videorecorder market. Both recorders and players feature automatic cartridge loading and are designed for both closed-circuit television and home recording. Referred to as Instavision, the system is the smallest cartridge loading video recorder and/or player to date. The public will have a choice of several models, all of which operate on batteries or household current in either black-and-white or color.

The Instavision system uses standard half-inch wide videotape enclosed in a small circular plastic cartridge. Like the EVR cartridge, the Instavision magazine is surrounded by a plastic leader strip which protects its contents. It is threaded and rewound automatically in the player. The cartridge will play for 30 minutes in black-and-white or color, or one hour in a non-standard "extended play" mode at half-speed. A two-hour version in the same cartridge is promised later. The cartridge is compatible with all other conventional reel-type recorders embodying the Type I standard. To operate the recorder/player, the cartridge is merely inserted in the recorder and the "record" or "play" button pushed.

Prices, based on forecast levels for today's closed-circuit market, will be approximately $800 for a monochrome player, $900 for a monochrome recorder/player or color player and $1,000 for a color recorder/player. Any model may be modified for color or recording capability after purchase with the addition of simple plug-in modules. An optional five-pound camera with zoom lens is $400. Thus, it it comparable in price with Sony and Panasonic portable camera-recorder combines. With development of mass markets, Ampex officials said prices could come down substantially.

Although no software-production plans are in Ampex's future, the company says it has program availability and talks are in progress concerning software tie-ups. Blank cartridges will sell for less than $13 for 30 minutes of recording time at the Type I standard, or 60 minutes in an extended play mode. Changing from standard to extended play is accomplished by a simple switch. Playing up to two hours will be offered in later designs.

The basic Instavision recorder/player weighs less than 16 lbs. with common flashlight or rechargeable batteries. It measures 11" x 13" x 4.5". It permits slow-motion and stop-action recording and elementary editing. Two independent audio channels permit flexibility in audio recording, including stereo playback. Rewind or fast forward controls advance the complete tape in one minute. A shoulder strap is included for portable operation. An accessory permits operation from an automobile cigarette lighter outlet.

Standard with each recorder or player is a separate power-pak that houses an AC power converter for plug-in operation, a battery recharger and optional electronic circuitry for color record or playback. The power-pak is designed as an attractive base for the recorder during any of these operations. The recorder is detached from the powre-pak for portable recording or playback.

The companion monochrome camera is of standard professional quality. It comes complete with an electronic viewfinder. The viewfinder, actually a miniature television receiver, permits precise scene framing, viewing of exactly what is being recorded, and pushbutton replay of recordings. A trigger control built into the pistol-grip enables one person to operate both camera and recorder easily.

Performance specifications for the recorder equal or exceed those of competitive systems announced to date. Color resolution is compatible with standard color television receivers.

The Instavision line has been designed by the Ampex Educational and Industrial Products Division, Elk Grove Village, Illinois. It will be manufactured by TOAMCO, the company's joint venture company with Toshiba in Tokyo, Japan. Toshiba will market the line in Japan, Ampex elsewhere in the world.

The new recorders are the first low-cost cartridge videotape recorders ever offered by Ampex. The company's broad line of one-inch closed-circuit recorders will continue to serve the more demanding segments of the closed-circuit market where higher picture quality, heavy duty construction and production features are required.

Philips, the pioneer company that established a worldwide standardization in the magnetic tape recording field, is now ready to join with other companies in a videocassette recorder standard. It has already set its own standards for the hardware systems it is now developing for commercial use. The goals are simplicity of operation, an incorporated recording facility, magnetic cassette programming, full color capability, one hour minimum playing time, and low consumer cost.

Philips has already eliminated the need for a TV adapter in its VCR system. In each VCR a color tuner is built in such a way that it represents a second television set, but without a viewing screen. This enables the use of the antenna input of the television receiver for playback purposes. Thus, while in its recording mode the VCR will take the signal to be recorded from its own incorporated color tuner. In this way a viewer can watch a program on his television receiver while he is recording another program on his VCR.

Although at the present time Philips is selling open-reel black-

and-white videotape recorders they are still in need of adaptors to be hooked up to present-day television receivers. The forthcoming videocassette recorder will be comparatively priced at $550, but at no extra cost for TV adaptors.

In November of 1969, Panasonic demonstrated a magazine type color video tape recorder developed by Matsushita Electric Industries in Japan. This particular model was designed primarily for the educational and industrial markets. In view of the type of applications prevalent in these fields, the magazine VTR included both playback and recording capabilities.

The Matsushita magazine VTR has several features. The magazine offers 30 minutes of color recording and playback on conventional magnetic videotape. Loading and unloading of the magazine is as easy as an audio cassette. The magazine can be inserted or withdrawn any time during the program without need for rewind. Color signals are directly recorded on half-inch tape without processing or use of a pilot signal. This is an achievement previously possible only on one-inch tape. The hardware unit is compact (14" X 14" X 5.1"), portable (33 pounds, including magazine and battery) and operates on external AC power or built-in DC battery. These characteristics were realized by the development of a special brushless DC motor.

In order to realize tape inter-changeability the tape format employed is "standard type - 1." The magazine houses two five-inch reels and the entire system is so designed that tapes can be removed from the magazine and played on a standard open-reel machine. Conversely, tapes recorded on an open-reel machine can be easily loaded into the magazine for convenient playback.

Matsushita has conducted and continues to conduct basic research in a number of areas related to the production, storage, and playback of audio/video information. At this time, the company remains committed to the use of the magnetic tape for video recording and playback systems. Matsushita believes the tastes and needs of the buying public will vary widely, and will encompass (1) playback of black-and-white and color pre-recorded materials equal in picture quality to current home TV systems, (2) recording programs "off air" for delayed or repeated viewing, and (3) prodution of "instant movies" by means of a camera input.

RCA's Holographic System

In October, 1970, a red-faced RCA rushed to demonstrate their home video player. Backs to the wall, they had little more to show than the individual components which actually make up their unit. Based upon the observation of numerous technicians present, RCA had several problems to overcome before marketing a successful integrated system. Their video element was blurry, and characters Chaplinesque in quality. Though it would not be difficult to lay sound into the RCA tape, there was none at the demonstration. RCA had chosen Selectavision as a trade name for its product, but legal obstacles over this nomenclature apparently caused them to back away. Of far more importance than the trade name is the fact that RCA's product will not be available to compete with CBS EVR for quite some time.

RCA's tape players will be the first consumer product utilizing lasers. Chase Morsey, Jr., executive vice-president of RCA, claims the initial price will be less than $400, with tapes costing under $10 for a 30-minute program—which is below the present videotape or film cost. The tape used in this process is far different from that which we commonly refer to as videotape, as employed by Sony in its Videocorder. Rather it is a 2-mil-thick completely transparent vinyl tape, very similar in appearance to that which is used to wrap chickens in supermarkets.

RCA's system employs a holographic rather than a photographic process. Both photography and holography are techniques to record subject matter images on film and tape. They differ in the way they record the image. Photography involves the registering of an image as a pattern of intensity variations produced by light reflected from the subject. In holography, the light source of a laser is split into two beams, one of which is directed at the subject and reflected onto a photographic plate and the other of which is sent directly to the plate. The first beam has a changed character (having been reflected from the subject) and interferes with the second direct beam. It is this interference that is photographically recorded in the form of a hologram. The hologram is implanted on clear vinyl tape. At least for the present, holographic tapes cannot be made directly from life, but rather from other media, such as movie films, videotapes, slides and photographs.

As RCA explains it, color programming emanating from a color TV camera, color videotape player, or the like, is recorded on conventional film by employing the electron beam recorder. This film is then referred to as the color encoded master. The master is then developed and a laser converts it to a series of holograms on a plastic tape which is coated with a photo-resist chemical. The chemical's molecular structure causes the tape to harden in varying degrees relative to the measure and strength of the laser light bombarding it. This tape then goes through a developing process. It is immersed in a chemical solution, eroding the hardened portions on the tape, resulting in a topographical map, the peaks and valleys and corresponding spaces in between representing the original program material in coded form.

The resultant tape is referred to as a master hologram. It is given a nickel coating which when stripped away leaves a nickel tape with the holograms impressed into it like a series of etchings. This is the nickel master. By feeding the nickel master through a set of pressure rollers, together with the transparent vinyl tape (the end product), the holographic etchings on the nickel master make an impression on the smooth surface of the vinyl tape in the form of a holographic relief. This same nickel master can churn out thousands of "prints" without any loss of quality.

The final holographic tape itself in raw form before coating and processing would cost about six cents per half-hour cartridge. The holograms occupy about one-third of the width of the tape. Color integration is also embossed in the same hologram by using two color sub-carriers, one for red and the other for the blue signal. The third color necessary for true color presentation, green, is derived from the other two color signals by the process of subtracting from the luminace or brightness information. The reason why RCA has gone to all the trouble of using holograms is the ease of operation, durability, and cheap duplicating cost which the mode offers. A production manufacturing plant could duplicate 2,000 or more high-powered color cartridges at the price of between $2 and $3 each, exclusive of rights costs.

Furthermore, a hologram tape can be cut into thinner and thinner plates, and each piece contains all the information needed to reconstruct a complete integral presentation of the program. Even with only one-tenth of the tape, the only thing lost would be picture resolution and contrast, but not content. This technical virtuosity makes holograms scratch-proof, dust-proof, and virtually indestructable. In addition, technical hardware problems, such as synchronization, are avoided. Thus, tape transport devices and feeder keys need not keep the images on the holograms in absolute accurate alignment and, since the light source from the laser unit inside the playback mechanism moves in parallel rays, the image of the hologram need not be carefully focused. Thus pick-up point is not critical.

The Fraunhofer hologram has excellent image immobilization properties and the two images are perfectly superimposed. Scratching, punching holes, wetting, or rubbing of the vinyl tape produce no observable difference in the picture produced on the television screen. Because of the nature of the hologram, when the low-powered 2mW laser housed within the unit passes a coherent light beam through the vinyl tape hologram, it creates a real image on the vidicon TV camera pick-up tube inside the playback unit. This image merely fades in and out as the tape moves along past the laser beam. This camera records the image reconstructed by the laser directly, as well as their NTSC colors as coded variations in the images, and mixes the two into an integrated color picture signal which it sends to the TV receiver. Unlike normal film projectors, it is possible for tapes to move at variable speeds and thus achieve a slow-motion effect or be stopped entirely without any damage to the tape and allow extended observation of but a single frame. The demonstration model moved at 7½ inches-per-second to reproduce normal movement.

No audio information has been included in the demonstration tapes presently seen, but the commercial version will undoubtedly utilize one—probably two—audio tracks, with an eye towards stereo response. These tracks will also be etched into the tape. The signal emanating from the RCA player is sent by wire through to the TV receivers' antenna terminals, which is identical to the EVR system. Thus the ability to hook up to multiple sets at the same time via a master antenna unit makes CATV use implicit for these systems.

In view of the hardware involved, cheap CATV programming may create millions of distributing stations. RCA's hardware marketing strategy is to put the playback unit in modular form rather than building it into its TV sets in order that potential users can place them anywhere in the home in combination with different TV receivers or futuristic wall screens. Its laser is said to be completely safe and has approximately 2,000 hours of life. The replacement cost is $25. Financial psychics predict that RCA's investment will reach $25-million before the first consumer units reach the home. Unlike CBS, RCA has the capability to both make and sell its machines, and will do so. CBS has turned to Motorola as an exclusive licensee. Many questions are raised in the RCA camp, however, and those suggest there are some high hurdles ahead for the process.

There is no doubt, however, that RCA is in the race to stay, and might win. The technical advantages in holography are its 3-dimensional image-reproduction capability and its potential use in giant wall screens. A breakthrough in either area could create tremendous momentum for the RCA product. Both Bell Telephone and Hughes Laboratories have had successful experimental results in projection of still 3-D pictures. Both are confident that within 15 years the system can be adapted to project motion pictures in 3-D. The technical hold-ups in this process are development of the slow-emulsion speed film necessary to produce the hologram and the present inability to photograph live subjects safely with the use of the laser beam.

The holographic process is the basis for the 3-D system. Its successful development as a home-consumer mechanism will make it possible for one to view an 8-foot tall John Wayne in three dimension —and even walk around him—in the living room. Panasonic has developed a 50-pound experimental set as a forerunner of wall screens.

Its demonstration model at the 1961 IEEE Show had fair resolution. Plans are for a new display panel with improved phosphor coating which will allow viewing even in a bright room. Even the demonstrated model had input for videotape recorders, closed-circuit cameras and other equipment. The 8" X 10.7" electroluminescent screen has 230 vertical and 230 horizontal electrode strips. A phosphor layer between these strips provides 52,900 picture elements. The 0.04" X 0.03" size of each element maintains the standard 4:3 picture ratio.

CBS' EVR

In December, 1968 CBS unveiled its entry in the video home entertainment market, calling its process Electronic Video Recording, or EVR—the system trade name. The system and its hardware were developed by a team headed by CBS Laboratories president, Dr. Peter Goldmark who—20 years ago—developed the long-playing record. CBS' 1968 development featured a black-and-white player at $400, and by March 1970, ahead of its own predictions, CBS unveiled its Color EVR player. The announcement was made in conjunction with Motorola, the exclusive licensee for hardware manufacture.

Basically, there are three elements to the EVR system. First, EVR, unlike Sony (videotape) or RCA (vinyl tape and holograms) uses photographic film. The EVR film has dual visual tracks and carries its sound in parallel magnetic-edge stripes. Forty frames will appear in a two-inch segment of film and will contain six times as much information as in a comparable strip of 16mm film. The film is 8.75mm wide, and synchronization is controlled through a series of indexing indicators running down the center of the film. These trigger the "electronic shutter" as the film moves along through the player. The dual video track allows twice the amount of time for black-and-white programming in a cartridge (52 minutes), whereas the color programming utilizes one of the rows of picture frames as the color code for the black-and-white image paralleling it (25 minutes). The color process works as follows: In the film, two rows of picture frames are recorded side by side. In one set of frames, an intense light registers the primary colors electronically. The registrations, which are concealed much as music is buried in magnetic tape, show just which color goes where. When projected, the hidden colors are exactly placed and are superimposed on the parallel images in black and white, reproducing the original full-color picture. Despite the miniaturization of the film, the image reproduced is sharper and of greater quality than conventional television pictures. Horizontal resolving power of up to a maximum of 600 TV lines per picture frame, with all the interlays, creates excellent picture quality. EVR's superiority to magnetic videotape is essentially due to its high-speed, low-cost mass duplication.

The second basic element in the EVR system is the cartridge which encases the EVR film. It is seven inches in diameter, resembles a 45 RPM record in configuration, and has a maximum capacity of 750 feet of film—which works out to 180,000 picture frames. It is constructed of molded, high-impact plastic, is approximately two-thirds of an inch thick, weighs one pound fully loaded, and is far more durable than an ordinary record. Compatibility is limited to the EVR player manufactured by Motorola and by any future manufacturer licensed by CBS. Motion pictures of 35mm, 16mm and one- and two-inch videotape are basic programming that is transferable to the EVR format. Video resolution is at least 500 lines horizontally; synchronization (as cited above) being controlled electronically from an optical mark running down the middle of the two monochrome channels where black-and-white programming is concerned and the same loci for color programming. Two magnetic audio tracks on the outer bands of the film, for black-and-white programming, integrate with the respective visual tracks alongside. With color, the dual track may be utilized for stereo or bi-lingual productions. Film speed is approximately six inches-per-second, and it takes approximately one minute to rewind a fully loaded cartridge. The EVR safety film is approximately 2¾ mil. thick. It threads from the cartridge with a reel-to-reel self-threading leader which engages a pick-up reel permanently within the EVR player. The film is for playback only and you will not be able to make your own recordings but will buy ready-made programming produced through CBS, its licensees and others producing in the EVR format.

Basically, EVR film is created in the following fashion: master film images are generated from an electron beam, its intensity varying with the signals coming from the picture source (which may be a TV camera, videotape or motion picture film). Electron beams can be brought to a much finer focus than white light and thus the picture frame can be extremely small and yet retain fine image resolution. Each frame is swept by 525 beam lines (the standard TV horizontal sweep rate) providing compatibility for playback through standard TV sets. This affords higher resolution than the 400 lines used in RCA black-and-white cartridge system.

The third component of the EVR system is the EVR player itself. Its nexus to the standard TV set is a coaxial cable to the external antenna terminals on the television receiver. The film cartridge is placed on the player spindle, the set turned to a channel not receiving local broadcasting, and the starter button is depressed. The film automatically threads itself from the cartridge spool past the flying spot-scanner to a take-up spool within the set. Little notches at the sides of the film trigger the player's automatic threading mechanism. The film is then viewable by the user. The electronic censor converts film images to electric impulses and then transmits these impulses, together with the sound, into the television set. The player itself features controls somewhat similar to those on any standard television set—such as focus, horizontal and vertical hold, and contrast.

The player is the size of a large attache case (20" X 18" X 8") and weighs 35 pounds. It is designed for portability, durability and simplicity of operation. The mechanism with capstan drive has fast forward, rewind, and "still control" for slow scanning of individual sequences so that one may freeze one of any of 180,000-odd frames without damage to the film or loss of resolution; resuming play, the picture and sound are immediately at normal speed. Because transmission to the set is direct, as in the case with RCA and the Sony video-tape methods, outside interference to sound and picture (such as jet planes, amateur radio operations, buildings) is eliminated.

Furthermore, unlike the Technicolor 1000 process or any 16mm or 35mm standard projector, there is no noise distraction to interfere with viewer concentration, conversation or tutorial instruction. It may be operated in a room with normal light, as is not the case with the Technicolor 1000 unit or any standard film projection system.

The player is equipped with a film position counter that can be set to zero for program reference. A channel selector is available on the color model manufactured by Motorola though it is used only when there is black-and-white programming, for then there are two available channels for programming. In color programming, one of the channels is utilized for the color-coded information and the other channel carries only a black-and-white picture—the mix creating the color picture on the TV screen.

Motorola, Inc. manufactures and markets the CBS Electronic Video Recording Player and is CBS' exclusive licensee. The company's Quincy, Illinois plant is capable of turning out 100,000 units annually. CBS, however, is already in negotiations with other manufacturers for EVR players when the Motorola contract expires. Rumor persists that CBS is negotiating with Sony as a potential licensee for the EVR players. The logic in such speculation is that it would hedge Sony's bet in the videotape area as there is little doubt CBS' process will be successful. Sony technology could make diversified hardware products to serve this market as well as its own videotape player. CBS is not going to manufacture the hardware, though considerable profit can be realized from licensing revenues from its manufacturer. They are focusing, rather, on sale and duplication of cartridges.

The purpose of the rather short exclusive licensing period to Motorola was CBS' desire to benefit from its marketing strategy which focuses upon the processing and sale of software cartridges—and this necessitates that there be sufficient players in the market. One company could not hope to provide all the necessary equipment or diversity in modular form that the American public would want. The competitive situation created by licensing several manufacturers would work to the benefit of the marketing strategy of CBS; thus Motorola was granted an exclusive license for a period short enough not to defeat this policy but long enough to justify its research and development exposure.

CBS, however, now finds itself victim of this rationale, since Motorola's strategy seems to cater to institutional and educational sales rather than the home consumer. It is the home market that will provide the real mass sales of cartridges that CBS looks forward to as the exclusive processor of cartridges. CBS, anticipating the crunch for EVR programming and deciding they will exclusively process the EVR cartridges, has constructed a 100,000 sq. ft. New Jersey plant. Projected statistics indicate that the plant will have to go a three-shift phase within the first year of operation in order to meet the anticipated demand of some 5-million cartridges. CBS will open with a two-shift, 3-million-cartridge output, and the first year's product is already sold out. Customers to date include Uplinger-Verna Sports, a California corporation marketing films on sporting events and physical improvement to hospitals and other large institutions. Computer Telejournal Corporation will produce a video periodical aimed at the computer market. Several large insurance companies, such as Equitable Life Assurance Society, have committed training information to the EVR process as well as being a heavy purchaser of the hardware players from Motorola. The initial EVR customer after the first public demonstration of the black-and-white unit in December, 1968 was the *New York Times* Book and Education Division. It will create educational films exclusively on EVR cartridges for elementary and secondary school distribution. Darryl F. Zanuck, then chief executive officer of 20th Century-Fox recommended that Fox convert their films to EVR five years after their initial theatrical release. The films would reach the public at a modest rental price.

Super-8: Technicolor 1000

Super-8 home projection units are also a competitor for the same home and industrial markets. There are at least seven manufacturing situations competing in the Super-8 market: Fairchild, Technicolor, Jay Ark, MPO, Bohn-Benton, Bell & Howell and Kodak. The first five all make an "endless loop" sealed cartridge system that fits only their own projection equipment. Bell & Howell and Kodak use non-sealed, plastic cartridges, both incompatible with the other. They automatically thread themselves through the system onto a take-up reel and when the end of the film has been projected, automatically rewind. Not only is there a lack of conformity in configuration of the cartridges and cassettes, but some use optical sound separation and others magnetic.

Rather than describe each of these hardware situations, we may examine Technicolor's operation as representative. The Technicolor 1000 series claims to be the instant movie projector for everyone. The projector is portable, weighing only 18 pounds and containing a built-in five-inch permanent magnet speaker with fair response and output jacks for larger, more dynamic speakers and amplification equipment. The clear plastic cartridges hold up to 29 minutes of sprocketless Super-8 film which utilizes an optical sound track. The 1000 Series features cartridge loading without threading or rewinding. The sprocketless film reduces wear and tear. A quartz halogen projection lamp has up to 40 hours of life. These features are combined with a solid state sound system requiring no warm-up, and pushbutton controls on a single panel with automatic shut-off in an aluminum housing. The unit works off a single power cord of 60-cycle 110 to 120 volts AC electric outlet.

There can be no error in loading the cartridge into the unit, since it is designed to fit into the projector only one way. Once inserted, the "on" button is depressed for instant sound movies. The cartridge can be removed at any time while the projector is running, but there is no reverse mechanism. The sound system is designed to give quiet trouble-fee performance, employing a solid state amplifier; its DC exciter lamp is good for 1,000 hours of life. Technicolor provides a one-year full guarantee against defective materials or workmanship. In future 1000 Series units—and with certain professional modifications in existing units—a provision will be available for single frame viewing by the use of a button on the top of the unit with no loss of focus on re-start and no flickering image. The new cooling features will permit indefinite single-frame viewing and intermittent stopping and starting at the user's discretion. The mechanism is geared to stop on complete frames and there is no sound distortion or deterioration of picture, which runs at 24 frames-per-second when the stop frame is released. The Technicolor 1000 Series provides wide-screen viewing at a far closer range than available in 16mm. In addition, Technicolor has a wide-angle lens system which fits easily on the existing lens and doubles the original picture size with no increase in projection distance. There is a full range of accessories from ear phones to rear screen projection equipment and carrying cases.

The Super-8 system has some rather obvious drawbacks. It requires a darkened room for effective viewing and no obstruction in the path of the projector's beam to the screen. This may be a short term virtue, since giant television wall screens have not yet come into being and viewing in all other processes is limited to a 21- or 23-inch color screen. The Super-8mm projection systems can, however, have a screen five or ten times as large. Educational utilization is hampered by need for a darkened room, which limits note-taking and other instructional purposes. Unlike all the other systems except Sony's, Super-8mm film editing may be accomplished in rather easy fashion.

Technicolor's 1000B heavy duty unit retails for approximately $400 and the economy unit for $100 less. Loading of a cartridge, exclusive of the cost of film and rights, costs under $6 including waxing and automatic stop preparation. The cartridges accommodate 580 feet of Super-8mm film and run 29 minutes. Instant program availability is an advantage of Super 8mm film, because Technicolor 1000 has a vast array of films available for the home and institutional market and an extensive catalogue listing all films available. They are geared for quick conversion of existing 35mm and 16mm films to Super-8mm cartridges. Technicolor and Warner Brothers will release a major package of post-1948 features for sale in Super-8 cartridges.

If Super-8 is to make a dent in the market, a solution to the darkened room projection problem must be found. It may come from Normande, a German company which has recently displayed an $850 device that can play Super-8mm movies into a standard color TV set. A small, three-year-old British firm, Vidicord of Great Britain, is moving fast to establish a beachhead in the European home video market before such giants as CBS and Philips get their versions rolling. The firm's Vidicord player uses black-and-white Super-8mm movie film, making it possible, says chief executive Leonard Cassini, "for anyone with a home movie camera to see his own films on his TV set." The player will cost $888, and cassette cartridges, available in four- to 45-minute lengths, will sell for around $1.20 a minute (about twice the cost of CBS' EVR). Because of the player's steep cost, Cassini will rent it for around $3 a week, which is about the same amount Britishers pay to rent color TV sets. (Most TV sets in the U.K. are rented rather than bought.)

There is the paramount problem of standardizing Super-8mm cartridges so they will be compatible to all cartridge players. In each of the five "endless loop" situations involving sealed cartridges only the manufacturer's projector can be used. Configurations differ among the cassettes, too. Undoubtedly the cassette unit will replace the reel-to-reel unit despite its self-threading, automatic rewind features. Furthermore, the cassettes and "endless loop" cartridges have two different configurations. The cassette builds in two reels, one of which is a take-up reel. The "endless loop" cartridges have one continuous reel feeding from the outside while simultaneously rewinding at the center of the same reel. Film in cartridges tends to stay cleaner because they are sealed. They are more efficient to run because there

is no rewind required, nor is there need for a professional projec-
tionist. Cassettes, on the other hand, permit the possibility of repair
or reversing film, as "endless loop" systems cannot be reversed or
easily edited. Furthermore, cassette packaging of film is far cheaper
than with the "endless loop" cartridges. Cartridges run from $6 to $10
for loading, with automatic stopping and waxing, but cassettes can be
fitted with film for under a dollar. While there is general agreement
that both the cassette and "endless loop" cartridges will stay on the
market, it is also generally agreed that compatibility must be solved.

Cartridge-cassette incompatibility is not the only factor plaguing
development of Super-8. Standardization of Super-8mm-sound is also
a problem. Both optical and magnetic are in use. Furthermore, the
number of frames separating the image and its corresponding sound
track locus—or more properly "sound separation"—differs between
systems. Current differences range from 125-frame advance to a 37-
frame retard. To fix an industry-wide standard would mean rendering
obsolete much of the existing equipment. The argument of magnetic
versus optical in terms of audio response has run the full gamut. The
only consensus is that magnetic track has slightly better range and
qualitative response. There is doubt whether the great increase of cost
over optical justifies its being the standard, for the audible difference
is insignificant. Most manufacturers utilizing optical sound tracks
claim magnetic is more expensive and not as durable. The magnetic
stripe tends to separate from the film, and there is always the problem
of accidental erasure. Kodak, however, has adopted the magnetic
standard which it processes more economically than its optical coun-
terpart. Kodak's film stock now comes with the magnetic stripe already
implanted on the film, thus preventing separation. Optical advocates
point to a diminished possibility of tampering with the sound track,
as opposed to its magnetic competitor.

Norelco

Norelco, a subsidiary of North American Philips Corporation,
has already found hardware and software distribution in the training
and educational fields. *PIP*, or Programmed Individual Presentation,
gains a market value by recognizing the fact that most training films
are composed of stills, which in effect wastes moving film stock.
Norelco's cassette unit therefore separates sound and picture in two
units, each similar in size and appearance to the familiar audiotape
cassette. The hardware, or Audio Viewing Unit, is a portable, 18-pound
self-contained machine for presenting learning programs mainly to the
individual, although it could accommodate small groups. Still pictures and moving pictures at any rate per frame are synchronized with
continuous sound without the usual problem of flicker. The picture is
displayed for viewing in a 4½" by 6" daylight screen.

Norelco estimates that software saving will come in ease of duplication and the celluloid economy of the PIP design. Comparing footage of a typical 20-minute program, a 400-foot reel could be converted to a maximum 50-foot presentation under the multi-media PIP system of stills and motion. The film cassette uses Super-8 color film which can be processed without extra cost at any color lab. Film and sound are tied together by pulses recorded on the sound cassette. Lip synchronization is possible.

Advantages to the Norelco system seem to be its interchangeability of sound and picture tracks, plus its multi-media approach for learning rather than for entertainment. The Audio Viewing Unit retails for $375. A sound cassette averages $1.25 and a blank video cassette will sell for $2.50.

Teldec Video Disc and MCA Plans

Recently unveiled in New York for its American premiere, the Teldec Video Disc promises to be one of the most innovative audio-visual devices in the hardware-software race. Created jointly by British Decca and Telefunken, the video disc is expected to be on the European market at a cost of $144 to $240.

The hardware system can be operated through any standard television unit. The user has only to plug the output from his Video Disc Player into the aerial socket of his TV set. Perhaps the most attractive feature of the Teldec unit is the low cost of its highly engineered software programming. The video disc looks much like a long playing phonograph record, but it is made of a very thin plastic foil which gives it a much more pliable quality. Teldec estimates that each disc will sell for $2.40 and will last up to 1,000 plays. Running time is five minutes for a nine-inch disc, and twelve minutes for a twelve-inch, long-play record. Stacking records on an automatic changer will virtually extend the play time for hours. In fact, a two-hour program would measure out to a stack of discs only 5mm high. Although the disc is only able to transmit black-and-white images at this time, a color video disc will be ready for distribution when the Teldec goes on sale to the public.

Compared to the grooves on an audio disc, video disc grooves are much closer together. By the development of a new vertical recording method it became possible to cut 130 to 150 grooves per millimeter, in contrast to the 10 to 13 sound grooves per millimeter of an audio recording. In order to trace the modulations or grooves on the surface of the video disc a new transducer had to be developed which could translate the programming into electrical impulses. The hardware unit, or Video Disc Player, incorporates such a transducer—which is called a pressure pick-up—much like the arm of a record player, but without the stylus. Instead of riding the grooves, the pick-up device senses the surface of the disc and translates the program pattern into electrical impulses. The arm moves across the disc via the movement of the turntable. For each rotation the pick-up moves over the surface of one groove. This method ensures accurate tracking and also reduces record surface wear. By eliminating the stylus the problems of bias and rumble are eliminated.

Since it is necessary to increase flow of information from the pressure arm to the disc, a special high-speed carrier was developed to take the place of the familiar turntable. The video disc foil is driven by a central carrier and rotates above a stationary plate. At 1,500 rpm a thin cushion of air is formed between the foil and the plate which has the effect of stabilizing the motion of the foil. Even at this speed the video disc corresponds to the United States television standards in use today. One complete rotation of the disc records one television picture. With this in mind, future developments by Teldec will incorporate a stop-frame facility. Other competitive factors are random access and repeat facilities. By allowing the pick-up to move only a few grooves for an automatic setting, any desired sequence of pictures can be repeated again and again. Video discs may also be instantly cued.

Teldec's Video Disc Player promises to be as simple to use as an ordinary record player. There are no expensive components to wear out and the use of the pressure pick-up arm means that the whole machine is so stable it could be operated upside down. Teldec hopes to maintain its hold alongside magnetic tape for two reasons. First, because of its high storage quality—the amount of information that can be programmed on a single disc; and second, the low expenditure for the operation of the hardware unit. These are the lowest costs incurred by any picture storage method at the present time. Sample programs demonstrated last fall by Teldec included popular singers, opera selections, ballet, animated children's films, a motor instructional film and a travel-oriented advertisement. The application of the disc may one day extend into newspapers and magazines where one might enjoy a replay of a news or sporting event.

No matter how promising the Teldec announcement seems, it was over-shadowed by another announcement by The Music Corporation of America on the same day. MCA, Inc. disclosed that it has been working on its own home entertainment device for over a year. The device, as of now kept under wraps, includes a disc which will permit 90 minutes or more of color and sound programming to be played without interruption through a home TV set. Although no technical details or preview dates have been set, the MCA disc is reported to be more advanced than the European system both in duration of playing time and color technology.

THE REWARDS

When one considers the enormous market television reaches with TV sets in 60-million American homes, the vast quantities of programming it devours, and combines those totals with the market for the record, tape, publishing and exhibition industries, the audio-visual cartridge market begins to take shape. Anything that can be read, seen or heard will find its way into this medium. Its potential is limitless, and its effect on all peripheral activity such as production are staggering.

The continuing rise in leisure time for Americans will contribute to the cartridge development. The Hudson Institute predicts that soon the average work week could be two hours shorter. A great upswing in the purchasing power will also contribute to the medium's success. The average family's allocation for personal recreation will continue to grow, and perhaps as much as 6.5% of the family's disposable income will be so allocated. (This compares to 5.6% in 1970). These two factors alone create the basis for future success of the audio-visual cartridge and the various playback systems it involves. The personalization of programming resulting from the individual-selection capability which the audio-visual cartridge offers will assure its success.

The First Wave: Institutional Market

The initial thrust appears towards industry, not the home. This market, too, is enormous. The institutional buyers who are being sought by large hardware complexes in the initial marketing phase are buying product as fast as it can be manufactured. Companies which desire to transmit instructional programming, sales data, and information of every other imaginable type to their personnel will make use of this effective and efficient process. The trend towards personalization of education—with its increased costs and the need for more in-home training—will create a still wider educational market.

The effect upon the classroom of both CBS' EVR and RCA's devices will be noticeable. The Carnegie Commission for Educational Television noted that a more versatile playback technology in Educational Television is the one element needed to return that classroom flexibility which is denied by present uses of broadcasting to the teacher—who can select the program, play it at the moment of his choosing, replay it at will in whole or in part, and interrupt it for comments. At this point, teachers must schedule class work around broadcast hours, and they have no control over what appears on the screen, and when. With cartridge technology, educators can more effectively integrate educational films into the smooth flow of the curricu-

lum. Teachers will be able to preview and choose, stop the program for
comment or general discussion, schedule lessons at their own discretion. Further, because EVR cartridges are considerably more economical, educators may no longer have to depend upon central or outside
audio-visual libraries, but can build their own libraries. Leading authorities could speak of new developments in their own fields, and
students would be able to study and learn at their own pace.

The Second Wave: Home Market

The range of material that will find its way into the audio-visual
cartridge medium is as diverse as methods of communication man-
kind now possesses. The new communicative possibilities could improve the quality of life immeasurably. There will be kinetic paintings
on giant wall-screens with stereo-audio aspect, matching color schemes
to rooms, personalities, or moods. One might proceed to learn a new
language at his own pace. Movies could be viewed over and over with
significant scenes and moments being put through on "instant replay."
Great lectures could be recorded and utilized as tools for adult learning. Instructional manuals on "how-to" home repair or carpentry
tasks could be included in cartridge form.

For the first time, a mass-produced visual aid can reach a segmented market without dependence upon mass distribution and acceptance. With a population base of 200 million, even small special-
interest groups could feasibly support the production of audio-visual
cartridges. Documentaries, special-interest films and features of all
lengths will be reproduced in this format. The enormous requirements
of programming which will be needed to service live TV, pay-TV,
theatrical exhibition, audio-visual cartridges, radio, books and other
periodicals will stagger the imagination. In short, the market is
limitless.

The economic implications of the new medium are already
obvious. Consider the EVR situation and what it might do for CBS as
a corporate entity in terms of profits. Several Wall Street analysts have
predicted as much as $.25 a share increase in CBS's after-tax earnings
in a situation which assumes only a 20,000-sale hardware year and the
sale of 2 million cartridges at a pre-tax profit of approximately $2 a
cartridge. CBS receives a 5% royalty from the manufacturer of the
player itself, as well as royalties on the broadcast EVR equipment
manufactured by General Electric which runs to over $30,000 a unit.
Great profit is realized in distribution, sale and processing of cartridges
for all of the existing television stations. And we must remember that
this profit situation is based upon an infinitesimal segment of the
available market. Even a cursory evaluation reveals that cartridges
will become the most important division in any one of the industries

mentioned. Its audience will encompass virtually all audiences for current feature exhibition, live television, pay-TV, legitimate theatre, literary forms, 16mm home exhibition, and educational and institutional communication.

As in the case with any new product, the range of sales forecasts is enormous. RCA's Chase Morsey foresees a $1-billion industry by 1980. Spindle Top Research, reporting under a grant from a Presidential task force on communications, forecasts $435-million in sales within one year after the players are in the consumer market. Arthur D. Little, Inc. reports the market closer to $150-million by that time.

In 1969 Americans spent over $6.35-billion for audio-visual entertainment alone. One-billion dollars was spent for motion pictures, $2.75-billion for TV programs, and $3-billion for TV sets—including $1.5-billion for repair of secondhand sets. Phonograph sales accounted for another $3.15-billion. These figures suggest a multi-billion dollar potential for the audio-visual cartridge medium. The explosive growth of the color TV market is an enormous incentive for marketers. By 1980 color TV will be found in 90% of all households—almost 70 million units. Heretofore, the audio-visual cartridge has attracted the interests of the leisure industries but the hardware price tag was not workable for mass marketing. Now, with units priced from $400 to $795, we can anticipate a goldrush. Even further price reductions, achieved by integrating players into TV sets, will create savings up to 50% and further stimulate the market.

VICTIMS AND VICTORS: THE COMBATANTS

In any race some win and some lose, but the stakes are such in the hardware situation that losers will not be punished too severely. Therefore, whether EVR, RCA process, Super-8 or videotape, the losses will be cut. The demographics of the market will help to provide a cushion. They are broad enough to assure hardware manufacturers that all plans can be practicable. To software manufacturers or those who own negative, the decision over which process to go with can, of course, be crucial if transfer of rights is exclusive with that process. Yet no one can sit and wait with negative to see which process triumphs. All of this works to make any system under full steam at least a partial winner. Videotape now appears to be leading.

Videotape manufacturers were first from the starting blocks. But they were not viable in the consumer market in the mid-1960's, and as a consequence manufacturers like Ampex regarded them as little more than hobby machines for the rich. A black-and-white non-cassette unit at $1,000, and almost $5,000 for a color reel-to-reel unit, was far too steep to create much interest in equipment. As a result development lagged with overstocked inventories, and the companies were unable to create a home-entertainment market with videotape players. When it became evident, however, that CBS and RCA were in the market with differing processes which would cut severely into the use of videotape as a consumer or institutional item, the videotape people up-graded their level of research and development.

The videotape player can offer the consumer greater range in that he may record live TV programming or, with the addition of a small portable camera, make his own live programming of home movies to play back through his television receiver. Advocates of both RCA and CBS systems believe, however, that the recording facet of videotape players will not appreciably increase acceptance over their own systems. Their conclusion is based upon a comparison of this fledgling industry with the audiotape industry, when a clear-cut market for pre-recorded material over self-recorded programming was established. Sony has no software programming strategy for its cassettes, but Ampex feels that if it is to be competitive, a full range of pre-recorded programming must be available in the videotape format. Avco will provide such programming.

This system, and the Super-8 industry as well, would benefit appreciably by standardization of cassettes or cartridges for interchangeability. Sufficient competition will be provided by CBS' EVR and Super-8 to make the videotape industry aware that it can ill afford the competition for programming to be further split among themselves. Without the production and availability of programming on an efficient and effective basis, the system will not achieve its potential. What most knowledgeable observers foresee is a videotape industry that is quite large—especially with the reduction of price for the videotape recorder player. It will likely follow acceptance of the CBS-EVR or RCA systems into the home and be an additional piece of hardware rather than the primary element.

The CBS and RCA investment is substantial enough to assure a steady level of software programming for their processes, but videotape people tend to rely upon either the consumer's ability to record off live TV or the independent marketing of software programming on videotape for their units. President William Roberts of Ampex feels that the advantage of being able to record a television sporting event, news, movies and other programming for viewing at a more convenient time will be a great enticement to many customers. Roberts predicts that the era of a $500 recorded player in color cassette form is close at hand—which is in line with Sony's planning and Avco's audiotape breakthrough.

The television networks are particularly wary of the videotape industry for it may mean a two-pronged attack at their main source of revenue. First, extensive viewing of pre-recorded programming could definitely erode the live television audience. More importantly, the potential for piracy and copyright infringement is manifest in this *modus operandi,* but it is virtually impossible to tinker with CBS' EVR or RCA's holographic process. CBS must certainly hope that its own programming format through EVR may capture any audience lost from its live television programming. NBC and ABC will have to rely upon the value of their live programming—and other programming made especially for any one of these processes—to capture revenues lost to the videotape industry alone. Undoubtedly all three major networks will be a major source of supply for programming to the audio-visual cartridge industry. In short, videotape recorder-playback equipment will make a significant dent in the market because of its unique capacity to record and instantly play back.

CBS-EVR—A Progress Report

Though CBS' EVR system may be today's leader in terms of its projected color-player price (manufactured by Motorola for $795) it is not likely that many of the units will find their way into the home. In fact, CBS' strategy is geared to the institutional buyer in the first stage of a two-stage marketing plan. This is essentially a result of the high price of the modular unit and of Motorola's plan to sell its hardware primarily to institutional buyers. Furthermore, RCA and several independent observers doubt whether Motorola can maintain a $795 color-unit price. It is felt that the retail price will be nearer to $1,000 for players on an individual basis. Serious de-bugging must continue in the EVR player, which is still in its initial development stage, where numerous technical problems persist.

Nevertheless, CBS has continued to gear its New Jersey plant to process cartridges for institutional buyers. The entire first year's output of 3 million cartridges was sold out. With the cost of a color cartridge at $25 for 25 minutes of programming—and the player at a minimum of $795—a home-consumer market is some time away. One must also consider that $25 covers only the physical cost of transferring existing programming to EVR—and obviously does not include the rights to acquire that programming, which would be amortized over the entire run of cartridges produced. But it is vital to recognize that a 20 minute 8mm film costs about $30 or more to print—and takes nearly as much time to copy as to project——whereas a 20-minute EVR black-and-white film can be mass duplicated in *13 seconds.*

CBS must complete three tasks before it can reach the home market. First, it must reduce the cost of the player to a reasonable level. In modular form $200 or $300 would be a most significant marketing cue for such a player. Second, the cost of a color cartridge will have to come down nearly 80% from the present level in order to cover the rights cost and create a 30-minute program for approximately $10. This would make purchase of the cartridge reasonable—otherwise a rental basis is required. Finally, CBS must come to grips with a distribution mode for the sale of its cartridges. It seems likely that rental will be the first approach, but as purchase prices become more realistic for home consumption a new approach will have to be explored. Distribution might utilize the CBS record division, Columbia Records, or any of the existing formats for distribution of physical product which RCA or CBS already employs. CBS is, incidentally, planning further miniaturization to increase its color cartridge length to 30 minutes.

The EVR system has numerous undeniable software advantages over the videotape and Super-8 systems. First, CBS has a huge inventory of programming which it could quickly convert, (and already has rights for) to EVR. Furthermore, it has a huge production staff in its network programming departments which quickly could gear up to produce product exclusively for the EVR format. The tremendous storehouse of information derived from its years of experience in production and exhibition of television programming will be a boon in the EVR staging. The vast Columbia record and music divisions will be drawn upon for specialized audio-visual packages and, more importantly, channels of distribution. In August 1967, CBS acquired the publishing house of Holt, Rinehart and Winston—paying $280-million for a firm whose earnings were only $6.6-million. Earlier in 1967 they had acquired Film Associates and Bailey Films, producers of educational films. In the entertainment field, CBS has a large reservoir of talent in radio and TV, in addition to its recording artists. The Columbia Record Club, with more than two million members, is a ready-made marketing organization. In short, CBS is extremely well situated to pursue its strategy, and it undoubtedly can capture a significant share of the market.

RCA: The Dark Horse

The short-term success of RCA's holographic process is far from assured. It claims to be reaching for the home market, but at the same time is not willing to concede the enormous educational and institutional markets to CBS, though this seems to be a foregone conclusion. RCA's holographic process is far from perfected. There are, however, several attractive advantages to the RCA system. Its film-embossing process on cheap vinyl plastic tape results in a color 30-minute cartridge at less than $10 including rights costs. RCA claims that its player price will be $400. Strategy is based on having "the cheapest razor blade," and the hope that CBS will not be able to reach the consumer with a player at under $1,000.

RCA intends to be a vital software source in service of its own process. Like CBS, it has purchased a publishing house (Random House). RCA claims that its research indicates that viewers are not terribly interested in recording their own TV programs off the air—either to play at a more convenient viewing time or to build a personal library. Nor is the public interested—RCA research says—in making their own home TV movies.

RCA has various divisions with effective already-existing channels of distribution for its cartridges. It will offer a starting library of 100 programmed cartridges, and has set aside $10-million to purchase rights to films, books, plays and other properties for the system. Through its NBC subsidiary, RCA shares many of the advantages in programming, information, distribution and production that are available to CBS, and these advantages point to a greater likelihood of success over videotape, Technicolor and Super-8 processes. RCA will manufacture its own hardware unit and will license others to do so. They will undoubtedly integrate players into entire TV-stereo units at a far lower cost, and make combinations with style and utility a great consumer feature, as Avco has done with its units.

Super-8: A Short-term Victor

The Super-8 process may well be short-run winner—but the likelihood of long-term success is questionable because of the aforementioned projection problems. This conjecture is based on the assumption that there will be no technological breakthrough such as projection of Super-8mm movies into a television receiver or giant wall screens without a darkened room. If these do succeed, Super-8 could be a viable process for the home entertainment market. It would still rely almost entirely on a rental distribution basis rather than outright sale because the cost of cartridges would be too steep. The non-recording capability would limit it in its competition with videotape. On the other hand, the capacity for making one's own home Super-8 movies and playing them through such equipment may compensate in some measure. It is unlikely, even on a rental basis, that feature movies could be available for this market at under $20 rental per showing.

VICTIMS AND VICTORS: THE SPECTATORS

Each combatant has a respectable chance of being a victor in the new market, but an equally interesting consideration is the possible impact of each one's success upon the aspects of the other's operations.

Victim Number One: Live TV

Whether network or local programming, live TV, VHF or UHF, will be affected drastically by cartridges, as well as by CATV, remains to be seen. There are only so many slices in the leisure-time pie. The home entertainment pre-recorded market will have margins that the live TV market cannot extend to, and the areas of service will be almost mutually inclusive. There will be certain areas, of course, in which live TV service will continue on an exclusive basis. These include news, live sporting programs, or any event or occurrence in which viewer-interest depends largely upon timeliness and the viewer's desire to see it as it happens. Even in this regard, CATV will be giving free TV a run for its money. Live TV will have to pay more for its pre-recorded programming because of fierce competition and may well move to a program pattern resembling radio's of recent years—though half-hour situation comedy and hour variety programs may still be standard fare. The large networks will probably move to create program product for the pre-recorded home entertainment market, because they already have production, distribution, and marketing facilities, as well as demographic information which will enable them to work effectively.

Program nature and quality, however, will be far different from that which is seen on television today, essentially because of a "segmented market." Thus greater profit may be realized from a program which might—on a live TV basis—receive a very small market share. If dependent on cartridge purchase or rental, however, such a program could be commercially viable. Whereas television seeks the broadest possible audience, the audio-visual cartridge programmer can successfully service the entire spectrum of entertainment needs. The network loss in live TV programming will be surpassed, however, by what they reap from pre-recorded cartridge programming for the consumer market.

Victim Number Two: Theatrical Exhibition

Ostensibly, the most severe threat posed by the pre-recorded home entertainment medium is to theatrical exhibition. Television's emergence two decades ago was regarded as the final blow against the theatrical exhibitors circuits, but a combination of forces worked to make the motion picture business as viable as ever. Considering the situation in retrospect, it is now clear that television could not have competed with the theatrical motion picture for several reasons. First, the quality of the picture was not as good. Second, color was not available. Third, screen size was a limitation to television on the one hand, and a drawing card for motion pictures on the other. Nor can one dismiss the fact that the level of entertainment of programming on television was far below what was accessible in theatrical exhibition. Still another factor which cannot be given short shrift is the communal or social experience of frequenting the movie house. Young people—the largest audience for the theatrical business—want especially to get out of the home, to be seen and to react with other people to an entertainment experience. This will remain an important stimulus to theatrical exhibition.

Questions regarding the effect of pre-recorded home entertainment cartridges upon theatrical exhibition are difficult to answer. More than 80 million movie tickets a week were sold in the mid-1940's and that figure was reduced to some 20.5 million a week by 1969. This drop is not entirely attributable to television's growth. The causal factors are the expansion of leisure time and easier credit—which have created genuine competition for the theatrical exhibition audience. With more Americans having more money and more leisure time in which to spend it, competition from boats, travel, second homes, expensive hobbies and other outlets and diversions for American society have worked to reduce theatrical exhibition. The cheap formula entertainment turned out by the movie companies in the early '40's is no longer the single means of escape for Americans, and only effective, stimulating, innovative features will draw audiences into the theatre. Despite television's intrusion into this market, it was the sale of features to TV that kept the motion picture business viable. Today a new situation prevails. The bulk of the present theatrical audience is between 18 and 35 years old and the product is designed for this group. The less affluent, less mobile—those outside the 18-to-35 age class—usually await a feature's sale to TV. Furthermore, specialized art films, feature sport films, documentaries and the like are unprofitable in the theatrical circuit.

Within five to ten years, however, the following is certain: large wall screens now in development will solve the problems of TV's physical limitations and permit the effective display of color, 'scope-type pictures. General Telephone and Electronics has recently developed a laser display system capable of projecting bright color TV pictures on large wall screens from a normal TV receiver. A stereo sound track will obviate the limitation of the three- to four-inch television speaker now commonly in use. Thus TV's eye-and-ear limitations *vis-a-vis* theatrical exhibition will be solved, if not improved, and combined with freedom of choice in programming in terms of content and scheduling. The cartridge permits the viewer to see the program when he wants, stop and start, see parts over again, examine single scenes, and totally enjoy the film beyond current theatrical exhibition and live-TV capabilities. Thus, freedom of choice in terms of programming is definitely an issue with regard to the future of theatrical motion pictures.

The real advantage the exhibitor will continue to have is the social experience—which, of course, can not be underestimated. Yet if exhibition is to survive and prosper a two-pronged approach must be adopted by exhibitors and those who sell to exhibitors. First, theatres must all be first-class houses with comfortable seating, and combined restaurants and bars. Such theatres could easily become centers for the sale of cartridge movies, because the combination would work to the benefit of both. The neighborhood house, as we know it, will probably be extinct.

Competition will be fierce because FCC control of mass-transmitted programming over the airwaves will be eliminated in the new system and the legal restrictions upon what can be sold and viewed in the privacy of one's home will more properly approximate present restrictions in books, thus yielding greater freedom and flexibility. The theatrical exhibition market cannot therefore rely on the advantage of being able to lure audiences out of their homes for the purely sexploitative qualities of films. The lure must still be taste, imagination and quality, and undoubtedly the whole movie market will mature as a result of the audio-visual cartridge experience.

Exhibitors are apprehensive of this new medium and rightly so. They have depended upon the studio to provide an exclusive, unending stream of product. When TV first became viable, only the movies which were no longer profitable for theatrical exhibition were sold to television. Then a perceptible erosion began. First it was seven, then five-year-old films, and recently films only one or two years off the circuit have been broadcast on television. The need for more films drove television networks into producing their own TV movies, and undoubtedly home cartridge markets will have movies made especially for them. Recently 20th Century-Fox announced plans to make their library of films five years or older available for EVR cartridges. This five-year barrier will quickly fall by the wayside if one of the big studios decides to release a less successful theatrical film directly to the audio-visual cartridge market.

Careful scrutiny of all facts suggests, however, that theatrical exhibition will be stimulated by this challenge. Exhibitors and distributors will have to re-evaluate their operation in order to offer an attraction that will bring audiences from their homes. The enormous Cinemascope screens, improved sound and projection systems, more comfortable entertainment complexes—combining food, drink, and entertainment—will be an attractive magnet. Another exciting format now on the horizon for exhibitors is the mixed media presentation that gained popularity at EXPO '67 in Montreal. The most popular attractions at the fair were several multi-screen theatres presenting imaginative uses of sound and picture. These theatres presented more than a movie—they offered a complete show that was a totally involving, sensory experience. Screens jutted at odd angles from walls and ceiling. Sound systems provided a 360-degree surround. Some theatres featured moving seats while others utilized sliding walls and screen panels. The theatre of the future may be no more than a hollow shell in which standard elements such as seats and screens are all moveable. The "road show" approach to exhibition may survive as giant mixed-media presentations that will be booked in for two years or more and will require unique interior design requirements. Bizarre though it sounds, this concept of exhibition is in line with the "showmanship" concept of marketing at which exhibitors and distributors have long excelled.

Thus the exhibitor must ponder the advantages he has over home units. The theatre must be a social center. In fact, if the exhibitor plans his strategy right, the motion picture theatre could well become the home entertainment center of its community. Speaking at a recent convention, Robert E. Brockway, President of the CBS-EVR division, said that the home town theatre "represents a partially utilized facility which ideally can be adapted as a marketing place" for cassette systems. Instead of being left out in the cold, theatre owners should plan now to utilize house time and space for more than just the presentation of feature films.

There is tremendous profit potential in rentals and sales of cassettes, either on a library basis or as promotional tie-ins and extensions of the theatre's current feature. By utilizing all the market possibilities behind the cassette phenomenon, theatre admissions could feasibly be lowered. There could be less of a reliance on the profits of candy, soft drinks and popcorn, although with greater attendance at lower prices those profits would also increase. Studies have shown that the public is interested in renting or buying cassettes as they leave the theatre. For instance, upon seeing Antonioni's *The Red Desert*, a theatre-goer or film buff may want to rent a copy of *Blow-Up* to view the next evening for enjoyment or critical comparison. With the incalculable variety of taste, the public rentals and purchase of film-programmed cassettes should be an extraordinary chance for the theatre to find a new life in the community. In the meantime, the great filmmakers will still be lured to the giant screen and its ability to present the motion picture format in its most effective fashion.

But whatever the reason, no force—exhibitors, studios, distributors, live or pay-TV, radio, or the publishing industry—will hold back the coming tide, for it is going to be damned profitable to be in this market. None of the giants wants to be left at the gate in this race.

Victor Number One: CATV

Further erosion of live TV will undoubtedly result from expansion of CATV, or pay-TV, which will originate programming. Many predict that a pay-TV system based upon CATV will take sports programming away from free TV. Some erosion appears inevitable, and thus networks are depending more and more upon acquisition of pay-TV or CATV companies and/or active participation in production and distribution of home entertainment pre-recorded programming.

The pre-recorded audio-visual cartridge home entertainment medium will also compete with CATV and pay-TV. In both cases the benefits are on the pre-recorded side. Since the viewer is playing the program directly into the television receiver or the giant wall screens, there will be no need to avoid ghosts, outside interference or poor reception. Thus cable-TV as a non-originating medium will be necessary only to improve the signal from live programming coming into the home. Pay-TV—whether through cable or otherwise—will be a competitor for programming with the pre-recorded home entertainment market, and will likely receive short shrift from the large programming sources. EVR may be a considerable bonus for CATV operators, in that the EVR cartridge is smaller than a 16mm motion picture or videotape reel which implies a savings of shipping cost and storage space.

Victor Number Two: The Studios

The great studios of the majors which are rushing to sell their land, rid themselves of their departments and trained and effective technicians, now turn out only 10 to 12 features a year plus several hours of television programming. If they gear up properly they will surely be participants in the boom. Training programs for cameramen and other crafts will be more realistic and effective. The need for product for all formats, pay TV, live TV, theatrical motion picture and, especially, the audio-visual cartridge will be so enormous that the only way the supply can possibly meet the demand will be to turn to the studio complex and its capacity for great productivity.

Victor Number Three: Unions and Management

Producers, writers and directors, as well as other ancillary crafts will be in short supply. The need for trained executive personnel will be staggering. Manpower with limited knowledge of supervision and production will be found in highly paid jobs. The search for technical talent will surpass the unions' wildest dreams. Great libraries of unproduced properties and infrequently used remake and sequel rights will become very valuable assets. It will revitalize the agencies and studios. There will be a renaissance in production.

A two-hour format will no longer be controlling in terms of feature films. Programming of every kind and description will come out of the giant studio complexes, and virtually everything imaginable will be prepared and marketed in an audio-visual cartridge. Perhaps the greatest difficulty in meeting these requirements will be effective management, especially in the creative area. Several large industries involved in programming are now searching for executives in this area.

Victor Number Four: The Publishing Industry

The publishing industry will definitely feel the impact of this new medium. An entire encyclopedia could be put on the 180,000-odd EVR frames in a cartridge—in effect replacing 26 volumes. Audio-visual periodicals and books on tape are a strong likelihood. This is not to say that the written word will disappear. It will only appear less frequently on paper and more in a film or tape form which may well reduce the cost and create greater audiences at greater profitability.

Victor Number Five: The Artist

The home entertainment industry of the future will resemble the book publishing industry much more than it does the current motion picture industry. Cocteau's dream will come true: film will be as accessible to the new filmmaker as pen and paper are to the writer and canvas to the painter. Having completed a film for a moderate amount, the filmmaker is free to show it privately or, if the film is good enough, have it distributed by a major manufacturer. Film companies will engage in financing, promoting and distributing much as major book publishers do today. The filmmaker need not strike a common cultural denominator; he need only appeal to a friendly minority. And with the costs of filmmaking substantially lower, it is more probable that a filmmaker can find his minority (in book publishing today, this minority can be as small as 5,000). In the cassette entertainment age, the film artist will be freer than ever before.

Whether individual artists—directors, producers, writers and performers—will benefit from audio-visual cartridge use of already produced films depends entirely upon whether profits from their sale will go into the total and, of course, whether they have a piece of that total. The motion picture industry has taken the firm position that sale of feature-length motion pictures (after they are released from the theatrical circuit) to an audio-visual cartridge medium is the same as the sale of a 16mm print to TV, and thus will not be specially computed but will round out the profit picture with profit participants sharing accordingly.

CONCLUSION

We have already discussed the marketing strategy in terms of software programming for the hardware manufacturer. But what might the revolution do for the producer? There are many ways to cash in on the enormous emerging market. If he is canny, the small entrepreneur might busy himself securing rights to already-produced material for audio-visual cartridge use, and thus—with some financial backing—possibly build a library of audio-visual cartridge offerings which would provide steady rental income or even income from outright sales. How the large studios, TV networks and entertainment complexes involved in leisure-time activities should cash in on this market in terms of programming and distribution is a more difficult question.

In epilogue, at least one suggested strategy for a move on the home entertainment market ought to be suggested. Such a strategy would be to initiate a three-phase operation. The first phase involves organizational staffing. This means a mass search for intelligent, imaginative executive management with sufficient experience in production and all its allied arts, and in distribution either of motion pictures, records or books.

The second phase involves acquisition of the information and negative with limited implementation. In the first step, one should choose that hardware situation which is sufficiently practicable in both an economic and qualitative sense, and utilize it as a testing mode. For whatever process eventually wins the day, one need only transfer the negative to it. The preferred choice at the present date would be either CBS' EVR system or Avco's system. Motorola is producing a sufficient quantity of EVR players and CBS' Rockleigh, New Jersey plant is busily processing cartridges.

The second step in this second phase would be to test-market the software programming for informational purposes. Because of the high cost of the players, the proposed approach might include a deal with large first-class hotels in five key cities throughout the country and five large apartment building complexes in each of those same cities. The approach would include putting players which are rented or purchased under special agreement in each of the apartments and hotel rooms. By hooking one, two or three players to the common antenna systems in each of the complexes and feeding the signal into the individual apartments, three unused channels could be utilized. This, however, would be a test of the pay-TV concept more than of the audio-visual cartridge concept, for under the first method a superintendent-programmer or bell-captain network chief would be controlling the programming selector for each of the viewers simultaneously. Operating the EVR player is so simple that hotel staffs could learn (and instruct any prospective guest) the use of the machine in a matter of minutes. A small booth could be set up which would contain available audio-visual cartridges from the most recent first-run features, older features, short subjects, and sports or documentaries. The guest would pay no additional charge for this service, since the hotel would bear the brunt of the cost as an exploitation and advertising device to attract prospective guests—much the same as is done with color television in every room. Arrangements could be made with feature length motion picture companies for a limited number of theatrical features for this audience, in the manner of in-flight motion pictures.

This second phase will yield valuable marketing data on such customer practices as stopping and starting movies, the nature of programming that entices them, and all the other information that is essential to a mass marketing program. This phase could also be profitable if expanded to cover the nearly three million hotel and motel rooms in the United States, the bulk of which already provide television receivers. It would also provide a base upon which to acquire negative product and—more specifically—needed demographic information.

The final phase involves full consumer implementation. The second phase gathered the essential basic information—whether prospective customers want to purchase, rent, use, re-use or return such programming. Now mass distribution centers and local distribution houses will have to be set up—either through existing theatres, record stores or even newly-created outlets. Mail order programming would be a possibility.

So much for strategy. Whatever the right strategy may prove to be, the cartridge revolution demands that those who want to join in get moving. The only wrong strategy is to sit back and wait for one hardware system to triumph. By that time, the ship will have sailed.

Appendices

APPENDIX I

NOTES ON THE SPONSORED FILM *

ROBERT RANDALL

Back in the early 1930's no neighborhood movie palace's program was complete without one or two "selected short subjects." Audiences—especially the kids—screamed with joy when the title of a favorite cartoon character's short subject flashed on the giant silver screen. And mature audiences responded positively to adult short subjects like *Pete Smith Specialties*, John Nesbitt's *Passing Parade*, and journalistic documentaries like those included in the *March of Time* series.

These shorts were made by the major studios. Some say they were "loss leaders"—never showing a profit but offered as an inducement to theatre managers to buy a studio's entire package of feature films in the days of block booking. With the demise of block booking and the advent of the double feature, major film producers lost interest in the money-losing short subjects. Audiences lost some, but not all, interest in the further extension of an already long double feature program.

So the majors long ago stopped producing theatrical short subjects. What has happened to theatrical short subjects since? Well,

ROBERT RANDALL works primarily with mass communication—ranging from words-on-paper through special presentations, film and television. His academic background includes Yale, Columbia and Oklahoma Universities. He is head of Media Development at American Telephone & Telegraph Co..

* EDITORS' NOTE: While this volume focuses upon the theatrical fiction film, it was felt that a brief description of theatrical potentialities for the "sponsored" film should be included.

they are still in evidence, but the production patterns have changed considerably and some of them are much more interesting than they were in the past. A few forward-looking museums are even storing away some new short films as examples of cinematic art, and thousands of young filmmakers are making thousands of short films—some with a careful eye on theatrical distribution. The latter include far-sighted people who are using theatrical shorts as springboards to propel themselves into full length feature films. The first time I saw Alan Arkin *as an actor*, he was playing the lead in a delightful theatrical short subject in which he convinced a welfare supervisor that life as a welfare client was much more fun than life as a welfare supervisor. Later, the first film I saw *directed by* Alan Arkin was a short fantasy called *People Soup*.

All this suggests that film graduates of over 500 colleges now teaching cinema might well consider theatrical short subjects as one of the proving grounds which will help separate professionals from dilletantes. A good film is a good film, regardless of whether it is 9- or 90-minutes long. It is easier for a beginner to prove that he can handle production problems in a short film—where many people who could not consider the expense of a feature film are willing to finance projects.

The chief sources of sponsorship, of course, are business corporations, foundations, government, educational media systems, and service groups. The money they are willing to spend frequently decreases as you traverse the line from business to service groups. Yet the amount of control they will want to exercise over the final product will vary from a great deal to none at all. It can be quite flexible, depending upon many factors.

What kind of money is actually being committed to such films? According to *Hope Reports*, sponsors spent more than $150-million on sponsored films in 1970 and $190-million in more prosperous 1969. Further, this was only for production costs. It does not include distribution expenses.

Only a small percentage of sponsored films are intended for the screens of admission-paid theatres, but this is still a larger percentage than most people would ever believe. That interesting (or lousy) travelogue you saw about Europe was sponsored by an airline which happens to have planes flying to Europe—if you should care to go. That funny theatrical short about a man who gets his Cadillac stuck between two other cars in a supermarket parking lot was—of course —a sponsored film. You can probably recall sequences where the camera held a bit too long on the (brand name) soft drink in his wife's grocery bag, or undue visual emphasis upon the fact that she trades with a grocer who gives away (brand name) merchandise stamps with every purchase. Some people say there was even an extra long shot of a (brand name) tea tin in the theatrical fiction film, *Rosemary's Baby*. There is nothing especially new about sponsored films which—directly or indirectly—push a commercial product. After all, Robert J. Flaherty's classic social documentary, *Nanook of the North*, was sponsored by a business organization, Revillon Frères.

Many sponsored films do not serve an explicitly commercial purpose. American Can sponsored a series of earnest interviews with blacks (*Making It*, produced by DeWitt Beall). Kaiser Aluminum sponsored a highly creative film on the subject of creativity (*Why Man Creates* by Saul Bass). And AT&T sponsored a short film (*Generations*) specifically to help its own managers better understand a new generation of customers and employees. Some corporations like Shell and General Motors have their own film production units. Others depend on over 700 independent film production organizations which specialize in making sponsored films. In recent years, some of these production companies have had more than 400 people continuously on their payrolls. Others have staffs which range downward in size to the one-man organization.

A few sponsored films are still being made by in-house production units for as little as $3,000 plus the hidden cost of the salaries and overhead for the in-house unit. Of course, independent film producers must charge more. Today it is not unusual to spend $100,000 on a 27-minute film. Some few "superbudgets" have gone above a half-million dollars for one film. Yet, the fact that a film is expensive does not make it better or more appealing to audiences. Here the sponsored filmmaker has learned the same bitter lesson the Hollywood companies have learned. A sponsor benefits from a film in direct relationship to: (1) how well he defines his own motives and goals before the filmmaking starts; (2) the skill, efficiency, and motivation of the filmmaker; (3) the kind and degree of rapport between the filmmaker and the sponsor; and (4) how well the finished product is promoted and distributed. So a wise sponsor does not try to buy films by the yard. He knows that in filmmaking the phrase "you get what you pay for" is not always true. There are low-budget sleepers and high-budget flops.

A sponsored short subject usually gets into a theatre through an organization like Modern Talking Pictures or Association-Sterling. These organizations specialize in short film distribution for a fee paid by the sponsor. This method has produced some impressive viewer figures. Modern reports that over 6,500,000 people have seen *Mayflower USA* in commercial motion picture theatres during the last three years. The picture was produced in 1957 and is still being used.

PERTINENT EXCERPTS FROM RECENT CONTRACTS OF MAJOR CREATIVE GUILDS AND CRAFT UNIONS

The Writers Guild of America:
        Theatrical and Television Film
Directors Guild of America, Inc.
Screen Actors Guild
International Alliance of Theatrical
        Stage Employees (I.A.T.S.E.) and Moving
        Picture Machine Operators (M.P.M.O.)

THE WRITERS GUILD OF AMERICA
THEATRICAL AND TELEVISION FILM
BASIC AGREEMENT

Ed. note: As the manuscript for this volume was in its final stages
of preparation in late 1971, the Writers Guild of America was still
some months away from concluding its new codified agreement. The
following selections, therefore, represent the basic 1963 agreement
with extensive 1966 and 1970 up-dates and changes. Initial selections
were suggested by Mr. Leonard Chassman, contract Administrator,
Writers Guild of America, West, Inc. The selections finally incorporated here deal with those areas of the agreement which, it is felt,
would be of greatest interest to the beginner in the field. The
reader is advised to regard the material as a mere introduction to
the more complex and lengthy document now undergoing codification.

DEFINITIONS

A "writer" is a person who is:

(i) employed by the Producer to write stories, adaptations,
treatments, scenarios, continuities, dialogue, scripts or screenplays
for use in the production of theatrical motion picture photoplays,
where the Producer has the right by contract to direct the performance
of personal services in writing or preparing such material or in making
revisions, modifications or changes therein;

(ii) employed by the Producer, who performs services (at
Producer's direction or with his consent) in writing or preparing
such material or making revisions, modifications, or changes in such
material regardless of whether such services are described or required
in his basic contract of employment; provided, however, that any
writing services described below performed by Producers, Directors,
Story Supervisors, Composers, Lyricists, or other employees, shall
not be subject to this agreement and such services shall not constitute such person a writer hereunder:

a) Cutting for time.

b) Bridging material necessitated by cutting for time.

c) Changes in technical or stage directions.

d) Assignment of lines to other existing characters occasioned by cast changes.

e) Changes necessary to obtain continuity acceptance or legal clearance.

f) Casual minor adjustments in dialogue or narration made prior to or during the period of principal photography.

g) Such changes in the course of production as are made necessary by unforseen contingencies (e.g., the elements, accidents to performers, etc.)

h) Instructions, directions, or suggestions, whether oral or written, made to writer regarding such material.

In addition to the foregoing, in the case of a person who at the time he performs services has not received at least two screen credits for story or screenplay, or both, as determined pursuant to Schedule A of this agreement, or Schedule A of the previous 1963 Theatrical Agreement or prior agreements, within a period of ten years (or has not received at least one of such credits within a period of five years) immediately prior to the rendition of such services, and who is employed solely in the capacity of the bona fide producer of a motion picture and whose employment does not include the requirement that he perform writing services, then, such person may, in addition to the above, perform the following writing services: make change in dialogue, narration or action, but not including significant changes in plot, story line or interrelationship of characters, and such services by such person shall not be subject to this agreement. If such person does make significant changes in plot, story line or interrelationship of characters, then such services by such person shall be subject to this agreement, except Article 5 hereof.

In addition to the foregoing, in the case of a person who at the time he performs services has received at least two such screen credits within such ten year period (and with at least one of such credits within such five year period) immediately prior to the rendition of such services, and who is employed solely in the capacity of the bona fide producer of a motion picture, and whose employment does not include the requirement that he perform writing services, then, if such person shall perform writing services in addition to those described in a) through h) above, such services by such person shall be subject to this agreement.

In addition to the foregoing, in the case of a person who at the time he performs services is employed solely in the capacity of the director of a motion picture, and whose employment does not include the requirement that he perform writing services, then, such person may, in addition to the above, perform the following writing services: make changes in dialogue, narration or action, but not including significant changes in plot, story line or interrelationship of characters, and such services by such person shall not be subject to this agreement. If such person does make significant changes in plot,

story line or interrelationship of characters, then such services
by such person shall be subject to this agreement, except Article
5 hereof.

In any event, if any producer or director shall receive screen credit
pursuant to the provisions of Schedule A attached hereto or is determined by a union credit arbitration committee to be entitled to such
credit pursuant to Schedule A and the union's credit rules relating
to the quantity and quality of the contrication necessary for such
credit in effect on the effective date of this agreement, then the
provisions of paragraph (h) of Article 5 hereof shall apply with
respect to such person.

With respect to a person employed solely as a producer-director, on
the motion pictures which he directs the director paragraph above
shall apply and on the motion pictures which he does not direct, the
producer paragraphs above shall apply.

This agreement shall not not is it intended to cover the employment
of Producers, Directors, Story Supervisors, Composers, Lyricists, or
other persons employed in a bona fide non-writing capacity except
to the extent that such employment consists of writing services
covered under this paragraph (a) (ii), nor the employment of Story
Analyists, at any time prior to the expiration of this agreement, in
the synopsizing of literary material, as referred to in sub-paragraph
1 (f) of the wage scales and working conditions of the current agreement between "Producer and I.A.T.S.E. & M.P.M.O. and Local #854 thereof."

The term "writer" shall not be deemed to include any corporate or
impersonal purveyor of such material or of rights therein.

WRITING CREDITS

A. Credit shall be given on the screen for the screenplay,
authorship of feature-length photoplays and shall be worded "Screen
Play By." The term "screen play" means the final script (as represented on the screen) with individual scenes and full dialogue, together with such prior treatment, basic adaptation, continuity,
scenario, dialogue, and added dialogue as shall be used in and
represent substantial contributions to the final script.

In the exceptional case where a writer has contributed to the
development of the final screenplay but is not given screenplay
credit hereunder, credit in the form "Adaptation By" may be given,
but such credit shall be subject to automatic credit arbitration as
provided in subdivision R of Schedule A.

B. The term "story," as used throughout this Schedule A means
all writing written substantially in whole by a writer or writers
while employed by the Producer, representing a contribution distinct
from screenplay and consisting of basic narrative, idea, theme or
outline indicating character development and action. The term

"source material" means all material upon which the screenplay is based other than story as hereinabove defined, including other material on which the story is based. Credit shall be given on the screen for story authorship of feature length photoplays to the extent and in the forms provided in the following subsections 1 to 5, inclusive.

1. When the screenplay is based upon story and upon no other source material, screen credit for a story authorship shall be given the screen writer, and shall be worded "Story By."

2. When the screenplay is based upon source material, screen credit for story authorship may be given by the Producer to the source material author, and may be worded "Story By."

3. When the screenplay is based upon both story and source material and the story is substantially new or different from the source material, credit for story authorship shall be worded "Screen Story By," which credit shall be subject to automatic credit arbitration as provided in subdivision R of Schedule A. The Producer shall not thereby be limited from giving credit to the author of source material, provided such credit shall indicate the form in which it is acquired. The following examples are illustrative and not intended to cover all situations: "From a Play By," "From a Novel By," "From a Saturday Evening Post Story By," "From a Series of Articles By," "From an Unpublished Story By," "Based on a Story By," "Ernest Hemingways's Old Man of the Sea," or other appropriate wording indicating the form in which it is acquired.

4. When the screenplay is based upon a sequel story written by an employed writer, story credit for such sequel shall be given in the form "Story By," and the author of the source material upon which such sequel is based may be given credit "Based Upon Characters Created By," or other appropriate form of credit.

5. The Producer may engage any person to write any source material (including, but not limited to the source material referred to in subsection 3, above), as an independent contractor and may guarantee source material credit to such person as above provided.

Upon the written request of a writer made prior to his acceptance of employment in connection with a designated photoplay, or upon the written request of a then employed writer made at the time of his assignment to a designated photoplay, the Producer shall notify him in writing of any then existing contractual obligation to give credit for source material in connection with such photoplay. The Producer shall not be thereby limited from making subsequent contractual obligations to give source material credit, as above provided, in connection with such

photoplay. Neither the existence of any form of credit obligation nor the giving of any such credit information shall relieve
a writer from his obligation to render services and otherwise
perform as provided in his employment agreement. A Producer
who furnishes a writer hereunder with inaccurate or incorrect
credit information shall not be deemed to be in breach of this
agreement or its employment agreement with such writer, if the
Producer at the time of giving such credit information believes
in good faith such information is correct.

The Producer shall be deemed to be contractually obligated
in any of the cases above mentioned if the Producer in good
faith considers itself so obligated.

Nothing herein contained shall limit the Producer from
using and purchasing source material, from entering into agreements to give source material credit therefor, as above provided,
from carrying out such credit obligations as may be therein
provided.

C. Screen credit on photoplays on which one writer or a team
has written both the story and the screenplay shall be worded "Written By."

D. Screen credit for screenplay will not be shared by more
than two writers, except that in unusual cases, and solely as the
result of arbitration, the names of three writers or the names of
writers constituting two writing teams may be used. A writing team
is: two writers who have been assigned at about the same time to the
same script and who work together for approximately the same length
of time of the script. The intention and spirit of the award of
credits being to emphasize the prestige and importance of the screenplay achievement, the one, two or at most three writers, or two teams,
chiefly responsible for the completed work will be the only screen
writers to receive screenplay credit. Story credit will not be
shared by more than two writers.

E. The limitations on the number of credits provided for in
subdivision D shall apply to all feature-length photoplays except
episodic pictures (such as Tales of Manhattan and If I Had A Million)
and revues. A revue is a feature-length photoplay in which the story
is subordinate to specialties, musical numbers or sketches, and in
connection with which star or featured billing is given to the actors,
singers, dancers, or musicians appearing in these separate specialties,
musical numbers or sketches.

F. Unless the screenplay writing is done entirely without the
collaboration of any other writer, no designation of tentative screenplay credit to a production executive shall become final or effective
unless approved by a credit arbitration as herein provided, in accordance with the Guild rules for the determination of such credit.

G. When more than one writer has participated in the authorship of a photoplay, then all participants will have the right to

agree unanimously among themselves as to which of them shall receive writing credits on the screen, provided that the form of credit agreed upon is in accordance with the terms of the Schedule A, and provided the agreement is reached in advance of arbitration, and provided that the form of such credit is not suggested or directed by the Producer. If such unanimous agreement is communicated to the Producer before a final determination of credits hereunder, the Producer will accept such designation of credits, and such agreed credits shall become final hereunder. The Producer will confirm such agreed credits by sending notice thereof to all participants and the Guild, in the manner hereinafter provided in subdivisions K and L hereof.

H. Writing credits as finally determined hereunder shall appear on the screen on a title card immediately preceding the cards on which appear credit to the Producer and the Director of the photoplay, provided that the card on which appears the credit to the Producer immediately precedes that of the Director, and otherwise the card on which writing credits appear shall immediately precede that of the Director. No other credits except source material credit, may appear on the card on which writing credits appear.

Source material credits (if they appear on the screen) and writing credits finally determined hereunder shall, subject to the foregoing, appear only in the following manner:

1. On one title card on which there appear only writing and source material credits.

2. On separate title cards on each of which there may appear any one or more of such credits, and no other credits.

3. On the main title card of the photoplay on which there may appear any one or more of such credits together with other credits.

Screen credit for the writer of the screenplay shall be accorded in the same style and size of type as that used to accord screen credit to the individual Producer or Director of the photoplay, whichever is larger.

Wherever source material credit, or source material and story credit given to the same writer, appears on the same title card as the screenplay credit, the screenplay credit must be the initial credit and must occupy not less than 50 per cent of the credit card in type at least as large in all respects as that accorded the source material credit. Wherever story credit, but no source material credit, appears on the same title card as the screenplay credit, the screenplay credit must be the initial credit and occupy not less than 60 per cent of the card. Wherever both a source material credit and story credit given to different writers are placed on the same title card as the screenplay credit, the screenplay credit shall appear in a larger size of type on the upper 60 per cent of such title card.

Such source material credit and this story credit shall appear in
a smaller size of type than that used for the screenplay credit and
shall appear on the lower 40 per cent of such title card which lower
40 per cent of such title card shall be apportioned equally among all
writers receiving such source material and story credit. Under the
circumstances described in the immediately preceding sentence, the
Producer shall have the right to place the source material credit
on another card without the limitations hereinabove imposed so long
as such other card is not inserted between the screenplay credit and
the Director's credit. The foregoing provisions of this paragraph
and the preceding paragraph shall not be applicable (i) to existing
contract commitments which contain terms contrary thereto, or (ii)
to photoplays for which the titles or advertising campaign material
have been made up prior to the effective date of the agreement to
which this is attached as Schedule A.

I. A writer who has participated in the writing of the screenplay, or a writer who has been employed by the Producer on the story
shall, for the purpose of this agreement, be considered a participant.
As a participant, he shall be entitled to participate in the procedure for determination of screen credits, and in addition, in the
case of a remake, any writer who has received credit either for story
or screenplay in connection with the most recent production of such
remake photoplay.

J. Prior to the final determination of screen credits, as
provided herein, the work of participants not receiving screen credit
may be publicized by the Producer. After such a determination of
screen credits only persons receiving screen credits or source material credit amy be so publicized. This provision shall be subject
to and shall not affect any publicity with respect to motion pictures
the principal photography of which commenced prior to June 13, 1960.

K. Before the writing credits for a motion picture are finally
determined (and in the case of a motion picture produced in Producer's
studios in the Los Angeles area, no later than three (3) business days
following completion of principal photography of such motion picture,
except where circumstances make it impractical), the Producer will
send to each participant and to the Guild concurrently a written
notice which will state the Producer's choice of credit on a tentative
basis, togehter with the names of all participants, their addresses
last known to the Producer, and if a participant is then also a
director or producer of the photoplay the notice will so indicate.
Where the Producer deems its record of participants incomplete, it
may comply with the foregoing by giving notice to each writer whose
name and address are furnished by the Guild within five (5) days after
the Producer's request for such information, in addition to giving
notice to each participant shown on its records.

The Producer shall on such notice of tentative credits, for the
information of the Guild and participants, state the form of any
source material credit which the Producer intends to use in connection

with the photoplay. Such credits shall not be subject to the provisions for protest and arbitration as hereinafter provided, but
the Guild shall have the right to object to the form of such a
credit.

At the Producer's request, the Guild may, but shall not be
obligated to, make a determination of screen credits and shall so
notify the participants. When a Guild determination is so made, it
shall be considered a final determination.

At the request of the Guild made to the Producer on commencement
of principal photography of such motion picture, the Producer shall
furnish the Guild with a list of all persons who, to the best of the
Producer's knowledge, are or were participants (See Section I above)
with respect to such motion picture. If thereafter any other writer
is engaged by Producer to render writing services in or in connection
with such motion picture during the principal photography thereof, the
Producer will promptly notify the Guild of that fact. If the motion
picture involved is a remake of an earlier motion picture produced by
the Producer, the list of writers to be supplied by the Producer pursuant to this paragraph shall include the name of any writer employed
by the Producer to render writing services with respect to the most
recent prior production by Producer of such earlier motion picture
and who received screen credit for such writing services.

A casual or inadvertent failure by the Producer to forward the
notices, lists, names or other information to the Guild or persons
specified at the times or places designated pursuant to this Section
K shall not be deemed to be a breach of this agreement.

O. Upon receipt of a protest or request to read the script,
the Producer will deliver a copy of the script to the Guild office
in Los Angeles for each participant who requests it, provided that
the Producer shall not be required to prepare additional copies of
the script, and the Producer shall notify the participants and the
Guild by telegraph informing them of the name of the protesting party
and the new time set for final determination.

P. If a unanimous designation of credits as provided for in subdivision G hereof or a request for arbitration as hereinafter provided
is not communicated to the Producer within the time limit set for the
final determination of credits, the Producer may make the tentative
credits final. The tentative screen credits shall become final where
the arbitration concerns only credits which are not to appear on the
screen.

Q. Any notice specified in the foregoing paragraphs shall, unless a specified form of service thereof is otherwise provided for
herein, be sent by the Producer by telegraphing, mailing or delivering the same to the last known address of the writer or may be delivered
to the writer personally.

R. Unless a unanimous agreement has been reached in accordance
with subdivision G hereof, any participant or the Guild, may within
the period provided for in subdivision N hereof, file with the Producer at its Studio and the Guild at its Los Angeles office a written
request for arbitration of credits. In any case where automatic
credit arbitration is required under Schedule A the Guild will be
deemed to have made a written request for arbitration of credits, at
the time the Producer submits the notice of tentative credits, and
in such case Producer will immediately make available to the Guild
the material as provided for under this subdivision.

The Guild through its arbitration committee shall, within ten
(10) business days thereafter, make and advise the Producer of its
decision within the limitations of this Schedule A. In the event
the decision of the arbitration committee is not rendered within said
period, as the same may have been extended by the Producer, the
Producer may make the tentative credits final, provided the terms and
provisions of this subdivision R have been fully complied with by
the Producer.

In the event of an emergency and upon the Producer's request
that the time for arbitration be shortened, the Guild agrees to
cooperate as fully as possible. If the material is voluminous or
complex, or if other circumstances beyond the control of the Guild
necessitate a longer period in order to render a fair decision, and
the Guild requests an extension of time for arbitration, the Producer
agrees to cooperate as fully as possible.

Prior to the rendition of the decision said committee may make
such investigations and conduct such hearings as may seem advisable
to it. Immediately upon receipt of said request for arbitration,
the Producer shall make available to the Guild three (3) copies of
the script, and three copies of all available material written by
the participants and three copies of all available source material,
provided, however, that if three copies of any such material shall
not be available, Producer shall only be required to provide such
copies as are available but in such case the time within which the
committee may be required to render its decision as provided for
herein shall be extended from ten days to twenty days. In addition,
the Producer shall cooperate with the arbitration committee to arrive
at a just determination by furnishing all available information relative to the arbitration. Upon request of the arbitration committee,
the Producer shall provide the committee with a copy of the cutting
continuity if it is available at the time of arbitration.

The decision of the Guild arbitration committee, and any Board
of Review established by the Guild in connection therewith, with
respect to writing credits, insofar as it is rendered within the
limitations of this Schedule A, shall be final, and the Producer
will accept and follow the designation of screen credits contained
in such decision and all writers shall be bound thereby.

S. The decision of the Guild arbitration committee may be published in such media as the Guild may determine. No writer or Producer shall be entitled to collect damages or shall be entitled to injunctive relief as a result of any decision of the Committee with regard to credits. In signing any contract incorporating by reference or otherwise all or part of this basic agreement, any writer or Producer specifically waives all rights or claims against the Guild and/or its arbiters or any of them under the laws of libel or slander of otherwise with regard to proceedings before the Guild arbitration committee and any full and fair publication of the findings and/or decisions of such Committee. The Guild and any writer signing any contract incorporating by reference or otherwise or referring to this Schedule A, and any writer consenting to the procedure set forth in this Schedule A, shall not have any rights or claims of any nature against any Producer growing out of or concerning any action of the Guild or its arbiters or any of them, or any determination of credits in the manner provided in this Schedule A, and all such rights or claims are hereby specifically waived.

T. In the event that after the screen credits are determined as hereinabove provided, material changes are made in the script or photoplay, either the Producer or a participant and the Guild jointly may re-open credit determination by making a claim to the Guild or Producer, as the case may be, within forty-eight (48) hours after completion of the writing work claimed to justify the revision of credits, in which case the procedure for determining such revised credits will be the same as that provided for the original determination of credits.

The Producer agrees to make revisions in advertising material previously forwarded to the processor or publisher to reflect such re-determined credits, provided that such revisions can physically and mechanically be made prior to the closing date of such processor or publisher and at reasonable expense and provided the processor or publisher has not yet commenced work on that part of the material which the change would affect.

U. No writer shall claim credit for any participation in the screen authorship of any photoplay for which credits are to be determined by the procedure herein provided for prior to the time when such credits have in fact actually been so determined, and no writer shall claim credits contrary to such determination.

V. In any publicity issued or released prior to the final determination of credits as herein provided, the Producer may include such screenplay or screenplay and story credits as the Producer may in good faith believe to be fair and truthful statement of authorship. After such final determination of credits, the Producer shall not issue or release any publicity which shall state screenplay or screenplay and story authorship contrary to such determination. No casual or inadvertent breach of the foregoing shall be deemed to constitute a breach by the Producer. Writing credit, but not necessarily in the form specified in this Schedule A, shall be included in publicity releases issued by the Company relating to the picture when the producer and the director are mentioned. The writing credit shall also be included in screening invitations issued by the Company where the credit of the producer or director are included. Prior to a final determination of credits the Company shall include those credits which it in good faith believes to be a fair and truthful statement of authorship.

Screenplay or screenplay and story credit in accordance with the final determination of such credit will be given on any paid advertising issued anywhere in the world, provided such advertising is prepared by the Producer in the Continental United States and is controlled by the Producer where such advertisement is used; it being understood that in such advertising prepared prior to final determination of screenplay and story credits, the Producer may include such screenplay or screenplay and story credit as the Producer may in good faith believe to be a fair and truthful statement of authorship. After final determination of credits, the Producer shall not prepare for issuance any advertising which shall state screenplay or screenplay and story authorship contrary to such final determination.

PAYMENT

Flat Deal Screen Minimums

	Effective from 6-16-70 to 6-15-73		HIGH BUDGET	
	Low* Budget	Medium* Budget	6-16-70 to 12-15-71	12-16-71 to 6-15-73
(1) Screenplay, including treatment	$5,600	$7,000	$11,000	$13,000
(2) Screenplay, excluding treatment	3,500	4,375	7,313	9,000
(3) Final Draft Screenplay or rewrite	2,100	2,625	3,688	4,000
(4) First Draft of Screenplay (alone or with option for Final Draft Screenplay):				
First Draft Screenplay	2,520	3,150	5,025	6,000
Final Draft Screenplay	1,680	2,100	3,350	4,000
(5) Treatment	2,100	2,625	3,688	4,000
(6) Original Treatment	3,100	3,625	5,025	6,000
(7) Story	2,100	2,625	3,350	4,000

(Flat Deal Screen Minimums, cont'd.)

	Effective from 6-16-70 to 6-15-73		HIGH BUDGET	
	Low* Budget	Medium* Budget	6-16-70 to 12-15-71	12-16-71 to 6-15-73
(8) Additional Compensation -Screenplay-No assigned Material (See revised Article 20 (b) in Article 13 of this Agreement.)	$1,000	$1,000	$ 1,500	$ 2,000

*NOTE: the minimum for a Screen Writer shall not be less than the "appropriate" television film minimum, consistent with the particular literary element and the length of the film.

Minimum Weekly Compensation

A writer shall be qualified:

(a) If he shall have had at least twenty-six (26) weeks of actual employment in the United States as a writer under an employment agreement or agreements in the motion picture industry; or

(b) If he shall receive a screenplay credit on a photoplay the cost of which is Two Hundred and Fifty Thousand Dollars ($250,000.00), or more; or

(c) If he shall receive screenplay credit on two photoplays regardless of cost; or

(d) If he shall receive teleplay credit on two (2) ninety (90) minute, or four (4) sixty (60) minute, or eight (8) thirty (30) minute filmed television programs.

It is understood that the employment of the writer need not be consecutive for the purpose of subdivision (a) above. If a writer shall once become qualified he shall thereafter continue to be qualified without regard to continuity of employment. The cost of a photoplay, for the purpose of subdivision (b) above, shall be the estimated budgeted cost thereof upon the date of commencement of principal photography.

Every writer employed on a week-to-week or term basis who shall be or become qualified as hereinabove provided, shall receive a salary at the rate of not less than the amount a week specified below for the respective period designated:

Week-to-Week and Term Employment of a Qualified Writer

Minimums	Effective through 6/15/72	6/15/72 - 6/15/73
Week-to-Week	$525.00 per week	$651.00
Term (Guarantees):		
14 out of 14 weeks	$487.00 per week	$604.00
20 out of 26 weeks	$450.00	$558.00
40 out of 52 weeks	$413.00	$512.00

Every week-to-week or term contract shall specify the exact compensation for each full week of services to be rendered thereunder.

If any writer under a week-to-week or term contract shall render services after the expiration of the guaranteed period of employment, then, for purposes only or prorating days worked in a partial work-week, (i.e., less than six (6) days), at the end of such employment, the writer shall recieve one-fifth (1/5) of the weekly rate for each day worked during such partial workweek, after the expiration of the guaranteed period.

Separation of Rights

(a) Definitions. For the purpose of this Article the following terms or words used herein shall have the following meanings:

(i) The term "dramatic rights" means the right of presentation in dramatic form on the speaking stage with living actors appearing and performing in the immediate presence of an audience, without any recordation, transmission or broadcast thereof intended for or permitting concurrent or future aural, or visual and aural, reception or reproduction at places away from the auditorium or other place of performance.

(ii) The term "publication rights" includes the right of publication in all writing forms and all writing media, excluding only comic books, comic strips and newspaper comics.

The provisions of this paragraph shall apply only to material subject to this Agreement and acquired after the effective date hereof under contracts subject to and enetered into after the effective date of this Agreement.

(iii) The term "sequel" as used with reference to a particular motion picture, means a new theatrical motion picture in which the principal characters of the first theatrical motion picture participate in an entirely new and different story.

(iv) The term "assigned material" means all material of every nature that the Producer has furnished the Writer (or to

which the Producer has directed the Writer) upon which material
the Producer intends the story (or story and screenplay) to be
based or from which it is to be, in whole or in part, adapted.
The term "assigned material" may include public domain material
or a character or characters proposed for use in the story (or
story and screenplay).

(b) <u>Initial Qualification</u>. The Producer agrees that if a
Writer, while in the employ of the Producer, writes an original
story (or original story and screenplay) including a complete and
developed plot and character development, he shall be initially qualified
for separation of rights hereunder. A Writer shall be deemed to have
written a complete and developed plot and character development if he
does so himself or if the product of the work of such Writer and writers
previously (but after June 13, 1960) employed hereunder together constitute such a complete and developed plot and character development.
Producer also agrees that if after the effective date of this Agreement it purchases from a person such a story (or story and screenplay) written by such person, then on condition that the material so
acquired had not theretofore been published or exploited in any manner
or by any medium whatsoever, and on the further condition that at
the time of such acquisition the person was a member of the Guild
in good standing, such person shall be initially qualified for separation of rights hereunder. If such person states that the material
has theretofore been published or exploited and if the Producer relies
on such statement, then such person shall not be entitled to separation of rights hereunder. If at the time of the transfer of rights
to the material so purchased there is in existence a valid agreement
for the publication or dramatic production of such material, then for
the purpose hereof such material shall be deemed to have been published
or exploited.

With respect to a Writer employed by the Producer, if there is
assigned material then:

(1) If the employment agreement (or written assignment delivered
by the Producer to the Writer, in the case of a term contract, week-
to-week contract, or multiple picture type employment) designates as
the assigned material upon which the motion picture is to be based,
or from which it is to be adapted, a story contained in a book, magazine, screenplay, play or other dramatic composition, treatment or
story in any other form, then the Writer, or any other Writer working
thereon, shall not be qualified for separation of rights unless:

(i) With the knowledge and prior or subsequent consent
of the Producer the Writer departed from the story contained in
such assigned material and created an original story (or original
story and screenplay) of the nature first described in this
Paragraph (b), to the extent that there is no longer any substantial similarity between such story written by the Writer and such
story contained in the assigned material; or

(ii) The assigned material designated in the employment
agreement or written assignment was not actually available to

the Writer, and the Writer creates a story (or story and screenplay) of the nature first described in this Paragraph (b).

If the Writer makes either of such contentions and the Producer and
Writer cannot agree thereon, either the Writer or the Producer may
submit the issue to arbitration and if it is determined by arbitration that the facts were as described in (i) or (ii) above, then such
Writer shall be initially qualified for separation of rights hereunder.

(2) If a character or characters furnished by the Producer constitutes all of the assigned material, and if such character (or one
of such characters) furnished by the Producer is intended by the Producer to be a principal character in the motion picture, and if such
character was taken from material, of any nature, theretofore published or exploited in any manner or by any medium, and if such character is used in the screenplay as a principal character, then the Writer
shall not be qualified for separation of rights hereunder. If, however,
any such character furnished by the Producer as aforesaid was
a minor character in previously published or otherwise exploited material, and with the prior or subsequent consent of the Producer was
converted by the Writer into a principal character in the story (or
story and screenplay) of the nature above described in Paragraph (b),
written by the Writer, and if no minor character as furnished by the
Producer (as distinguished from such character or characters as developed by the Writer) constitutes a substantial contribution to the final
screenplay, and if no principal character furnished by the Producer
remains a principal character in the motion picture, then such Writer
shall be initially qualified for separation of rights hereunder. If
such character or characters furnished by the Producer constitutes all
of the assigned material and were not taken from material theretofore
published or exploited in any manner or by any medium, and if the
Writer were otherwise qualified for separation of rights hereunder,
the Writer shall not be deprived of such separation of rights, unless
such character or characters furnished by the Producer constitute
a substantial contribution to the final screenplay, in which latter
event such Writer shall not be qualified for separation of rights hereunder.

(c) <u>Final Qualification</u>, If it is determined, in the manner
provided in Schedule "A" attached hereto, that the Writer of the story
(or story and screenplay), initially qualified for separation of rights
as above provided, is entitled to receive "story by" or "written by"
or "screen story by" credit, he shall be entitled to separation of
rights in the following areas:

(1) Publication Rights. Publication rights throughout the world
in the "separable material," as hereinafter defined, shall be
licensed exclusively to the Writer on a royalty free basis both
for the original term of copyright and for any extensions and
renewals thereof, without the necessity for the execution by the
Producer of any further instrument, except as expressly provided
below and subject to the provisions of Section (5) of Paragraph
(g) hereof and to the following:

(i) No publication rights may be exercised by the
Writer prior to the expiration of three (3) years
from date of the employment contract (or the date of
the assignment of the Writer in the case of a term
contract, week-to-week contract or multiple picture type
employment) or three (3) years from the date of acquisition in case the material is purchased, or prior to
the expiration of six (6) months following the general
release of the motion picture, whichever is earlier.

(ii) The Producer shall be entitled to and shall own
the exclusive right to make, publish and copyright or
cause to be made, published and copyrighted in the name
of the Producer or its nominee, serially or otherwise,
in any and all languages and throughout the world, syn-
opses, summaries, resumes, adaptations, stories and
fictionalized versions of and excerpts from any screenplay or photoplay, in any form and in any publication
media (with or without illustrations) for the purpose
of advertising, publicity or exploitation, of the
motion picture based on such material, provided that
any single publication may not exceed 10,000 words in
length.

(2) If a Company desires to publish, or cause to be published,
a "paperback" type of novelization for the purpose of publicizing
or exploiting such motion picture, the Company shall have the
right to do so (and without being subject to any limitation on
the number of words) provided such publication shall not take
place earlier than six (6) months prior to the initial scheduled
release date of the motion picture. Such publication shall
occur in accordance with the following procedure: The Company
shall give written notice to the writer entitled to separation of
rights, with a copy to the Guild, specifying such Company's desire
for such publication and the name(s) of publisher(s) who are
acceptable to the Company. Within 10 days, the Guild shall give
the Company written notice of the name of the writer ("Guild-
named writer") who intends to negotiate for the publication of
such novelization and the name of the agent who will negotiate
for such writer. The Guild-named writer shall only be the writer
entitled to separation of rights for such motion picture or
another accredited writer for such motion picture should the
writer entitled to separation of rights desire not to write the
novelization. Such agent shall keep the Company fully informed
of the status of the negotiations. Any publication agreement
entered into by the Guild-named writer shall provide that the
Company shall have control of the time and locale of the publication and release and of the cover, title, credits, legends,
advertising material, stills and other elements furnished by
the Company (referred to herein as the "art work"), and the
Company shall have the right to arrange for, and keep as its sole
property, payment to the Company respecting such art work. All

payments for the right to publish or cause the publication
of the novelization shall be made to and retained by the Guild-
named writer. If the Guild does not give the Company the aforementioned notice within the aforementioned 10-day period, or if
the Guild-named writer does not consummate a publication agreement
with a publisher within 45 days after the Company's notice to
the Guild naming such publisher as acceptable to the Company, the
Company shall have the right, on such terms as it may elect, to
cause the novelization to be published by such publisher as it
may elect. The compensation to be paid the person writing such
novelization shall not exceed that offered to the Guild-named
writer in his negotiation with the publishing company unless the
Guild-named writer is first given an opportunity to write the
novelization for such increased compensation. Copyright in any
novelization written pursuant to this paragraph 2 shall be taken
and remain in the name of the Company or its nominee. If the
Guild-named writer does not enter into the publication agreement
within the aforementioned 45-day period, the Company will nevertheless pay or cause to be paid to the writer, if any, entitled
to separation of rights, amounts equal to 1/3 of the monetary
compensation, including royalties, if any, paid for his writing
services to the person engaged to write such novelization by the
publisher or by any other person, firm or corporation authorized
by the Company. The term "novelization" as used in the preceding
sentence means a novelization which is based upon the separable
material and utilizing the separable material in a manner which
would constitute a copyright infringement of such separable
material of the writer if the writer were the sole copyright
owner thereof. At the request of Company in case of conflict
between the time periods delineated hereinabove and the release
schedule of the picture, the Guild will give reasonable waivers
to reduce the 45-day period for negotiation by the Guild-named
writer.

      (iv) If the Writer exercies any of the publication
rights, and on each occasion that the Writer exercies the
publication rights licensed to him hereunder, copyright in
the published work shall be taken and remain in the name
of the Producer or its nominee; Writer shall cause the
publisher to comply with all necessary copyright formalities;
and the Producer shall have, and is hereby granted all rights
of every nature in an to the published work, including the
right to extend or renew the copyright, except for such
rights, if any , as may have been expressly reserved by the
Writer under and pursuant to his employment agreement or in
the agreement for the purchase of unpublished and unexploited
material from a Guild member, and excepting also the publication rights and dramatic rights therein, to the extent that
publication and dramatic rights are licensed to and permitted
to be used by the Writer under all the terms and provisions
of this Article 35. If the Writer arranges for the publication of a novel or short story, as permitted hereunder, all
royalties and other monies received by such Writer under

the publication agreement between the publisher and the
Writer shall be the sole property of the Writer.

(v) If the Writer exercises any publication rights
licensed him hereunder, the Writer shall have the right
to make his own arrangements for publication of the novel
or short story, as permitted hereunder, and shall have
exclusive control of all matters relating to such publication, except as expressly provided in subdivision (v) in
connection with such exercise. As soon as practical after the
Writer has the same, but in any event within a reasonable
period prior to the publication thereof, the Writer will
submit to the Producer a copy or proof of the work in form
in which it is to be published together with a reasonably
detailed statement of the manner in which the publication
will be made. The Writer will not use the title of the
motion picture as the title of his published work without
the prior written consent of the Producer; and if the Producer requests the Writer to use the title of the motion
picture as the title of his published work, the Writer agrees
to do so. If prior to the release of the motion picture by
the Producer it is determined that the Writer is entitled
to separation of rights, in the manner hereinafter provided,
and if prior to such release the Writer exercies any publication rights licensed hereunder, the Producer may, but shall
not be be required to, use the title of the published work
or any translation or adaptation thereof as the title of
the motion picture.

(c) Sequel Payments

(1) Notwithstanding the fact that the Writer is entitled to
separation of rights hereunder, he shall have no sequel rights
in or to the motion picture or the separable material; however,
on each occasion that the Producer produces a theatrical motion
picture which is a sequel to a theatrical motion picture as to
which a Writer has been granted separation of rights hereunder,
the Producer will pay to the Writer an amount equal to 25 percent
of the fixed compensation paid to the Writer for his writing
services in the writing of the story (or story and screenplay)
involved. For such purposes, the compensation of a term contract
contract writer will be apportioned in accordance with the Producer's normal accounting procedure, but in no event shall the
payment made to any term Writer on account of the production of
a motion picture sequel exceed the sum of $20,000.00. If the
Writer entitled to separation of rights hereunder did not write
the story (or story and screenplay) while in the employ of the
Producer, but sold such material to the Producer, then the motion
picture sequel payment shall be 15 percent of the fixed payment
initially made to the Writer at the time of acquisition.

(2)   If the writer is entitled to separation of rights under this Article 35 and if the separable material contained a character or characters which are used as the basis for a television series produced primarily for broadcast over "free" television, the Producer will pay to the Writer $178.20 for each 15-minute episode of such television series produced and broadcast, either live or by film. $297.00 for each one-half hour episode of such television series so produced and broadcast, $564.30 for each one-hour episode of such television series so produced and broadcast, and $742.50 for each ninety-minute or longer episode of such television series so produced and broadcast.   All of the foregoing is subject to the following conditions:

(aa) The parties acknowledge that the payments to be made under this paragraph (e) (2) are at present equal in amount to the so-called television sequel rights minimum payments provided for in the Television Film Basic Agreement, exclusive of any so-called re-run or royalty payments.   If such television sequel rights minimum payments (exclusive of any such re-run or royalty payments) are increased during the term of this agreement, then with respect to any material written after the effective date of such increase and for which payments are to be made under this paragraph (e) (2), such payments shall likewise be increased to correspond with such television sequel rights minimum payments, exclusive of any so-called re-run or royalty payments in each case.

(bb) If the writer receives more than $50,000 and if the contract involved so provides, the Producer shall have the right to credit upon the aforesaid payments, the amount in excess of $50,000.   In determining whether the amount exceeds $50,000 there shall be included all monies paid or payable to the writer by reason of percentage payments, participations, or deferments.

(cc) If the Writer's contract provides for any payment based on profits or any other revenue derived from the television series, the payments to be made under this paragraph (e) (2) can be recouped from or offset against such payments based on such profits or other revenue.

(dd) No so-called re-run or royalty payments shall be payable hereunder.

(ee) If any so-called television sequel rights payment is paid or payable to any writer under the Television Film Basis Agreement then in effect, no payment shall be payable under this paragraph (e) (2) with respect to the television series involved.

(ff) If more than one writer is entitled to payment under this paragraph (e) (2) with respect to the television series involved, then all such writers shall be considered as a unit and shall share equally in such payment.

(gg) The provisions of this paragraph (e) (2) shall apply only
to material subject to this agreement and acquired after
the effective date hereof under contracts subject to and
entered into after the effective date of this agreement.

GENERAL

Acquisition of Rights by Producer. If at any time prior to the
disposition or exploitation by the Writer of publication or dramatic
rights in separable material, as permitted herein, and either before
or after the Producer has acquired or employed the Writer to write
such material, Producer shall wish to acquire either or both of such
rights, it shall so notify the Writer and the Guild. The Guild agrees
that within fourteen (14) days after such notice, a paid negotiator,
whose fees and expenses shall be paid by the Guild, shall meet with
the Producer for the purpose of negotiating a purchase price for the
rights sought to be acquired by the Producer. It is agreed that the
negotiator will promptly thereafter quote a price at which the desired
rights may be acquired by the Producer. Producer shall have the right
to acquire the rights in question for the quoted price within thirty
(30) days after the Producer receives such quotation. If the Producer shall fail to purchase the rights in question at the price quoted
by such negotiator, the Writer may thereafter sell such rights to any
other person, firm or corporation at any price; provided that, if the
Producer has acquired, or employed the Writer to write, such material
the Writer shall first give the Producer fourteen (14) days written
notice thereof, within which time Producer may acquire such rights
at such price as has been offered to Writer in good faith by such
other person, firm or corporation. If a negotiator is not made available within the fourteen (14) day period first above mentioned, the
Producer may negotiate directly with the Writer or his representatives.

Writer Teams. If two or more Writers collaborate in or separately contribute to the writing of a story (or story and screenplay) which
satisfies the requirements for separation of rights under the provisions
of Paragraph (b) hereof, and it is determined that such Writers are
entitled to share a credit specified in Paragraph (c) hereof, then
all such Writers shall be regarded as equal tenants in common in the
rights herein granted with respect to the separable material, and the
separable material written by each of such Writers shall be included
in the separable material so owned in common by all of such Writers.

Speculative Writing.

(a) The Producer and the Guild agree that there shall be no
speculative writing, nor shall either party condone it as a practice.
As used herein, the term "speculative writing" has reference to any
agreement covered hereunder which is entered into between the Producer
and any writer whereby the writer shall write material, payment for
which is contingent upon the acceptance or approval of the Producer,
or whereby the writer shall, at the request of the Producer, engage
in rewriting or revising any material submitted under the terms of
this agreement and compensation for the writer's services in connection
with such material contingent upon the acceptance or approval of the
Producer.

(b) The Producer and the Guild recognize that there is possibly an area wherein the proer and constructive exchange of ideas and criticism between a writer and a Producer may be claimed by the Guild to be speculative writing. Whenever the Guild feels that speculative writing has occurred, the case will be referred to grievance and arbitration and the Producer's intent as determined by the facts shall be an important factor in the consideration. It is understood in this connection that nothing in this Article shall limit the submission of original stories or prevent the Producer from discussing with any writer any ideas suggested by such writer, or discussion with any writer any ideas or any material suggested by the Producer in order to determine the writer's thoughts and reactions with respect to any such idea or other material to determine the writer's suitability for an assignment.

Writer's Right to View Rough Cut and Sneak Preview

The Producer will afford the following writers a reasonable opportunity to view a rough cut of a photoplay, and will notify such writers of the time and place of the first "sneak preview" of such photoplay if such preview is held:

(a) Prior to the final determination of credits, as provided in Schedule "A" attached hereto, all writers who have been employed in the writing of the final screenplay;

(b) After the final determination of screen credits, as in Schedule "A" provided, only those writers who have been accorded screenplay credit,

provided, however, that any inadvertent failure on the part of the Producer to give any such notice or to afford such an opportunity shall not be deemed to be a breach of this agreement or a default on the part of the Producer. An alleged default or breach of the provisions of this Article 24 may not be submitted to conciliation or arbitration hereunder but may only be submitted to the Producer-Writer Cooperative Committee and any determination reached by it in such regard shall be final. Information concerning the time and place of any sneak preview shall be confidential. The writer will not advise any other person or persons of the time or place of any such sneak preview and in the event of any violation of such confidence by the writer the Producer shall thereafter be relieved of any obligations with respect to such writer under the provisions of this Article 24.

COMPACT DEVICES (Cable TV, Cassettes, etc.)

Exhibition of product by means of devices now known or hereafter devised, utilizing cassettes, cartridges, discs, tapes or wire (such as the EVR, RCA and other new processes) shall be governed by the following:

1. If the Company employs a writer or purchases material for a film intended primarily for exhibition on compact devices, the terms of this agreement relating to theatrical films shall apply; provided, however, if the film packaged in such compact device is produced primarily for exhibition on free television, then the terms

of this agreement relating to television film shall apply; provided further that nothing in this Article 53 B. is intended to include any film or transaction specifically excluded from this agreement pursuant to any other provision of this agreement.

2. With regard to television film which is packaged on such devices and licensed for theatre or home use, the theatrical use payments required for the theatrical release of television film shall be due.

3. With regard to theatrical film which is packaged of such devices,

a. if licensed or sold for broadcast on free television, the television licensing payments required elsewhere in this agreement shall be due;

b. if licensed or sold for any other use, no payments for such exploitation shall be due under this agreement, except as may flow from the exercise of one of the options set forth below.

4. With regard to all of the forms of exhibition of product on compact devices set forth above, the Guild shall be permitted to choose either of the following options:

a. Accept the terms of any agreement relating to such licensing or sale negotiated between the AMPTP or its member companies and the Screen Actors Guild (pro rata to SAG's television licensing formula in the ratios of SAG's and WGA's 1960 Theatrical MBA's).

b. Terminate this agreement upon sixty (60) days' notice, which may be given any time after April 15, 1972, for purposes of negotiating provisions relating to such licensing of sale.

DIRECTORS GUILD OF AMERICA, INC.
BASIC AGREEMENT OF 1968

ARTICLE I

Recognition and Definition of Employees Recognized

SECTION A: RECOGNITION
The Guild is recognized by the Employer as the sole
collective bargaining agent for all Directors, Unit
Production Managers and Assistant Directors in the motion
picture industry.
The phrase "motion picture" and the phrase "motion
picture industry," wherever used in this Agreement, shall be
deemed to mean the production of all types of motion pictures
on film or tape or transferred from tape to film or film to
tape, or otherwise, of any guage or size or type, whether for
public or private showings as theatrical, television, industrial, religious, educational, commercial, documentary or
government films, and whether produced by means of motion
picture cameras, electronic cameras or devices, tape devices
or any combination thereof, or other means, methods or devices
now known or yet to be devised, in connection with which a
Director, Unit Production Manager or Assistant Director renders
services as an employees.
The Guild and the Employers, through the Association of
Motion Picture and Television Producers, Inc., as a group
will endeavor promptly to arrive at an agreement for separate
rates and provisions for the problems encountered in producing
industrial, religious, educational, documentary, government
films, television and theatrical commercials, and video tape.
The parties agree to commence negotiations not later than 60
days after written request.

SECTION B: DEFINITION OF EMPLOYEES RECOGNIZED
    1.   Director
A Director is one who directs the production of motion
pictures, as the word "direct" is commonly used in the industry.
The fact that he may also render services as a Producer and/or
Writer or in any other capacity shall not take him out of the
classification of Directors, with reference to any work performed by him as a Director, and during the period of such work.

2. Unit Production Manager

A Unit Production Manager is one who is assigned by the
employer as a Unit Production Manager of one or more motion
pictures as the term "Unit Production Manager" is customarily
used and understood in the motion picture industry. A Unit
Production Manager may be assigned to work concurrently on
one or more productions, whether theatrical and/or television.
No Unit Production Manager need be employed on any production.
Where no Unit Production Manager is assigned to a production,
the functions of a Unit Production Manager shall be deemed
included as part of the work of the First Assistant Director,
but without any adjustment in compensation.

Where both Unit Production Managers and Assistant Directors
are employed by an employer or where a Unit Production Manager
is occasionally employed on individual productions, the functions
of the Unit Production Manager relate substantially but not
entirely to business functions and those of Assistant Directors
relate substantially but not entirely to functions more directly
under or with the Director.

There shall be no delegating to other employees (except
First Assistant Directors where no Unit Production Manager is
assigned to the production involved) the duties of Unit Production Managers. However, nothing contained in this agreement
shall be construed to preclude any persons employed in the
following categories from performing the functions of their
employment as such functions are normally and customarily performed in the motion picture industry and which may at times
include segments of the functions of a Unit Production Manager.
Such employees shall not be subject to this Agreement:
Producer (including Associate Producer and Assistant Producer
when performing functions which in their absence would be
performed by the Producer); Location Auditor and personnel
(other than clerical) of Location, Production and Budget or
Estimating Departments.

It is an element of good faith of, and part of the consideration for, this Basic Agreement that no Employer will
make a general rearrangement of duties among such categories
or change classifications of employment for such categories
for the purpose of eliminating Unit Production Managers who
otherwise would have been employed hereunder.

3. First Assistant Director

A First Assistant Director is one who is assigned by the
Employer as the first assistant to the Director.

4. Second Assistant Director

A Second Assistant Director is one who is assigned by
the Employer as an assistant to the First Assistant Director.

ARTICLE II

Guild Shop

SECTION B: LISTS EXCHANGED: MAINTENANCE OF GUILD SHOP
2. Guild's Lists

Within fifteen (15) days after the execution of this
Agreement, the Guild will deliver to the Employer a complete

list of all members of the Guild in good standing as of the
effective date of this Agreement. The Guild agrees that it
will furnish to the Employer, from time to time, supplemental lists showing the names of all of its members who
are or have subsequently become members of the Guild in
good standing, and as well, will promptly notify the Employer
in writing of all persons employed by Employer who have
ceased to be members of the Guild in good standing.
        Any inquiry by the Employer to the Guild as to the date
of "first employment" of a Director, Unit Production Manager
or First or Second Assistant Director shall be answered by
the Guild.
        If any Director, Unit Production Manager or First or
Second Assistant Director employed by Employer fails or
refuses to become a member of the Guild in good standing,
the Guild shall promptly notify, in writing, the Employer.
        3. Reliance on Lists
        Each party shall be entitled to rely upon such lists
and information concerning "first employment" furnished by
the other party. Should any Employer employ or continue to
employ any Director, Unit Production Manager or First or
Second Assistant Director who has ceased to be a member of
the Guild in good standing prior to written notification from
the Guild of such changed status, such employment shall not
be a violation by the Employer of the provisions of Section A
of this Article II.
        4. Disputes, How Settled
        Should the Guild dispute the Employer's designation of
the duties of any individual for Guild membership, such
disagreement shall be submitted to the Employer-Director
Cooperative Committee, hereinafter mentioned, and if not
there determined, may be submitted to Grievance and Arbitration
pursuant to the provisions of this Agreement.

                          ARTICLE III

Disputes

SECTION A: MATTERS SUBJECT TO ARBITRATION PROCEDURES
        The following matters shall be subject to Arbitration
Procedures as described in Article V, except as otherwise
provided in that Article or hereafter in this Article:
        (a) Alleged violations of the terms of the Basic
Agreement.
        (b) Disputes concerning interpretation of the
terms of the Basic Agreement.
        (c) Money claims for unpaid compensation.

SECTION B: COURTS
        Nothing herein contained shall be construed to prevent,
as between individual employer and employee, or the Guild,
as the case may be, recourse to the courts at any time prior
to the happening of any of the following events: (i) mutual
agreement to arbitrate; (ii) a final determination of the
dispute by the Grievance Procedure or in any other manner;
and (iii) with respect to the employee if the Guild and the
Employer have mutually agreed to arbitrate the same issue,
question or matter.

SECTION C: ARBITRATION REQUIREMENT
     Employer and the Guild will be bound to arbitrate any
issue, question or matter arising between them under this
basic Agreement if arbitrable hereunder, except that neither
the Employer nor the Guild shall be required to agree to such
an arbitration in any case where the Employer or the Guild
feels that the issue, question or matter can best be determined by a court.

SECTION D: RIGHTS
     The pendency of any mutually agreed arbitration procedure
shall not be deemed a waiver or limitation or suspension of
any of employee's or Employer's rights of suspension, termination or injunction except to the extent, if any, that such
a waiver, limitation or suspension is required by and specifically agreed to in the agreement to arbitrate.

ARTICLE VI

Minimum Salaries and Working Conditions of Directors

SECTION A: MINIMUM SALARIES OF DIRECTORS FOR THEATRICAL MOTION
             PICTURES (EXCLUDING PICTURES MADE FOR FREE TELE-
             VISION)
     Employer agrees that the minimum salaries and working
conditions set forth in the following schedule and footnotes,
both inclusive, shall govern the employment of such Directors
employed on theatrical pictures:

Type Of Picture	Rate Per Week	*Guaranteed Period Of Employment	**Prepa- ration Time	***Cutting Allowance Pay
Free Lance				
A. Director's First 3 Feature Films:				
Any picture budgeted under $40,000	$1,000.00	3 weeks and 3 days	1 week	3 days
Any picture budgeted $40,000 up to $85,000	$1,000.00	4 weeks	1 week	3 days
Any picture budgeted $85,000 to $200,000	$1,000.00	5 weeks	1 week	3 days
Any picture budgeted $200,000 up to $500,000	$1,000.00	6 weeks	2 weeks	1 week

Type Of Picture	Rate Per Week	*Guaranteed Period of Employment	**Preparation Time	***Cutting Allowance Pay
B. 4th and Subsequent Feature Films:				
Any picture budgeted under $500,000	$1,000.00	7½ weeks	2 weeks	1 week
C. ALL FILMS budgeted $500,000 and over	$1,000.00	10 weeks	2 weeks	1 week
Term	$1,000.00	20 or more out of 26 weeks or any multiple of such period	0	0
Daily (where permissible)	1/4 of $1,000 ($250 per day)			
Free Lance Shorts	$1,000.00	1 week and 1 day per film (see Art. VI, Sec. B, Par. 6)	2 days	0
Second Units	$1,000 per week $250 per day	1 week or 1 day	Art. VI Sec. B Par. 2	0

Interchange of Assignment - Theatrical - Television
With respect to Directors, there may be complete interchange of assignment between production of theatrical films and television films. Whenever such interchange takes place, such Director shall receive not less than the respective minimum pay and working conditions pertaining to theatrical motion pictures or television motion pictures, whichever is applicable to the assignment on which the Director is employed at the time in question.
The Daily Rate for daily employment, as such, shall be $250 per day.

SECTION B: FREE LANCE CONTRACTS
1. Cost of Photoplay As Basis Of Rate Of Salary
The cost of a photoplay as estimated by the Employer in good faith at the time of the employment of a free lance Director, shall be the cost of such photoplay for the purpose of the schedule set forth in Section A above. For the purpose of this clause, any deferment of "direct" production costs

shall be deemed to be part of production costs. Where the
Director feels the budget is not accurate and it affects
his salary, he can bring the matter before the Cooperative
Committee or proceed through the Grievance and Arbitration
procedure.
    2. <u>Second Unit Work On Weekly Or Daily Basis and
        Applicable Preparation Time</u>
    A Director may be employed for second unit work on a
weekly basis.
    4. <u>Travel To Distant Location</u>
    All transportation, meals and accommodations to distant
location for Directors shall be first class or the best
obtainable if first class transportation, meals and accommodations are not available where and at the time required
by the Employer.
    5. <u>Compensation On Recall For Particular Services</u>
    Should a Director be recalled, after having been closed,
for additional work, including but not limited to retakes,
added scenes, sound track, process shots, transparencies,
or trick shots, trailers, changes, or for any other purpose,
compensation for such additional services shall be payable
at the weekly rate provided for in his contract of employment
covering such picture, but shall be payable only for the days
on which such services are actually performed. In computing
compensation for such services rendered for a period of less
than a full week, the weekly rate shall be prorated in the
manner provided in paragraph 6, below. It is agreed, however,
that no compensation shall be payable for such services to
the extent that they are rendered within the guaranteed period
of employment.
    The Employer shall give advance notice to the original
Director if another Director is to perform such services, the
anticipated nature of the work to be done, and the name of
the Director, if known.
    6. <u>Compensation For Fractional Week</u> (For Theatrical
        Pictures)
    In computing compensation to be paid any free lance
Director on a weekly basis, with respect to any work period of
less than a week following the guaranteed employment period,
the compensation per day during such partial "workweek" shall
be computed and paid for at one-fifth (1/5) of his weekly
rate. In computing compensation to be paid any free lance
Director of shorts on a weekly basis, with respect to any
work period of less than a week, following a full "workweek,"
the compensation per day during such "partial workweek" shall
be computed and paid for at one-fifth (1/5) of his weekly rate.

SECTION E: SUSPENSION AND TERMINATION
    Suspension of payment of salary permitted by the so-called
"force majeure" clause of employment agreements with Directors
shall be limited with respect to each continuous cause of
suspension as follows:
        (a) <u>Directors Under Term Contracts Receiving</u>
            (1) less than $2,000 per week may be suspended
                for 4 weeks without salary,
            (2) $2,000 per week or more shall be subject to
                individual negotiations between the Employer
                and the Director.

(b) <u>All Directors Other Than Term Contract Directors
     Receiving</u>
     (1) the minimum compensation, may be suspended
         for 4 weeks without salary,
     (2) above the minimum compensation, but less
         than $2,000 per week, may be suspended
         8 weeks without salary,
     (3) $2,000 per week or more are subject to
         individual negotiations between the Director
         and the Employer.

After the expiration of the period of limitation above
mentioned, the Employer may not again suspend the Director for
the same cause during the further contuance of the same cause
of suspension, but if, after the termination of such cause,
there is a new occurrence of the same or any other cause of
suspension, the Employer may again exercise its rights under
said "force majeure" clause.

SECTION G: MINIMUM CONDITIONS - PREPARATION, PRODUCTION AND
            POST-PRODUCTION
            <u>PREAMBLE</u>

The Director's professional function is unique, and
requires his participation in all creative phases of the film
making process.

He works directly with all of the elements which
constitute the variegated texture of a unit of film entertainment or information.

The Director's function is to contribute to all of the
creative elements of a film and to participate in molding and
integrating them into one cohesive dramatic and aesthetic whole.

The following provisions of this Section G are therefore
agreed upon:
  1. <u>Disclosure and Consultation With Respect to Commitments</u>
      (a) Prior to the employment of the Director, or in
the case of a Director employed under a term contract or multiple
picture contract or under option, prior to his assignment to a
picture Employer shall inform him of the following in relation
to the picture in question:
                (i) the names of artistic and creative personnel
                already employed;
                (ii) all existing film contemplated to be used;
                (iii) any rights of script approval or cast
                approval contractually reserved to any person
                other than the Employer and the individual
                Producer; and
                (iv) the top sheet (summary) of any theatrical
                budget which has been established and any
                limitations thereof, if any;
                (v) the story on which the motion picture is
                based and the script, if any exists, shall be
                made available to the Director.

        It is the intention hereof that Employer shall
make full and complete disclosure to the Director of all of the
existing artistic and creative commitments with respect to the
picture for which the Director is to be employed prior to his
actual employment, or prior to his assignment to the picture if
previously employed or optioned without such an assignment.

(b) After the Director is employed, or in the case
of a Director employed under a term contract or multiple picture
contract or under option, after his assignment to a picture, he
shall participate in considerations, if he is reasonably available, with respect to any changes in the elements of which he
has been previously notified, of proposed casting and the
employment of other artistic or creative personnel, and of any
rights of approval thereafter granted to third parties. The
Director shall participate in considerations and advise and
consult with the Employer or the individual Producer and present
the Director's views and opinions with respect to casting, the
employment of artistic and creative personnel, as well as with
respect to the script and all revisions thereof, and the production schedule, and the Director's advice and suggestions
shall be considered in good faith.

2. Preparation

If there is no approved script prior to the assignment of
the Director, it shall be submitted promptly as possible. Any
changes or additions in such script shall be submitted to the
Director promptly, and before such changes or additions are
made available for general distribution. The individual Producer, or other responsible person, will confer with the
Director to discuss and consider the Director's suggestions
and opinion with respect to such changes or additions and will
confer with the Director to discuss and consider any script
changes or revisions which the Director may desire to recommend.

3. Production

Consistent with the orderly progress of photography, the
Director shall see the dailies of each day's photography at a
reasonable time. No one shall be present at the screenings of
such dailies except those persons designated by the individual
Producer, the Employer, or the Director, and all such persons
shall have a reasonable purpose for attending such dailies.
The Editor assigned to the picture shall be present at all
screenings.

In the event second unit work shall be contemplated, the
Director shall be informed thereof and shall be given an
opportunity to consult with the individual Producer and participate in considerations as to the person to be engaged to
direct such second unit work and also, shall be given the
opportunity to consult with the Second Unit Director with
respect to the manner in which the second unit work is to be
performed.

Prior to the completion of principal photography, the
Director shall be advised of and shall participate in considerations with respect to the utilization of the following:

        trick shots
        process plates
        inserts
        montages
        miniatures
        transparencies
        backgrounds
        stock film
        glass and matte shots
        optical devices

After principal photography, the Director shall be
consulted and participate in considerations with respect
to the foregoing, subject to his availability.
    4.   Editing and Post-Production
    The Director shall be responsible for the presentation
of his cut of the motion picture (herein referred to as the
"Director's Cut") and it is understood that his assignment
is not complete until he has presented the Director's Cut to the
Employer, subject to the terms and conditions of this Agreement,
as soon as possible within the time period hereinafter provided
for.
        (a)   The provisions set forth in this subsection 4
shall apply to a Director with respect to the editing of any
motion picture directed by him; subject to the following
further terms and conditions:
            1)   any time spent following the close of
        principal photography shall, except for the cutting
        allowance herein elsewhere provided for, be without
        additional compensation;
            2)   such provisions shall be subject to the
        Director's availability during the Employer's
        post-production scheduling.
        (b)   The Director shall prepare the Director's Cut of
the film for presentation to the individual Producer, and if
the individual Producer shall not have final cutting authority
over the picture, then also to such person or persons as shall
have final cutting authority over the picture. In pursuance
thereof, the following procedure shall be followed:
            1)   The Director shall see the assembled sequences
        as soon as the Editor has assembled them. The Director
        shall then be entitled to make changes therein without
        major elimination of scenes or dialogue; provided that
        with respect to television, the Employer shall cause
        the sequences to be assembled and made available for
        viewing by the Director as soon as possible following
        the close of principal photography. As to television,
        such changes shall be made by the Director working with
        the Editor and in consultation with the individual
        Producer.
            2)   Such changes shall be accomplished within the
        following time periods:
                (a)   Theatrical Motion Pictures
                    (i)   As to features budgeted at $1,000,000
                or less, within two weeks after the close of
                principal photography.
                    (ii)   As to features budgeted at $2,500,000
                or less, but more than $1,000,000, within four
                weeks after the close of principal photography.
                    (iii)   As to features budgeted in excess of
                $2,500,000, within six weeks after the close of
                principal photography.
            3)   When the Director's Cut is ready, the Director
        shall screen such cut for the individual Producer, or
        such other person or persons referred to above. It is
        the intention of the parties that if the individual

Producer does not have final cutting authority over
the picture the person or persons who have such
authority will not delegate final authority for the
purpose of avoiding the provisions of this Agreement.
During such screening, the Director shall be entitled
to make such recommendations or suggestions for
further changes in the final cut as the results of
such screening may indicate.

5)   It is understood and agreed that the Director's
right to prepare his Director's Cut is an absolute right,
subject to the terms and conditions of this Agreement.

6)   With respect to a theatrical motion picture
which is subject to this Agreement, and the principal
photography of which is commenced during the term of
this Agreement, if such motion picture is licensed by
Employer for United States network free television
exhibition under a contract which provides that the
network may edit the motion picture for such television
exhibition, the Employer agrees to obligate the network
or the distributor to consult with the Director of such
motion picture with regard to such editing done by the
network, subject to conditions.

5. Previews
With respect to theatrical motion pictures, the Employer
will give the Director reasonable advance notice of the time and
place of all previews (excluding press previews) at his last known
address. If the Director cannot be reached, the Guild must be
notified. The Employer will also give the Director reasonable
advance notice of the time and place of the first trade-press
preview which is held either in Los Angeles or in New York.

7. Compensation In Case Of Lending (Theatrical Motion Pictures)
If the services of a Director under a term contract are loaned
to another employer, the terms of such loanout shall be deemed to
include services of the nature mentioned in this Section G performed by such Director for the borrowing Employer, and such
Director shall be entitled to receive from the lending employer
such compensation, if any, as is applicable to such services.

8. Additional Scenes and/or Retakes
Should additional scenes and/or retakes be made, the original
Director shall have the opportunity to do them, unless the Employer
assigns another Director. If another Director is to be assigned
for this work, the original Director shall be notified and advised
by the Employer of the nature of such work to be done and the name
of the Director to be assigned, if known.

9. Looping and Narration
a)   The looping of dialogue for scenes already photographed and the recording of narration for any motion picture
film shall be directed by the Director of the picture, provided
that

(i)   such services do not delay the orderly
procedure of photography on the film, and
(ii) the Director's availability for and the
rendition of such services does not increase
the normal cost of looping or recording of
narration, at the time and place scheduled by
the Employer, and

(iii)   the Director receives no additional compensation for directing loopings and narrations, and
(iv)   the Employer shall not be required to send the Director to the place of looping or recording for narration if the Director is not available at such place.
    b)   Should it be impracticable for the Director to attend such looping or narration recordings, the Employer shall consult with the Director, if he is available, as to what person is available and fitted to direct such loopings and narrations. The final decision in the selection of such person (who may, but need not be a person subject to this Agreement) shall remain with the Employer, but the Director of the film shall be given the opportunity, if practicable, to explain to such person his ideas as to the content and qualities of the work to be done.

    10.   The Dubbing Of Sound and Music
    The Director, if available, shall participate in considerations with respect to the dubbing of sound and music.
    12.   Employer's Decision Final
    The Employer's decision in all business and creative matters shall be final, but this provision shall not release the Employer or the Director from their respective obligations hereunder.

SECTION H: CREDITS (FOR THEATRICAL MOTION PICTURES)
    2.   Size and Location Of Credit
    In giving such credit on 24 sheets, the Director's name shall appear in type not less than 5" in height, and on other forms of advertising covered hereby, the Director's name shall appear in type not less than 15% of the height of type used for the title of the photoplay in marketing advertising and 30% of the title in the United States motion picture industry trade paper advertising.   In all cases, the location of the credit shall be discretionary with the Employer.   In no event shall the minimum Director's credit be less than the minimum credit required to be accorded any other person under the collective bargaining agreement entered into by the Employer covering such person.
    4.   Screen Credit
    The Director shall be given credit on all positive prints in print not less than 40% of the size of the title and no other credit shall appear on such card, which shall be the last title card appearing prior to principal photography.   If more than one Director is given such credit, in accordance with the provisions of paragraph 6 below, then such 40% may be reduced to 30% for each.   The Employer shall give notice to the Guild of the contents of main titles before the prints are made, for the purpose of checking compliance with the credit provisions of this agreement.
    6.   Guild To Determine Controversy Over Credits
    Should more than one Director do substantial work on a photoplay, the Guild and all such Directors (other than Directors of second units) shall be notified in writing as to the directorial credit intended to be given.   Should any such Director be dissatisfied with such determination, he may immediately appeal to the Guild and notify the Employer in writing that he is doing so.

8. Restriction On Use Of "Director" On Screen Or In Paid Advertising
   (a) The Employer will not hereafter and during the term hereof enter into any agreement with any guild, craft, union or labor organization where it agrees to accord members thereof screen or paid advertising credit which includes the word "Director," "Direction" or any derivation thereof, but the foregoing shall not apply to a guild or craft with which the Employer heretofore entered into an agreement requiring such credit, and
   (b) that except as required by agreements heretofore executed by the Employer, and agreements permitted by (a) to be hereafter executed, Employer will not grant to any individual, other than a Director, any screen or paid advertising credit which includes the word "Director," "Direction," or any derivation thereof.

ARTICLE VII

Minimum Salaries and Working Conditions Of Unit Production Managers and Assistant Directors

SECTION A: MINIMUM SALARIES
   1. Minimum Salary Schedule and Conditions
   Employer agrees that the minimum salaries and conditions of employment set forth in the following Schedule and paragraphs shall govern the employment of Unit Production Managers and Assistant Directors. Term contracts shall be for a minimum of 23 out of 26 weeks or multiples thereof.

| | Free Lance Daily Per Day | | Free Lance Or Term Weekly Per Week | | | |
Type of Employment	5-1-68 thru 4-30-70	5-1-70 thru 4-30-72	5-1-68 thru 4-30-70 Studio Workweek (5 days)	Distant Location Workweek (7 days)	5-1-70 thru 4-30-72 Studio Workweek (5 Days)	Distant Location Workweek (7 days)
Unit Production Manager	$137.50	$143.75	$550.00	$750.00	$575.00	$775.00
First Assistant Director	$131.25	$137.50	$525.00	$725.00	$550.00	$750.00
Second Assistant Director	$ 76.25	$ 80.00	$305.00	$400.00	$320.00	$420.00
Trainee (See page 55)						

6. Workweek, Partial Workweek and Prorating Of Fractional Payroll Weeks
(a) A full workweek for weekly schedule employees shall consist of five (5) consecutive days, excluding a studio Saturday and studio Sunday. Provided, however, the workweek shall be extended to seven (7) consecutive days when Saturday and Sunday are distant location days, at the distant location weekly salary provided in Article VII, Section A, 1, above.
In any workweek (other than a full seven (7) days distant location workweek) which consists of only distant location days or a combination of studio and distant location days, each studio day shall be paid for at 1/5 of the studio workweek rate and each distant location day shall be paid for at 1/7 of the distant location workweek rate, as provided in Article VII, A, 1, above, but such employee shall not receive less than the studio workweek rate for such full workweek of employment.
(b) In computing compensation to be paid an Assistant Director or Unit Production Manager on a weekly basis, with respect to any work period of less than a week following the guaranteed employment period, the compensation per day, including all distant location days, during such partial workweek shall be computed and paid for at one-fifth (1/5) of his weekly rate.
(c) The day of departure for and the day of return from distant location shall be deemed location days.

SECTION B: WORKING CONDITIONS
1. Interchange
(a) Interchange Of Classifications:
Nothing herein shall prevent Unit Production Managers or First or Second Assistant Directors from being interchanged, or from accepting employment in other capacities, at prevailing rates of such other classifications. A Second Assistant Director with less than one hundred and four weeks experience in the motion picture industry as a Second Assistant Director (or seventy eight weeks for Second Assistant Directors employed prior to May 1, 1968) shall not be elevated to a First Assistant Director during such first one hundred and four weeks (or seventy eight weeks, as the case may be) except in case of an emergency, in which event the Guild shall be notified as soon as practicable. (Such one hundred and four weeks or seventy eight weeks shall commence with the date of his first employment as a Second Assistant Director.) Any Second Assistant Director may be elevated to Unit Production Manager, in which event the time any such Assistant Director has worked in the motion picture industry as a Second Assistant Director shall apply not only towards the one hundred and four weeks or seventy eight weeks of experience referred to above, but as well towards the period he would otherwise have to work as a Unit Production Manager before becoming eligible to work as a First Assistant Director. Any First Assistant Director who hereafter becomes a Unit Production Manager may perform services either as a Unit Production Manager or as an Assistant Director. Any Unit Production Manager who has been employed as such in the motion picture industry for at least four years may perform services either as a Unit Production Manager or as an Assistant Director.

A Unit Production Manager who, on November 28, 1966, is not
on the Assistant Directors Industry Experience Roster must
be employed as a Unit Production Manager in the motion
picture industry in Los Angeles County, California for at
least four years on and after September 15, 1964 before he
may be added to the Assistant Directors Experience Roster or
be interchanged as an Assistant Director.
    Unless it is agreed upon at the time of hiring, an
employee hired as a First Assistant Director or Unit Production
Manager need not later accept an assignment as a Second Assistant Director during the said employment and his refusal to do
so shall not eliminate the obligation for completion of assignment pay.
    Employees initially assigned on a particular picture
by an Employer in a capacity other than a Director, Unit
Production Manager (who is interchangeable with an Assistant
Director, as provided above) or Assistant Director shall not
later be assigned on such picture by Employer as a Director
or Assistant Director except in the case of a bona fide
emergency, in which event the Guild shall be notified as soon
as possible.
    (b) Interchange of Assignment:
    Subject to (a) above, with respect to Unit Production
Managers and Assistant Directors, there may be complete interchange of assignment between production of theatrical films
and television films.
    3. Employment Conditions
    (a) Assistant Directors
    A First Assistant and Second Assistant Director shall
be employed on each motion picture and free television motion
picture including, without limitation, commercials, trailers,
talent tests and promos, nontheatricals, industrials and documentaries, westerns, serials and shorts.
    (b) Unit Production Managers.
    A Unit Production Manager may be assigned to work
concurrently on one or more productions, whether theatrical
and/or television.
    13A. Assistant Directors Industry Experience Roster
    (a) An Industry Experience Roster has been established
for Assistant Directors composed of those qualified and available
persons who, as of May 1, 1964, i) have had experience as
First or Second Assistant Directors in the production of
theatrical or television motion pictures with Employers in
Los Angeles County, California, and who have qualified and been
placed upon said Roster by Employer on or before October 4, 1965.
    13B. Unit Production Managers Industry Experience Roster
    (a) An Industry Experience Roster has been established
for Unit Production Managers composed of those qualified and
available persons who i) as of November 28, 1969 have had
experience as Unit Production Managers in the production of
theatrical or television motion pictures with Employers in
Los Angeles County, California and who have qualified and been
placed upon said Roster by Employer on or before June 12, 1967.

13C. <u>Trainee Program</u>
(a) The parties have established the Directors Guild-
Producer Training Plan (herein referred to as the Trust Fund)
which is a jointly administered formal program for training a
sufficient number of qualified Assistant Directors and Unit
Production Managers to meet the needs of the Industry. Such
program provides the method for placing such qualified persons
on the Assistant Directors Industry Experience Roster.
The Trust Fund shall administer the formal
training program through a Board consisting of at least fourteen
(14) Trustees with Employers and employees at all times equally
represented.
(6) A trainee must work under the supervision
of a Second Assistant Director at all times, and there shall be
only one trainee employed on any day on any production unit.
16. <u>Duties Of Assistant Directors and Unit Production Managers</u>
No one shall perform the customary and usual duties of a
Second Assistant Director except a Unit Production Manager (to
the extent that such interchange is permissible under this
Agreement) or a First or Second Assistant Director.
No one shall perform the customary and usual duties of a
First Assistant Director other than a Second Assistant Director
who is qualified hereunder for interchange, a First Assistant
Director or a Unit Production Manager (to the extent that such
interchange is permitted by the terms of this Agreement).
No one shall perform the customary and usual duties of a
Unit Production Manager other than a Unit Production Manager,
First Assistant Director or a Second Assistant Director (except
to the extent provided by paragraph 2, Sec. B of Article I)
hereof.
17. <u>Screen Credit For First Assistant Directors and Unit
Production Managers</u>
As long as the practice of giving screen credits to any
individual (exclusive of the individual Producer, Director and
cast) prevails, the Employer shall also give screen credit in
a prominent place on all positive prints to Unit Production
Managers and First Assistant Directors.

ARTICLE IX

<u>Miscellaneous Provisions</u>

SECTION A: COOPERATION BETWEEN EMPLOYER AND GUILD
1. <u>No Strike Provision</u>
The Guild agrees that during the term hereof it will not
call or engage in or assist any strike, slowdown or stoppage
of work affecting motion picture production against the
Employer. The Guild agrees that it will use its best efforts
in good faith to require its members to perform their services
for the Employer, even though other persons or groups of persons
may be on strike. The Guild and the Employer mutually agree
that during the term of this Agreement they will endeavor to
promote good will, mutual understanding and real cooperation
between members of the Guild and the Employer.

6. <u>Any Member Of Guild May Obtain Better Terms</u>
Nothing in this Agreement shall prevent any person from
negotiating with and obtaining from the Employer better
conditions and/or terms of employment than those provided
for in this Agreement. The terms herein provided are minimum,
and not maximum. The Guild will not by the adoption of By-Laws
or otherwise seek to prevent the inclusion in contracts of
employment with Employers of any terms or conditions not
violative of this Agreement.
7. <u>No Waiver Of Minimum Terms</u>
No waiver of the minimum terms herein provided (unless
specifically authorized by the provisions of this Agreement)
may be granted except by the Guild.
10. <u>Pension Plan</u>
(a) Employer and Guild are parties to the "Directors
Guild Of America - Producer Pension Plan" (herein called the
"Pension Plan") and Employer agrees to contribute to the
Pension Plan with respect to each employment of a Director,
Unit Production Manager or Assistant Director upon a theatrical
or television motion picture under this Agreement, an amount
equal to 5% of the Director's, Unit Production Manager's and
Assistant Director's salaries earned by such Directors, Unit
Production Managers and Assistant Directors. Such amounts shall
be contributed to the Pension Plan as and when such salary is
paid to such Director, Unit Production Manager or Assistant
Director.
11. <u>Directors Guild - Producer Health and Welfare Plan</u>
A separate Health and Welfare Plan shall be established
and known as the "Directors Guild - Producer Health and Welfare
Plan," herein referred to as the Welfare Plan. It is to be
funded as follows:
12. <u>Post '48 and All Theatrical Motion Pictures Commenced
Prior To May 1, 1960</u>
As to all theatrical motion pictures, the principal
photography of which commenced prior to May 1, 1960, the Guild
does not and will not make any claim for compensation for the
exhibition of such motion pictures on television.
19. <u>Nondiscrimination</u>
The parties mutually reaffirm their policy of nondiscri-
mination in the employment or treatment of any Director,
Assistant Director or Unit Production Manager because of race,
creed, color or national origin.

PRODUCER—SCREEN ACTORS GUILD
MEMORANDUM AGREEMENT OF 1971

1. Term and Effective Date

   The term hereof shall be three years commencing July 1, 1971.
   The provisions hereof shall be effective on and after said
   date except as specifically otherwise provided and shall
   apply to existing contracts of employment or contracts of
   employment entered into on or after said date.

2. Minimums -- 15% increase, per schedule attached.

3. Theatrical Pictures -- Principal photography of which starts
   after June 30, 1971:

   A. Free Television -- The present contract provisions of
      the Codified Basic Agreement of 1967, hereinafter "Basic
      Agreement",(General Provisions, section 5) relating to
      payments to actors for the television exhibition of
      theatrical motion pictures shall apply except that the
      percentage of base payable with respect to the second
      plateau of Distributor's Gross Receipts ($125,000 to
      $199,999) shall be 10%. (For convenience, the present
      contract provisions, as so modified, are referred to in
      this memorandum as the "revised theatrical formula.")

   B. Supplemental Markets ("cassettes," pay-type CATV, pay TV)--
      50% of the "Distributor's Gross Receipts" shall be included
      in the revised theatrical formula, in combination with the
      gross covered by A, and payment is to be made to the actors
      accordingly.

   C. Pension and Health and Welfare contributions shall be made
      with reference to payments to actors under A and B, at
      6-1/2%, subject to the theatrical Pension and Health and
      Welfare ceilings.

   D. Wherever reference is made to pay-type CATV or pay TV such
      reference shall be deemed to include only those uses of
      motion pictures where a charge is actually made to the
      subscriber for the program viewed or where the subscriber
      has the option, by additional payment, to receive special
      programming over one or more special channels.

"Free television" shall include televising of theatrical or television motion pictures where no such program charge or special channel charge is made to the subscriber in addition to the general cable charge including but not limited to programming taken from another free TV transmission or originated by the CATV facilities and such exhibition shall not be included among "Supplemental Markets."

4.   Theatrical Pictures -- Principal photography of which started after January 31, 1966, but prior to July 1, 1971:

A.   Free Television -- The present contract provisions of the Basic Agreement (General Provisions, section 5) relating to payments to actors for the television exhibition of theatrical motion pictures shall apply as to payments made to actors after July 31, 1971, except that payments shall be computed under the revised theatrical formula, and shall be subject to Pension and Health and Welfare contributions at 6½%. If free television revenue has already been received on a picture covered by this paragraph, so that the second plateau payments have already been made, the applicable payment for the next plateau shall be 2½ percentage points less than the amount specified in the theatrical formula (for example, if the next payment triggered is the third

plateau payment, the percentage shall be 22 1/2%, plus the 6 1/2% Pension and Health and Welfare contribution). Only one such 2 1/2% reduction shall be made.

B.   Supplemental Markets (as defined above) -- 50% of the distributor's gross receipts from this source shall be included in the revised theatrical formula only for the purpose of computing and paying Pension and Health and and Welfare contributions, at 6 1/2%. Individual actors shall be given credit for qualification and benefit purposes on the basis of the revised theatrical formula although no payment of compensation is to be made to the actors with reference to income from this source.

C.   The Pension and Health and Welfare contributions provided for in A and B are subject to the theatrical Pension and Health and Welfare ceiling. There shall be no duplication of Pension and Health and Welfare contributions calculated with respect to any particular plateau of Distributor's Gross Receipts.

D.   If the Association makes a "better deal" with the Directors Guild or the Writers Guild with reference to the release of theatrical motion pictures principal photography of which started prior to July 1, 1971, the Screen Actors Guild shall have the right to re-open this contract on this subject, or to accept the better deal. Any dispute as to whether or not a "better deal" has been made with either of said Guilds shall be arbitrable.

5. <u>Television Motion Pictures</u> -- With respect to all television
motion pictures produced between July 21, 1952 and June 30,
1971, and all television motion pictures produced during the
term hereof:

    A.   Supplemental Markets ("cassettes," pay-type CATV and pay TV,
as defined above) --

        (i)   Subject to clause (ii) below, the revised theatrical
formula relating to payments to actors for the television exhibition of theatrical motion pictures shall
apply, plus Pension and Health and Welfare payments,
at 6 1/2%, but for this purpose the Distributor's
Gross Receipts to be included in the formula shall be
50% of the actual Distributor's Gross Receipts.
Such payments shall be subject to the Pension and
Health and Welfare ceilings referred to in Paragraph
6A below for television motion pictures of one hour
or less duration released as such, and shall be
subject to the $100,000 ceiling referred to in
Paragraph 6B below in the case of television motion
pictures having a running time in excess of one hour,
including shorter programs combined into a single
feature type picture.

        (ii)   The initial exhibition in such markets shall trigger
a payment to the actor of 20% of the applicable base
amount; payment to the actor of an additional 10%
of the applicable base amount shall be triggered
when the included Distributor's Gross Receipts from
such markets equals $62,500.

    B.   "Inflight" -- The "Inflight" market shall be considered
to be a supplemental market for the purposes of this
paragraph 5, except that 100% of the Distributor's Gross
Receipts from this source shall be included, and except that
if such gross receipts are included in the first plateau,
payment to the actor of the full 30% of the applicable base
amount shall be triggered.

6. <u>Pension and Health and Welfare</u> --

    A.   Television Ceilings:

        1/2 hour programs $3,500

        1 hour programs $6,000

        1 1/2 hour programs $7,500

        2 hour programs $10,000

    B.   Theatrical Ceiling: Present contract to apply.

    C.   <u>Adherence to Plans</u>   --   By signing this agreement Producer
hereby becomes a party to and is bound by the SAG-Producers
Pension Plan Trust Agreement and the Pension Plan adopted
thereunder; and the SAG-Producers Welfare Plan Trust Agreement
and the Welfare Plan adopted thereunder.

Producer further hereby accepts and agrees to be bound by
all amendments and supplements heretofore and hereafter
made to the foregoing Agreements and documents.

Producer hereby accepts the Producer Plan Trustees and the
Alternate Producer Plan Trustees under said Trust Agreements
and their successors designated as provided therein.

7. Television Motion Pictures -- Network Reruns --

The rerun formula for the United States and Canada referred
to in Section 15 of the 1967 Screen Actors Guild Television Agreement, hereinafter referred to as the "Television
Agreement," is modified with respect to the second
and third runs if such runs include the telecasting of
the picture over a television network in prime time:

A. Second Run -- Player shall be paid 50% of his total applicable
    minimum salary, plus the percentages set forth below of the
    difference between the actor's total applicable minimum salary
    for the program and the actor's actual salary for the program,
    which for this purpose shall be deemed not to exceed $1,500:

        Programs made for the 1971-72 season -- 10%

        Programs made for the 1972-73 season -- 12%

        Programs made for the 1973-74 season -- 15%

B. Third Run -- Same as A, except that the reference
    to 50% shall be to 40%.

C. Where an individual contract existing on July 1, 1971 provides
    for re-run compensation for the 2d or 3rd run in network prime
    time in excess of 50% or 40% respectively of the Player's
    total applicable minimum salary, the payment hereinabove pro-
    vided for in excess of 50% or 40% respectively of the Player's
    total applicable minimum salary shall be credited against such
    re-run compensation provided for in the Actor's individual
    contract which is in excess of 50% or 40% respectively of the
    Player's total applicable minimum salary.

D. The provisions hereof shall not apply to television motion
    pictures principal photography of which was completed prior to
    July 1, 1971.

8. Initial Employment for Pay TV and Cassettes -- The second
paragraph of Section 8 of the General Provisions of the
Basic Agreement is deleted. The third paragraph shall
include "cassettes," so that there shall be negotiations
for minimum wages and working conditions prior to the
employment of actors for production of cassettes or pay
TV product.

9. Educational, Religious and Industrial Films -- Not
covered by this contract.

10.   <u>Preference of Employment</u> --

    A.   Section 14 of the General Provisions of the Basic Agreement shall apply to all free lance players in theatrical and television and three-Day players in television, except as follows:

        (i) Weekly players guaranteed compensation equal to at least twice minimum; three-Day players guaranteed compensation of at least twice the three-day minimum. Guarantee of double minimum referred to above to be either in length of employment or salary, or both.

       (ii) Free lance players, three-Day players and Day players,less than 18 years of age.

    B.   Preference of employment to apply in the 300-mile zone as to three-Day and free lance players and the 150-mile zone as to Day players. Zones with respect to SAG branch offices to be applied as presently applicable to Day players.

    C.   Damages for Breach: $250.00 for Day players; $350.00 for three-Day players; $500.00 for weekly players. Damages shall be doubled in cases of willful misrepresentation or falsification of facts by Producer. Such damages shall not be compounded with union security violation penalty.

    D.   The present provision with respect to military personnel shall be expanded to cover any governmental personnel where the same conditions presently specified exist, as to Day players, three-Day players and free lance players.

    E.   With respect to special or unique vehicles or equipment not available to Producer without employing the owner or an operator appointed by owner, preference of employment shall not apply to the owner-operator or designated operator.

    F.   A joint Producer-SAG committee shall be appointed to resolve claims arising under this Paragraph. If such committee cannot agree, the claim shall be arbitrable.

    G.   Where the exception provided in Section 14 D(6) of the General Provisions of the Basic Agreement (first employment) is utilized by the Producer, it shall present in writing to the Guild facts showing that the employee has had sufficient training and/or experience so as to qualify for a career as a professional motion picture actor and that such person intends to pursue the career of a motion picture actor and intends to be available for employment in the motion picture industry.

H.   If an actor is employed under one or more of the
      exceptions provided for in subdivisions (1), (2),
      (3), (4) and (5) of Section 14D of the General
      Provisions of the Basic Agreement, the preference
      provisions shall apply to the subsequent employ-
      ment of such person.

11.   Union Security -- Section 2F of the General Provisions of
      the Basic Agreement limiting initiation fees shall be
      eliminated. The union security violation penalty is in-
      creased to $275.00 per violation. The 15-day reporting
      provision is changed to 25 days with respect to engagements
      on "overnight" locations. The inquiry referred to in Section
      2D of the General Provisions of the Basic Agreement by the
      Producer to the Guild may be made before, on, or one business
      day after the date of employment.

12.   Loan-outs -- An actor borrowed from a domestic company or a
      foreign company shall receive the same working conditions as
      those provided in the Televison Agreement or Basic Agreement.
      Union shop and Pension and Health and Welfare provisions shall
      apply where the lending company is a signatory to the Basic
      Agreement or Television Agreement whether such company is a
      domestic or foreign company, provided the services are
      performed under the jurisdiction of this contract. The
      obligation to make the payment of Pension and Health and
      Welfare contributions is the obligation of the lending
      company. Producer shall give reasonable notice to SAG
      prior to the commencement of the term of the loanout where it
      borrows the services of any actor from a non-signatory
      lending company, foreign or domestic, to render services
      within the jurisdiction of this Agreement.

13.   Emergency Suspension -- The emergency suspension provisions
      of Schedules B, C, and E (directly or by reference) of the
      Basic Agreement and of Section 57 of the Television Agree-
      ment with reference to illness of another member of the cast
      or the director, are amended to provide that if the suspension
      has a duration of 5 days or more, in the case of theatri-
      cal, or three days or more in the case of television, the
      suspension may be effective as of the beginning of the
      event, but if the duration is less than the number of
      days stated, the suspension is not effective.

14.   Flight Insurance -- The Producer will provide a minimum
      coverage of $50,000.00 of flight insurance for each actor
      when required by the Producer to travel by airplane, or
      $100,000.00 flight insurance when required by the producer
      to travel by helicopter.

15.   Per Diem -- The travel provisions of the various schedules
      containing the provision entitled "Engagement of Actor --
      Other Areas" shall be changed to provide a $40.00 per day
      allowance instead of the present $30.00 per day allowance.

16. <u>Coding of Motion Pictures</u> --

   A.   Producer hereby authorizes television stations to make available to representatives of SAG its station logs to verify the station plays of programs.

   B.   Regarding a possible system of coding product which appears on television, a joint Producer-SAG committee will be established to consider any working system when it is available, and such committee shall investigate and make recommendations,which will be given consideration by the producers.

17. <u>Tape Rates</u> -- The payments provided for in Section 59(a) of the Television Agreement shall be increased to $181.50 and $230.00, respectively. With respect to prime time network re-runs, the actor shall be paid such rate or the amount provided in paragraph 7 hereof, whichever is the greater.

18. <u>Interviews and Auditions</u> -- A Schedule B or C Actor shall not be kept waiting for an interview or audition for more than one hour after the time scheduled for the interview or audition. The type of interview or audition referred to is an interview or audition for a specific picture, not a general or get-acquainted type of interview. If the actor is more than five minutes late, the above rule shall not be applicable. It is not the intent of this provision to limit the duration of the interview or audition itself. If an actor is detained for more than the permitted period he shall be compensated for the excess time he is required to wait at his straight time hourly rate in one-half hour units. If no salary has been agreed upon before the interview or audition, and if the Actor and Producer cannot agree on the applicable salary, the salary rate at which such Actor shall be compensated for such excess time shall be determined by conciliation, and if conciliation fails, by arbitration in accordance with the applicable provisions of the Basic Agreement. However, claims for violation of this Section must be filed by SAG not later than 15 days after the date of the alleged violation.

19. <u>Nudity</u> --

   A.   <u>Notification</u>: The Producer's representative will notify the actor (or his representative) of any nudity or sex acts expected in the role (if known by management at the time) prior to the first interview or audition.

   B.   <u>Closed Set</u>: During any production involving nudity or sex scenes, the set shall be closed to all persons having no business purpose in connection with the production.

   C.   <u>Production Stills</u>: No photographs will be permitted other than production stills made by a photographer

assigned to the production, or photographers authorized by the Producer to explcit the motion picture.

D.   Consent: The appearance of an Actor in a nude or sex
      scene or the doubling of an Actor in such a scene shall
      be conditioned upon his or her prior written consent.
      Such consent may be obtained by letter or other writing
      prior to a commitment or written contract being made
      or executed. If an actor has agreed to appear in
      such scenes and then withdraws his consent, Producer
      shall have the right to double. Producer shall also
      have the right to double children of tender years
      (infants) in nude scenes (not in sex scenes).

20. Looping -- Free lance players may be recalled to loop
     (record soundtrack) after completion of principal photo-
     graphy at one-half day's pay for a four-hour looping ses-
     sion. If the session exceeds four hours, a full day's
     pay shall be payable.

21. Definition of Network -- Section 15(b)(4) of the Television
     Agreement and Section 5A(2)(b) of the General Provisions of
     the Basic Agreement are amended to include not
     only NBC, CBS and ABC, but also any other network hereafter
     established for exhibition of entertainment product by any
     means, including CATV or satellite distribution; provided,
     however, that such newly established network shall only
     be deemed included as a "network" if it exhibits sub-
     stantially simultaneously (taking into account time changes
     and delays) in overall markets substantially comparable to the
     markets in which NBC, CBS or ABC networks presently exhibit.

22. Late Payment of Residuals -- Sections 15(e) and 16(c) of
     the Television Agreement, and Section 5D of the General
     Provisions of the Basic Agreement are amended to
     change the late payment penalty to 1-1/2% per month on the
     unpaid balance, commencing to accrue from the date of the
     delinquency, in the case of the Television Agreement, and
     ten days after notice in the case of the Basic Agree-
     ment.

23. Photography of Legitimate Stage Plays (Instant Movies) --
     Section 30 of the General Provisions of the
     Basic Agreement is amended to include in addition to
     a legitimate stage play, any ballet, opera or any other
     stage performance.

24. New York Studio Zone -- Sections 32F of Schedule A,
     44B of Schedule B, 41B of Schedule C, and 32B of
     Schedule E of the Basic Agreement, are amended to provide
     for a New York studio zone identical to that applicable to
     the New York extra players (Section 33, New York Extra
     Players Agreement, 1970).

25. Undirected Scenes -- Public Event -- The right to photograph professional entertainers shall be unqualified and not subject to Guild approval, provided they do not take part in the public event by arrangement with the Producer, are not under the direction and control of the Producer and are not performing in their capacity as professional actors.

26. Trailers --

   A. Scenes photographed simultaneously with a separate camera (behind scene shots) are to be interchangeable with clips in trailers, and subject to the same limiations (Section 18, General Provisions, Basic Agreement and Section 31 of the Television Agreement).

   B. 12-minutes (or less) Promotional Films for Theatrical Motion Pictures -- Actors receiving $25,000 or more per picture may agree to make such films or permit use of clips from the picture without additional compensation, subject to individual bargaining. All other actors appearing in such films or clips must be paid on the basis of individual bargaining but with Day player minimum as the base compensation. Such films may not be combined to make "specials." If Producer does not obtain permission of the actor for use of such clips or if more than one actor is involved and one of them does not agree, the provisions of Section 22 of the General Provisions of the Basic Agreement shall apply.

   C. Section 31 of the Televison Agreement is amended to provide that the Producer shall be entitled to freely bargain with Actors engaged at a salary of $2000.00 or more per week for the use of clips or sound track in trailers on the same basis as for the making and use of trailers.

27. First Class Transportation -- If six or more actors travel together on the same flight and in the same class on jet flights, the coach class for such actors shall be deemed to be first class transportation. This does not include "economy" flights.

28. Work Past Midnight -- Subject to the overtime provisions, where the total engagement for any week of the Actor's services is night work and where the last day of such week goes past midnight, the work past midnight does not count as an additional day. For this purpose night work is defined as a call for 4:00 p.m. or later.

29. Meal Periods -- The first meal period on location must commence six hours following the time of first call for the day.

30. Re-takes, Added Scenes, etc. (TV Series Players) -- In the provisions regarding re-takes, added scenes, etc., as to TV series players, the references to "the last three episodes" are to be changed to "any three episodes."

31. Free Lance Players "On or About" Date -- With respect to television pictures, the one-day "on or about" provision will apply if a written employment contract is submitted to the Actor at least three days before the designated start date.

32. Forms of Hiring - Television -- The provisions relating to the forms of hiring for Players employed under Series Contracts referred to in Sections 5, 6, 7, 8, 9, and 10 of the Television Agreement, shall be amended, as appropriate, by adding the following to the forms of hiring:

   A. In all forms of hiring where at least 13 episodes are guaranteed by Producer in writing prior to start of services and where Producer has completed an initial group of episodes (not fewer than 13), Producer shall have the right, once in each production year, to thereafter recall Player for services in additional episodes beyond those comprising the initial group, provided that all of the following conditions are complied with:

      (1) Player shall be guaranteed employment in a number of additional episodes equal to the difference between the number of guaranteed episodes in the initial employment period, and 22 episodes.

      (2) The employment period for such additional episodes shall commence not later than 60 days after the completion of principal photography of the initial group.

      (3) Player shall be given not less than 5 days' advance notice of the starting date of his services in such additional episodes.

      (4) Producer shall be entitled to Player's services in such additional episodes for a number of work days determined as follows:

         Multiply the number of episodes by the following number of days as applicable:

1/2-Hour Programs	5 days
1-Hour Programs	6 days
1-1/2-Hour Programs	8 days

      (5) The overall production period allowed for the production of the additional episodes shall be in the same proportion as the number of episodes guaranteed in the

original production period bears to the original overall
production period specified in the Television Agreement,
which is expressed in the following formula:

Number of Guaranteed Episodes in Original Production Period		No of Guaranteed Episodes in Additional Production Period
Original Overall Pro- duction Period Specified in TV Agmt.	=	X (new production period)

B. In all forms of hiring where less than 13 episodes are guaranteed
by Producer in writing prior to start of services and where
Producer has completed the initial group of episodes, Producer
shall have the right, once in each production year, to
thereafter recall Player for services in additional episodes
beyond those comprising the original group, provided that
all of the following conditions are complied with:

(1) Player shall be guaranteed employment in a number of
additional episodes equal to the difference between
the number of episodes included in the initial
employment period, and 12 episodes.

(2) The employment period for such additional episodes
shall commence not later than 60 days after the completion of principal photography of the initial group.

(3) Player shall be given not less than 5 days'
advance notice of the starting date of his services
in such additional episodes.

(4) Producer shall be entitled to player's services in
such additional episodes for a number of work days
determined as follows:

Multiply the number of episodes by the
following number of days as applicable:

1/2-Hour Programs	5 days
1-Hour Programs	6 days
1-1/2 Hour Programs	8 days

(5) The overall production period allowed for the production
of the additional episodes shall be in the same proportion as the number of episodes guaranteed in the
original production period bears to the original overall
production period specified in the Television Agreement,
which is expressed in the following formula:

Number of Guaranteed Episodes in Original Production Period		No of Guaranteed Episodes in Additional Production Period
Original Overall Pro- duction Period Specified in TV Agmt.	=	X (new production period)

C. Whenever Producer notifies Player of an additional group of
episodes to be produced, it may extend the work time and
float time on a pro rata basis for any extra episodes which
may be added to the additional group provided such notice is
given prior to expiration of the overall production time
calculated as provided above.

D. Paragraphs 5, 7 and 9 of the Television Agreement shall be
amended to eliminate reference to salary breaks for float
purposes. The minimums will permit the applicable maximum
employment period.

E. Series Contracts - 1 Hour or More (2 or more series Presented in a Combined Series Format (e.g. "Bold Ones"))

In those instances where Producer receives an initial
order for less than 13 episodes in cases where the
network plans to broadcast 2 or more different series
presented in a combined series format during a given
broadcast year, Producer shall have the right to employ
the Player for 6 episodes or all episodes initially
ordered in the subject series, whichever number is greater.
Such employment shall be on the basis of the following
minimums, work time and overall production period:

	Minimum Per Episode	Work Time Per Episode	Overall Production Period
1 Hour	$757.00	1 wk. plus 1 day	6 episodes in 8 wks., plus 6 days for each add'l. episode.
1-1/2 Hour	$1,022.00	1 wk. plus 3 days	6 episodes in 12 wks. and 3 days, plus 8 days for each add'l. episode.

If the guaranteed number of episodes exceeds 6, the overall period
shall be extended proportionately.

F. Series Contracts - $10,000 or More per Episode

(i) With respect to Players whose employment contracts provide
for payment of $10,000 or more per episode, Producer shall
be entitled to work days and float days as follows:

	Work Days	Float Days
1/2 Hr.	5	6
1 Hr.	7	9
1-1/2 Hr.	10	12

(ii) With respect to employment contracts with Players who
are guaranteed any of the following bases:

(a) $20,000 per episode; or
(b) $100,000 per series when such series is one of
a number of series presented in a combined
series format (e.g. "Bold Ones")   or
(c) $150,000 for a 13 episode guarantee

Producer and Player may freely bargain for work time, overall production time and options.

G. Options -- Sec. 20 (b) -- The Television Agreement is amended to provide that a Producer may not exercise an option on a Series Player who receives less than $3500 per episode or per week for an additional contract year unless such Player shall have been employed during the then current contract year for a minimum of 22 episodes under the 13 out of 13 form of hiring, or 12 episodes under the 7 out of 13 form of hiring, or as provided in subdivision (ii) of said Section 20 (b). With reference to the form of hiring referred to in subparagraph E of this paragraph 32, a Producer may not exercise an option on a Series Player who receives less than $4000 per episode or per week, for an additional contract year unless such Player shall have been employed during the then current contract year for a minimum of 6 episodes, or as provided in subdivision (ii) of said Section 20 (b). The present provisions of Section 20 (b) with reference to Series Players in one and one-half hour programs remain unchanged.

33. Exclusivity - Television

Amend Paragraph 19(a) (2) and (3) of the Television Agreement to change the money figure of $2,000 to $7,500 for 1/2-hour program, and $10,000 for all programs 1 hour and over in length.

34. Other Provisions -- Except as hereinabove specifically amended or modified all of the provisions of the Basic Agreement and the Television Agreement shall be deemed incorporated herein by reference and shall be applicable during the term referred to in Paragraph 1 above.

35. Formal Contracts To Be Executed -- It is understood that the parties intend hereafter to execute formal contracts to be designated respectively:

"Producer-Screen Actors Guild Codified Basic Agreement of 1971,"

covering production of Theatrical Motion Pictures, and

"1971 Screen Actors Guild Television Agreement"

covering production of television motion pictures, incorporating the terms of and superseding this Agreement. Pending the execution of. said formal agreements, this Agreement shall be a binding agreement between the parties.

SCREEN ACTORS GUILD, INC.

By _____

By _____
Charles Boren
On behalf of the member companies
of the Association of Motion
Picture and Television Producers, Inc.

SCHEDULE OF NEW MINIMUMS

DAY PLAYER (Theatrical and TV)

Actor   138.00
Stuntman   138.00
Airplane Pilot (Studio)   186.00
Airplane Pilot (Location)   242.00

Singers:

	Theatrical	Television
Solo & Duet	161.00	150.00
Groups 3-4	138.00	132.00
Groups 5+	115.00	115.00
Mouthing 1-16	115.00	104.00
Mouthing to play-back 17+	86.00	86.00

WEEKLY PLAYER (Theatrical and TV)

	Theatrical	Television
Actor	483.00	
Stuntman	518.00	
Airplane Pilot	518.00	
Airplane Pilot (Flying or Taxiing – daily adjustment)	159.00	

Singers:

	Theatrical	Television
Solo & Duet	489.00	483.00
Groups 3-4	443.00	
Groups 5+	403.00	
"Step Out"	+ 23.00 per day	

3-DAY PLAYER (Television only)

Actor & Singer
  (1/2 or 1 hr. snow)   352.00
Stuntman (1/2 or 1 hr.)   380.00
Actors, Singers & Stuntmen
  (1 1/2 hr. show)   414.00

MULTIPLE PICTURES- WEEKLY (TV only)

Other than Stunt men or
Pilots: (1/2 & 1 hr. show)   324.00
         (1 1/2 hr. show)   382.00
Pilots & Stunt men:
         (1/2 & 1 hr. snow)   518.00
         (1 1/2 hr. show)   575.00

TERM PLAYERS (Theatrical and Television)

10 out of 13 weeks:
  per week   414.00
20 out of 26 weeks:
  per week   345.00
Beginners:
  0-6 months   186.00
  6-12 months   207.00

SERIES (TV only)

1/2 hr. 13 out of 13   483.00
  Less than 13   552.00
1 hr. 13 out of 13   580.00
  Less than 13   649.00
1 1/2 hr. 13 out of 13   773.00
  Less than 13   876.00

TV TRAILERS (Sec. 31B)

Off Camera   138.00
On Camera   173.00

EXHIBIT A (Non-commercial billboards)

Principals - use on 13 shows   483.00
  Additional days   138.00

Singers:
  1-2   373.00
  3-4   352.00
  5+   324.00
  Additional days   138.00

SIGNATURES ONLY

1-2 singers   324.00
3-4 singers   255.00
5 + singers   221.00
  Additional days   138.00

THE STANDARD BASIC AGREEMENT BETWEEN THE
INDEPENDENT MOTION PICTURE INDUSTRY EMPLOYER AND THE
INTERNATIONAL ALLIANCE OF THEATRICAL STAGE EMPLOYEES (I.A.T.S.E)
AND MOVING PICTURE MACHINE OPERATORS OF THE
UNITED STATES AND CANADA (M.P.M.O.)

West Coast Studio Locals of I.A.T.S.E

II.   SHOP AGREEMENT

      Employer agrees that each and every employee, hired by the Employer to perform services in the County of Los Angeles, or hired by the Employer in the County of Los Angeles to perform services outside said county in the crafts and classifications of work referred to or described in Articles III and IV hereof,

---

*Excerpts outlined by Walter F. Diehl, Assistant International President

shall be and remain a member in good standing of the International Alliance and its appropriate West Coast Studio Local on and after the thirtieth day following the beginning of his first employment as hereinafter defined or the effective date of such respective agreements between the Employer and affected unions, whichever is the later. The foregoing reuirements of union membership as a condition of employment shall be subject to the obligations of the parties under the law.

The International Alliance warrants that it and/or each of its local unions herein referred to and provided for represent a majority of the employees of the Employer, or have been certified by the National Labor Relations Boards and are the bargaining representatives.

The Employer recognizes the International Alliance on behalf of its respective West Coast Studio Locals as the exclusive collective bargaining representatives for his employees within their respective classifications as herein provided for.

III. SCOPE OF AGREEMENT

The crafts and classifications of work subject to this agreement are those over which the above referred to International Alliance and its locals have jurisdiction, and referred to in Article IV of this agreement, and such other crafts and classifications of work in which the Employer shall hereafter recognize the International Alliance and/or a West Coast Studio Local chartered by the International Alliance as the collective bargaining agent of the employees in such crafts of classifications, or in which the International Alliance and/or a West Coast Studio Local chartered by the International Alliance shall be designated by the National Labor Relations Board as the collective bargaining agent of such employees. Upon such recognition or designation as aforesaid, this agreement shall immediately become effective and operative with respect to such employees.

V. BARGAINING AGENCY

It is hereby agreed by and between the parties hereto that all of the crafts and classifications of work covered by this agreement shall constitute during the term of this agreement, an indivisible and integral bargaining unit of which the International Alliance shall, during the term of this agreement, act as and be the collective bargaining agency.

VI. INSIGNIA OF THE INTERNATIONAL ALLIANCE

(a) The insignia of the International Alliance is copyrighted and is the sole property of the Alliance. The Employer hereby agrees to display the insignia as herein authorized unless or until otherwise directed on any and all motion picture films or substitutions thereof such as picture tapes, wires, etc., recorded by any media and produced under the terms and conditions of this contract which carry a screen or air credit title or titles. Said insignia to be clear and distinct, and shall appear on a sufficient number of frames to sustain a minimum of tenseconds of viewing. It shall not be smaller in height than one-fifteenth (1/15th) of the vertical title card or frame used to produce the title. Its other dimensions are to be proportionate in accordance with a facsimile of said insignia as displayed on the inside of front cover of this agreement. The letters "A.F. of L.-C.I.O." below insignia, or any other letters or numbering, shall be an additional dimension of not less than one-third (1/3rd) of the height of the insignia. The letter "R" in circle must be used; it designates registration.

(b) The Employer further agrees to permit the application of the insignia by persons authorized by the Alliance on other products used in the production of Motion Pictures as long as the application does not mar, harm or in any way deface or interfere with the use of said products.

(c) FOREIGN PRODUCTION

The Employer agrees that in the event he contemplates Motion Picture production outside the continental limits of the United States and Canada, he will, before proceeding further with said plans or with the execution of same, notify the International Alliance through its International Representative, or its designated officer, os such contemplation, and will meet with said representative or officer, at which time the question of employment of I.A.T.S.E. members on the production will be discussed and a decision will be made as to the use of the insignia.

IX. PREFERENCE OF EMPLOYMENT TO PERSONS HAVING
EXPERIENCE IN THE MOTION PICTURE INDUSTRY

With respect to employees hired by the Employer to perform services in the County of Los Angeles, California, or hired by the Employer in the County of Los Angeles to perform services outside said county, the Employer shall give preference of employment to persons having experience in the motion picture industry in said Los Angeles County, in the crafts and classifications of work subject to this agreement. The definitive terms of such preference or seniority shall be those contained in the industry experience seniority roster systems as, by agreements, have been set up and maintained industry-wide between Employers on the one hand and the International Alliance and/or the respective West Coast Studio Locals on the other hand. In the negotiation and maintenance of such definitive terms, the parties consider, among other things, the length of service of such persons in the motion picture industry in the respective crafts or classifications of work, described in Articles III and IV hereof, and/or as employees of the Employer.

XII. VACATIONS

Because employment in the independent field is intermittent in nature, gene-rally, and time off with pay for vacation purposes is not practical or feasible, it is agreed that the Employer shall pay in lieu of such vacation time a sum of not less than four per cent (4%) of the straight time earnings, including hours worked on night premiums at straight time, for all daily scheduled employees, and four per cent (4%) of the guaranteed weekly earnings for all weekly scheduled employees, and the same to be paid currently with weekly pay checks, unless in lieu thereof other arrangements are made between the Employer and individual local unions named and provided for herein.

XIII. HOLIDAYS

New Year's Day, Memorial Day, Independence Day, Labor Day, Thanksgiving Day and Christmas Day shall be recognized as holidays. If any of the above-named holidays fall on Sunday, the following Monday shall be considered the holiday.

XV. HEALTH AND WELFARE FUND

In accordance with Article V, Sections 1 and 2 of such Welfare Fund, the Employer shall, for the period commencing with the effective date of this agree-ment and continuing to and including January 31, 1973, pay into the Welfare Fund twenty-two point fifty-five cents (22.55¢) for each work hour guaranteed an employee by such Employer, or each hour worked by an employee for such Employer under the terms of this agreement, including straight time and overtime hours on any day worked.

XVI. PENSION PLAN

   (a) Employer's Contributions
       In accordance with Article III, Sections 2 and 3 of the Pension Plan,
and commencing as of the effective date of this agreement and extending to and
including January 31, 1973, the Employer shall pay into the Pension Plan a total
of twenty-five point ninety-five cents (25.95¢) for each work-hour guaranteed
an employee by such Employer, or hour worked by an employee for such Employer,
including straight time and overtime hours on any day worked. Where a minimum call
is applicable and the employee works less than the minimum call, then the minimum
call shall constitute time worked. Employees subject to this agreement employed
for full weeks under guaranteed weekly salary schedules, shall be credited with not
less than the hours guaranteed the employee under such guaranteed weekly salary
schedule. In the event such employee works in excess of such applicable number
of hours guaranteed in such weekly schedule, then additional contributions shall be
made on such excess hours worked. For the purpose of this provision, studio employment under "On Call" weekly schedules shall be considered as fifty-four (54) hours
for a full work-week, or eleven (11) hours per weekday in a fractional work-week;
and on distant location sixty (60) hours for a full work-week or ten (10) hours
per week-day in a fractional work-week. "On Call" contributions shall be based
on such number of hours only.
   (b) Employee's Contributions
       In accordance with Article III, Sections 4 and 5, of the Pension Plan,
every employee covered by this agreement shall, for the period commencing as of
the effective date of this agreement and extending to and including January 31,
1973, pay into the Pension Plan sixteen point four (16.4) cents for each work
hour guaranteed such employee by Employer or for each hour such employee works
for Employer under the terms of this agreement, including "straight time" and
"overtime" hours on any day worked, as above defined. Studio employment under
"On Call" weekly schedules shall be considered as fifty-four (54) hours for a
full work-week, or eleven (11) hours per week-day in a fractional work-week;
and on distant location sixty (60) hours for a full work-week, or ten (10)
hours per week-day in a fractional work-week. "On Call" contributions shall be
based on such number of hours only. Accordingly, commencing as of the effective
date of this agreement, Employer shall deduct daily or weekly from the compensation of such daily or weekly employees the amount of such contribution due from
such employee as above provided, which deductions shall be paid by Employer into
the Pension Plan on behalf of such employee as the employee's contribution to the
Pension Plan, as herein required. Such money paid by Employer on behalf of employee
into the Pension Plan shall not constitute nor be deemed to be wages due to the
individual employee subject to this agreement, nor shall said money paid into the
Pension Plan in any manner be liable for or subject to the debts, contracts, liabilities or torts of such employees.
       Any change in conditions or rates of contribution to the Industry Pension
Plan other than those herein provided for that may become effective in the
industry at any time hereafter up to and including February 1, 1973, shall likewise apply to this Employer in a like manner.

XVII. INDUSTRY PENSION PLAN RETIREES' HEALTH
       AND WELFARE COVERAGE

   (1) Three and one-quarter cents (3¼¢) for each work-hour guaranteed an employee
by such Employer or hour worked by an employee for such Employer, under the terms of
this agreement, including "straight time" and "overtime" hours on any day worked.

Where a minimum call is applicable and the employee works less than the minimum call, then the minimum call shall constitute time worked. Employees subject to this agreement employed for full weeks under guaranteed weekly salary schedules shall be credited with not less than the hours guaranteed the employee under such weekly salary schedule. In the event such employee works in excess of such applicable number of hours guaranteed in such weekly schedule, then additional contributions shall be made on such excess hours worked. For the purpose of this provision, studio employment under "On Call" Weekly Industry Pension Plan, through its Administrator, as agent, for transmittal Schedules shall be considered as fifty-four (54) hours for a full work-week; and on distant location sixty (60) hours for a full work-week, or ten (10) hours per week-day in a fractional work-week. "On Call" contributions shall be based on such number of hours only.

XVIII. PRE '60 THEATRICAL PICTURES; PAY TELEVISION

(a) The exhibition of any motion picture by television where a charge is paid by or assessed to or collected from the viewing audience, including subscription, telemeter, or any other method whereby a charge is paid by the viewing audience, for the right to view such motion picture, is herein referred to a "pay television."

A "free television" picture is a motion picture initially released on television, other than pay television.

As to all motion pictures, it is recognized and acknowledged that the Employer has the unrestricted right to use, exhibit and market the same for any purpose, in any manner and by any method now known or hereafter developed, and that the Employer does not hereby relinquish or surrender any of its property rights therein. The exhibition of a motion picture by pay television is theatrical exhibition, and is merely an extension or substitute for the theatrical box office.

XIX. POST '60 THEATRICAL MOTION PICTURES

(a) Theatrical motion pictures produced by Employer with employees employed directly or indirectly by Employer under the Basic Agreement of 1961 between these parties the principal photography of which commenced in the period between February 1, 1960, and January 31, 1967, both dates inclusive, which motion pictures are released to Free Television shall be governed by Articel XIX of such Basic Agreement of 1961. Provided, however, that as to such motion pictures the principal photography of which commenced after January 31, 1965, Section 10) Article XIX of such Basic Agreement of 1961 shall not apply, but Section 10) of Article XIX of this agreement shall apply.

The following provisions of this Article XIX relate and apply only to theatrical motion pictures produced by employer with employees employed directly or indirectly by Employer under this agreement the principal photography of which commenced after January 31, 1967, which motion pictures for the first time are either during the term hereof or at any time thereafter released to Free Television. (Such motion pictures are referred to in this Article as the "motion picture" or "motion pictures.")

(b) As to each such motion picture, the Employer will pay nine percent (9%), hereinafter referred to as the "percentage payment," of the Employer's accountable receipts from the distribution of such motion picture on free television, computed as hereinafter provided and subject to the following conditions:

1) Three-fourths (3/4) of such percentage payment shall be paid, as hereinafter provided, to the Motion Picture Industry Pension Plan (herein referred to as the "Penion Plan").

One-fourth ($\frac{1}{4}$) of such percentage payment shall be paid, as hereinafter
provided, to the Motion Picture Health and Welfare Fund (herein referred to as
the "Health and Welfare Fund").

2) The term "Employer's gross," as used herein, means the world-wide total
gross receipts of Employer derived from the distributor of such motion picture
(who may be the Employer or a distributor licensed by the Employer) from licensing the right to exhibit the motion picture on free television. If the distributor of the motion picture does not distribute the motion picture directly to free
television, but employs a sub-distributor to so distribute the motion picture,
then the "Employer's gross" shall be the world-wide total gross receipts derived
from such sub-distributor from licensing the right to exhibit the motion picture
on free television. In case of an outright sale of the free television distribution rights, for the entire world, or any territory or country, the income derived
by the seller from such sale, but not the income realized by the purchaser or
licensee of such rights, shall be the "Employer's gross." If any such outright
sale shall include free television exhibition rights and other rights, then
(but only for the purpose of the computation required hereunder) the Employers
shall allocate to the free television exhibition rights a fair and reasonable
portion of the sales price which shall, for the purpose hereof, be the "Employer's
gross." In reaching such determination Employer may consider the current market
value of free television exhibition rights in comparable motion pictures. If the
Pension Plan shall contend that the amount so allocated was not fair and reasonable,
such claim may be determined by submission to arbitration as herein provided; and in
the event the Board of Arbitration shall find that such allocation was not reasonable and fair, it shall determine the fair and reasonable amount to be so allocated.
If the outright sale includes free television distribution rights to more than one
motion picture, Employer shall likewise allocate to each motion picture a fair and
reasonable portion of the sales price of the free television rights; and if the
Pension Plan contends that such allocation is not fair and reasonable, the question
may be determined by submission to arbitration as above provided. If the Board
of Arbitration shall find that such allocation was not fair and reasonable, it shall
determine the fair and reasonable amount to be so allocated to each motion picture.
The price received on the outright sale of only free television distribution rights
in a single motion picture shall not be subject to arbitration. Sums paid to any
advertising agency in connection with any exhibition of a motion picture on free
television shall not be included in Employer's gross.

3) The term "accountable receipts," as used herein, means the balance of the
Employer's gross after deducting an arbitrary forty percent (40%) of the Employer's
gross for distribution fees and expenses; except that in the case of an outright sale
of free television distribution rights, there shall be deducted only an arbitrary
ten percent (10%) of the Employer's gross for sales and commissions and expenses
of sale.

4) Employer's obligation shall accrue hereunder only after accountable receipts
are received by the Employer; but as to foreign receipts such obligation shall accrue
only when such receipts can be freely converted to U. S. dollars and are remitted
to the United States, and until such time no frozen foreign receipts shall be included in accountable receipts. Payments of amounts accruing hereunder shall be
made quarterly on the basis of quarterly statements, as hereinafter provided. Frozen
foreign receipts from free television shall be deemed to be released on a first-in
first-out basis, unless the authorities of the foreign country involved designate
a specific period that would render such basis inapplicable. Such released funds
shall be allocated between the motion picture and other motion pictures distributed
by the distributor in the same ratio that receipts, derived from the distribution
of the motion picture on free television within the foreign country, bear to the
total receipts derived from the distribution of the motion picture and all other

motion pictures on free television within the foreign country, during the applicable period, unless the authorities of the foreign country involved require another method of allocation in which case such other method shall be used. Foreign receipts shall be accounted for in U. S. dollars at the rate of exchange at which such receipts are actually converted and remitted, and should any discounts, taxes, duties or charges be imposed in connection with the receipt or remittance of foreign funds, only so much of such funds as remain thereafter shall be included in accountable receipts. Employer shall not be responsible for loss or diminution of foreign receipts as a result of any matter or thing not reasonably within the control of the Employer. The Pension Plan and the Health and Welfare Fund shall be bound by any arrangements made in good faith by the Employer, or for its account, with respect to the deposit or remittance of foreign revenue. Frozen foreign receipts shall not be considered trust funds and the Employer may freely commingle the same with other funds of the Employer. No sums received by way of deposits or security need be included in Employer's gross until earned, but when the Employer is paid a non-returnable advance by a distributor, such advance shall be included in the Employer's gross.

5) If any license or outright sale of exhibition rights to the motion picture on free television includes as a part thereof any filmed commercial or advertising material, the Employer shall be permitted to allocate a reasonable amount (in accordance with then current standard charges in the industry) to such commercial or advertising material, and the amount so allocated shall not be included in Employer's gross hereunder.

6) Such payments made hereunder to the Pension Plan and Health & Welfare Fund are not and shall not in any manner be construed to be wages due to any individual employee, nor in any manner be liable for or subject to the debts, contracts, liabilities or torts of any employee.

7) Employer will furnish to the Pension Plan and Health & Welfare Fund written reports showing the Employer's gross received from the sale, lease, license and distribution (whether by Employer or a distributor) of each such motion picture on free television. Such reports shall be furnished quarterly during each fiscal year of the Employer. Concurrently with the furnishing of each such report, the Employer will make the payments shown to be due by such report. All required payments shall be made by check payable to the order of and delivered to the Pension Plan and the Health & Welfare Fund entitled thereto. Each such quarterly statement shall designate the title of the motion picture involved. On request the Employer shall make available to the Pension Plan and Health & Welfare Fund all accounting statements delivered by a distributor to the Employer, but only insofar as such statements relate to the Employer's gross. The Pension Plan and Health & Welfare Fund shall have the right, at reasonable times, to examine the books and records of Employer insofar as they relate to the Employer's gross. Employer shall not be required to furnish any quarterly statement hereunder with respect to the motion picture prior to Employer's receipt of any Employer's gross with respect to the motion picture, or for any quarterly period during which no Employer's gross from the motion picture is received by the Employer.

XX. CONTRACT SERVICES ADMINISTRATION TRUST FUND

Employer shall for the period commencing as of the effective date of this agreement, to and including January 31, 1973, pay to the Industry Pension Plan through its Administrator, as Agent for transmittal to the Contract Services Administration Fund, the following:

For the period commencing February 2, 1969, to and including January 31, 1970, one cent (1¢) per hour, for the period commencing February 1, 1970, to and including January 31, 1973, one and one-fourth cents ($1\frac{1}{4}\cancel{c}$) per hour, for each workhour guaranteed an employee by such Producer, or hour worked by an employee for such Producer on or after February 2, 1969, for employees who are subject to the Retired Employees Fund (on the same weekly and daily formula as the contributions paid under the Retire Employees Health and Welfare Fund); provided, however, that in place and stead of the above cents per hour payments, such payment with respect to employees of laboratories shall be at the rate of three-quarters of one cent ($3/4\cancel{c}$) per hour for the period commencing February 2, 1969, to and including January 31, 1973.

XXI. MEANING OF TERM "MOTION PICTURES"

The parties confirm their mutual understanding and agreement that the term "motion pictures" as used herein and in all prior agreements between the parties means and includes, and has always meant and included, motion pictures whether made on or by film, tape or otherwise, and whether produced by means of motion picture cameras, electronic cameras or devides, tape devices or any combination of the foregoing or any other means, methods or devices now used or which may hereafter be adopted.

XXII. EXCULPATORY CLAUSE

The Employer agrees that he will not make any claims or institute or join any suit or proceeding in any tribunal against the International Alliamce by reason of, or otherwise seek to hold the International Alliance responsible for any acts, conduct or omissions on the part of any chartered local union or any of its members, unless such acts, conduct or omission were actually and in fact instigated or done by the International Alliance. In respect to any such questions of alleged liability of the International Alliance, it is agreed that the General Executive Board or the International President, or his duly designated International Representative, shall be the only body or person authorized to act as agent or representative for and on behalf of the International Alliance.

The International Alliance, its officers, agents and members shall not be held liable in any manner whatsoever for any strike, slow-down, work stoppage or any other form of action which results in cessation, stoppage or delay of work or production, unless such action is offically authorized by the International Alliance, nor will the International Alliance be held liable for any unauthorized acts or activities of its officers, agents or members. The International Alliance agrees that it will, upon receipt of notification from the Employer of such acts or activities, promptly adivse its members that such acts or activities are unauthorized by the International Alliance, and will use its best efforts to require a discontinuance of such cessation, stoppage or delay of work or production.

XXVI. NON - DISCRIMINATION

The parties to this agreement agree that under this agreement there shall be no discrimination due to race, creed, color, or national origin.

INDEX